Memories of Nine Years in 'Akká

Memories
of
Nine Years in 'Akká

Dr. Youness Afroukhteh

Translated from the original Persian

by

Riaz Masrour

GEORGE RONALD
OXFORD

George Ronald, Publisher
Oxford

Youness Afroukhteh, *Kháṭirát-i-Nuh-Sáliy-i-'Akká*,
first published 109 B.E. (1952), Tehran

© This translation Riaz Masrour 2003
All Rights Reserved
Reprinted 2005

A catalogue record for this book is available from the
British Library

ISBN 0-85398-477-8

CONTENTS

A *Note from the Translator*   xiii
A *Note from the Publisher*   xviii
Preface to the First Edition, 1952   xix
Foreword   1

Chapter 1

Journey to Baghdad	3
Through Russia to 'Akká	8
Arrival in Badkubih and leaving Russia	9
The life of the pilgrims in 'Akká	20
Visiting the Shrine of Bahá'u'lláh	24
Feasts	29
Morale of the believers in the days of hardship	30
The schemes of the Covenant-breakers	33
The dwarfish old man	41
The Covenant-breakers' means of livelihood	42
Types of Covenant-breakers	44
My duties on this pilgrimage	45
'Abdu'l-Bahá's words	48
The suckling babe	58
The rebellion of Mírzá Áqá Ján	60
The Covenant-breakers' planned rebellion through Mírzá Áqá Ján and Ṭábúr Áqásí	67
Events after Mírzá Áqá Ján's rebellion	69
A story	74
The nature of 'Abdu'l-Bahá's cares in those few days	75

The story of Áqá Mírzá Ḥasan	79
Dismissal	83
The story of the package and my mission	90
Tehran	92
The story continued	93
Alláh'u'Abhá / Alláh'u'A'ẓam	95
The effect of the story of Áqá Mírzá Ḥasan	96

Chapter 2

Departure from Tehran	103
Pilgrimage at 'Akká with an American, Mr. Hoar	104
My feelings during the first days in the Holy Land	106
Description of my duties in those days	109
Haifa in 1900 A.D.	110
The morale of the believers of Haifa and 'Akká in those days	113
Six months in Haifa	115
'Abdu'l-Bahá's visits from 'Akká to Haifa	116
Construction of the Shrine of the Báb	117
'Abdu'l-Bahá's words in those days in Haifa	121
Three pistol shots at 'Abdu'l-Bahá	122
The renewal of confinement	126

Chapter 3

Circumstances surrounding the renewal of confinement	132
Details of the renewal of confinement	134
Release of the Covenant-breakers from prison due to the Master's intercession	135
My return to 'Akká	135
"O Breakwell, O my dear one!"	138
The pilgrimage of Mr. Dodge's sons	142
Madame de Canavarro and Mr. Phelps	144
Mr. Dreyfus and Miss Sanderson	148
The late Dr. Arastú Khán	150
Mrs. Lua Getsinger	150

Arrival of a Covenant-breaker from Bombay, Ḥusayn-'Alí Jahrumí, surnamed Fiṭrat	156
Establishment of an English class	158
News of the upheavals of Yazd and Isfahan	160
The realization of one of 'Abdu'l-Bahá's predictions: Mírzá Badí'u'lláh's story concluded	163
The return of Mírzá Badí'u'lláh to the fold	166
Conduct, manners and attitude of Mírzá Badí'u'lláh	172
Mírzá Badí'u'lláh breaks his vows of repentance	173
Rapid progress of the Faith in East and West and the sending of the Arch-breaker of the Covenant's agent to America	174
Burdens, sorrows and labours of 'Abdu'l-Bahá	177
The effect of difficulties and sorrows on 'Abdu'l-Bahá	180
A story	183
One task does not distract Him from another	185
Kashkúl or pumpkin bowl?	188
The effect on the pilgrims of meeting 'Abdu'l-Bahá	193
The manner of revealing verses	195
Fridays	202

Chapter 4

The Prison City again – one year later	208
The arrival of certain Western believers wearing the *fez* in the Ottoman style	213
Mr. and Mrs. Winterburn	215
Mr. Frank Frank	217
Further progress of the Faith in the East; Construction of the Mashriqu'l-Adhkár in 'Ishqábád	222
Rapid progress of the Cause of God in the West	227
The condition of the Covenant-breakers	231
Visits by non-Bahá'í Westerners	233
Account of the conversion of an American lady in 'Abdu'l-Bahá's presence	239
Servitude	242
A bitter-sweet story	246

Medicine	249
Trusting the road to the highwayman	253

Chapter 5: Various Miscellaneous Events

"The triumph of the Cause of God is in his hands"	257
The definitive date for the end of the Covenant-breaking period	260
Collapse of the domes	261
"Once I was embarrassed"	263
The sweet fragrance of some of the letters	264
You conquered my heart before I ever existed	266
The name of the first Japanese Bahá'í was Yamamoto	268
His gait and bearing defy words	270
A story to illustrate a point	272
The Master on health	273
Another illustrative story: "Six years of hard work did not go to waste!"	276
Charity devoid of hypocrisy	279
Infiltrating the Faith of God	282
The meaning of generosity	283
"Eat the bread, but don't drink the wine"	287
What sort of place was 'Akká?	291
One "effulgence" of the Prison, the thirty-day fast	294
"My wellbeing and its opposite are in the hands of the friends"	298
A grand feast	301
Love	303

Chapter 6

Again, never-ending tasks and severe hardships	308
'Abdu'l-Bahá's utterances in these days	310
My own circumstances at this time	311
The Persian Consulate building	313
Miss Barney and *Some Answered Questions*	314
A change in conditions: The arrival of biased officials	319

CONTENTS ix

My journey to Europe — 322
Arrival at Marseilles — 324
Arrival in Paris — 326
Return to 'Akká — 328
A brief visit to Beirut — 331
'Abdu'l-Bahá's teachings on how to attract divine
  confirmations — 332
Moving to Beirut — 334

Chapter 7 — 341

Multiple investigators, both secret and open — 345
Interpretation of Mírzá Núru'd-Dín's dream — 347
Intrigues of the Covenant-breakers — 348
The situation in 'Akká as the Covenant-breakers awaited the
  impending chaos — 353
The arrival of Sulṭán 'Abdu'l-Ḥamíd's officials, and their
  departure due to the cannon blast of divine confirmation 354
This is the letter from Núru'd-Dín-i-Zayn — 357
The fulfilment of the prophecies of 'Abdu'l-Bahá, now
  and in the future — 366

Chapter 8

Arrival at Beirut — 369
What sort of place was Beirut? — 373
The conditions of this servant in Beirut — 375
That grenade that missed the breast of Sulṭán 'Abdu'l-
  Ḥamíd struck the liver of the Covenant-breakers — 379
Another look at Beirut — 380
The everlasting disgrace of the Covenant-breakers was
  simultaneous with the removal of Sulṭán 'Abdu'l-Ḥamíd — 381
When did Satan ever give me a chance? — 382
Manufacturing a dream with the intention of slandering
  the Faith of God — 384
I consider such words to be meaningless — 385
Conclusion of Chapter 8 — 386

Chapter 9

We believers were not without our faults	390
What is a homeland and who is a patriot?	394
What was happening on the moon?	396
By God, you're right!	399
What is fortune?	402
Return to Beirut	404
Three medical cases	406
News from Iran and the Ottoman States	412
The end of the Most Great Prison of 'Akká	414
Describing the indescribable	416
Return to Iran	419

Apology 425

Selected Biographical Notes	427
Bibliography	445
Notes and References	451
Index	483

LIST OF ILLUSTRATIONS

Between pages 44 and 45:
'Abdu'l-Bahá, the Master
The house at the Cave of Elijah on Mount Carmel
Driving from Haifa to 'Akká along the sands
The land approach to 'Akká
The pilgrims' first view of the Mansion and Shrine of Bahá'u'lláh at Bahjí
The Shrine of Bahá'u'lláh
The House of 'Abdu'lláh Páshá from the street
The garden in the courtyard of the House of 'Abdu'lláh Páshá
The Khán-i-'Avámíd, the caravanserai where several Bahá'ís lived

Between pages 172 and 173:
Hájí Mírzá Haydar-'Alí of Isfahan
Mishkín-Qalam, Mírzá Husayn of Isfahan
Zaynu'l-Muqarrabin, Mullá Zaynu'l-'Ábidín
Áqá Muhammad Ridáy-i-Qannád of Shiraz
Áqá Husayn-i-Áshchí of Káshán
The original building of the Shrine of the Báb on Mount Carmel
The Shrine of the Báb, alleged by the Covenant-breakers to be "a strong fortress"
Dr. Youness Khán and Dr. Arastú Khán

Between pages 268 and 269:

  Thomas Breakwell
  Hippolyte Dreyfus
  Lua Getsinger
  William Hoar
  Isabella Brittingham
  The Master's carriage, driven by his faithful servant Isfandíyár
  The Bahá'ís of 'Ishqábád, carrying materials for the construction of the Ma<u>sh</u>riqu'l-A<u>dh</u>kár
  The 'Ishqábád House of Worship under construction
  The streets of 'Akká: a view down Saladin Street
  Báhá'is in front of Tel-i-Fa<u>khkh</u>ár, with the Mansion of Bahjí in the distance

Between pages 396 and 397:

  Shoghi Effendi in childhood
  The first Persian edition of *Some Answered Questions*
  Laura Barney
  Ethel Rosenberg
  Kanichi Yamamoto, the first Japanese Bahá'í
  Believers in Paris in the early 1900s
  'Abdu'l-Bahá's tent in the courtyard of the House of 'Abdu'lláh Pá<u>sh</u>á
  Dr. Youness Afroukhteh
  Dr. Youness Afroukhteh with his wife Zarintaj and daughters Nirvana and Farzaneh in about 1926
  Doctors at the Sehat Hospital, Tehran
  "The Holy One walks"

A NOTE FROM THE TRANSLATOR

"Jináb-i-Khán", the title by which Dr. Youness Afroukhteh (Yúnis Afrúkhtih) was honoured by 'Abdu'l-Bahá, was a writer, an interpreter, a wonderful poet, a magnificent orator, a brilliant physician and an indefatigable teacher of the Faith of God. He was also a first class humourist. And it is this heavenly quality of wit and humour that infuses this volume with a mood rarely seen in similar literature and thus makes reading these pages such an interesting and delightful experience.

My father had been a patient of this beloved servant of 'Abdu'l-Bahá and used to tell me, in my youth, about him and the wonderful stories of his famous memoirs. Once, gazing at a portrait of the beloved Jináb-i-Khán which my father kept in his study, I remarked that he looked so radiant that it was almost as if the picture emitted light. The observation seemed to transport my father to another place and time. His eyes glazed over and remained fixed on a far-off point in space, as a wistful smile found play on his lips. After what seemed like a long pause he said, "That is the light of 'Abdu'l-Bahá. Jináb-i-Khán was at that Threshold for nine years. That is why the light is so intense." All this made my first reading of these memoirs much more meaningful. It was "light" writing about the "Sun"; a physician describing the true Healer; it was the utterly devoted lover writing about Love personified.

Over those nine years (1900–1909), Jináb-i-Khán served 'Abdu'l-Bahá as secretary, translator, envoy and physician. His account of some of the most significant events of the period, his graphic and stirring depictions of the various attributes and moods of 'Abdu'l-Bahá, and the description of his own emotions – all expressed in a lively and at times mischievous language of humour and wit, and made ever more meaningful by the addition of the verses of poetry (including some of his own) interspersed throughout the book, make this volume uniquely memorable.

On his return to Persia, as he began his brilliant career in medicine, Jináb-i-Khán continued to serve the Cause of God with ever-increasing passion. He describes in his memoirs in some detail the teaching firesides he held at his home in Tehran in times when such activities could have spelled doom. In 1925 he travelled to the United States where he spoke at large gatherings and imparted to the friends in that region the light of faith and certitude he had absorbed from the Master. A few years later he embarked on an extensive European tour where he not only introduced the life-giving principles of the Faith of Bahá'u'lláh to many a gathering, but also was a living demonstration to the friends of the spirit of love and fellowship which flows from the practice of those principles.

In a moving passage from his wonderful memoirs he recounts that once as he made his report to 'Abdu'l-Bahá of his visit to Paris, where he had been sent by the Master, he made mention of the fact that his appearance among the French believers and his words to them seemed to have a deeply profound effect on them.

> Suddenly 'Abdu'l-Bahá halted, and turning His blessed face to me asked, "How many years have you been with us?"
>
> "Four years," I replied.
>
> "In these four years you don't know what I have given you; you have no idea what you have absorbed from Me!"

In addition to his international teaching services, Jináb-i-Khán was also active in Bahá'í administration. He served on the National Spiritual Assembly of Persia as well as the Spiritual Assembly of Tehran for many years, until advanced age and the onset of a chronic illness deprived him of the energy to continue. His health deteriorated over time until on 28 November 1948 he left this earthly abode for his heavenly home, so that once again he might gain admittance to the heavenly threshold of his Beloved Master. His "In Memoriam" may be found in *The Bahá'í World*, volume 12, pages 679–681.

At each reading of Jináb-i-Khán's memoirs one tends to come away with a new impression, a fresh realization, a deeper understanding of the words of that heavenly Reality, 'Abdu'l-Bahá. In the course of my last reading of the book and as I replaced Persian words and concepts with their English equivalents, I caught something significant that had escaped me in previous readings. Absorbed and captivated by the warmth that radiated from these pages I began to visualize myself as a player in the story, an observer of the events, a resident of the pilgrim house. So I too began to experience, in a daydream state, the joy and thrill of nearness to the beloved Master, and as I pounded the computer keys I too basked in the sunshine of His love. Along with the rest of the friends, we seemed to be in the midst of Paradise while living in the Most Great Prison. No-one wished for anything but to be near Him and to live out his life in a sort of spiritual ecstasy, as if there was nothing else to life.

Then one day quite suddenly, just after the dismantling of the Most Great Prison, the Master voiced his long-cherished desire: "I have to spread the teachings of God around the world." Before His re-incarceration in the city of 'Akká He had repeatedly mentioned the fact that, "Were it not for the safeguarding of the Most Holy Shrine, I would travel and teach the Faith." And now that He felt that the Shrines were safe He was making plans to do exactly that. For me, reading those words, came a sudden awakening – as if He seemed to be telling me that we have a duty in this world to perform. We are not here to simply enjoy each other's company and the comforts of life. It is not enough to remain good Bahá'ís and simply lead a passive life. We must follow Him and win the hearts of men by our conduct, actions and words.

Jináb-i-Khán distinguished himself in following the Master's exhortations for the remaining days of his life. He himself became an unforgettable example of devotion, service and sacrifice for all the lovers of 'Abdu'l-Bahá the world over.

I began the translation of the 124 B.E. (1968) revised edition of the book in the summer of 1996 and gave to it my utmost effort, although there always remains room for improvement. I have translated much of the poetry and have tried to keep intact the weight of the original verse and the beauty of the rhyme which are such indispensable features of classical Persian poetry. My English translations of 'Abdu'l-Bahá's unpublished Tablets and prayers, whether from Arabic or Persian, remain provisional and are so annotated. There is so much here that despite my best endeavours this translation can never hope to match the beauty and zest of the original. My hope is that English-speaking believers, not unlike myself, may take this spiritual journey with Jináb-i-Khán and in doing so enrich their lives, strengthen their resolve in service to the Cause and, God willing, share with him, in whatever may be their portion, the extraordinary joy of experiencing nearness to the magical presence of the Centre of the Covenant, 'Abdu'l-Bahá.

I wish to thank my dear friend Mr. Adel Shafipour for his help in translating some of the Arabic Tablets and deciphering certain Arabic passages which escaped my level of competency but not his. I am indebted to Dr. Houshang Sharifi for his assistance with translation of further Arabic text. Mrs. May Hofman's editing of the manuscript was truly a service of love. With the precision and skill of a surgeon she performed the invaluable service of sorting out words, sentences and paragraphs and making sure that the outcome was an "English" document.

I wish to express my deep gratitude to my dear friend and colleague Dr. Ahang Rabbani, through whose suggestion I began the project and whose constant encouragement and invaluable assistance in reviewing and refining of the text enabled me to complete it.

A NOTE FROM THE TRANSLATOR

This translation is dedicated to my beloved wife Nazli Masrour, whose all-consuming devotion and constant care and attention spurred me on from beginning to end. I know of no other handmaiden of 'Abdu'l-Bahá who has happily accepted so many of the household burdens and responsibilities, given more of her time and industry, and generally fussed over her husband more intently and with more vigour and love in support of his pursuit of a goal. Without it this translation would have carried the name of another of 'Abdu'l-Bahá's servants than mine, and in recognition of her support my heart is filled with humility and gratitude.

Riaz Masrour
August 2003

A NOTE FROM THE PUBLISHER

Many people have assisted in making possible at last the full English translation of *Kháṭirát-i-Nuh-Sáliy-i-'Akká*. In addition to those already mentioned by the translator, the publisher would like to thank the following: Nirvana Farhoumand Afroukhteh and Farzaneh Yazdani Afroukhteh, daughters of the author, and Minerva Douglas, his grand-daughter, for their interest and support; Saeed Khadivian, whose unpublished translation of these memoirs in the early 1980s provided a useful point of reference to the non-Persian-speaking editor of the present translation; Mr. 'Alí Nakhjavani for his continued encouragement; and the following for their technical help in providing information and materials: Laura Barnes, Arthur Lyon Dahl, Roger Dahl, Iraj Khodadoost, Diana Kitanova-Samii, Erica Leith, Minou Moarefi, Mahmud Samandari, Shapur Rassekh, Robert Stockman, and Mina Yazdani. We wish also to thank the staff at the Bahá'í World Centre who read and revised the provisional translations of writings by Bahá'u'lláh and 'Abdu'l-Bahá.

The writing of *Kháṭirát-i-Nuh-Sáliy-i-'Akká* was finished in the year 99 B.E. (1942), but its first publication did not take place until ten years later in 109 B.E. (1952). A revised edition appeared in 124 B.E. (1967), and that edition, reprinted in 1983 by Kalimát Press, is the version used in this translation. The most recent Persian edition was published in Germany in 2003. To assist the reader, the publisher has added explanatory endnotes and a section of biographical notes on many of the people mentioned in the book. These do not form part of the original text.

PREFACE TO THE FIRST EDITION, 1952

In the Name of God, the All-Glorious!

Memories of Nine Years in 'Akká, written by Dr. Youness Afroukhteh, is a remarkable book. Using delightful expressions and in the sweetest choice of words, the author records those momentous and horrifying events related to the uprising of the breakers of the Covenant and the sorrow and anguish of the Centre of the Covenant.

Among those works dealing with the history of Covenant-breaking, this book is pre-eminent in its clear establishment of truth from falsehood. It has been honoured by the approval and praise of the beloved Guardian and his explicit instruction, to this Assembly, that it should be published and disseminated. Its author was favoured after his passing by the following cable from the beloved Guardian, words of infinite bounty from the heaven of mercy and generosity:

HEARTS GRIEF-STRICKEN PASSING BELOVED YÚNIS AFRÚKHTIH DISTINGUISHED PROMOTER HOLY FAITH HERALD COVENANT TRUSTED SECRETARY BELOVED MASTER STAUNCH SUPPORTER HIS TESTAMENT. HIS SERVICES ENRICH ANNALS BOTH HEROIC FORMATIVE AGES FAITH. INSTRUCT ASSEMBLIES ALL PROVINCES HOLD BEFITTING MEMORIAL GATHERINGS. INFORM VARQÁ ERECT MY BEHALF MONUMENT HIS GRAVE. ARDENTLY PRAYING ALMIGHTY'S INESTIMABLE BLESSING HIS SOUL.

Signature of the Guardian

These words of the Guardian serve as a true indicator of the character of the esteemed author and eliminate the need for any further description of his praiseworthy qualities and virtues, or of the record of his services.

The publication of this book will no doubt bear many fruits. It will bring increased awareness to the friends of God of the significance of the divine Covenant, the necessity of eschewing Covenant-breakers, and the deceit and treachery of this loathsome group. Further, it will familiarize young Bahá'ís who have not personally witnessed the upheaval of Covenant-breaking and have not encountered the seditious and corrupting deeds of these destroyers of the foundation of the Faith of God, with their malicious actions.

This Assembly recommends to all the friends the in-depth perusal of this wonderful book.

'Alí-Akbar Furútan
Secretary of the National Spiritual Assembly of Iran

FOREWORD

Some thirty-seven years have passed since the occasion of my first pilgrimage to the threshold of the incomparable beloved, 'Abdu'l-Bahá. It is my purpose, therefore, to record for posterity the recollections of my three-month residence in the Most Great Prison city of 'Akká, and then to continue these reminiscences and share with the reader my memories of the nine years of my second pilgrimage, which took place thirty-four years ago.

It seems now as though I had a dream lasting three months some thirty-eight years ago, and another, nine years in duration, which began thirty-four years past and ended twenty-five years ago. I shall, therefore, set out to record under the title of *Memories of Nine Years in 'Akká* an account of my spiritual discoveries during those dream-like journeys. In so doing, I shall attempt to refrain from relating unsubstantiated tales and hearsay traditions, and shall leave the interpretation of these dreams to posterity. My hope is that future generations of believers may become acquainted with past events and, unlike the followers of other religions who have largely remained incognizant of the traits and attributes of past Manifestations, obtain an understanding of the character, personality, and manners of one such divinely-inspired Personage.

This account covers certain historically significant events, for the largest portion of these memoirs relates to the activities of the Covenant-breakers in the time of 'Abdu'l-Bahá.

Since Baghdad was the initial site of their rebellion, I shall begin the story with my journey to that city.

I should state at the outset that to remember events that took place a quarter of a century ago is no easy task, especially in my case, for I have always suffered from a pronounced frailty in this faculty. However, highlights of these events have left such an indelible impression on my mind that even if after thousands of years the minute particles of my remains – having since been cast into limitless space by the hand of nature – were to be recovered and analysed, the memories of those past events might yet be detected by any attentive observer. It is this hidden power, residing in the recesses of my memory, which encourages and propels me to recount the events of the past for the generations of the future.

Having said this, in relating this story I still find myself unable to depend solely on those brain cells that house the record of my lifelong memories. Moreover, I do not intend to depend on any assistance from those unidentified microscopic beings. Instead I shall place my hope and trust in the divine assistance of 'Abdu'l-Bahá. My prayer is that His spirit may shine forth from the Concourse on High with the luminous light of His bounty and generosity, and aid the hosts of feeble and unlettered ones such as this servant. And so it is in that heavenly and holy Being that I place my wholehearted reliance, as I take up the pen and begin the story.

CHAPTER ONE

Journey to Baghdad

When the Blessed Beauty ascended to the Abhá Kingdom in 1892, Nabíl described the event thus: "Verily, the Sun of Bahá has set", signifying the date of His passing in the abjad[1] system. The late Shokuhi,[2] too, mourned His ascension with the words, "Alas, verily, He who was our Lord has hid from our eyes".

Although still very young, I was inconsolably grieved and utterly shaken by the gravity of that event. But sustained reading and study of the Writings of Bahá'u'lláh filled me with hope and expectation that the Sun of Divine Beauty would continue to shine unabated from a different horizon and manifest its splendour in a new human temple. Reading the Kitáb-i-'Ahdí[3], especially, filled me with confidence and hope.

It was then that Writings emanating from the pen of 'Abdu'l-Bahá began to descend upon the believers like copious rain, following the Supreme Pen with utterances that filled the hearts with such gifts of spirit, such sweetness of expression and delicacy of meaning, and creating such an aura of spiritual sensitivity that I was prompted to conclude that while the words of Bahá'u'lláh were like multi-coloured flowers of the garden of spirit, the words of 'Abdu'l-Bahá were the quintessence of their beauty and fragrance.

As I continued to read the Tablets of 'Abdu'l-Bahá I

gradually became so enraptured and enamoured with His Writings that in the third year after the ascension of Bahá'u'lláh I petitioned for permission to visit the Holy Land as a pilgrim. However, before the arrival of the response, I eagerly set out towards Baghdad, hoping to receive it in that city and so expedite my journey to 'Akká through Damascus and Aleppo.

This unplanned and hastily-arranged journey, however, undertaken in the dead of winter and utilizing various means of transportation such as mule, donkey and carriage, took some forty days to complete. But since permission for pilgrimage had not yet arrived, and, in any case, it would have taken an additional fifty to sixty days to reach 'Akká through Damascus and Aleppo, I decided, utterly exhausted, to return to Tehran and await the receipt of the permission there, and then set out again, this time through Russia and Istanbul, toward the goal of my desire.

In Baghdad I met and became closely associated with Mírzá Músá, surnamed Ḥarf-i-Baqá. It was there that I began to hear rumours that a certain person, through the devious suggestions of a dervish-like individual, had become a proponent of the Greater Branch[4] and had lost faith in the divine Covenant. This led to consultation amongst the friends, which brought out the question: "Of what benefit is the meddling of the other Agḥṣán[5] in the affairs of the Cause?" The answer to such a question was clearly simple, for men of understanding can readily discern that the Sun of Truth cannot shine from two horizons, and that absolute truth can in no wise accept multiplicity. In the face of these rumours, I could also observe and feel the enthusiasm and devotion of the friends, the support and encouragement given them by Mírzá Músá and his efforts in safeguarding the community.

While in Iraq I travelled to Karbilá and Najaf[6] and visited the Islamic holy shrines, and on my return to Baghdad I took advantage of the many opportunities to meet with the friends and enjoy their companionship. But since permission to travel to 'Akká had not arrived, I decided to return to Tehran.

During the course of my arduous journey, the possibility of the rebellion of the Aghṣán consumed my thoughts. Was not the verse, "We have chosen 'the Greater' after 'the Most Great'"[7] sufficient for Muḥammad 'Alí? Could the Aghṣán be contemplating opposition to 'Abdu'l-Bahá? Did they intend to follow in the footsteps of Yaḥyá[8]? These were the concerns which tormented my soul during the journey to Tehran.

On my arrival in Tehran I received 'Abdu'l-Bahá's Tablet that indeed included the glad tidings of permission to visit 'Akká. My excitement knew no bounds, but before I set out towards Russia I realized that I had neither a passport nor sufficient funds to undertake such a journey. So I reconciled myself to returning to my work.

I should sit back and follow the path of patience,
I should take up life where I had left it off.

I therefore reapplied for a position in the same international bank where I had formerly worked as a clerk. I was accepted and began to bide my time until another opportunity to travel should present itself.

Of the rumours of Covenant-breaking in Baghdad I confided in no one and instead began my personal teaching efforts in earnest. Suddenly rumours filled the town that the Hands of the Cause were disunited and had differing views about the station of 'Abdu'l-Bahá. Ismu'lláh'u'l-Jamál had put forward the argument that the Shrine of Bahá'u'lláh possessed a higher station than the person of 'Abdu'l-Bahá, emphasizing the point that since Bahá'u'lláh was the Truth, so were His garments and so was His body and therefore so was His Shrine. The Hand of the Cause Ákhund 'Alí-Akbar argued, "If His garment is the truth and His hat is the truth, how could His Most Great Branch not be the same truth?" These arguments began to attract attention and little by little reached the ears of the friends in remote villages.

At the same time news reached Tehran that the friends in Baghdad had begun to call the Greater Branch by his given name of Mírzá Muḥammad-'Alí, had torn his pictures to shreds and consigned the pieces to the oblivion of the flame.

Meanwhile, there streamed from the pen of 'Abdu'l-Bahá heart-rending Tablets which ignited the souls of the friends, creating much agitation and turmoil, the effect of which the great Na'ím described as a rift which placed the believers into two columns of "ayes" and "nays", referring to those who were prepared to sacrifice their lives for 'Abdu'l-Bahá and those who had chosen to become the violators of the Divine Covenant.[9]

The veil had now been removed and the secrets of the hearts exposed. Soon the infernal writings of the enemies of the Cause of God began to reach the friends in Tehran and the rift became public knowledge. These writings contained the news that the Aghṣán and the Afnán[10] were firmly united and were directing the community of the friends to remain faithful to the Aghṣán. The believers rejected these claims and returned them in batches, and took their grievances to 'Abdu'l-Bahá.

As was heard in those days and subsequently confirmed, the rebellion in Baghdad had been initiated by an agent of Mírzá Muḥammad-'Alí who had begun to sow seeds of doubt about the station of 'Abdu'l-Bahá. Having gained one adherent, he then journeyed to Mosul or Damascus. There, he informed the Arch-breaker of the Covenant about the results of his work and the generally favourable atmosphere for further intrigue. With this news in hand, Mírzá Muḥammad-'Alí began to dispatch seditious writings to Baghdad in the hope that the friends would weaken in their resolve, become attracted to the promises of the Aghṣán, and fall in with their designs. But on the contrary, these heretical writings proved the infidelity of the Covenant-breakers and strengthened the friends in their courage to arise and do whatever was necessary to protect the Cause.

In Tehran, however, the actions of the Covenant-breakers were different in nature and much more intense in their effect. The opposition was begun by one of the most renowned and revered Bahá'í scholars of the time, Áqá Jamál

[Burújirdí], later known as the "Old Hyena". This man had been busy devising ways to deceive the simple-minded believers. And since he had been a member of the Islamic clergy, an *ákhund*, he believed that having one half-witted follower was more valuable than owning title to the entirety of a sizeable piece of property. Eventually, he found two followers whose names I cannot now recall, and thus became the proud owner of two large properties.

At the ascension of Bahá'u'lláh, this man secretly established contact with the Covenant-breakers and informed them that with his power and influence he was readily able to enlist a large segment of the Bahá'í community of Iran under his own authority. At the same time he was corresponding with 'Abdu'l-Bahá and seeking to establish, with the Master's consent and support, a place of honour and a position of leadership for himself within the Faith. When I finally succeeded in attaining His presence, 'Abdu'l-Bahá made repeated reference to these letters and explained how because of His rejection of these requests, the Old Hyena had become more and more resentful and dangerous.

Áqá Jamál undertook a journey to the Holy Land, and since at that time the believers and the Covenant-breakers had not been formally separated he began secretly to attend the meetings of the violators of the Covenant. He participated in devising plans for opposition and gained their assurance of receiving a prominent role in the future administration of the Faith. On his return to Tehran, he began his seditious whisperings, and in response to the title "He Whom God hath purposed" bestowed upon 'Abdu'l-Bahá in the Kitáb-i-Aqdas,[n] he made up the title "Those whom God hath chosen", and considered that all consultation on matters relating to the Cause should include himself as well as the other Aghsán.

'Abdu'l-Bahá was entirely aware of the details of all of his activities. However, He closed His eyes to these machinations and with loving advice and wise counsel directed the friends. Alas,

> *Of what benefit is advice to the blackhearted?*
> *How can a nail penetrate the rock?*

Áqá Jamál did not cease his nefarious activities. He remained in continuous contact with the Covenant-breakers and published and circulated their writings in Tehran. In the meantime, news reached the city that since the Covenant-breakers had made their activities public, 'Abdu'l-Bahá had journeyed to Tiberias heartbroken and dejected. This news was immediately followed by reports that the Aghṣán had changed their ways and pleaded with 'Abdu'l-Bahá for forgiveness, and that the Master had returned from Tiberias.

Emotions were running high in the Bahá'í community of Iran. Joy and sadness filled the hearts at the same time. To the tragedies of the ascension of Bahá'u'lláh on the one hand, and the maltreatment of the friends by the government on the other, were added the rebellion of the violators of the Covenant and the rejoicing of the enemies of the Faith. But what kept the friends hopeful and confident, and motivated their every deed, was the success of the teaching efforts. Streams of seekers attended secret firesides and readily enrolled in the Cause of God.

This, in brief, was the beginning of the rebellion of the Covenant-breakers. Now let us return to the story.

Through Russia to 'Akká

This emotional and spiritual turmoil finally brought me to a point where the cup of patience overflowed, and so it was in the mid-winter of the fifth year of the ascension of Bahá'u'lláh that I again resigned my post at the bank and together with Áqá Mírzá Fadlu'lláh, son of Ashraf, set out on a journey toward Qazvín.[12] Due to the extraordinary harshness of the winter that year we took five days to reach Qazvín, where we went to the home of the honoured Samandar, who also expressed interest in accompanying us on the pilgrimage. After five days of rest, we resumed our journey by mule and mule-drawn carriage towards Rasht.[13] Again, because of repeated snowstorms and forced stops in several poor villages along the road to Rasht, this leg of the journey took eleven days. On our arrival in Rasht we heard some depressing news. The road to Istanbul from Russia, which we had selected for the continuation of our journey, had been closed to Iranian travellers, as everyone was concerned about the cholera epidemic in Mecca and the Ḥajj pilgrims.

In the home of the honoured Arbáb, where we had stopped, we had many opportunities of meeting the friends and were shown great hospitality by all. The reports of cholera did not stop us from continuing our journey, although the honoured Samandar decided to stay behind. Nevertheless, the two of us pressed forward with unquenchable longing towards Anzali,[14] with Badkubih[15] as our main destination for that leg of the journey. But the Russian boats were prevented by stormy seas from entering the harbour at Badkubih, leaving us stranded in Anzali.

Finally, after twelve days of waiting as we gazed out with tearful eyes at the Russian ships passing in the distance, we were able to board the *Neynay*, a Russian steamer, and reached Badkubih in three days.

Arrival in Badkubih and leaving Russia

The friends in Badkubih enjoyed free and delightful spiritual gatherings. However, despite their concerns, we did not accept their wise counsel to terminate our journey and return to Tehran; we encouraged each other to strive to remove any and all obstacles on our way. As has been said:

Some sacrifice all to attain the Beloved,
and some leave it to the whim of destiny.

And so, disregarding the advice of the friends, we found someone who was even more impetuous than we were, obeyed his seemingly imprudent advice and proceeded toward Tbilisi[16] in the hope of coming a few steps closer to our goal.

In Tbilisi we received wonderful hospitality from the Ahmadov brothers. Here, no one had yet detected the foul odour of the rebellion of the Covenant-breakers. We spent several days in prayer and meditation while the preparations necessary for the continuation of our journey were made. With much difficulty we were at last able to obtain Customs clearance, for the officials had strict instructions to stop the passage of Iranian travellers from Batumi[17] to Istanbul. But having succeeded here, we were destined for even greater hardships.

In Istanbul we were promptly handed over to the police, for the Turks were at war with the Greeks and the massacre of the Armenians was at its peak. To complicate matters still further, the corrupt officials in Batumi had not stamped our passports properly. This created a great many problems and severely jeopardized the journey. At all times, however, we were content and thankful to be closer to our ultimate destination.

Having at last cleared this hurdle we were set free to continue our journey and thus with hearts filled with gratitude and love for divine providence, we sailed for Beirut and afterwards for Haifa. On the ship we met several of the friends from Baghdad and finally arrived at our destination. In a state of great excitement, spiritual attraction and with a prayerful attitude we alighted at Haifa in the early hours of the evening.

In Haifa, we were told that 'Abdu'l-Bahá was in seclusion at the Shrine of Elijah[18] and only two or three of the believers were permitted to attain His presence. This general ban applied to everyone except friends from Iran who had received specific permission from 'Abdu'l-Bahá to make the pilgrimage. This horrific news left us shaken and grieved, as we realized that the rebellion of the Covenant-breakers was much more widespread and serious than what had been reported to us in Tehran. At the same time, our desire and longing to attain the presence of 'Abdu'l-Bahá robbed us of all patience.

Since we had arrived in the evening, we were informed

that our meeting with the Master had been scheduled for the afternoon of the following day. We were then taken to the home of Ḥájí Siyyid Taqí Man<u>sh</u>ádí where we were welcomed and greeted by a few of the friends who visited us briefly, after which we were assigned a small room for the night. My fellow traveller was a man of humour and devotion and so we passed the night chanting prayers and poetry.

The following morning, Man<u>sh</u>ádí took us out for a stroll in the streets of Haifa. While sightseeing, we stopped and purchased some necessary food items and then returned to the house. As it had been several days since we had enjoyed a good meal, we hastily prepared a very large omelette, of which we all ate generous portions complemented with lots of yogurt, cheese and a mountain of bread. Our stomachs satisfied, our spirits revived too; our knees stopped shaking and our devotion to the Cause of God found new vigour. Once recovered physically, we began to lose all patience with Man<u>sh</u>ádí, who seemed less than serious in making the necessary arrangements for us to attain the presence of 'Abdu'l-Bahá.

At last, after hearing all the "maybe"s and "God willing"s, we set out towards the slopes of Mount Carmel, arriving at the Shrine of Elijah at dusk. The cool mountain air, combined with all the joy and longing of attaining the Master's presence, had elevated our spirits to such a level that we could hear earth and heaven and indeed every piece of rock exclaiming "Yá Bahá'u'l-Abhá!"

We had not climbed more than a few steps up the slope when suddenly we beheld the luminous countenance of the Centre of the Covenant of God walking down the slope on a narrow track, headed towards the wide open fields.

Once in His presence, each of us communicated in his own way to the Beloved of hearts, expressions of utter humility and devotion. With smiles that melted the hearts, and repeated words of welcome, the Master told us to go to the upper level and wait for Him. There were two small, modestly furnished rooms, one for 'Abdu'l-Bahá and the other for the pilgrims. What there was in the way of kitchenware and bedding consisted of a copper pan, a small grill, two plates, one tray, one quilt, a small samovar and two teacups. There was also a very courteous yet agile ten-year-old Indian child who stood ready to assist in any way we might need. This is all that there was to fill the needs of 'Abdu'l-Bahá in His seclusion. Along with two of the friends resident in Haifa, we entered the pilgrim room, sat down, and began to converse while tea was being served.

We were told a great deal about the seditious activities of the Covenant-breakers. But they spoke with apprehension. It was clear that they were not permitted to speak openly, and besides, they could not take us into their full confidence as yet. But at the same time they gave us the joyful news of the great successes in various teaching projects in the West. In any event, the situation was similar to the one in Iran.

About two hours after sunset, the pilgrims from Iran and Baghdad were taken individually into the presence of 'Abdu'l-Bahá. I was the second to be summoned. With a burst of excitement and speed I entered the room, and found myself before the blessed person of 'Abdu'l-Bahá. As I fell to my knees and placed my brow at His feet, my pent-up tears of joy and longing were finally released, and as I wept, His gentle hand helped me to my feet and into His arms. I was transported into another world, the highest paradise. And as my spirit soared in that spiritual atmosphere, He helped me to sit on bent knees just opposite Him as He began to speak to me. I did not comprehend a word.

> *Think not that words can penetrate my being,*
> *I turn a deaf ear when good advice is offered.*

One moment I was overwhelmed by the heavenly beauty of that wondrous Countenance, the next I felt shame and fear for any past deeds and conduct unworthy of such surroundings. Who am I? Where is this? How did I ever become worthy to be present in this heavenly place? How did I ever become worthy of receiving, first hand, the blessings of

'Abdu'l-Bahá? Suddenly another thought invaded these musings: What if this is but a dream? What will I do if I awake to discover that this, in fact, has been a dream? As these thoughts filled my mind I could not hold back my tears, and began to weep loudly. But again, 'Abdu'l-Bahá's love enveloped and consoled me. Gradually I recovered my senses and began to listen and commit to heart the words of the Master.

As He paced the floor, He spoke to me: "They say that Jonah was swallowed by a fish and spent three days in its belly. This means that the onward march of the Cause of God was delayed for three days. This is also the same three days that Jesus spent in heaven after His ascension and before His return."[19]

Of course, these are not His exact words, but they contain their meaning and essence. 'Abdu'l-Bahá continued His utterances, imparting to me words of counsel:

"I wish the friends of God to give forth light like this lamp. The Sun of the Abhá Beauty has set, so the beloved of God must shine brightly as the lamp."

I said to myself: may my life be sacrificed for this present and manifest Sun, whose warmth and brightness cause my tears to flow uncontrollably.

> *I wipe away the tears with my fingertips,*
> *Otherwise the oncoming Caravan will surely sink in the tear-laden mud.*

With a glance expressing unquenchable thirst, I beheld the wondrous figure of the incomparable Beloved and my heart spoke the words of Saʿdí:

> *The eyes that beheld you likened you to the tall cypress –*
> *Consider the shortsighted who is blind to such beauty.*

At last, with the words "Go in the care of God", He dismissed me from His presence. Each of the pilgrims, one by one, were taken to His presence and as they emerged I could see in their faces the same emotions that dominated my being: lost in utter wonderment, weeping one moment and breaking into joyous laughter the next, as they took their places in a corner of the room.

The late Ḥusayn Effendi, who was in charge of serving tea and attending to the pilgrims' needs, had upon instructions from the Master prepared our dinner in town and brought the food, along with some bedding, to the room. We ate in silence. I was lucky enough to receive some leftover portions of 'Abdu'l-Bahá's food, which I consumed with great relish. One of the friends reminded us that the Master had not been sleeping well and that He was in the habit of leaving His quarters before the break of day and taking long walks in the fields, spending the time in prayer and supplication.

After dinner our bedding was spread on the floor of the room next to 'Abdu'l-Bahá's and we retired. But who could sleep?

> *Sleep does not come when you are so near,*
> *The game of love is not for the head that seeks a pillow.*
>
> *All is peaceful and the hour is past midnight,*
> *But the eyes that have lost sleep are Venus' and mine.*

At dawn I awoke, walked outside, entered the front enclosure of the sanctuary and enquired about 'Abdu'l-Bahá. A young man who was both guard and doorkeeper told me in Arabic that the Effendi had gone out. As we had been told, the Master had gone out before the break of day into the fields, walking and praying; this solitude had been chosen by 'Abdu'l-Bahá to relieve the fatigue and stress of the sadness and pain inflicted upon Him by the rebellion of the Covenant-breakers.

In the pure air of dawn, and in this spiritual atmosphere which the prophets knew, I chanted a prayer and visited the renowned cave called the retreat of Elijah. After that, I performed my morning obligatory prayer and then returned inside for tea with the friends. The Master soon returned and summoned the friends into His presence. Now I had regained my senses and was in complete control of my faculties, and so I was all ears and ready to hear and understand every word of 'Abdu'l-Bahá. With those loving and heart-warming smiles, He gave us permission to be seated, and then enquired about the friends in Tehran and Baghdad. He spoke many kind words about the friends in those two cities. He then spoke briefly about the greatness of the Cause of God and divine tests and difficulties, and bestowed on us words of loving counsel. While He was speaking and as everyone was listening intently, the young man who guarded the area walked in and whispered in 'Abdu'l-Bahá's ear. The Master gently asked us:

"Leave now, so that those who are waiting may attend. I will summon you again." We all rose, and with heavy hearts, bowed and left the room.

As we walked out, we met two men who were waiting to be admitted into the Master's presence, one an Ottoman officer and the other a Persian with a long black wavy beard, dressed in a long *'abá*.[20] The Persian greeted us with the conventional Muslim greeting of *"Salám"* [Peace], in the Ottoman style. I returned his greeting and walked away. Mírzá Faḍl'u'lláh immediately objected to my returning the Persian's greeting:

"Why did you return his *'Salám'*? Did you not recognize that the man was none other than Mírzá Badí'u'lláh, the rebellious half-brother of 'Abdu'l-Bahá?"

"How do you know?" I asked.

"That young man there communicated the information to me through facial gestures," he replied.

"The curse of God be upon him! Where did that beast come from? It seems we cannot find a moment's peace without having a shameless intruder sticking his unwelcomed nose into our affairs!"

Thus I expressed my feelings. While everyone laughed heartily at my comments, I felt shame and regret for my transgression and so in repentance I repeated the Greatest Name several times. And this was no childish act on my part. Later on, in many of His talks with us, 'Abdu'l-Bahá confirmed that the Covenant-breakers used the ploy of greeting the friends with the word "*Salám*" with the intention of confusing them and shaking their confidence. I shall say more about this in future chapters.

A few minutes after the conclusion of His meeting with those men, we were summoned again into 'Abdu'l-Bahá's presence. At first, one could readily detect the signs of sorrow in His blessed face. But since the company of the devoted and the sincere always brought Him joy, it was only a few minutes before the Master's countenance began to glow with divine radiance, as He spoke to us about the prophecies of the Blessed Beauty concerning the future victories of the Faith.

After further words of loving counsel, 'Abdu'l-Bahá instructed us to proceed directly to the Shrine of Bahá'u'lláh and chant the Tablet of Visitation three times, once on our own behalf, once on 'Abdu'l-Bahá's behalf and once for the Covenant. The horse-drawn carriage had been made ready to take us to Bahjí.[21] On the way, I began to review the words of 'Abdu'l-Bahá with two of the resident Bahá'ís. Each, based on his own recollection and understanding, discovered new significances in those heavenly words. And with these thoughts, which had filled our hearts with love for 'Abdu'l-Bahá, the world and all that was therein seemed to us the very incarnation of the promised paradise itself. We were in the highest heaven, associating with the dwellers of the Concourse on High.

At first, the green fields and the gentle breeze gave us a taste of true paradise, and as we approached the sea the billowing waves were but a reflection of the spiritual excitement of the friends. It seemed as though we were beholding throngs of angels worshipping, glorifying and praising the Blessed Beauty. The spiritual intoxication was such that we were utterly unaware of ourselves. Heavenly melodies could be heard from all sides, enrapturing us and transporting us to the world of reality. As we passed, our fellow travellers from Haifa described the major sights of interest: "This is such and such a river that passes through the Garden of Riḍván;[22] this spot offers a beautiful skyline of 'Akká; this is the gate to the city; this is 'Akká's suburban city park, the establishment of which was encouraged by 'Abdu'l-Bahá; to the right is the cemetery, the grave of 'Abdu'l-Bahá's mother is here;[23] to the left, the building with the white dome is the shrine of the prophet Ṣáliḥ[24] where Ḥusayn Effendi[25] is also buried; ahead is the famous Mansion of Bahá'u'lláh; adjacent to the Mansion, the Shrine of Bahá'u'lláh can be readily seen."

With tearful eyes we all bowed our heads. In front of the Shrine there was a cypress grove with large pine trees providing ample shade. The Blessed Beauty used to raise His tent here and spend some time in peaceful leisure.

As we listened in astonishment and wonder to the descriptions of these delightful places, there suddenly appeared in the distance a group of people, adults and children, clad in a combination of Arab, Persian, Turkish and Western dress, some in long Eastern cloaks and some in short jackets and leather belts with *fezzes* on their heads, all looking perturbed and staring at us with unwelcoming and ghastly faces. We were told that these people were the Covenant-breakers.

"May they be accursed of God!" was my reaction. "What are they doing here?"

"They live in the Blessed Beauty's Mansion," I was told.

How strange! Why could we not have a moment's peace without these parasites sticking their ugly noses into our affairs?

We alighted from the carriage and were taken to an unfurnished room in the basement. This was the land of the Covenant-breakers. They just stood there watching us, grinning and whispering to each other. We were told to take no notice and not to pay them any attention: "These people are just looking for an excuse to create a disturbance" – and so we remained calm and unperturbed. Realizing at last that we had no intention of engaging them, they withdrew one by one and thus we began our ablutions. We washed and cleansed ourselves and in utter humility focused our attention on the sanctified Shrine.

The fresh appearance of the fragrant flowers and the resulting perfumed air of the surroundings had so attracted the hearts that our thoughts were totally centered on the Incomparable Beloved; we were reminded that this pilgrimage was on behalf of the loving Master, and as we knelt before the threshold of the Blessed Beauty we were overtaken by such transports of joy and attraction that the unpleasantness of confronting the Covenant-breakers melted away completely. This was the place of pure and utter spirituality. In the words of the poet:

> *In our hearts there is no place except for the Friend.*
> *Give both worlds to the foe; sufficient unto us is the Friend.*

We then entered the Shrine itself, applied rosewater to our faces and fell to our knees again, and as bidden by 'Abdu'l-Bahá, chanted the Tablet of Visitation three times. And then we bared our hearts, our souls, the very depths of our beings and our very essences before our Lord. After a time, softly, with unburdened hearts and in utter humility we stepped back and out through the door and without looking around; avoiding any possible confrontation with the Covenant-breakers which would have spoiled our happy and spiritual state, we began our journey back to 'Akká.

The panorama of the Blessed Beauty's Most Great Prison City left a strange impression on our souls, and the interior of the town with its narrow winding streets brought out our deepest emotions. To behold those very streets, alleys, houses, bazaars, all of which had at one time held the gaze of Bahá'u'lláh or had been blessed by His footsteps, cleansed the heart from any trace of sorrow. Every passageway was His pathway; every spot was the Point of Adoration; every step was the place of prostration; every site was a place of history.

We stopped at last at a caravanserai[26] and entered a

crowded, noisy reception area, climbed a few worn-out broken steps and entered the main room. This room looked out onto the Mediterranean and was very pleasant. We met with other friends already there and with joyful spirits greeted and embraced all of them. White tea,[27] fragrant and delicious, was made ready and within minutes other friends began to gather until the renowned Zaynu'l-Muqarrabín and Mishkín Qalam arrived.

Each introduced himself and Mishkín Qalam, as part of his introduction, gave me a few strands of his own hair, both white ones and yellowed ones. He said: "It's my thin beard and crooked body that are my passport to fame!" To which I responded in jest: "I too have helped, for I have always said that Mishkín Qalam does not need to tell jokes to get laughs – his face and body serve the purpose all by themselves!" Everyone broke out in hearty laughter and this opened the door to more light-hearted comments and merry-making. The friends each contributed with wit and humour and created a warm and joyful meeting. The late Mírzá 'Azízu'lláh Khán Varqá was one of our fellow travellers whom I came to know well and with whom I spent a great deal of time.

Our days and nights were filled with happiness. The chanting of divine verses, prayers and poetry was quite popular, especially Bahá'u'lláh's Tablets revealed in honour and praise of 'Abdu'l-Bahá. Also popular were the rebuttals written by the Persian friends in response to the publications of the Covenant-breakers; these always provided a hot topic of discussion. We were well aware of the wolves dressed in sheep's clothing who were milling about, but we did not dare express our thoughts.

In any event, it was now two or three days that we had been in 'Akká, anxiously awaiting the arrival of 'Abdu'l-Bahá. In the first few days of our pilgrimage we had become so intoxicated with the wine of reunion that we were utterly forgetful of ourselves and only conscious of Him. But now that heavenly effect was wearing off, and we were in need of another cup of His love. Although the sweetness of His nearness would have been unforgettable even after a thousand years, yet the venom of separation was too bitter to endure.

It takes a more bitter poison than separation from you
To make me forget the sweetness of your nearness.

This is because the memories of 'Akká can never fade and the sweetness of attaining the Master's presence will forever endure in the deepest recesses of our hearts.

What was unusual at that time was that the Covenant-breakers seemed to be more active in their opposition to the Faith than the friends were in its defence. Their strategy included soliciting the help of non-Bahá'ís, with whom they were in constant secret communication. These they encouraged to participate in their gatherings, in the hope of discovering the plans and activities of the friends and also to make themselves appear to the non-Bahá'í community as a forthright and friendly people. In fact, the appearance of Mírzá Badí'u'lláh and the Ottoman officer in Haifa was one such manoeuvre.

After a few days, the Sun of the Beauty of the Covenant appeared over the horizon of 'Akká and our joy knew no bounds. First, prominent members of the non-Bahá'í community arrived to pay their respects, after which He summoned the friends and the pilgrims. From this day on, life in 'Akká became organized and friends from Iran, Baghdad, Egypt and even India began to arrive in groups.

The life of the pilgrims in 'Akká

The pilgrim house, as already mentioned, was a pleasant and happy place. It consisted of a storage room, a kitchen and a warehouse. Regardless of their number, the pilgrims stayed there in contentment and joy. Áqá Muḥammad Ḥasan, the custodian of the pilgrim house, sometimes by himself and at other times with the assistance of a helper, attended to the needs of the pilgrims, kept the house in pristine condition and generally coordinated and organized the affairs of the pilgrims with such efficiency and dedication that nothing short of divine confirmation could inspire such perfection.

As to the residence of 'Abdu'l-Bahá[28]: its simplicity and spiritual atmosphere was beyond description. The building itself was old and immense, and had formerly belonged to a prominent family of 'Akká. One upper and one lower apartment had been leased by 'Abdu'l-Bahá. Another apartment belonged to the Protestant missionaries who had turned the lower apartment into an infirmary for the Arabs and every morning taught the patients the principles of Christianity. The front yard, which covered an area of about 200 square metres, had been landscaped in accordance with the Master's instructions. This natural verdant garden, with beautiful flowers in bloom, two palm trees in their midst and a grape vine in one corner, filled the air with heavenly fragrance, especially at the hour when the Master, pacing back and forth on the paths, summoned the pilgrims to the Abhá Paradise.

The lower level, consisting of a few rooms, was the *bírúní*[29] and was called the *darb-khánih*.[30] The upper floor was the *andárúní*, which consisted of two rooms. One was His office and the other, simply furnished with two or three couches, was the reception room where He entertained guests. Three windows of this room looked out to the sea and to the stone walls that had been built as a defence of the citadel of 'Akká. Although the splash of the billowing waves against the stone walls of the fortress was daunting, yet the sunsets were overwhelmingly beautiful. These are some details relating to the life of the pilgrims at that time.

The pilgrims were usually awakened in the morning by the beautiful prayer chanted by one of the friends, such as Mírzá Faḍlu'lláh. After the observance of the morning obligatory prayer and having had tea and a small breakfast, everyone walked over to the *darb-khánih*, which consisted of one large room and a coffee room. Here they met the friends, conversed on various Bahá'í topics and read aloud from letters containing references to the Faith received from their hometowns. This would continue until 'Abdu'l-Bahá, on His way out of the house, would greet the pilgrims before departing; at times He would stop briefly, say a few words, and extend His love to the pilgrims before leaving the house. At noon the friends would return to the pilgrim house and be served a prepared lunch, after which no one missed the *qaylulih*, as it was commonly known in 'Akká, an afternoon rest of half an hour to an hour.

Following the nap, tea was served and then we strolled toward the *darb-khánih*. As night fell, the friends arriving from their homes or their places of work began to assemble in the *bírúní* area of 'Abdu'l-Bahá's residence and shared news about the Faith, whether from abroad or locally, which they had received that day. This continued until 'Abdu'l-Bahá's arrival, when He would occupy a chair and address the group. Or He would walk up the stairs to the *andárúní* area, summon the friends individually or collectively, and acquaint them with the divine teachings as He saw fit. At times non-Bahá'ís or town dignitaries would be granted permission to visit 'Abdu'l-Bahá on Fridays and Sundays, which were days of rest referred to as the Days of Visitation. On these days the friends, whether pilgrims or residents of 'Akká, were expected to visit the Shrine of Bahá'u'lláh, of which I shall write more later.

On Bahá'í holy days, the friends passed time in the beautiful Firdaws or Riḍván Gardens, or attended festivities at the House of 'Abdu'l-Bahá. Of course the afternoon visit to the Shrine of Bahá'u'lláh was mandatory.

The duration of the pilgrims' stay in 'Akká or the length of pilgrimage was not predetermined. Depending on personal situation, weather conditions, Covenant-breakers' intrigues, mischief of the enemies, or other causes the significance of which may not have been evident to us, a pilgrim could remain in 'Akká anywhere between two days and four months.

During these days, as the pilgrims observed the divisive actions of the Covenant-breakers and the hostile activities of the enemies of the Cause directed against the Centre of the Covenant, and heard His heart-rending utterances, they became so inflamed with the fire of the love of God that they illumined any land they travelled to with the light of divine love. In fact, I did not meet a single pilgrim who did not desire to lay down his life for the Faith. This was especially likely at that time, since for those who did not observe prudence and caution a variety of perils typically leading to long prison terms and even martyrdom were realities which could be anticipated as a matter of course. Completion of pilgrimage and departure from 'Akká was announced to each pilgrim at a day's notice. Áqá Muḥammad Ḥasan, who coordinated the activities of the pilgrims, had received from them the title of Michael, the Angel of Life, as he was the one who usually brought the glad tidings of 'Abdu'l-Bahá's summons for the friends to attain His presence. On the last day of pilgrimage, however, he was renamed 'Izra'il, the Messenger of Death, for bringing the bad news – that is, the end of someone's pilgrimage. How happy were the times when he arrived proud and joyful and announced: "The pilgrims are summoned," and alas the day when he arrived disconcerted, his head hanging low, to announce: "In accordance with 'Abdu'l-Bahá's instructions, such and such a pilgrim is to take his leave tomorrow on such and such a ship."

The daily routine of the pilgrims consisted of correspondence with their home lands, the transcription and copying of sacred verses and various other Writings, and at times the conveying of 'Abdu'l-Bahá's instructions to others, if they were so bidden. Another activity that engaged almost all the pilgrims in both work and recreation and had become a customary occupation since the inception of the pilgrim house, was wheat sifting. This was a service easily accomplished, entailing no major responsibility. What performed the work were the eyes and the tips of the five fingers, leaving the ears, the tongue and the intellectual faculties free; this encouraged many pleasant activities such as the telling of anecdotes and humorous stories. Chanting and singing songs were also permitted. Normally

Mírzá Faḍlu'lláh, who had a melodious voice, took over with beautiful songs.

A more detailed description of the wheat sifting process is as follows: in the mornings after breakfast the servant attached to the pilgrim house would spread a large tablecloth on the floor and place a round low table at its centre. He would then carry inside bags of wheat, already machine sifted and washed. The friends would empty the bags onto the table, sit around the table and sift the wheat manually so that it could be sent to the mill. Every day a portion of the flour received from the mill was made into dough and the resulting baked bread was consumed with the famous Persian stew, *abgusht*.[31]

Visiting the Shrine of Bahá'u'lláh

From the first year following the ascension of the Blessed Beauty, visiting His Shrine was, in accordance with 'Abdu'l-Bahá's instructions, a required duty as well as a sign of devotion and faith. And so the pilgrims and the residents were required on Fridays and Sundays to leave 'Akká and in a state of utter humility and lowliness approach that blessed Spot while chanting prayers. In the proximity of the Shrine there was a place where everyone stopped to rest and refresh themselves before approaching the Shrine and performing the rites of visitation. Before the second incarceration of 'Abdu'l-Bahá and while He was still permitted to leave the city, He would frequently accompany the friends on these visits to the Shrine and in fact would Himself chant the Tablet of Visitation. From the second or third year after the ascension of Bahá'u'lláh, certain ceremonial details were added to the visits, which made the overall experience a profound spiritual event full of meaning and significance to friend and stranger alike. This practice had gained such renown that both friends and foes, and especially government officials – including military officers, civil servants, judges, and even the muftis who were the religious authorities of the Ottoman government – having observed the grandness of the spectacle and overcome by the spiritual intensity and humble devotion of the pilgrims, displayed a great desire to participate in that solemn act of pilgrimage.

The visits to the Shrine of Bahá'u'lláh were performed on two occasions: first, on weekends, i.e. Fridays and Sundays, and second, on Bahá'í Holy Days.

Pilgrimage on Fridays and Sundays

Just outside the House of 'Abdu'l-Bahá was the courtyard where the stable and the carriage were located. 'Abdu'l-Bahá owned two carriages: a large one which could seat nine and was referred to as the American carriage, and a conventional one capable of seating only four. On Fridays and Sundays a few hours before sunset, 'Abdu'l-Bahá's renowned carriage driver, Isfandíyár, prepared one of the carriages and drove it out into the courtyard where any of the pilgrims and residents who arrived in time could board. As to the seating arrangement, the pilgrims enjoyed first priority. Isfandíyár would drive the friends in groups to Bahjí. 'Abdu'l-Bahá Himself, however, covered the distance on foot, either alone or in the company of one or two of the believers. In the first years after the ascension of Bahá'u'lláh a small room on the ground floor of the Mansion had been used by the pilgrims for a short rest before entering the Shrine itself. But shortly afterwards the Covenant-breakers took possession of that room and 'Abdu'l-Bahá found another place for the friends to assemble.[32]

Sometimes 'Abdu'l-Bahá travelled by carriage, but most often on foot. Arriving at Bahjí, He would rest briefly in the room adjoining the Shrine and then summon the friends inside, where in complete silence He would disperse rosewater on each and every visitor. After kneeling to kiss the threshold, He would rise to chant the Tablet of Visitation. As I write these words I can see with the eye of spirit 'Abdu'l-Bahá standing before the threshold in supplication and I can hear His sublime powerful voice chanting the beautiful verses. Here memory plays no part, for it is the heart and the soul that in a state of utter attraction commit to the treasury of spirit every word that leaves the blessed lips of 'Abdu'l-Bahá. My feeble heart trembles at the vibrations of His blessed voice as if there were a direct connection between that celestial chant and the nerve centre of my heart.

As He chants the verses in utmost humility, repeating the passages twice: "Waft, then, unto me, O my God and my Beloved, from the right hand of Thy mercy and Thy lovingkindness, the holy breaths of Thy favours, that they may draw me away from myself and from the world unto the courts of Thy nearness and Thy presence" – the holy breaths of divine favours are indeed wafted and the divine fragrance is in truth inhaled by the spirit, cleansing the heart from attachment to the world and summoning the spirit to the divine rosegarden. The physical body is released from all that is earthly and the spirit is transported to the courts of nearness. O God, what world is this? How I long never to return to the world of darkness or hear the satanic whisperings of the evil ones. Ah, how I wish that I could live in a world where none but 'Abdu'l-Bahá would have a claim on my heart. O God, keep our hearts faithful in the love of 'Abdu'l-Bahá, for He is the light that will guide us to the Abhá paradise.

As the chanting of the Tablet of Visitation ends, we step back slowly out of the Shrine and once more put on our shoes. 'Abdu'l-Bahá is nowhere to be seen. The friends stand around, waiting. Suddenly that celestial Being appears and silently walks out of the Shrine. Their hearts filled with the love of 'Abdu'l-Bahá, the believers follow Him like a company of angels. There is absolute silence. Ah, what an atmosphere. Now 'Abdu'l-Bahá begins to chant some verses from Bahá'u'lláh. Surely, ears were given to us to hear such melodies. O, God, please, deprive not these servants of such bounty. O, behold the distinguished figure of 'Abdu'l-Bahá.

The graceful peacock and the strutting partridge,
Will cease their flaunting once they behold your gait.

Soon we arrive at the town gate and enter the Most Great Prison. It is dusk. People watch us with curious eyes. We enjoy the experience all the more. Now we are at the door of 'Abdu'l-Bahá's residence. The Beloved of the hearts climbs the stairs. We enter the reception room downstairs and take our seats. The chanter[33] of the Qur'án arrives and begins to chant the verses: "I take refuge in Alláh from Satan the accursed. In the name of Alláh, the most benevolent, ever merciful. Verily I saw eleven stars…"! Now we come to our senses again.

O my dear readers, if perusing these lines thrills and inspires you and makes you thirst for a similar pilgrimage, do not despair; do not lose hope. In the presence of the Guardian of the Cause of God, as he chants the Tablet of Visitation at the Shrine of 'Abdu'l-Bahá, you will experience the same emotions. So hasten, hasten; attain, attain.

Pilgrimage on Holy Days

A number of flowerpots containing flowers of various hues were usually brought and placed in the *birúní* of the House of 'Abdu'l-Bahá, ready to be transported to the Shrine of Bahá'u'lláh. On Holy Days all the pilgrims and residents assembled at the House of 'Abdu'l-Bahá about two hours before sunset or when the heat of the day was not excessive. They would all be dressed in their best clothes. Each would place a flowerpot on his shoulder and take his place in one of two columns, ready to depart on foot towards the Shrine. During my time in 'Akká the starting point was not the House of 'Abdu'l-Bahá, because of the machinations of the Covenant-breakers and the evil whisperings of the enemies of the Faith. In those times the flowerpots would be brought to the gate of 'Akká and placed there for the pilgrims. The exodus, then, began from that point as 'Abdu'l-Bahá, not unlike a General in the field, walked sometimes in front and sometimes at the side of the columns, a flowerpot on His shoulder. Issuing instructions and commands as the march continued, this General of the hearts led the army of light toward its destination. The two or three pilgrims who had melodious voices chanted beautiful verses, such as Bahá'u'lláh's Mathnaví,[34] His Sáqí Namih,[35] or sometimes the poetry composed at the time of the Blessed Beauty for that particular occasion. In this vein the procession would progress, slowly and with great dignity and order, until the Shrine could be seen at a distance. At the command of 'Abdu'l-Bahá everyone would stop and place the flowerpots on the ground, and then someone would chant a prayer in a resonant voice:

"O, my God, my Desire and my Beloved! Thou art my origin and unto Thee do I repair. Illumine my heart with the light of thy knowledge."[36]

I am utterly incapable of describing the atmosphere generated or the heightened spiritual state which dominated our inner beings. It was truly a different world. The Arabs standing nearby watching us were silent and utterly fascinated by what they observed. Once the flowerpots were delivered at the Shrine, another prayer was chanted and then everyone would enter a room where tea and pastries were served and the friends had an opportunity to rest and perform their ablutions before entering the Shrine.

At this point 'Abdu'l-Bahá, who had already entered the Shrine, would invite the friends to enter. After the chanting of the Tablet of Visitation as previously described, He would ask the friends to be seated. Then verses revealed for that occasion were chanted by one or two of the believers; at times some chanted some of the mystical verses of Bahá'u'lláh such as "Hálih-Hálih-Yá-Bishárát".[37]

On the first Holy Day that I visited the Shrine, after the chanting of the Tablet revealed specifically for that occasion, 'Abdu'l-Bahá selected to be chanted the Tablet revealed in my honour during my youth: "He is the speaker before the faces of all men. Verily the gate of the highest paradise was flung open, whereby emerged the incomparable Beauty, and passing above all heads He called out with a great calling, 'O denizens of the earth and the heavens...'"[38] In this Tablet I am addressed by name and encouraged and commanded to teach the Faith. The selection of this Tablet and especially the reference to my name left me in state of euphoria.

As previously described, the friends would depart and proceed toward 'Akká, all circling like moths around that divine Candle which illuminated their hearts.

Feasts

Two types of feasts were held in 'Akká. One was the public feast, which was held in either the Garden of Riḍván or the Mansion of Bahjí. The other was a special feast observed for the pilgrims at the House of 'Abdu'l-Bahá. At the public feasts it was typical for one type of food to be served, such as Chinese kebab or pot kebab,[39] the selection and preparation of which was under the direction of the Master. In such cases He would appear for just a few minutes to supervise the service. The absolute simplicity and cleanliness of the dinner table created an atmosphere of love and spirituality. This type of feast was normally held on Holy Days. The special or private feasts for the pilgrims were distinctive and beautiful events. The table was wonderfully decorated with flowers of assorted colours which not only revived the spirit but also stimulated the appetite. This feast was, in all its details, conducted and supervised by the Master. He would summon the friends to the table, seat each one individually, moving fluidly around the table and serving each guest with His own hand. Then He would leave the room briefly, allowing the friends to concentrate on the food. He would then return, and while speaking of happy things, replenish any plate in need of another helping. Here, there were multiple types of food, all Persian dishes but placed on the table in European style,[40] which looked very appetizing. Since the number of guests usually exceeded the table placements and chairs, the food was served in two sittings. The atmosphere of the second sitting was just as wonderful as the first. Once the first group was finished, all the dishes would be collected and the tablecloth replaced with a fresh one, and thus the cleanliness and beauty of the table would remain intact. As to the Master himself, He ate at the third sitting. He would summon all the servants around the table and they ate together.

The first time I was present at such a feast, I noticed that the pilgrims were so totally enthralled by 'Abdu'l-Bahá's presence and so captivated by His walk and His bearing that no-one touched his food. Once He noticed us gazing at Him with worshipping eyes, He emphatically commanded us to begin eating. It was then that I recovered my senses and decided not to lose the opportunity. Therefore, as a service to myself and on behalf of all the believers and devoted servants of God, I performed my duty conscientiously and ate as much as I could. As the great Sa'dí has said:

> *In the feast that is hosted by the Beloved*
> *The glutton thinks of nothing but food.*

Since this meal was composed of both physical and spiritual nourishment, its pleasing flavour will forever remain intact in my memory.

Morale of the believers in the days of hardship

In those difficult and perilous times, the believers' thoughts and morale were quite peculiar and not readily understandable by today's standards, unless one had observed or experienced the events of that time first hand. Those faithful old resident believers[41] who had accompanied the Holy Family since the beginning of the exile to Baghdad, Adrianople and Istanbul up to their arrival at the Most Great Prison and during their subsequent release and move to the Mansion of Bahjí had been witnesses to the ever-growing rank and the exalted position of the Master. This was clear, as He was held in the highest regard by the Blessed Beauty while commanding the obedience and devotion of both the Afnán and the Aghsán. Now these believers had to endure the pain of beholding that radiant Being, that heavenly Beloved, in such harsh and humbling circumstances. They were sorrow-stricken and heartbroken.

Hardly a day passed without a new plot being devised or a new intrigue planned. Covenant-breakers' accusations and charges against 'Abdu'l-Bahá were so widespread that the whole of Syrian citizenry had utterly misunderstood 'Abdu'l-Bahá, and even those whose very daily livelihood was provided through the charity of the Master had also rebelled against Him.

Those dignitaries of 'Akká, Haifa, Beirut and Damascus who had themselves attested to the Master's spiritual power and ascendancy and had even claimed to have witnessed miracles, now expressed disgust behind His back, and contributed to the cause of the Covenant-breakers in vilifying 'Abdu'l-Bahá. Yet in His presence they became the very embodiments of loyalty.

The number of His loyal non-Bahá'í devotees was on the decline, while the number of troublemakers increased daily. The friends' sorrow, pain and anguish at this state of affairs knew no end. However, 'Abdu'l-Bahá's presence, His kind and loving words and cheerful demeanour, brought the light of hope to their hearts and infused new vigour into their drooping souls.

In those days, the sun of the Cause of God had but recently risen on the Western horizon. Each week, large numbers of enrolment cards and letters containing religious and philosophical questions were received from Western scholars, some of which were read in translation to the friends in the *bírúní* of the House of 'Abdu'l-Bahá. Those friends who had suffered for the Faith and had tasted the pain of incarceration and humiliation in the path of God considered the Cause to be an Eastern religion and could not imagine that such an intensely spiritual philosophy could spread so quickly in the West or that Western materialistic scholars would show any interest in drawing spiritual sustenance from such a divine Source.

At the same time, however, the flood of polemic writings by the Covenant-breakers was pouring into Iran, all of which – along with the decisive and categorical rebuttals written by the friends containing incontestable proofs of the legitimacy of the position of the Centre of the Covenant – were sent to 'Abdu'l-Bahá. The Master kept some of them and permitted others to be read aloud in either the pilgrim house or the *bírúní* of His residence.

These joyful tidings from the Westerners, indicating the depth of their faith and commitment to the Cause, revived the hearts and brought joy to the souls. And the potent and unequivocal proofs that the friends in Iran extracted from the divine Tablets and the various Biblical scriptures generated a sense of excitement and exuberance in the believers. They became so exhilarated and inspired that they gave speeches and wrote essays proving the heresy and infidelity of the violators of the Covenant of God.

Since at that time the Covenant-breakers could not be readily distinguished from the believers, there were always some of them in the group, wolves in sheep's clothing. These unfaithful renegades recounted whatever they had heard in the House of 'Abdu'l-Bahá to the Covenant-breakers in the Mansion, encouraging them to widen the scope of their seditious activities and to reach a larger area with their published materials. And so the struggle continued, leaving neither the resident believers nor the pilgrims any peace. One moment they were happy and the next they wept.

When we were in 'Abdu'l-Bahá's presence, His words of assurance and the glad tidings of the ultimate victory of the Faith created such an atmosphere of attraction and enthusiasm that one would utterly lose oneself and become wholly absorbed in the Master. Examples of such words may be found in the various prayers and Tablets of 'Abdu'l-Bahá.[42] Today it is time to review those prophecies and experience joy and delight at their fulfilment.

Such was the morale of the friends at that time. Now read about the ploys of the Covenant-breakers.

The schemes of the Covenant-breakers

A short account of the schemes of the Covenant-breakers has been presented previously. Those friends who are acquainted with the words of 'Abdu'l-Bahá are of course aware that the Arch-breaker of the Covenant had shown signs of faithlessness while in Baghdad. Furthermore, during his mission to Bombay to publish Bahá'u'lláh's Writings, he had altered a number of the words of the divine verses in order to undermine the concept of the Covenant. His secret agreements with the Old Hyena are described at the outset of this account. After the ascension of Bahá'u'lláh, as the friends are aware, he stole certain of the divine verses and began a systematic alteration of the revealed Text. These events have been amply described by 'Abdu'l-Bahá in His talks and Tablets.[43]

From the day that the Kitáb-i-'Ahd was read in 'Akká, the Arch-breaker of the Covenant gathered around him the Aghṣán, the Afnán, and a group of his own cronies who had been secretly supporting him, and formed a council [*hai'át*] to oppose the divine Covenant. This group exerted its utmost to create disunity among the friends of God. They utilized deceptions and schemes which one would only read about in stories and legends, the description of which is not worthy of mention.

Through the powers of discovery and invention, the mind of man has conquered the world of nature, has brought to light the secrets of the power of magnetism and electricity, and has in so doing extended the civilization of humankind. But at times, it also has enhanced man's capacity to destroy itself. In the same way, the minds of the Covenant-breakers, who were utterly devoid of the understanding of the truth of the Faith and the Divine Will, had perceived ways, devised methods, and created plots which they thought would guarantee them ultimate success. Since they were ignorant of the spirit of the Faith, they considered the progress of the Cause to be a political matter and imagined that expediency and political strategy would in the end bring to them the power to control the Faith of God.

They took great pride in their internal unity and had placed their investigators and spies in especially sensitive areas of the city, with the ultimate intention of establishing a Caliphate-like form of theocracy after the Sunni pattern and accordingly: Relegate 'Alí to his own house rather than the House of the Caliph.[44] For example, as the sons of the "Great Effendi", which is how Bahá'u'lláh was known to the Turks and Arabs, they had established direct liaison with the political centres of the Ottoman Empire, their agents continually travelling back and forth between 'Akká and Istanbul. In order to establish these contacts, they had made gifts to the enemies of the Faith of a number of precious articles which they had purloined from the House of 'Abdu'l-Bahá. The continuation of this form of bribery, however, eventually served to expose these various secret relationships. It came to light that many of the Ottoman civil and military authorities in 'Akká, Haifa, Beirut, Damascus and even in Istanbul had been brought into the camp of the Covenant-breakers by frequent acts of bribery.

For instance, when Kaiser Wilhelm, the German Emperor, paid an official visit to the Ottoman capital as a guest of the government, he decided to make a tour of the holy sites of Palestine. Before his arrival in Haifa, Mírzá Badí'u'lláh had persuaded the Emperor's chamberlain to permit him to present a gift of welcome to the Emperor. As the Emperor disembarked at Haifa port, his very first steps landed on the cherished and priceless Persian carpets offered by Badí'u'lláh as unworthy gifts to the threshold of the Emperor. He was subsequently introduced to the Emperor as a son of Bahá'u'lláh. It is obvious how precious and exquisite must have been the gifts which merited presentation at such an occasion and through what intrigues they must have fallen into the hands of the Covenant-breakers, and how painful such a shameful and obscene act must have been to the believers.

The Covenant-breakers, however, were ecstatic, overjoyed at the Emperor's acceptance of their gift; for them it was an occasion for celebration and merrymaking. They supposed that after completing their mastery of the Ottoman Empire and control over the prominent members of the ruling class, Germany, its government and its people would be next on their list of conquests! They considered the Emperor of Germany as prey to be successfully trapped by the bait of two Persian rugs. One might have said: "You unfortunate creatures, the prey came, snatched the bait and laughed at your foolishness!"

So these were their plans in the political arena. As to their thoughts regarding religious and spiritual matters, they had devised many plots, engaged themselves in many conspiracies and laid assorted traps for newly enrolled Bahá'ís, as well as for those of uncertain or shaky belief – plots that no one could dream up or imagine. Their spies attended all Bahá'í meetings, mixed with the friends, especially the pilgrims, and seemed to be loyal, staunch and faithful believers in the Covenant – so much so that everyone praised their level of dedication and faithfulness. Then, while exhibiting great love and devotion for 'Abdu'l-Bahá, they would begin to point out the faithlessness and disloyalty of one of the most prominent and dedicated believers, gradually increasing the number and severity of their accusations until they succeeded in making him appear to be a Covenant-breaker.

The poor uninformed pilgrim, basing the validity of such intelligence on the spiritual dedication of the source, which had already been amply demonstrated to him, would share this information with others. Before long this created a tumult and the allegations would spread far and wide. A newly enrolled Bahá'í, still lacking the knowledge and wisdom to assess the situation, would on hearing these fabrications about the Covenant-breaking activities of one of the most trusted teachers of the Faith, begin to be attracted to the cause of the Covenant-breakers themselves. In this way, the devotion and resolve of the friends were undermined, and if such a believer while investigating the situation unwittingly confided the matter to another Covenant-breaker, he would be further deceived in the same preplanned process.

The Covenant-breaker would begin by exaggerating the rank of 'Abdu'l-Bahá, stating that His station was even loftier than that of Bahá'u'lláh Himself. While praising the Covenant, he would level a series of accusations against the entire group of the true believers. He would refer to 'Abdu'l-Bahá by His titles of "Him Whom God hath purposed", or "Him round Whom all names revolve" instead of the title of "Master" which had been used by Bahá'u'lláh and subsequently exclusively used by the friends.[45] He would then claim that, while in the act of prayer, he focused his thoughts and mental faculties on the person of 'Abdu'l-Bahá, since 'Abdu'l-Bahá was no less sacred than the House of the Ka'bih in Mecca. Right after this, he would level a series of complaints about the faithful believers and accuse them of disloyalty to the Faith. The poor pilgrim was then guided to yet another more crafty and devious one, who supplied him with an armful of Covenant-breaker writings for his information and edification.

At that time 'Abdu'l-Bahá always referred to the Covenant-breakers in His many talks as evil ones, and prohibited the friends from any association with them, similar to Bahá'u'lláh's interdiction regarding association with Mírzá Yaḥyá's followers. 'Abdu'l-Bahá's emphasis on His prohibition was definitive and unequivocal. In the words of Ḥa'fiẓ:

> *Our wise old man, may his soul rest in peace,*
> *Warned us to refrain from speaking with those that break the Covenant.*

In truth, whoever fell into the trap of the Covenant-breakers was deprived of salvation, lost beyond any possibility of redemption.

One of the ploys used by the Covenant-breakers was to

select, without any apparent logic, one of the more naive and innocent pilgrims and then fabricate a story about the poor man's Covenant-breaking activities and relate them to as many ears as were willing to listen. Their agent would spread the rumour that he had seen the man in conversation with a Covenant-breaker and even noticed that he was carrying Covenant-breaker writings in his pocket. "I saw him bow to Mírzá Muḥammad-'Alí in the street," or "I noticed that he did not rise from his seat when 'Abdu'l-Bahá entered the room."

For a while they would continue to spread false accusations until a commotion would ensue and the unfortunate pilgrim would become embroiled in the suspicion and contempt of the friends. Then they would corner him and tell him that the friends suspected him unjustly, saying, "How can someone as faithful and loyal to the Faith of God as yourself become suspected of cooperating with the Covenant-breakers? Obviously something must be wrong. This shows that not all the Covenant-breakers are truly disloyal. There must be one or two main culprits who truly are the enemies of the Faith, but surely the rest are only going through a terrible test. And consider the unfairness of the friends, who have completely abandoned them as outcasts. What is important is to be acceptable at the threshold of the Blessed Beauty, let people say whatever they want." These words were enough for the gullible pilgrim to be plunged from the heights of faith and fidelity to the abyss of doubt and apathy.

Another of the Covenant-breakers' ploys was to denounce, in their sinister publications, those friends who were closest to 'Abdu'l-Bahá and make them appear as the real trouble-makers and firebrands. "They it was", they would proclaim, "who broke 'Abdu'l-Bahá's heart with these unfounded allegations against us loyal servants." In these publications they would sometimes unexpectedly, and without any apparent reason, praise the qualities and character of one of the true believers and exalt his position to exaggerated heights. This precipitated the suspicion of the friends towards that individual, and the subsequent circulation of rumours would undermine his good reputation and standing in the community.

In one such published document they expressed great praise and admiration for Mírzá Abu'l-Faḍl in order to throw suspicion on him and subject him to the believers' scorn and rebuke. But that blessed soul issued a clear and eloquent response in refutation of the contents of that document and sent it to 'Abdu'l-Bahá. This response was read aloud in the *bírúní* of the Master's house. In his refutation, Mírzá Abu'l-Faḍl denied the grandiose eminent station to which he was elevated in the Covenant-breaker publication, adding: "I am not the person for whom you have expressed such praise. I happen to be the person who is the subject of your hatred and rejection. And if you have detected any virtues in me, it is 'Abdu'l-Bahá's friends who should acknowledge and admire them and not the likes of you."

Another trick of the Covenant-breakers was that whenever their founder and chief – who had been officially cast out of the Bahá'í community and had no association with any of the friends – encountered a pilgrim in the street or in the marketplace, he greeted him with a great show of humility and apparent sincerity. To the eyes of a passerby, the lack of any response by the believer to such an expression of friendship and kindliness could be misinterpreted as an outright insult by the pilgrim, which reflected poorly on 'Abdu'l-Bahá and was of great benefit to the Covenant-breakers.

In short, they used a multitude of ruses and deceptions in 'Akká and other cities just to compromise a soul and bring sadness to the heart of 'Abdu'l-Bahá. In those times the great majority of the Master's words pertained to tests and difficulties and He went to great lengths to explain and elaborate the issues in order to awaken the friends to such ploys.

As detailed in many of His Tablets revealed in those days, He had concealed the disunity and faithlessness of the Covenant-breakers for years, tolerating their enmity and hatred without mentioning a word to anyone until they themselves, by sending their publications to Iran, at last disclosed their own disloyalty and subsequent break from the Faith of God.

The Master used to say, "One day Mírzá Díyá'u'lláh came to pay a visit. I noticed he kept staring at his fingers, which were stained black, waiting for me to enquire about them. I said nothing until he explained: 'Last night we were busy until dawn writing and printing our publications for shipment to Iran, and that is why my fingers are stained.' He added, 'Last night my brother [Mírzá Muḥammad-'Alí] produced some writings which we printed and shipped this morning.' I admonished him, 'Verily, I testify that there is no God but God, soon a day will come that Mírzá Muḥammad-'Alí will say, "How I wish my fingers had been broken so that I could not take up the pen and announce my violation of the Covenant." I concealed the matter for four years and did not reveal it to the friends. But now it is out of My hands and I can no longer conceal the matter, for you have exposed yourselves.'"

While the writings of the Covenant-breakers, containing all sorts of lies, half-truths and accusations, were being hurled like double-headed darts at the hearts of the faithful friends, they never denied the verse revealed by Bahá'u'lláh: "Turn your faces toward Him Whom God hath purposed,"[46] but they continued to complain, make accusations and advance claims without openly questioning 'Abdu'l-Bahá's authority. And while I had not read any such writings myself, I knew their nature from the rebuttals which had been formally issued by the friends. One such claim was that 'Abdu'l-Bahá was not infallible but had claimed divinity and had rejected the Aghṣán's counsel on matters relating to the Faith. In short, since we considered them the violators of the Covenant of God because of their opposition to the Centre of the Covenant, they in turn referred to us as infidels, since we had excluded them from participating in the administration of the Faith.

The Covenant-breakers attended secret meetings in which they planned their goals and devised ways to accomplish them. 'Abdu'l-Bahá was, of course, always well aware of these plans and intrigues, and at receptions where He entertained the pilgrims and the residents – among whom a goodly contingent of the Covenant-breakers was usually present – He would disclose and describe their strategies. This alerted the believers to become mindful of the dangers associated with such conspiracies. At the same time, the Covenant-breakers were made aware of His complete knowledge of the situation and the secret informers discovered that their secret was out. But the Master never named names, thereby manifesting and demonstrating His heavenly qualities of mercy and concealment of sins.

As pointed out earlier, the strategy of the Covenant-breakers was implemented through political and religious channels, or by accusing 'Abdu'l-Bahá of injustice towards them. In fact, this third approach was their most effective weapon. Such accusations, of course, were devoid of truth and the friends were aware of 'Abdu'l-Bahá's intentions and actions. But on local non-Bahá'í residents these complaints left the desired impression. For instance, all the believers were aware that after the ascension of Bahá'u'lláh the Covenant-breakers had pilfered whatever they could from His personal belongings including some priceless items, as well as Bahá'u'lláh's personal storage chest which contained many of His Tablets and His personal seal. However, once in the presence of their non-Bahá'í friends, they always complained of their miserable impoverished lifestyle. They sent written accounts of their pitiful condition to all the acquaintances of 'Abdu'l-Bahá in Palestine, Damascus and old Turkey, tearfully expressing their grief and anguish for what had befallen them.

Having perused 'Abdu'l-Bahá's sublime and eloquent literary style, the vast majority of the divines of the region had developed a special regard and deep reverence for Him. Nevertheless, the Arch-breaker of the Covenant sent each one of these men, in his own hand, letters filled with accusations against 'Abdu'l-Bahá, imploring them for justice and assistance. Those divines who were not acquainted with 'Abdu'l-Bahá, or those who harboured hatred in their hearts for the Master due to religious prejudice, considered these letters to be ample justification for rising in opposition against Him. Others, who bore no resentment towards the Master, sent Him the letters and asked for an explanation. One of these divines was the Mufti of 'Akká, who having received such a letter forwarded it to 'Abdu'l-Bahá. The Master responded thus: "O Mufti, thou hast pronounced judgement upon us while we are a prisoner and have fallen into the clutches of the company that returned from the banks of the Euphrates after precipitating that which caused the lamentation of earth and heaven."[47]

The dwarfish old man

On this pilgrimage, whenever 'Abdu'l-Bahá summoned us to His presence in His reception room I often saw an old man, short in stature with white beard and dark complexion, who would arrive after everyone else, prostrate himself, kiss the threshold, and then enter the room and bow almost to the waist before 'Abdu'l-Bahá. He would then take his seat near the entrance door when motioned to do so by the Master. I had often intended to enquire about the identity of the stranger but somehow I failed to remember to do so. The obvious reason was that while in the presence of 'Abdu'l-Bahá, we were so intoxicated by the wine of His bounty and love that the last thing I could think of was to ask about someone's identity.

One day when I was in His presence and seated near the doorway, I saw the old man arrive. First he prostrated himself and kissed the threshold of the antechamber where visitors removed their shoes, then he walked in and again prostrated himself and kissed the threshold of the room before entering. He then bowed in a grand style and stood motionless until he received the Master's permission to sit near the door. As he took his seat with downcast eyes I continued to remain baffled as to his identity and why it was that I had not seen him among the believers of the community. At the end of His remarks, which took about thirty minutes, 'Abdu'l-Bahá motioned to the stranger to chant a prayer. The old man instantly took out a prayer book from his pocket and began to chant one of Bahá'u'lláh's moving prayers in a voice becoming his age and stature.

Once we were dismissed from His presence and took the stairs to the lower floor, the stranger went in the direction of the *andárúní*. I immediately asked someone who he was, and was told he was none other than Mírzá Áqá Ján.

"Which Mírzá Áqá Ján?" I inquired.

"He is the 'Khádimú'lláh'[48] or 'Abd-i-Hadír', of whom you have surely heard," I was told.

"May he be accursed of God!" was my ready reaction. "Just can't find a moment's peace with these trouble-makers around," I concluded.

Khádimú'lláh had been out of favour since the days of Bahá'u'lláh and now at this time the Covenant-breakers were actively looking for him, intent on taking his life.

"What is he doing here?" I asked.

"He has taken refuge in 'Abdu'l-Bahá's house," I was told.

As I reflected about this old man, rejected and disliked by all, I had no idea that within two weeks he would play a significant role in the affairs of the Faith, the memory of which would never fade, and that I would be one of the observers of that performance.

The Covenant-breakers' means of livelihood

In those days, while 'Abdu'l-Bahá and His family were experiencing great hardship, the Covenant-breakers were living most comfortably. Their home was the Mansion of Bahjí, with its beautiful spacious living quarters and full furnishings. They received their expenses directly from 'Abdu'l-Bahá, Who provided for them no matter how dire were the circumstances. This was the lifestyle of the Covenant-breakers, while 'Abdu'l-Bahá lived in the conditions that have been described in earlier pages of this book.

Three individuals were in charge of the household's

annual, monthly and daily purchases of groceries and other needed provisions. Áqá Riḍá Qannád, one of the exiles and prisoners of Baghdad, who enjoyed 'Abdu'l-Bahá's complete trust, made purchases of wheat, charcoal, firewood, barley, hay, cooking oil, sugar and tea and other items of need which were in season. Typically, one of the friends would bring a list of the necessary daily food items to town and Áqá Riḍá or Áqá Asadu'lláh made the daily purchases and delivered them to the house.

On a few occasions I heard from resident Bahá'ís that the Mansion's daily expenditure for food was quite extravagant and that their lifestyle resembled that of a king who was holding official banquets. One day, quite by chance, I was shown a list of their required provisions and was astonished at the items requested which not even the wealthiest and most extravagant of households would indulge in. For example, in addition to requests for chickens, roosters and young chicks (although they already had chickens in the barnyard at Bahjí), they had specified several types of fish. The purpose of this strategy was to sap 'Abdu'l-Bahá's strength and energy and break Him physically.

In the meantime, they had concocted and spread a rumour that the payments of Ḥuqúqu'lláh[49] regularly sent by the believers to 'Abdu'l-Bahá were not in fact reaching Him. They claimed that members of His family had stolen His seal and were stamping the draft transfers and stealing the money for themselves. Because of this very rumour, the believers actually stopped sending their Ḥuqúqu'lláh, not knowing if their contributions reached 'Abdu'l-Bahá. The Covenant-breakers, who were aware of this, intended to apply as much pressure as they could to cause the Master to weaken and ultimately collapse. They thus came up with a list of essential necessities, the description of which is beyond the scope of this narrative.

Once, when I arrived at 'Abdu'l-Bahá's house and entered the reception room in the *bírúní*, 'Abdu'l-Bahá was in the process of giving instructions to Áqá Riḍá. As I entered the room the Master was saying: "Very well, go ahead and borrow some more money and make the purchases and deliver them to the Mansion." After 'Abdu'l-Bahá left I asked Áqá Riḍá about the discussion they had been having.

"I don't know what they are doing with all that food," he replied. "They must be either selling it or burning it. It has been only a few days since I sent them a complete supply of the provisions they requested. And now they are asking for more, while 'Abdu'l-Bahá's debts are mounting. I do not know what to do."

In short, this was another of their many ploys to exert as much pressure as possible on 'Abdu'l-Bahá in order to weaken Him and render Him powerless.

Types of Covenant-breakers

When the event associated with the verse "When the ocean of my Presence hath ebbed" came to pass,[50] and the Sun of the Beauty of the All-Glorious was hid from mortal eyes behind the clouds of mystery, and the divine Lote-Tree gave way to its fairest fruit of servitude and utter evanescence, and the verse "Servitude is the very essence of divinity" found its true significance in the person of 'Abdu'l-Bahá – at such a time, the leafless and fruitless Agh̲ṣán, who had lost their way and become lifeless, were finally severed from the tree of life and cast out of the community of the believers.

After that, each of the Agh̲ṣán employed a different attitude and strategy. The Arch-breaker of the Covenant Mírzá Muḥammad-'Alí, like his predecessor Yaḥyá Azal, secluded himself in a corner of the Mansion but directed Mírzá Badí'u-'lláh, his brother, in their struggle against 'Abdu'l-Bahá. Mírzá Ḍíyá'u'lláh, the other brother, who was an unstable and fickle individual, became an intermediary between 'Abdu'l-Bahá and Muḥammad-'Alí.

The activities of these three were quite obvious to all. All day long, Mírzá Badí'u'lláh ran about in all directions hoping to create as much dissension, devise as many schemes, and

'Abdu'l-Bahá, the Master

The house at the Cave of Elijah on Mount Carmel can be seen on the right of the top picture. Here 'Abdu'l-Bahá would stay during the summer months, in the upper storey shown in the photograph below. Youness K͟hán describes first meeting the Master here.
(Photographs by Edward Getsinger, c.1900)

Driving from Haifa to 'Akká along the sands (top): "as we approached the sea the billowing waves were but a reflection of the spiritual excitement of the friends". Below, the land approach to 'Akká.
(Photographs by C. M. Remey, 1908)

The pilgrims' first view of the Mansion and Shrine of Bahá'u'lláh at Bahjí. 'Abdu'l-Bahá would walk here from 'Akká, while on Holy Days He would be accompanied on foot by all the pilgrims and resident believers, carrying vases of flowers as described in Chapter 1.

The Shrine of Bahá'u'lláh in the time of 'Abdu'l-Bahá

The House of 'Abdu'lláh Páshá from the street, showing the main entrance under the archway. Here the Master lived and received pilgrims and visitors. Shoghi Effendi was born in the room above the arch in March 1897. To the right may be seen the wooden structure on the roof, built by 'Abdu'l-Bahá as a retreat where He could go to pray without interruption.

The garden in the courtyard of the House of 'Abdu'lláh Páshá. The Master's study is on the upper floor, just behind the palm tree.

The Khán-i-Avámid, the caravanserai where several Bahá'ís lived. (Photograph from the nineteenth century, École Biblique, Jerusalem)

initiate as many provocations as he could. Since this required association with different classes and types of people, and as he endeavoured to play his role to perfection, he had become a man of a thousand faces, dealing with each group in accordance with its own customs and expectations.

He therefore participated in all sorts of gatherings and assemblies and did whatever necessary in order to find acceptance with those groups and attract their sympathies towards the plans of the Covenant-breakers. It was said of him that he had involved himself in many immoral pursuits and even participated frequently in sessions of drunken debauchery in assorted garbs and guises.

As for the late Mírzá Ḍíyá'u'lláh, that poor unstable clown was never sure of anything. At times he was firm in the Covenant, and at other times he would become a violator. He was never sure of anything, including himself. He was usually the one who brought the messages of the Covenant-breakers to 'Abdu'l-Bahá.

As to the rest of the Covenant-breakers, they were of three types: first, those who were cut off from the Faith, who acted discourteously and were openly offensive in the presence of 'Abdu'l-Bahá; second, those who were entirely severed from the Faith and wandered about 'Akká with no further connection to the Cause. The third group comprised the trouble-makers and evil-doers who associated openly with the friends and were the informers and spies, carrying messages and reports to the Covenant-breakers on the basis of which they devised their next plans and hostile actions against the Faith.

My duties on this pilgrimage

While sifting wheat was an easy, trouble-free service entailing no responsibility and in fact bringing great pleasure, yet it seemed that God had destined me to perform a service even more pleasant and entertaining. In accordance with the Master's instructions I started a French class, teaching two or three young men for an hour each day. Furthermore, since the rays of the Sun of Truth had just begun to illumine the American horizon, pure-hearted men and women who had awakened from the stupor of heedlessness to the reality of the glad-tidings of Bahá'u'lláh were sending to 'Abdu'l-Bahá declarations of their acceptance of the Faith, and publishing proofs of the truth of the revelation of the Lord of the Age.

Reading, translating, and distributing of these papers sent by those holy souls, especially in the face of all the sinister and heinous publications of the Covenant-breakers, brought great joy and happiness. Whenever any of these translations contained interesting insights meriting public attention, the Master instructed me to read it to the believers in the pilgrim house, or send the document to Iran directly. The spiritual intensity and attraction of some of the American friends resembled that of the early believers in Iran and had the same effect on the American believers at large. This also applied to the resident Bahá'ís [in 'Akká] who, having suffered so much for the Faith, found great joy and encouragement in those letters.

Each day, nay every hour, we received another heartbreaking report about a fresh accusation or slander against 'Abdu'l-Bahá. At the same moment glad tidings would reach us from the West expressing endless love, devotion and joy and imparting news of the declaration of yet another group of God-intoxicated seekers; this quickly washed away the dross of sadness and melancholy. For example, we would receive news that in Iran the Covenant-breakers and the followers of Yaḥyá had united and so the enemies of the Faith were celebrating this event.

> *The town constable and preacher made a friendly pact,*
> *One evildoer became the helpmate of the other.*

But then news would reach us that such and such an American scholar, who had been a bitter opponent of the Faith for a long time, had declared and announced his conversion in the very church to which he had previously belonged.

Among the good news from America was an article

written by Ibráhím K͟hayru'lláh [Kheiralla] at 'Abdu'l-Bahá's request, which offered proofs of the validity of the Faith. In accordance with 'Abdu'l-Bahá's instructions I translated the article during the course of my stay[51] and on my departure was commanded by Him to take the document to Tehran and deliver it to Mírzá 'Alí-Akbar K͟hán Rawhání for circulation.

In short, the receipt of such news and the distribution of this type of publication brought great joy to the hearts of the friends but also added to the intense hatred and enmity of the Covenant-breakers. In Iran, they invented fresh designs each day and conceived of new plots in order to plant the seeds of corruption and disunity. In the Ottoman realms they spread the germs of hatred and discord. They did what they could to find their way into America, and caused the fall of K͟hayru'lláh, leading him astray like themselves. At the time, K͟hayru'lláh had gained the great respect of the American Bahá'í community, which he had founded, and I used to translate his writings which the friends valued greatly and carried off with them as testimonials.

During this time I enjoyed the unique distinction of being the only one familiar with foreign languages. As this unique position highlighted my virtue and yet at the same time concealed my assorted shortcomings, I was assigned to translate and distribute, day and night, any news received from K͟hayru'lláh. Since this activity pleased 'Abdu'l-Bahá and was a source of happiness for the friends, I gradually – and mainly due to the Master's infinite kindness and blessing – developed a great staunchness in the Faith and an uncommon insight in identifying those of the Covenant-breakers who misrepresented themselves in gatherings as true believers.

Additionally, I had acquired boldness in speaking openly in meetings on such issues without discretion, and fearlessly said what needed to be said. While the friends resident in 'Akká and Haifa had to conduct themselves with more caution and prudence because of their old friendships or possible kinship with these Covenant-breakers, I, fortunately not being bound by any such considerations, openly spoke out in the pilgrim house, disclosed what was hidden and exposed what was untrue.

Because of this, both the pilgrims and the resident believers had developed great affection for me and so each night in the pilgrim house the meetings were fraught with emotion and excitement. The elders of the community came to visit the friends and participate in the all-night sessions of fellowship. Frequently, the poems of Varqá were chanted melodiously and at times I myself composed a few lines of verse which, once approved by 'Abdu'l-Bahá, were read aloud at these meetings.

In short, despite all the problems and pains, when we came together we were in great joy and excitement. Of course, 'Abdu'l-Bahá's kindness and blessings towards me were constant and immeasurable, and considering my many shortcomings, I felt pangs of shame in receiving so much bounty in the face of such unworthiness. But His generosity exceeded my expectations and His infinite favour and grace concealed my countless faults and failings.

'Abdu'l-Bahá's words

At such a time, when the Faith of God was the target of the darts of disbelief and dissension, when the winds of test and trial were blowing with great intensity, when the ark of the Cause of God was surrounded by devastating storms, the rudder of the ship rested in the mighty grasp of the Centre of the Covenant, Who with the power of His utterance and Writings guided the ship towards the shores of deliverance and directed humankind towards the highway of salvation.

Even should the traces of His pen on paper not last forever, the effect of the words of 'Abdu'l-Bahá shall be so deeply engraved on the hearts and minds of His hearers as to eternally endure, passing from one heart to another.

In those days, the utterances of 'Abdu'l-Bahá, like His Writings, covered a variety of subjects and were revealed in response to the prevailing circumstances. First were His countless blissful prophecies concerning the future of the Faith. He likened the present time, so fraught with unhappiness and hardship, to the days of Muḥammad and Christ, painting a vision of the future when the triumph of the Faith of God would be realized and His Kingdom on earth established. He regarded the final victory of the Cause as an absolute reality and enabled us to visualize the ultimate ascendancy of the religion of God and the hoisting of the banner of this divinely ordained Dispensation upon the world's highest peaks. He often gave examples of the battles of the Prophet Muḥammad, especially the battle of Khandaq,[52] in which the believers, while engaged in fighting the infidels, had fastened pieces of rock around their waists to mitigate the pangs of hunger. While they were building the moat to defend their position, which gave its name to the subsequent battle, the Prophet loudly declared with each stroke of the pickaxe: "With this stroke the lands of the kings are conquered and the legions of the Caesars defeated."

Some of the believers who were not yet deepened in their devotion and understanding mocked and laughed secretly, wondering how they could conquer the countries of Asia, Europe and Africa when they were in such depths of misery and affliction. But when the conquering Arab legions won new territories and countries endowed with food in plenty, and when they tasted the sweetest fruits – which they swallowed whole without even minding the pits – then they cried out for joy, "This truly is what the Prophet of God promised us, this truly is what the Prophet of God promised us."

The Master spoke too of the time of the rising of the sun of Jesus and all the afflictions and anguish that He and His disciples had to endure. He spoke of their detachment, their courage and their forbearance in the face of unbearable difficulties, and how they established their sovereignty at last and achieved everlasting salvation.

Then the Master described in glowing terms the magnificent future of the Bahá'í Faith and the heights of glory and eternal happiness that awaited its faithful followers.

'Abdu'l-Bahá expressed these visions with such heavenly power and spiritual force that they penetrated the hearts and souls, creating such an aura of confidence and certitude that the friends could visualize their fulfilment, not in the distant future but at that very instant, and moreover saw themselves as the fortunate participants in that glorious age. The promised eternal glory and everlasting joy seemed so real and within reach that dimensions of time and space had no place in that world of reality. Past, present and future were not different times, but one unchanging dimension. These prophecies of 'Abdu'l-Bahá were so clear, so sublime and pleasing, and the promise of their realization so conclusive, that even God's most exalted angels could not have hoped to raise our souls to a loftier spiritual state.

Best of all, many of 'Abdu'l-Bahá's prophecies have already been fulfilled much sooner than anyone could have estimated. For example, when no one could possibly imagine that a small impoverished village like Haifa could develop into a beautiful and established international port, become the cross-roads of Asia, Europe and Africa, and at the same time gain the everlasting honour of holding the remains of the Supreme Manifestation of God and thus become the Point of Adoration[53] for the world, 'Abdu'l-Bahá described a vision of a city that was beyond the comprehension of the mind of man. Now we can all see the great structures of the port of Haifa surpassing the great ports of the world, gaining such prominence that nearby countries have become concerned that before long Haifa may develop into the centre of world commerce and industry.[54]

Another of 'Abdu'l-Bahá's prophecies which has been wholly realized pertains to the construction of Bahá'í edifices. At a time when the first signs of recognition and acceptance of the new Faith in the West were little by little reaching the Holy Land, while at the same time in the East the Faith of God was still wrapped in veils of caution and discretion, 'Abdu'l-Bahá gave us the joyful tidings of the construction of the Russian and American Houses of Worship.

And this was at a time when the daily requirements of food for the pilgrim house could hardly be met. To us at the time it seemed these tasks would have to be assigned to the angels in heaven.

Praised be God, the American House of Worship has been completed.[55] Alas, the construction of ours is just starting. Praised be God that the national Ḥaẓírátu'l-Quds[56] of various countries and the Bahá'í centres of various cities are announcing the call of the divine kingdom to the people of the world. And it was 'Abdu'l-Bahá Who told us of such days to come.

Another subject of 'Abdu'l-Bahá's talks was the expression of His yearning for martyrdom. As His calamities and afflictions multiplied, so increased His zeal and longing to bear the pain. The names of the great martyrs of the Faith flowed from His lips in glorious terms: "The illustrious Varqá, may my soul be sacrificed for his sake; the illustrious Rúḥu'lláh, may my soul be sacrificed for him; the honoured Sulaymán K͟hán, may my soul be sacrificed for his sake." And as He repeated these, the souls of His listeners were plunged into the depths of the great ocean of renunciation in the path of God.

At such poignant moments when 'Abdu'l-Bahá expressed His longing for suffering, sacrifice and martyrdom in the path of the Blessed Beauty, I was reminded of the great Persian poet Sa'dí, who so movingly tells the story of the candle and the sacrifice of the moth. Oh, but the sacrifice of the moth is unworthy of mention when compared to the sacrifice and renunciation of the lighted Candle of this heavenly assemblage, for the sacrifice of the moth lasts but a moment, while the sacrifice of this Candle has lasted a lifetime, imparting the light of guidance while being consumed by the flame of love and renunciation.

> *I remember, one sleepless night I heard the moth say to the candle,*
> *"I am in love, so I deserve to burn. Why weep and shed these tears?"*
> *Said the candle, "O my poor one, I have lost my sweet beloved."*

> *Tears dropped perfidiously down his face as he said this.*
> *O false one, loving is not for you, who possess neither patience nor*
>   *forbearance.*
> *While you flee a feeble flame, I have stood straight in the fire.*
> *While the fire of love singes your wings, I burn from head to foot.*

My purpose in telling this story is to show that it is the Manifestations of the divine will and the radiant and heavenly souls of each Dispensation who are the first to enter the arena of sacrifice and impart the celestial rays of guidance. They are then followed by the inspired moths that circle around these heavenly Candles. Thus according to the blessed verse, "I was a hidden treasure and wished to be made known,"[57] the love emanating from God and His Manifestations is superior to the love expressed by His creatures. In fact, the love expressed by God's creatures is simply a reflection, a manifestation of that great and all-embracing love of those dawning-places of divine light. Therefore, if His servants sacrifice a thousand lives in His path, this is but an effulgence of their love for their Beloved, a love from sanctified hearts which have been illumined by the light of faith and selflessness. Sacrifices made as expressions of such love cannot be compared to the martyrdom suffered in the path of God by the great martyrs of the Cause, the mirrors of whose hearts are brighter and more radiant and thus reflect a much larger portion of those heavenly rays. Examples of these are the King of Martyrs, or the esteemed Varqá, or the much loved Rúḥu'lláh, may my life be sacrificed for them, who hastened to the glorious field of martyrdom while we, the helpless and unfortunate who have witnessed the ascensions of both the Blessed Beauty and 'Abdu'l-Bahá, are still slumbering in the beds of comfort and heedlessness.

> *Come, my beloved, and witness, my misery is plain to see,*
> *You are gone and I endure, see how heartless I can be.*

'Abdu'l-Bahá's description of the many blessings associated with sacrifice and martyrdom in the path of God, and His ability to make us see with the eye of the spirit the joy and bounty awaiting the friends in the Abhá Kingdom, created such feelings of excitement and attraction that the friends began to conceive of ways, and invent plans, to make martyrdom a reality. One expressed the intention that once he reached Tehran he would proceed directly to the Shah Mosque, ascend the pulpit and raise the Call of God. Another declared that he would attend a *rawdih-khaní*[58] and in the presence of the most orthodox and fanatical Muslim divines, where all the elements of self-sacrifice would be at hand, do whatever it would take to achieve his end. And so, while everyone entertained similar plans, each had a particular preference as to how this goal should be achieved. One insisted that he would first convert a hundred seekers before succumbing to the pain of martyrdom. Another explained that true teaching was performed by each and every drop of blood shed in the arena of service. A third desired torture and pain, while a fourth yearned to be beheaded.

Once, while on our way from the pilgrim house to the *darb-khánih*, Mírzá Faḍlu'lláh and I were having a conversation on this very topic. He declared that he favoured martyrdom through the agony and torture of having lighted candles inserted into stab wounds made in various parts of his body (as in the manner of martyrdom of the renowned Bábí leader Sulaymán Khán). I, being young and adventurous and enjoying a bit of showmanship in everything, was in favour of a little more excitement and clamour at my scene of martyrdom and therefore expressed the desire to die by being blasted by a cannonball while strapped to the mouth of the barrel. Mírzá Faḍlu'lláh did not find my choice seemly. This fuelled a debate which reached its peak just as we arrived at the *bírúní* reception room, where we could hear 'Abdu'l-Bahá speaking clearly and forcefully. Slowly we approached the entrance. 'Abdu'l-Bahá was pacing back and forth as He uttered these words: "One should die in the path of the Blessed Beauty by having lighted candles inserted in his stab wounds." My challenger in this heated argument, he who had disagreed with my choice, threw me a quick glance full of meaning, as if to say, "I told you so". Immediately 'Abdu'l-Bahá's words followed: "One should die in the path of the Blessed Beauty by the blast of a cannon." I gave him a not-too-gentle nudge in the side, expressing my satisfaction at having the last word.

Now, friends, consider, that in these past thirty-seven years neither did he die of any stab wounds packed with lighted candles, nor did I suffer any indignities from the blast of a cannon. However, in those days, and because of 'Abdu'l-Bahá's utterances, we all entertained such thoughts and desired such sacrifices. But that thought and that desire no longer exist today, since the promises of 'Abdu'l-Bahá have been fulfilled. The clergy have been vanquished; the Covenant-breakers have lost all support and are utterly disgraced; these colourful dome-like turbans of green, white and blue have collapsed. Today, service to the Cause of God and contribution to the ultimate triumph of the religion of God is achieved by spreading the message, establishing the institutions and administering the affairs of the community. Happy are the ones who will taste the sweetness of success in this path.

Another theme of 'Abdu'l-Bahá's utterances at that time pertained to the awakening of souls in the face of the many machinations of the Covenant-breakers. As described previously, He familiarized the believers with their manner of conduct and their many types of deception. He also explained that the method of prevention of that infectious and deadly disease was to suspend all association with such people and leave them to their own devices. Using reason and logical proofs, and speaking like a teacher of physical education, He described the many symptoms of that dreaded disease, which He could readily diagnose by understanding the contents of each heart. For example, He would say that whereas physical health is only moderately communicable, physical disease is highly contagious. By the same token, the effect of spiritual health is also very gradual and slight, while spiritual disease is communicated quickly and potently. This is because a patient struck down with a spiritual disease does not seek a cure; in effect he hides his malady and thus communicates that condition covertly. 'Abdu'l-Bahá likened the disease of the violation of the Covenant to many physical ailments, as is highlighted in the Tablet to the late Dr. Hádí Khán to whom I had taught the Faith: "O physician! Make an effort, find a cure and heal the odious disease of that Old Hyena," etc. Once the doctor received the Tablet he instantly realized that he was being deceived by Áqá Jamál and that 'Abdu'l-Bahá was alerting him to that danger. Straight away, he severed all connection with him and published the Tablet; the nickname "Old Hyena" became Áqá Jamál's new identity.

The truth is that had we not been blessed with these divine teachings, the many evil machinations and deadly deceptions of the Covenant-breakers would have shaken, nay, destroyed the very edifice of the Faith of God. 'Abdu'l-Bahá further explained and elaborated on the perils awaiting the violators of the Covenant and their tragic ends. The prophecies of 'Abdu'l-Bahá all came true and His heavenly counsel produced the expected results.

Once a group of pilgrims, who were just returning from a meeting with 'Abdu'l-Bahá, expressed great joy and happiness at their visit, yet at the same time evinced a feeling of concern and sadness, for they had heard from the blessed mouth of 'Abdu'l-Bahá: "Soon you will see that Mírzá Badí'u'lláh will encounter such hardship and misery that he would be willing to haul manure between Haifa and 'Akká to earn a living, and yet will fail to find such work." Apparently He had been so emphatic and forceful in drawing the attention of the friends to this that the group was unanimous in their recollection of all the details of the story.

After this event I was puzzled as how to interpret such a prediction, for while it was quite possible to imagine Mírzá Badí'u'lláh as a hauler of manure, it was difficult to conceive that he might search for such employment and yet fail to find it. Only four years later did 'Abdu'l-Bahá's prediction come true in all its details and with such accuracy that I said to myself: "How right you were, 'Abdu'l-Bahá!" The details of this story will be described more fully in a later chapter.

Another topic of 'Abdu'l-Bahá's discourse at that time was the necessity of deepening and consolidating the newly-enrolled believers, which warranted at least temporarily a higher priority than even the duty of teaching itself. Once, when we had the bounty of being in the presence of 'Abdu'l-Bahá in the reception room of His residence, He said the following concerning the deepening of the new believers: "Is it not true that the Blessed Beauty, may my life be a sacrifice for His loved ones, has advised wisdom and discretion in performing service related to the Faith? The purpose is to conduct that work in a manner consistent with the requirements of the time. At a given time a particular approach may be effective and it is that approach which should be followed. For example, there was a time when teaching was all-important and everyone was emphatically encouraged to participate. Today, teaching is not beneficial. This is the time for deepening and confirming the friends in the principles of the Faith." And then He pointed towards the foundation of the building and added, "Armed with pickaxes, the Covenant-breakers are tearing into the very foundation of this Faith. What good is there in adding another floor to the edifice? Wisdom requires us to prevent them from destroying the foundation of the structure first. Before long the day will come when this foundation will grow strong, and then I will command all to teach the Faith. But for now, confirmation of the souls is more important than any other task."

In brief, because of this, it soon seemed as though the entire company of the friends were going through the deepening process over and over again. Since I am unable to recall 'Abdu'l-Bahá's exact utterances regarding the deepening and confirmation of the souls, I therefore present to the attention of my honoured readers an example of 'Abdu'l-Bahá's words as revealed by His own pen:[59]

He is the All Glorious!
O thou who hast drunk from the fountain of life: Verily, the caravan of the Kingdom set out into the wilderness of the heavenly Realm and sent forth its search party to find water in a dark and gloomy well. As they lowered the pail they announced, "Joyful tidings: behold, the youth of the Covenant who, falsely accused, was abandoned in this deep well by His brothers and was subsequently sold [into slavery] for a paltry price. Woe, then, unto them for that which they have done, and glory be upon those who acquired Him from His brothers."

Another series of 'Abdu'l-Bahá's utterances concerned moral education and training. In this the Master was very emphatic. In every gathering in which He spoke about the glorious station of martyrdom, He usually followed that by alerting the friends to the many ploys of the Covenant-breakers, then gave glad tidings of the ultimate triumph of the Faith, and finally spoke fervently on the improvement and refinement of morals and more particularly on the subject of detachment from all things save God. His words were so penetrating, so effective and so transforming that every member of His audience became the very personification of a detached spirit; the world and all that was therein seemed less than a wisp of straw in their eyes. The most significant utterances of Bahá'u'lláh, His Tablets and other verses such as the Hidden Words, Ṭarázát, Ishráqát, Tajallíyát and others[60] were explained by 'Abdu'l-Bahá in simple and yet clear language for all to understand.

This is a brief account of the various topics that 'Abdu'l-Bahá spoke about most frequently. However, as to His way of speech, His mode of expression, and His manner while speaking, neither the pen nor the tongue are capable of adequate description. This servant has had the opportunity to be in the presence of several great Bahá'í speakers such as Nabíl-i-Akbar, whose eloquence, lucidity of language, and sheer force of expression not only convinced every listener but left them irresistibly humble and submissive. His method of reasoning and demonstration of proofs subdued and vanquished the most sceptical of foes. I had always imagined that 'Abdu'l-Bahá's words would be similarly detailed, scholarly, eloquent and sophisticated, and that to understand them would require a great deal of attention and reflection. But I was entirely wrong. I discovered that the great speakers chose to use eloquent language full of embellishments in order to properly unfold and develop the truths they were expounding, describe in detail the meaning of their arguments and at the same time capture the attention and admiration of the listener by the use of such elaborate language. But the utterances of 'Abdu'l-Bahá covered the basic and fundamental principles and truths and were proffered in language of such simplicity, sublimity and precision that it could be likened to a stream of crystal-clear water flowing gently and quenching the burning thirst of the true seeker's longing for truth, or like a flash of electricity penetrating and illuminating the hearts of the believers, and whose magnetic quality captivated their souls and elevated them to the highest paradise. Happy were the ones who attained and drank their fill.

And it was not only we Bahá'ís who were enthralled by the beauty of speech and sublimity of manner of that incomparable Beloved, and who thirsted after the crystal waters of His utterance. Non-Bahá'ís, too, were utterly fascinated and enamoured by 'Abdu'l-Bahá's powers of expression. High-ranking Ottoman officials came to hear 'Abdu'l-Bahá speak in Turkish, while groups of Arab scholars came to listen to His splendid Arabic.

> *O, what clamour at thy door, as thy lovers assemble,*
> *As caravan's commotion approaches the oasis.*

The suckling babe

Since I have committed myself to writing all I observed on this journey and also to include, as far as I remember, expressions of my heartfelt emotions, I will not forgo the story of the suckling babe, which follows:

The elders of those days, whether pilgrim or resident, who were acquainted with the history of the Faith and had from the dawning of the Sun of Truth seen many of the major events associated with the establishment of the Cause, found a great resemblance between the behaviour of the Arch-breaker of the Covenant and that of Bahá'u'lláh's half-brother, Yaḥyá Azal. While reminiscing about the past, they also engaged in speculation about the future. The severing of the unfaithful branch and the remaining violators of the Covenant from the blessed tree of the Faith of God was a matter of certainty. Therefore, the question that emerged was: "How will this affect the future of the Faith?"

But I did not find this type of discussion very pleasant, and refused to speculate about the future or participate in such discussions, for I could not bear the thought that one day 'Abdu'l-Bahá would leave us forever. Then I heard the whisper that from the sacred lineage [of Bahá'u'lláh], a new babe had been born and had been named Shoghi Effendi. Although my whole being was thrilled by the news, I did not wish to associate the dawning of this sparkling star with the setting of the shining sun of the Divine Covenant. In so doing I prevented myself from deviating even as much as a hair's breath from the blessed verse: "Turn your faces toward Him Whom God hath purposed."[61]

I convinced myself that worrying about the future was of no use; that today was the day for confirmation and education of the believers and that tomorrow was in the mighty hand of the sovereign Lord of the Faith of God who was able and unconstrained.

For some time the residents of the pilgrim house had shown great interest in seeing Shoghi Effendi; they pleaded continually with the illustrious Afnán[62] in the hope that such longing by so many might be realized. Quite by chance one day, this babe of only four months was brought to the *bírúní* of 'Abdu'l-Bahá's house. The friends were beside themselves with joy and I, too, hastened to pay a visit to that beloved infant. But I made every effort to look at him in no other light than as a Bahá'í child. However, a strong urge compelled me to bow my head and observe the deepest respect. For about a minute I was utterly captivated by the beauty of that face. I gently kissed the soft hair of his blessed head, and as I did so I felt an indescribable quality in that infant. I could see his likeness to the pictures that I had seen of the infant Jesus in the arms of His mother Mary. For several days an image of his shining face was before my eyes, but gradually it faded.

I had similar emotional experiences twice more: once when he was in his ninth year and once when he was eleven. Since Mírzá Ḥaydar-'Alí and I were intimate friends and often shared each other's secret thoughts, I related to him the details of my visit and the nature of my impressions, and found that he shared my understanding of the situation, and so we decided to keep the matter quiet. Praised be God that the Will and Testament of 'Abdu'l-Bahá has been read and the secret revealed at last.

The rebellion of Mírzá Áqá Ján

For several days a general atmosphere of melancholy, gloom, and concern had dominated the hearts and spirits. The emotions of excitement and attraction that had previously filled our souls had given way to a subdued and uneasy feeling and foreboding. 'Abdu'l-Bahá's tone of voice, too, lacked its former quality. It was said that all this was due to the approach of the seventieth day of Naw-Rúz.[63]

At last the day arrived, and we were told that the night of the following day was the eve of the anniversary of the Ascension of Bahá'u'lláh. We were informed that after an all-night vigil of mourning, we were to set out at first light to visit the Shrine of the Blessed Beauty. The following day, the day of the Ascension itself, a feast organized by Mírzá Áqá Ján was to be held.

That night all the pilgrims and resident believers of Haifa

and 'Akká arrived at the pilgrim house, chanting the divine verses and prayers and weeping openly as they mourned the passing of Bahá'u'lláh. The Centre of the Covenant arrived too. Signs of sorrow and pain were to be seen everywhere. When 'Abdu'l-Bahá left the gathering, several of the younger friends insisted that I should compose some verses of poetry in observance of the event and recite them at the Shrine the following morning. Although I had no talent in the composition of elegies, the thought of the opportunity of reciting poetry in the presence of the Master and in a gathering assembled at the Shrine was so exciting and inspiring that I was able to compose the piece before dawn, right there in the overcrowded pilgrim house. But pending 'Abdu'l-Bahá's approval I did not share it with the friends.

At dawn we were all summoned by the Master and each was given a bottle of rose-water and a lighted candle. Before the first light of dawn, two parallel columns of believers moved through the city gate and in a state of sorrow and grief began their procession towards the Shrine of Bahá'u'lláh. A few of us who had melodious voices were commanded by 'Abdu'l-Bahá to take turns in chanting prayers. Mírzá Faḍl'u'lláh, of course, had first priority. As we walked, the Master moved about, issuing instructions and directing all activities.

From the intensity of emotional expression one would have feared for our very lives. Prayer followed prayer and verse followed verse until we arrived and entered the Shrine. As commanded by 'Abdu'l-Bahá, we poured the rose-water into the flowerbeds at the entrance of the Shrine and placed the lighted candles in the surrounding soil. Then 'Abdu'l-Bahá, as was His custom, chanted the Tablet of Visitation. The signs of intense sorrow on the face of 'Abdu'l-Bahá broke our hearts and our tears flowed unabated. Having completed the chant, 'Abdu'l-Bahá left us and entered the adjacent room, adding to our pain. It was impossible to stop the flow of tears, especially when we remembered the tearful eyes of the Master as He chanted the Tablet. The uncontrollable weeping and sobbing prevented any further attempts at chanting of prayers. At last the tears ended, but the moaning and lamentation continued. As the poet says:

> *When tears dry up, the heart pours out instead;*
> *When water subsides, the spring produces only mud.*

At last we regained our composure, calmed down and began to chant prayers. As the sun rose we left the Shrine and moved to the Bahjí pilgrim house located behind the Mansion, where we enjoyed a well-deserved rest while sipping tea. Now I sent to 'Abdu'l-Bahá the unworthy verses that I had composed for the occasion. He returned them with a few corrections and commanded Mírzá Faḍl'u'lláh to chant it. After the break we returned to the Shrine, and following a few prayers Mírzá Faḍl'u'lláh gave a moving rendition of my elegy:

> *Once again is the time for mourning, grieving, O Bahá,*
> *For the people of Bahá comes the day of lamenting, O Bahá!*
>
> *From the eye of creation flowed tears of blood,*
> *World's order was shattered by confusion, O Bahá!*
>
> *In the midst of that grief He yearns for death to descend,*
> *Who has loved that glory, that beauty, O Bahá!*
>
> *The creation shed tears of blood at this disaster, so sudden,*
> *As though death's spear had struck deep in its heart, O Bahá!*
>
> *The heart of existence was set ablaze, the pillars of life were torn,*
> *Once that mighty Beauty hid in His realm of glory, O Bahá!*
>
> *The fire of Thy loss engulfed all beings in the world,*
> *Heart and body did it melt, burned our souls, O Bahá!*
>
> *Thy ascension caused my heart to fall into deepest grief,*
> *Thou didst ascend to heaven, pain filled my soul, O Bahá!*

THE REBELLION OF MÍRZÁ ÁQÁ JÁN

*As the eye of man became deprived of meeting its Lord,
That glowing sun became deprived of its light, O Bahá!*

*Separation from Thee has spread darkness across the world,
Who can find Thy light of nearness, O Bahá?*

*Out of this loss and from earth to heaven there rose high
The cries of O Bahá, and O Bahá and O Bahá!*

*The spring-like eye of every Bahá'í doth weep tears of blood,
Our broken hearts are bleeding through our eyes, ceaseless, O Bahá!*

*The river Oxus was astounded at the flowing flood of our tears,
A hundredfold more than the Oxus flowed those tears of grief, O Bahá!*

*But for a time was the temple of joy here for His lovers,
Now a house of pain is standing in its place, O Bahá!*

*However much joy filled our hearts when Thou wert near,
A hundredfold is our share of grief and pain this day, O Bahá!*

*What can I say of the fire that was ignited within?
Thou knowest well what transpired in our hearts, O Bahá.*

*Suffice it that in this time of heart-rending grief,
Tears of sorrow covered the eyes of 'Abdu'l-Bahá, O Bahá.*

*Praised be God that the rays of bounty shining from the light of Bahá
Found their dawning place in the temple of the Mystery of God, O Bahá!*

*This Thy servant, like Youness [Jonah] swallowed by the fish,
In the endless ocean of grief has been drowning, O Bahá,*

*Praised be Thee, O Beauty, O Mystery, King of Bahá,
Our broken hearts were mended through Thy bounteousness, O Bahá!*

Again we left the Shrine and prepared to have lunch, after which we had an hour's rest. But spirits were low, hearts were grief-stricken and thoughts agitated and distressed. We could tell that the Covenant-breakers were up to something. One could see non-Bahá'ís moving about in the area. Before long we were to discover what was going on.

Following afternoon tea we returned to the Shrine. In the meantime, chairs were being placed outside the Mansion under the upper hallway balcony.

"What is going on?" some inquired.

"Mírzá Áqá Ján wishes to speak," we were told.

What? That same dwarfish old man who always sat at the doorway with his head hanging low? Now he was standing on a stool so that everyone could see him. He began to speak. But he was not coherent. The more I listened the less I understood. He jumped from point to point. I strained to grasp the purpose of the talk but failed to do so. I was looking at a monster whose limbs were trembling and whose soul was in agony. He was saying, "... while kneeling in prayer I fell asleep and Bahá'u'lláh came to me in a dream and said, 'This note written in green ink has just fallen into My hands. Why have you remained silent? Why, Áqá?'"[64]

Exhaustion due to lack of enough sleep, combined with the boredom of listening to this nonsense, robbed me of all patience. I rose to my feet. So did the honoured Áqá Mírzá Maḥmúd Káshání, one of the resident Bahá'ís. He shouted out in protest, and soon there was a great uproar. As I walked over to the wash-basin near the stairs to wash my hands and feet, 'Abdu'l-Bahá suddenly swept past me in a state of fury. Observing the situation, Mírzá Áqá Ján beat a hasty retreat towards the entrance of the Shrine with the late Mírzá 'Alí-Akbar in hot pursuit. Suddenly we heard a loud cry. The Master entered the Shrine while we stood outside watching the events unfold. We were all shocked and upset.

Covenant-breakers and a group of Ottoman officials, standing on the steps as well as on the upper floor behind the windows, were staring down, ready to charge us. Before long, calm returned. The pilgrims were asking each other what the problem was. How could Mírzá Áqá Ján, so humble and resigned, decide to advance a claim of succession as the Guardian of the Faith? Somebody said that since in his waking hours he was expelled from the Faith by Bahá'u'lláh, now in sleep Bahá'u'lláh has bestowed upon him the station of guardianship! I wondered in what trance-like state could such an unfortunate creature have reached such a fantastic conclusion? Suddenly Áqá Mírzá 'Alí-Akbar emerged from the Shrine carrying what seemed to be a large bundle of papers. 'Abdu'l-Bahá now instructed everyone to enter the Shrine, dispensed rose-water to each one as before, and began to observe the rites of visitation.

There was no sign of Mírzá Áqá Ján. Everyone was stunned at what had transpired; the atmosphere of mourning had given way to a state of incredulity. Which should we weep for, the ascension of the Blessed Beauty, the endless suffering of 'Abdu'l-Bahá, or the precious Faith of God which had become the target for the assault of the enemy, the plaything of the hateful? This was saddest of all. For this, tears of blood must be shed; this sorrow was above all other sorrows. Eyes were dry, faces pale and breath short. I felt so distressed that no amount of tears could sooth the state of my agitation.

When tears are gone at last, blood will flow in their place.
What will flow from those eyes when the blood dries up?

In such a state we left the Shrine at last and began our journey back towards town. Silence filled the air. A general state of melancholy, reflection and bewilderment dominated our thoughts as we slowly continued on our way.

But there was one amongst us who did not share the sadness. He strolled along happy and smiling, talking to the friends in a whisper. When we reached 'Akká we realized that whether consciously or unconsciously, he had performed a great service and had in fact prevented a major upheaval from taking place. This person was none other than Mírzá

'Alí-Akbar, the son of Mishkín Qalam. It was he who had saved the day by informing 'Abdu'l-Bahá of Mírzá Áqá Ján's intention to announce a claim as Guardian of the Faith. Had he been able to do so, there would have followed – as the Covenant-breakers hoped – a major confrontation between them and the believers, and this would have necessitated the intervention of Ṭábúr Áqásí, 'Akká's Chief of Police, who had been monitoring events from the upper window of the Mansion and along with his cohorts was prepared to charge and make arrests – and in so doing inflict irreparable damage on the reputation of the Faith. This would have brought about the ultimate realization of the well-laid plans of the Covenant-breakers, of which more will be said in a future chapter.

Another reason for Mírzá 'Alí-Akbar's happy mood was his discovery and appropriation of the Covenant-breaker materials found on the person of Mírzá Áqá Ján. When he had pursued Mírzá Áqá Ján into the Shrine and heard him shouting and cursing, he had grabbed him. But at that very moment, 'Abdu'l-Bahá arrived on the scene and prevented him from continuing the confrontation. However, while they wrestled, some papers fell out from under Mírzá Áqá Ján's *'abá*; these were quickly recovered by Mírzá 'Alí-Akbar and shown to 'Abdu'l-Bahá. The Master in turn ordered a thorough search of all his pockets; during this a bundle of Covenant-breaker materials were discovered, and now lay on the table in 'Abdu'l-Bahá's *bírúní*. The Master opened the papers. There were about one to two *man*[65] of crumpled, torn and twisted papers, all bearing writing either in pencil or ink and most of them signed and sealed. Each sheet was addressed to a renowned devoted believer in a style similar to that of the Tablets revealed by Bahá'u'lláh, except in an indignant and angry tone and containing among other things insulting references to the Master. A few of the papers were read; these gave an idea of the nature and intent of the rest of the batch. After that, the meeting ended, the gathering dispersed and we returned to the pilgrim house.

As we had gained a clearer understanding of the situation, everyone felt better. Our minds were at rest. We had a good night's sleep and in the early morning presented ourselves at 'Abdu'l-Bahá's *bírúní*. The papers were brought out for a second look. 'Abdu'l-Bahá arrived too and spoke at length about their contents. For a few days the papers were made available for all to see. The pilgrims reviewed the papers, took notes, and discovered the intentions and goals of the Covenant-breakers from their own handwritten materials. They also listened carefully to 'Abdu'l-Bahá and recorded every word uttered by Him.

The Covenant-breakers' planned rebellion through Mírzá Áqá Ján and Ṭábúr Áqásí

In the earlier section "The schemes of the Covenant-breakers" (see above, p. 33) I did not see sufficient justification to include the rebellion of Mírzá Áqá Ján. However, the matter will now be briefly described. At the time of the ascension of Bahá'u'lláh, Mírzá Áqá Ján had already been expelled from the Faith and was unwelcome in Bahá'í circles. He lived a life of general misery and disgrace. However, due to Bahá'u'lláh's generosity he had accumulated a sizeable fortune. The Covenant-breakers had secretly planned to seize his wealth either by killing him or by demonstrating that they considered it clear injustice for someone who had displeased Bahá'u'lláh to be walking around on God's earth in such a condition of affluence and contentment. But Mírzá Áqá Ján had discovered the conspiracy and sought refuge at 'Abdu'l-Bahá's door; repenting his past conduct he found a haven in the sanctuary of the Master's home.

The Covenant-breakers were outraged at such a development and spread a rumour that Bahá'u'lláh's death had been caused by two poisonous pills introduced into His food by Mírzá Áqá Ján. Their purpose was to create dissension and take advantage of its likely outcome in ways beneficial to themselves. On the other hand, any possible danger from such a mischief would be directed at Mírzá Áqá Ján alone, because of his hand in the alleged crime.

And so they secretly established communication with him and encouraged him to rebel. As previously mentioned, having deceived him, the Covenant-breakers instructed and trained him, fed his ego and on the strength of his eminent position as the recorder of the verses of revelation received by Bahá'u'lláh, induced him to lay an independent claim to divine inspiration. Their purpose, of course, was provocation – to create chaos in the hope that it would lead to a full-scale rebellion against the Faith.

The foolish Mírzá Áqá Ján then spent a great deal of time preparing letters containing a description of the dream he had concocted, in which he claimed to have been admitted into the presence of Bahá'u'lláh and through divine revelation and inspiration to have received and written down words expressing God's indignation and outrage. It was these messages that he had planned to send to various devoted believers. In one case he claimed that he had received directly from heaven a Tablet inscribed in green ink commanding him to rescue the Faith from the clutches of the infidels. The writings contained the same accusations and insults hurled at 'Abdu'l-Bahá by the Covenant-breakers, except in much harsher and more venomous language.

He had planned to hand over these papers to the Covenant-breakers on the day of the anticipated revolt. Their intention was to copy the contents in the hand of Mírzá Majdu'd-Dín, who had been Bahá'u'lláh's amanuensis during the latter part of His life, and then disseminate them among the friends. That is why, on this day, he was carrying the papers under his *'abá*, fastened around his waist. He was hoping to incite a riot, draw the friends into confrontation and then give the appearance of being rescued and given asylum by the Covenant-breakers. This was the Covenant-breakers' covert design. Their plan consisted of the intervention of Ṭábúr Áqásí, an Ottoman official and their close friend and well-paid agent, with whom they had a longstanding relationship. He had previously participated in many of their devious activities and operations, including receiving and forwarding to Beirut and Istanbul their many complaints and grievances filled with allegations and false charges; in return he earned a substantial profit. On the day when the believers were in mourning, Ṭábúr along with a few others had been brought to the Mansion to be on the lookout for any signs of conflict, at which time he was supposed to charge out with his cohorts, stop the riot, make formal charges against the participants, inform Istanbul of the results and recommend the banishment of the Master. This action was supposed to deliver into the hands of the Covenant-breakers the Shrine of Bahá'u'lláh and in his view stop any further troubles in the future.

I should also add that the Covenant-breakers' main complaint to the authorities was that while Bahá'u'lláh had been a recluse and a dervish, it was the Master's plan to elevate His station to the level of divinity in order to fulfil His own political and military aim, which was nothing short of rebellion against the government. It was for this very reason that Ṭábúr had been called, so that the violators of the Covenant could justify their argument in his presence, hoping ultimately to take possession of the Shrine of Bahá'u'lláh and become the recipients of the gifts and contributions of future pilgrims. Praised be God for His mercy, as at the first sign of commotion Mírzá 'Alí-Akbar had immediately informed 'Abdu'l-Bahá of the situation and His very presence on the scene cooled the tempers and subdued the tense atmosphere. The Covenant-breakers, who had made ready for a fight, stood motionless as statues; Mírzá Áqá Ján ran away; and the mischief was cut short.

Events after Mírzá Áqá Ján's rebellion

Mírzá Áqá Ján did find sanctuary with the Covenant-breakers, but left his papers behind. All the efforts of the Covenant-breakers had gone for naught. Their intentions were revealed and their secrets uncovered. Those papers, the contents of which the breakers of the Covenant were about to alter and amend to suit their purposes and then send out to various destinations, all penned by the hand of the pretended recipient of revelation who claimed the office of Guardianship, were now lying on a table in 'Abdu'l-Bahá's *bírúní* and giving rise to mockery and laughter. The friends read them, laughed, and at times took notes. He had expressed a great deal of malice towards 'Abdu'l-Bahá, stating it a deadly sin to attain His presence. Furthermore, in papers addressed to various faithful believers he had brought false accusations against the most renowned defenders and champions of the Faith. He had accused Mírzá Abu'l-Faḍl and certain other scholars and teachers of the Faith of misdeeds which are unworthy of mention here. For example, he had called Áqá Mírzá Faḍl'u'lláh "seditious", while from the very depths of his diabolical mind had revealed in my honour the following abominable verse: "O Youness! O thou tyrant! God, the Beloved, warns that verily he who disbelieves in God has committed the greatest injustice." Those of the friends who had been named in the papers each received their own documents. As soon as things returned to normal, and peace and calm were restored, the friends recaptured their old enthusiasm and the pilgrim house became filled once more with the humour and laughter of the believers. The sadness and melancholy of the anniversary of the Day of the Ascension had passed; once more the intoxicating pleasure of nearness to the Master and beholding His beauteous countenance brought joy and delight to the hearts. The friends, young and old, who had all tasted my sharp playful wit and untimely humour, had found a perfect way to retaliate. In these lighthearted moments, before I could utter a word I would suddenly find myself addressed by my honourable title of "O Youness! O thou tyrant!" for which I was unable to find a suitable response since I could not possibly address them in turn by their "given titles". If you only knew what joyful and spiritually fulfilling times we had! Everyone was happy, everyone was forgetful of self. Morning, noon and night we attained the presence of the Beloved and were utterly inebriated with the wine of His tender love and bounty.

But, alas, alas, this joy and happiness did not last long. We had moments of spiritual ecstasy, but they were all too short. Again the dark clouds of oppression and tyranny covered our sun of good fortune and happiness. The Beloved of our hearts became once more the object of unjust attacks by the government, and dealing with them consumed all His time. The doors of reunion were shut; we spent many an hour in 'Abdu'l-Bahá's *bírúní*, sighing, yawning and just waiting to behold His heavenly face again. He was either not at home, or He was in meetings with non-Bahá'ís and enemies, or He was at the Government House defending the Faith and Himself. He would leave early in the morning for destinations unknown to us, and would return home very late at night. From a distance, as He passed swiftly by, we would bow our heads, to which He would respond with a quick but loving gesture. The friends were all concerned, all frightened, all anxious. But the saddest of all were the pilgrims whose time of pilgrimage might suddenly come to an end, their lifetime dream of attaining the presence of the Beloved of the world and tasting the sweetness of His nearness remaining unfulfilled.

For a period of ten to twelve days, although He was near, we suffered the pangs of separation. At night in the pilgrim house we were engaged in chanting prayers and reciting the "Remover of Difficulties". During the day, as the saying goes, "These are they who cling to any handle" – we would reach for whoever and whatever could help us attain the presence of the peerless Friend. But nothing worked. We could neither ask a question nor receive an answer.

One evening 'Abdu'l-Bahá arrived just before sunset. The friends naturally assumed that there would be sufficient time for a visit. But alas, the visit was all too short. Looking weary and unwell, He said, "I am tired. With the permission of the friends I will retire," and went swiftly up the stairs.

Sorrow and grief filled the room. Everyone was heartbroken; anguish was to be seen on all faces. But I, having through no merit of my own been the frequent recipient of 'Abdu'l-Bahá's endless kindness and generosity, and therefore considered by the believers to be a favourite of His threshold, now became their last resort. So they left it in my hands to come to some solution and find a way to reach the Master. They told me that at times when 'Abdu'l-Bahá's pain and anguish became too intense, a mere visit by devoted and loving friends was a panacea which seemed to relieve and dissipate His anxiety and stress. Having known these friends for some time, and feeling quite confident of their devotion and unconditional love for the Master, I decided to communicate to Him, through a few verses of poetry, our misery and pain at separation from Him, and to leave the rest in God's hands. So I sat down in a state of excitement on the bottom step of the staircase and wrote these verses in pencil on a crumpled old piece of paper:

> *O 'Abdu'l-Bahá! We are the lovers of Thy countenance standing expectant at Thy door,*
> *Step outside so that we may gaze on that wondrous face!*
> *The Covenant-breaker considers such a gaze a sin;*
> *He is oblivious that we are in the midst of paradise.*
> *That precious foot with which Thou tread'st the ground*
> *Place on our heads, so we may soar to the heavenly throne.*

Straight away, I found the twelve-year-old servant boy, K͟husraw, and gave him the paper to deliver. Within the space of one minute he returned, having delivered the message to 'Abdu'l-Bahá. Suddenly I grew anxious and uneasy; my heart began to pound rapidly and my spirit seemed intent on leaving my body. In this agitated state I looked up and beheld the Sun of the countenance of the Covenant appearing, as it were, from the Abhá paradise. Holding a few flowers in His hand, He began to come down the stairs. Then He stopped, and looking down at us said: "The friends are many and our flowers but a few, and I do not know who to give them to?" I immediately remembered the poem that says,

*In your hand there's a flower and you wonder who to give it to,
I am the most deserving, O king of the righteous, to me, to me...*

I began to laugh. He looked down at me, smiling, and said humorously, "Don't you laugh, you TYRANT!"

He descended the stairs gently, and as He landed on each step, He repeated: "You tyrant, you tyrant!" On the fourth repetition it occurred to me that once they heard of this the Covenant-breakers would have ample justification to spread all sorts of rumours and accusations against me. As He reached the bottom of the stairs and entered the yard, the friends circled around that divine Candle like moths. These words were then revealed; they are a close paraphrase of the actual words of 'Abdu'l-Bahá:

"In every Dispensation, the enemies fabricate certain charges and accusations. For example, since the Apostle of God Muḥammad had no sons, they gave Him the title 'He who is barren of progeny'. 'Alí, who had a rather large midriff, was called 'pot-belly' by his enemies. When we were in Baghdad, the followers of Yaḥyá had named Bahá'u'lláh 'the Great Idol'. I am called the 'Stone', and so you should accept the title of 'tyrant'!"

(By 'Stone', 'Abdu'l-Bahá was referring to the Black Stone, *Hajaru'l-Aswad*, in Mecca, the Point of Adoration for the Muslims).[66]

Radiating immense joy and gaiety as He made these remarks, He strolled towards the front yard of the *bírúní* and placed those few flowers in a hollow area of the flowerbed. We, who numbered about fifty or sixty, followed Him out and stayed in the front yard for about two hours while 'Abdu'l-Bahá spoke to us, sometimes standing and sometimes pacing about in a happy and joyful mood. Afterwards we were dismissed from His presence and returned to the pilgrim house. Our happiness knew no bounds as we embraced and congratulated each other in an atmosphere of spiritual joy and fulfilment.

The friends flooded my face with kisses. Although the hour was late, the illustrious Afnán arrived just to express his many congratulations for this great success and give the happy news of 'Abdu'l-Bahá's joy and satisfaction. He asked me if I had taken the flowers deposited by Him in the frontyard flowerbed. I responded negatively. He said that while 'Abdu'l-Bahá had expressed great satisfaction with all the friends, He had mentioned, "I put the flowers there for Jináb-i-Khán." It was a wish come true! I excitedly jumped up and started to run outside to fetch the flowers. However, it was late and the friends advised that it could wait till the next day. That night I dreamt of nothing but flowers and blossoms. Before dawn, I awoke, ran outside and retrieved the flowers, and out of sheer joy ate one of them. For the life of me, I cannot remember what I did with the rest. Fortunately, from that day forward these hardships were replaced with peace and tranquillity. The gates of reunion were flung wide open as we attained 'Abdu'l-Bahá's presence daily and sometimes in the evening. Yet the flames of dissension and rebellion remained dormant beneath this seeming air of harmony and calm.

A story

After Mírzá Áqá Ján's revolt, his papers remained scattered on the table outside 'Abdu'l-Bahá's *bírúní* while the believers read them and discovered the secrets of the evil ones and the thoughts and plans of the wicked. Some copied passages to take home with them and shock their unsuspecting friends. I had no interest in writing down any part of that rubbish – I was in general satisfied with the document which carried my own name. At times, when He entertained the friends, 'Abdu'l-Bahá would say a few words about them. One day, as He picked through the papers with His own blessed hands, He found a document that caught His eye. He read it aloud and showed the signature and seal to the friends. I was standing at some distance, listening. 'Abdu'l-Bahá asked me to move closer and witness the seal on the document. I bowed at His command and took a few steps closer. But again He insisted, "Come and look." I took another step and bowed again. With that I meant to imply that 'Abdu'l-Bahá's remark was of course correct. The third time, He was emphatic as He invited me to "Come closer and look!" Helpless, I approached 'Abdu'l-Bahá and peered down at the signature and seal as He had instructed. Afterwards, I began to wonder why the Master had been so insistent that I should actually move closer and witness the signature and the seal for myself. What was the wisdom of His insistence, when for me His words were the very essence of God's will? And while my eyes and ears could be subject to human error, His words were the quintessence of truth. I concluded that there must be a defect or at least a weakness in my faith of which I was unaware.

In brief, dark thoughts agitated my mind and continued to torture me. Every time such thoughts occurred, I prayed to be protected from temptation and evil and that the wisdom of this matter might be revealed to me. This continued until my return to Iran. One day, in a conversation with a friend regarding Mírzá Áqá Ján, I was asked about some details of that event which, because of my first-hand knowledge, I was able to clarify and remove all doubts. I then realized the wisdom of 'Abdu'l-Bahá's insisting that I should examine the document closely, for armed with that knowledge I had been able to apprise a group of uninformed friends of the truth of the matter. My joy and contentment knew no bounds and I praised God for such a blessing. The details of this incident will be discussed in a later chapter.

The nature of 'Abdu'l-Bahá's cares in those few days

On the day when Mírzá Áqá Ján's rebellion took place, the carefully devised plan of the Covenant-breakers to create a riot and a confrontation was defused by the unexpected entrance of 'Abdu'l-Bahá on the scene. With that, their final dart of hatred and enmity went astray; moreover, their papers fell into the hands of the faithful. Then the violators of the Covenant, advised by Ṭábúr Áqásí, prepared a formal complaint and submitted it to the Ottoman authorities.

Not long afterwards a number of hearings were convened in 'Akká. The nature of the complaint was twofold: one was official and was handled by Ṭábúr himself, and the other contained a number of personal allegations, of which I remember five. They stated that:

1. The Great Effendi [Bahá'u'lláh] was a man of the highest religious station, a saint, and His days and nights were spent in meditation. However, the illustrious 'Abbás Effendi ['Abdu'l-Bahá], has exaggerated His station to the level of divinity in order to advance His own political aspirations and to provoke an uprising and a revolution.

2. Our friends, who are numbered in the thousands in Iran and India, have been deliberately misguided by His propaganda to shun further communication with us and to consider us their enemies.

3. The funds and numerous gifts regularly received in the name of Bahá'u'lláh are not shared with us.

4. He has taken possession of our paternal inheritance and deprived us of any part thereof.

5. His behaviour towards us is in flagrant conflict with the requirements of the Will and Testament of Bahá'u'lláh.

These were their major complaints. However, they emphasized the first point and gave it special significance. Unfortunately for them, they were ignorant of the wisdom behind Bahá'u'lláh's injunction forbidding the teaching of the Cause throughout the Ottoman Empire. They imagined that the reason for this instruction was fear of the ensuing persecution and hardship once Bahá'u'lláh's claim to divine rank was made public. Obviously, a heart bereft of the fear of God is not informed of the divine will. They never imagined that the Kitáb-i-'Ahd would be made public in the enquiry and Bahá'u'lláh's own claim to divine authority would come to light. It was learned later that in the hearing 'Abdu'l-Bahá openly presented Himself as the authoritative interpreter and promoter of the sacred Faith of Bahá'u'lláh, voluntarily submitting the Kitáb-i-'Ahd in its entirety and basing His responses to the five categories of complaint against Him on that Book. In one case He made reference to the verse, "God hath not granted them any right to the property of others",[67] and added that if the people of Persia were devoted Bahá'ís, they would not, in accordance with this verse, part with a penny towards them (the Covenant-breakers). Furthermore, 'Abdu'l-Bahá clarified that according to the Text, the Aghṣán, the Afnán and all other believers must in all cases turn to Him. How, therefore, could those who opposed and vilified Him, who spread the vilest rumours and accusations against Him, and who proclaimed themselves to be His avowed enemies, expect to be revered by the people of Bahá? He also added: "For four years I concealed their enmity toward myself until they themselves divulged their hatred and animosity in writings which they signed and dispatched to Iran."

Regarding the subject of inheritance He explained: "In the opening passages of the Book, Bahá'u'lláh clearly states: 'Earthly treasures We have not bequeathed, nor have We added such cares as they entail.' However, He has left two priceless items, either one of which I will happily hand over to them any time they make their choice. One is a holy Qur'án, and the other is Bahá'u'lláh's prayer beads." The fame of these two items had reached every corner of the Ottoman Empire; all the dignitaries of 'Akká had seen them and were well aware that the Arch-breaker of the Covenant had stolen them and that currently both items were in the possession of the enemies of 'Abdu'l-Bahá and were in fact being passed from one to another. Once one of the Covenant-breakers, at the instigation of the Arch-breaker of the Covenant, had shown the prayer beads to 'Abdu'l-Bahá and had asked: "How much, in your view, is this worth?" 'Abdu'l-Bahá had been heard to respond, "It depends in whose possession it is."

This, then, is a brief account of 'Abdu'l-Bahá's cares and difficulties in the days following the passing of Bahá'u'lláh. His days and nights were spent in meetings with the officials defending Himself and the Faith against the claims and accusations of the Covenant-breakers. And as the troublemakers little by little simply exhausted all their ploys and complaints, and 'Abdu'l-Bahá began to find some free time to visit with the friends, He always spoke briefly and in guarded language about the ongoing events. Whenever the subject was brought up, He would say, "I know that before I reach the top step of these stairs, the Covenant-breakers will be aware of everything I have said tonight. I wish, at least, they would quote me using My own words." And especially when any Covenant-breaker attained His presence, 'Abdu'l-Bahá would address him on the subject directly and openly, with clear evidence and unequivocal proof, until he felt shame and disgrace at his action or the action of his co-conspirators.

For example, He would frequently address some of the Covenant-breakers in these words: "I adjure you in the memory of the Blessed Beauty to be truthful. Did you not come to me with the story that the Covenant-breakers intended to kill Mírzá Áqá Ján in such-and-such a place and throw his body down a well because, they claimed, he had sent two pills to Bahá'u'lláh and the ingestion of the first caused His death? Now, I am not saying that Mírzá Áqá Ján was responsible for the death of Bahá'u'lláh, but why was it that such a despicable person suddenly became their favourite and was encouraged to oppose Me?" This is an example of the frankness with which 'Abdu'l-Bahá addressed the Covenant-breakers. And usually they remained utterly silent, sometimes even confirming His words.

In short, the episode of Mírzá Áqá Ján proved to the Covenant-breakers – who at that time were still freely associating with the friends and claiming devotion to the Faith –

that they had been clearly identified and their actions had come to light.

The story of Áqá Mírzá Ḥasan

During that three-month pilgrimage I discovered numerous facts and ascertained the truth of manifold issues, none of which, outside that particular time frame, would have been comprehensible to me or understandable to others regardless of my best attempts to explain them, unless the evidence and proofs of such issues emerged independently and their true meanings came to light.

For example, a particular aspect of meeting the Master was that if a hundred pilgrims were in His presence and 'Abdu'l-Bahá spoke on certain issues of His own choosing (completely unrelated to the personal questions or problems of any of the pilgrims), each pilgrim would discover the answer to his own problems or questions in His words, and would consequently consider himself to have been the intended addressee of 'Abdu'l-Bahá's remarks and the sole recipient of His bounty and blessing.

> *So freely is His grace lavished on every soul*
> *That each servant can say the Lord is his alone.*

And if that gathering of one hundred souls could have revealed to each other their inner thoughts and secrets, and in that light examine and explore the true meaning of 'Abdu'l-Bahá's words, they would have discovered in those words the same life-giving spirit which when imparted by raindrops and sunlight causes each seedling to become strong, verdant, fragrant and fruitful, each in accordance with its own latent capabilities.

For instance, a mystic or a poet or an historian or an artisan or a champion wrestler or a simple labourer all have different natures, tastes, thoughts and talents. Yet regardless of their talents and capacities, this rain of bounty and sun of generosity would cause each one to grow into full bloom. The seed of knowledge would produce the fruits of knowledge; the seed of courage and strength would produce the fruits of courage and strength.

> *The rain whose life-giving nature none can deny,*
> *A tulip it raises in the garden, in the salt-marsh a thorn.*

I learned this truth at that time, and later in Tehran I was able to put it to the test, of which I shall write more later.

One day in the pilgrim house we welcomed a few newly arrived Persian friends from Egypt. As was the custom, each pilgrim introduced himself by giving his first and last names and his profession. One of these introduced himself as Ḥasan and added, "I am not one of you. I am here to investigate the Faith. If it is true, I will accept it. Otherwise, I will go my way and you can go yours." When he began to introduce himself, his fellow travellers sitting across the room made it clear, by the aid of facial gestures and wrathful smiles, that we should not believe a single word. And of course we did not. When Mírzá Ḥasan left the room his fellow pilgrims expressed deep concern about him: he was a troublemaker, a wicked man, well-known among the vile and the evildoers of Egypt, and in fact a collaborator and agent of the Islamic clergy of Egypt who had resolved to harass and torment the friends. Having recently received financial support from his backers, he had journeyed here with the intent of concocting a series of questions and answers and publishing them in Egypt to defame the name of the Faith. We were all dejected and upset by this news, as the presence of such a despicable person obviously undermined our freedom to communicate with each other in the pilgrim house.

Some two hours later, the group of the friends from Egypt was summoned to the presence of 'Abdu'l-Bahá. Mírzá Ḥasan, too, followed the group inside. On their return, as he walked ahead of the group, I cornered him with obvious curiosity:

"So, how did it go? What did the Master talk about?" I enquired.

"It was all kindness and generosity, all kindness and generosity," he replied.

In his absence I asked others if he had been addressed by 'Abdu'l-Bahá. The answer was unanimous. He had not received the smallest measure of notice or attention from the Master. The next time around, the entire contingent of the pilgrims was summoned and this time I paid careful attention to see if he might receive favourable notice from 'Abdu'l-Bahá. In fact, in that gathering he was almost nonexistent, receiving neither any particular attention nor the merest acknowledgement. As we walked out I asked him, "What was your impression?"

"It was all bounty and generosity," he responded.

In the pilgrim house, when Mírzá Ḥasan was around we were guarded in our speech regarding the nature of the problems within the Faith. 'Abdu'l-Bahá, however, openly and without regard to Mírzá Ḥasan's true identity and his mischievous intentions, spoke about the Covenant-breaker issues as He normally was wont to do. Having thus heard the Master, we too threw caution aside and began to express ourselves without care or hesitation.

Gradually, we noticed that Mírzá Ḥasan was presenting arguments and proofs, albeit in Islamic terminology, against the Covenant-breakers and in support of the Faith of God. In the pilgrim house most of our conversations revolved around issues related to the Covenant, and Mírzá Ḥasan began to contribute to the discussions. Soon his zeal became so intense that he would not take a back seat to anyone in presenting arguments and providing proofs, although his speech was innocent of conventional Bahá'í terminology.

In short, in the fourteen-day stay of the Egyptian pilgrims, Mírzá Ḥasan received hardly the slightest recognition from the Master, and yet with every passing day he seemed happier and more radiant. And when, having completed their pilgrimage, the Egyptian pilgrims finally received instructions to depart, Mírzá Ḥasan surprised me by showing a fervent eagerness to teach the Faith. The afternoon before the day of their departure we were all in the presence of 'Abdu'l-Bahá in the *bírúní* of His house. As the Master entered the room Áqá Siyyid 'Alí-Akbar approached Him and whispered a few words to Him; the Master replied in a rather harsh tone of voice and in the following words:

"What question? What answer? We are not an ecclesiastical authority; We have not put forth any claims; We have neither advanced a claim to the office of prophethood nor that of Imámate – why should any questions be brought to Us? I am but a servant among Bahá'u'lláh's multitude of servants and I serve the cause of humanity through His message of love and brotherhood. If Mírzá Ḥasan has any questions, he can refer them to the many scholars, doctors of religious jurisprudence, men of learning and teachers of religion who are in the business of solving abstruse problems and complicated questions. We have no claim to the possession of any special knowledge or erudition, why should he bother with us!" While 'Abdu'l-Bahá was speaking with such intensity and emotion, I looked round and located Mírzá Ḥasan standing on the far side of the flowerbed, his head low, looking meek and bowing incessantly. I was perplexed. I told myself, this unfortunate, miserable man is leaving the fountainhead of bounty and generosity without taking the smallest share and without achieving his goal. This blessed Being, 'Abdu'l-Bahá, whose breast has been the target of painful darts of the enemy, has withheld His blessing from this unfortunate man. I thought that the action of 'Abdu'l-Bahá must have been prompted by a wisdom the nature of which I was unable to grasp.

In the morning, the Egyptian travellers were summoned to the presence of 'Abdu'l-Bahá for the exchange of farewells. On his return from the farewell session, Mírzá Ḥasan could hardly contain his joy and kept telling us of his many plans for what he would do once he was back in Egypt. Again I asked him what, if anything, 'Abdu'l-Bahá had said to him. The whole group unanimously answered, "Nothing". As they prepared to leave, suddenly 'Abdu'l-Bahá's messenger, looking exhausted and out of breath, rushed in. Mírzá Ḥasan had been summoned by 'Abdu'l-Bahá. At this news Mírzá Ḥasan dashed out in a state of euphoria. After about thirty minutes he returned beaming with joy: "'Abdu'l-Bahá has commanded me to teach the Faith in Egypt!", he said, his face radiant and filled with emotion. Praised be God, we have seen all sorts of strange things and have invoked the name of the "transformer of hearts" in prayer; now we await the result of this latest transformation.

At last the travellers left. A week later we received the news that Mírzá Ḥasan had confronted his patrons and sponsors and had staunchly defended the Faith of God, presenting conclusive proofs and convincing evidence in its support.

Dear reader, this is not the end of this story, which will be continued later. However, you should know that the telling of this story in Tehran guided one of the most eminent and high-ranking Muslim clerics to accept the Faith and eventually distinguish himself in rendering great service to the Cause of God. That is when I finally understood the true meaning of this event. I shall tell that story later. Be patient.

Dismissal

This account has distracted me from pursuing the events associated with the rebellion of Mírzá Áqá Ján. As previously described, although the fire of this rebellion was dormant, yet its menacing smoke stung the eye of friend and foe alike as 'Abdu'l-Bahá endeavoured mightily to extinguish its emerging blaze. While due to the relaxation of certain restrictions on the Master the door of reunion was not entirely closed to us as had been over the previous few days, yet all additional applications for pilgrimage from the friends in foreign lands were being denied. 'Abdu'l-Bahá repeatedly told us, "This land is in turmoil." Gradually, and according to His instructions, His foreign correspondence was reduced and my translation work declined notably. He had instructed that letters from the West should no longer be forwarded from Port Said but were to be retained there until further notice. The volume of correspondence from Iran, too, was reduced and the pilgrims one by one received their notices to depart. At all times His words pertained to the rebellion of the Covenant-breakers, the general social disorder in 'Akká and a host of other problems which He felt made it necessary for as few of the friends as possible to remain in His care. He even encouraged the resident friends to leave the city and relieve the overcrowding of the believers in 'Akká.

In the meantime, news was being received that clearing Customs in Istanbul, Beirut and some of the frontier locations was becoming more and more troublesome for the friends, as they were being regularly searched for written materials. This was convincing proof that the actions of the Covenant-breakers and the officials of 'Akká had borne fruit and had reached a much wider circle.

At this time the residents of the pilgrim house comprised Mírzá Hájí 'Abdu'lláh Khán, the father-in-law of Varqá the martyr; Mírzá Azízu'lláh Varqá; Mírzá Fadlu'lláh, the son of Ashraf; and myself. The local situation, however, was not dire enough in my estimation to require my departure from 'Akká. But then, I had not received any intimation from the Master one way or another.

One day as I, along with a group of the resident believers, was having a joyful time in the pilgrim house, the "Angel of Death" suddenly arrived carrying 'Abdu'l-Bahá's instruction for the departure of the whole lot of us. We had a week's notice. I could hardly believe this frightful message about myself, but its accuracy was soon confirmed. Petrified, I hurried to the presence of the Beloved to present my case.

I argued, "Since I have no responsibilities or attachments in this world, I had thought that I would always remain at this threshold, especially since this was my father's wish and desire."

With a world of love, compassion and gentleness, He said, "Very well then, you must stay here with us."

My happiness knew no bounds as I ran back to the pilgrim house in a state of utter delirium. I rushed in and announced that I had dodged the Angel of Death and gained new life.

That night, however, sleep abandoned me. I wondered why I had not simply obeyed the will of the Master. I remembered my father's repeated advice on the subject of obedience and what I had heard of similar situations in the time of Bahá'u'lláh. I came to the conclusion that I had erred and that I should strive to completely eliminate any trace of my own will. Next afternoon, I found my opportunity to be in 'Abdu'l-Bahá's presence as we walked in the empty streets of 'Akká.

I bared my heart. "May my life be a sacrifice for You, last night horrible thoughts kept me awake all night. I was frightened by the thought that I had been disobedient and that your loving permission for me to stay was the result of my presumptuous behaviour, my impertinent and bold plea to remain here, and that I would soon taste the bitter penalty of regret and remorse."

The ocean of love and compassion surged. "God forbid, God forbid, this was my will. Be assured. There is no remorse in anything except breaking the Covenant of God. Ask whatever you desire, for that shall be my will and my desire. Be at peace." The following two or three days were spent in joy and peace. But terrible news kept pouring in from various parts of Iran, Egypt and India. The writings of the Covenant-breakers had shaken the Cause of God in all parts of the world. Sedition and turmoil were evident everywhere. Hardly a day went by without the receipt of sorrowful and depressing news from various points around the globe.

The followers of Yaḥyá had found a fresh opportunity to join forces with the Covenant-breakers to conspire and plot. 'Abdu'l-Bahá was quite distressed and broken-hearted. His pen was never still. Although the upheaval in 'Akká had dissipated somewhat and the friends were able to attain the presence of the Master regularly, yet the effect on the person of 'Abdu'l-Bahá of the pain associated with the severity of the incoming news was beyond description. And because of it He repeatedly mentioned and even emphasized to the friends the advantages and benefits of departing from 'Akká and travelling to other destinations, even those in close proximity to the town.

'Abdu'l-Bahá explained that if the believers would disperse, even for a short time, He would be better able to defend the Faith against the onslaught of the government officials, especially those who would arrive later from Istanbul to investigate the recent events. Furthermore, since the friends were either immigrants or prisoners, if they left immediately they would not be held responsible for anything, and if they travelled to Iran, India, Egypt or Russia and described their observations and experiences of the events in 'Akká, the accusations and calumnies of the Covenant-breakers would cease to further weaken the faith and resolve of the believers in those areas. 'Abdu'l-Bahá had made the same remarks to us before the incident of Mírzá Áqá Ján, and He now repeated them with emphasis and urgency.

At times He gave examples. Since the Turks were then fighting the Greeks, 'Abdu'l-Bahá said, "Sulṭán 'Abdu'l-Ḥamíd pays a great deal more attention to his generals in the field than to his ministers and courtiers who mill around at Court. He continually reinforces and arms those in the field, where a single soldier is more valuable and worthy than this minister or that director who is near him and away from the action. In the Faith of God the same logic applies. The hosts of the Kingdom always accompany those who are engaged in the field of service and sacrifice, and I too accompany them in spirit and pray continually for their success." In short, He frequently gave such examples and repeatedly emphasized this principle.

These words of 'Abdu'l-Bahá created such excitement in my heart that I sent a message to Him announcing my readiness, if He deemed me worthy, to perform any required service at whatever destination that He wished. His response was that I should depart for other destinations even if only for three months, and then return. I was thrilled with such glad-tidings, and so the next time I attained His presence I enquired, "I await your command; in which direction do you wish me to embark?"

After showering me again with many tender expressions of His love and kindness, He said, "Whichever destination you choose will serve the purpose."

"I have no will or desire of my own," I explained, to which He responded, "Go, meditate, and choose." Returning almost immediately, I submitted a note expressing my inability to decide, and that my mind commanded me to "place my affairs in God's hands, as He is well aware of His servant's condition". When He had read the note, a number of people including non-Bahá'ís being present, He adorned my head with the crown of honour and glory, picking up His pen and, while repeating words of praise and admiration revealing in the margin of my note a Tablet which also contained a powerful prayer:

"O thou who art enkindled by the fire which blazes in the tree of the Covenant! Arise and like a flame of fire ignite the horizons of the world. Depart towards other destinations and immerse thyself in every sea. Drink from every soft-flowing and pristine fountain, raise the cup of the Covenant and quell the schemes of the heedless ones..."[68]

Straight away I returned to the pilgrim house and handed my passport to the servant to obtain the necessary signature. But where to, no one knew. I asked him to enquire the destination of 'Abdu'l-Bahá. The Master indicated that I should travel with the three pilgrims bound for Iran. That night my passport was ready and next morning, after observing the rites of pilgrimage at the Shrine of Bahá'u'lláh, we attained the presence of 'Abdu'l-Bahá. He imparted to us heavenly counsel and words of wisdom. As we said our farewells, each of us in his own way expressed sentiments of deep devotion and utter servitude to the threshold of the Master. We then returned to the pilgrim house and said our goodbyes to a group of friends present while two porters carried our luggage out. As we started down the steps, a messenger suddenly rushed in bringing heavenly tidings: "The Master instructs that Jináb-i-Khán is to stay."

What wonderful news! My spirit soared. Leaving my luggage at the pilgrim house I accompanied the travellers to the city gate; on my return I proceeded straight to the House of 'Abdu'l-Bahá. 'Abdu'l-Bahá arrived at the same time. When I attained His presence, He said: "Jináb-i-Khán, you have been left alone!" – to which I responded,

"May my life be sacrificed for you:

> *Each member of the circle of the friends left for a destination,*
> *Except I and the thought of you, for each have found a home in the other.*"

Around noontime I returned to the pilgrim house where I greeted and renewed my acquaintance with the illustrious Zayn and the honored Mishkín Qalam, almost as though I had left for Iran and had just returned. From that time I began a solitary life in the pilgrim house, where the simple broth cooked with that same wheat which we had sifted while singing and chanting gave me strength of body and soul.

But I had nothing to do all day, for there were no pilgrims and all correspondence with the West had been suspended. Afternoons were spent in taking leisurely strolls in the Firdaws and Riḍván Gardens, and evenings in attaining the presence of the Master. In other words, I had developed into one of the lazy and unproductive members of the group resident in 'Akká. This went on for ten or twelve days.

One afternoon I was in 'Abdu'l-Bahá's *bírúní* when suddenly the Master arrived. Addressing me He said, "Jináb-i-Khán, tomorrow you will be on your way."

I was so shocked that for a moment I was unable to find my wits. He looked at my confused face and smilingly said, "Well?"

I struggled to speak. "You had not mentioned anything about leaving," I said. "I wrote the letters you asked for."

"What else do you want?" 'Abdu'l-Bahá replied.

"I want....", I began, but tears started to stream down my face.

"You know the conditions here," said the Master. "I want you to leave in the same joy with which you came." Then He asked me, "Laugh". As I struggled to find humour in the midst of heartbreak, He suddenly said rather loudly, "Come on, man, laugh!"

The sound of my laughter filled the room. He began His slow climb up the stairs as He repeated the words, "Marhabá, Marhabá!" [Well done, well done], approving my joyful reaction to that heart-rending news. This joy remained with me until three or four months later in Tehran when I awakened from that spiritual dream, but I shall describe the details of that later.

That same day I packed my luggage again. Next morning I observed the rites of pilgrimage at the Shrine of Bahá'u'lláh, gazed at His blessed portrait, and in the afternoon received the Master's summons for a farewell meeting. As I approached the entrance, I could hear 'Abdu'l-Bahá's voice, intense, shrill and indignant. I stood there, quite shaken at the turn of events. I asked the illustrious Afnán what had happened. He said that upsetting messages from the Covenant-breakers had been brought in by some of the women. At last 'Abdu'l-Bahá stepped into the *bírúní* reception room; seeing me standing there He said, "Jináb-i-Khán, you see what they are doing to Me. When you arrive in Iran, speak openly of all that you have seen here. I concealed their actions and intentions. But you are to openly reveal all."

He then handed me a large envelope, which I was to deliver to someone in Istanbul, and gave me much instruction regarding that mission. I understood that the suspension of my recent instruction to depart from the Holy Land had been brought about so that I might undertake this particular mission.

In short, the many blessings that were bestowed upon me by the Master at that meeting were beyond words. I only know that in a state of joy and ecstasy I asked God to assist me, unworthy as I was, to serve the Faith of God in such a way that I might merit His love and generosity.

The story of the package and my mission

When 'Abdu'l-Bahá handed me the package, He repeatedly emphasized its significance and how it should be closely guarded. I was instructed not to part with it at any time and therefore not to pack it in my suitcase, but to keep it on my person at all times. As soon as I was dismissed from His presence and went down the stairs, the illustrious Afnán again brought a message from 'Abdu'l-Bahá instructing me to purchase a carrying bag for the package once I reached Beirut. I was to keep the bag concealed underneath my clothes and make sure that it was not stolen. Soon the importance of the package became very clear to me. That night I arrived at the house of the late Ḥájí Siyyid Táqí Manshádí in Haifa. When I told him the story of the package, he became very concerned and informed me that in Beirut and Istanbul the Ottoman officials were examining and inspecting all written materials. He suggested, therefore, that it would be prudent for me to buy postage stamps, stick them on the package and have it postmarked at the Post Office the next day. At first I accepted this suggestion, but later I concluded that deviation from the instructions of the Master would be a mistake. Furthermore, to make an attempt at any other option was also out of the question, since 'Abdu'l-Bahá had said nothing regarding such an eventuality. Therefore I decided not to take any action, lest I unnecessarily endanger the mission by the possibility of having the package confiscated at the Post Office and in so doing disgrace myself in the eyes of the Master.

The following morning, meeting not the slightest difficulty from the officials at Haifa who were friendly towards the Faith, I boarded the ship. But in the afternoon in Beirut we were stopped for inspection. One of the officials, having examined my passport, ordered his assistant to search me carefully, adding, "He is coming from Haifa and 'Akká, search his pockets and inside his clothing with great care."

I stood there helpless as the second official began to conduct a thorough and rather harsh probe. But what kind of search did in fact take place? He discovered the package immediately, but without so much as a glance at it, and almost mindlessly, handed it back to me as if it had no relevance to the search in progress, and then began a careful and detailed examination of some ready-for-trash pieces of paper which he had found on me.

Praised be God, His bounty has such astonishing effects! I pray that I may at all times remain under the shadow of His divine will. In a joyful mood I purchased a bag in Beirut and quickly returned to the ship.

Taking the event as a good omen, I became certain that divine assistance would accompany me no matter where I went and that in fact the package was my protector rather than the other way round. On my arrival in Istanbul, they searched my luggage and examined the Tablets I was carrying for some of the friends without any protest, since Iran had been noted as the destination. Then they took me into another room where they carefully conducted a body search. Not only did they check each pocket and inspect each piece of clothing, they even separately examined the lining of each garment. But what do you think they did to the rather large bag that was hanging under my arm? Several times they pushed it aside so that they could reach my shirt pocket, without showing the least curiosity or paying any attention to a bag of that size. I could do nothing but laugh at the poor inspector's obvious deficiency in his powers of sight and touch, as he struggled to find the incriminating evidence that was under his very nose.

The ease with which I passed through the Customs inspection filled me with such happiness that I began to jump around in the streets of Istanbul like a child, as I had done in the streets of 'Akká. Next day, with divine assistance and as I had desired, I completed my mission and prepared for the last leg of my journey back to Iran. But the road to Russia was closed. For about forty days, a few friends and I made every effort to leave, both in Istanbul and in Trebizond. At last the road was opened and we continued our journey. In Tbilisi we were once more received by the Ahmadov brothers, who showed us much love and hospitality. We quickly passed through Badkubih and visited the friends in Anzali, Rasht and Qazvín; finally, having said goodbye to my companions as they proceeded on their way to their own destinations, I reached Tehran alone.

Tehran

Tehran in those times was, as 'Abdu'l-Bahá used to say, the centre of tests and difficulties and the hub of sedition and conspiracy. The Old Hyena, who had been rejected by 'Abdu'l-Bahá and was regarded by the faithful as a despicable figure, had lost his influence and power, and old age had dissipated his skill in both words and action. And yet he and his cronies still lost no opportunity to find, confuse and dishearten the new believers. As I have stated previously, since the excitement and devotion that had been generated in the hearts of the friends had accelerated the teaching work, the enemies of the Faith under the direction of the Covenant-breakers of 'Akká were, in response, busy planning and plotting in every corner.

While open Bahá'í firesides and confidentially arranged introductory meetings were being held on a regular basis both at fixed locations as well as on a rotating basis at different homes, the evil ones nevertheless lost no opportunity to present themselves at these meetings in order to create, in whatever manner possible, doubt and suspicion in the hearts of the listeners.

In other words, the same tricks and deceptions prevalent in 'Akká had now infected Tehran. Their purpose in creating doubt and suspicion, in trivializing the divine verses and resorting to abstract and vague arguments in support of their views, was to create disunity among the believers and, as had happened in past religions, to break the Faith into separate sects based on varied perceptions of religious leadership and authority.

The Covenant-breakers felt that in so doing they would emerge as a separate and yet legitimate faction of the Faith with a leadership all their own. In other words, in order to satisfy their unscrupulous ambitions and corrupt inclinations, they intended to splinter a theophany for the sake of which many a lover of the Abhá Beauty had accepted all manner of sacrifice and martyrdom.

After arriving in Tehran I spent some two months visiting the friends and speaking at various gatherings. I then applied to be reinstated at the bank. However, since I had resigned from my position twice before, my application was rejected. But those same angels of bounty, who had saved my life when I was on my way to Istanbul and helped me to complete my mission of delivering 'Abdu'l-Bahá's package, again came to my aid and before I knew it I was sitting at my desk in my office at the bank, pen in hand. As I sat there reflecting on my recent experiences, I realized that I had been away from this bank for nine months and that three of those months had been spent in a dream-like state. Wonder, joy and inspiration at what I had seen lingered in my mind and soul. From that time on I established a fireside, open to all, in my home, the spiritual effects of which brought my heart and soul indescribable joy.

The story continued

In all the meetings and gatherings of the friends, the story of Mírzá Áqá Ján's rebellion was a subject of conversation for a time. Sometimes I felt that the information I had shared with them was received differently by different friends. Some had already heard stories that were completely untrue. It became clear that unknown sources were spreading false information, and so I recounted to them everything that I had seen with my own eyes. These eyewitness accounts helped many of the friends to discover the falseness of what they had heard and to see the truth. And yet I wondered to myself if the wisdom would ever be demonstrated to me of the Master's insistence that I should actually witness with my own eyes Mírzá Áqá Ján's signature and the seal on that document on that fateful day.

One day an old friend whose purity of heart and devotion to the Faith was exemplary came for a visit. Two years earlier, it had been our intention to journey to 'Akká together, but the emergence of certain difficulties had prevented me from accompanying him and so he had completed his pilgrimage before I set out on mine. In describing my journey, I gave him an account of the many difficulties and dangers I had experienced on my way to Istanbul and my subsequent joyful times in 'Akká. I then related the story of Mírzá Áqá Ján. He immediately protested, voicing the view that the hatred and enmity that some of the believers felt for Mírzá Áqá Ján had prompted them to forge that infamous document in his name, and that in fact it was they who had spread those lies and accusations to defame and denigrate him. At this I became outraged, and recounted my personal observations with much emotion. But I soon realized that his mind was made up and that there was nothing I could do to change it. Again I repeated for him the events as I had witnessed them, and when I mentioned the fact that I had actually seen the document bearing the signature and the seal of Mírzá Áqá Ján with my own eyes, he cut me short and asked whether I had actually witnessed the signature myself or had merely heard about it from others. When I assured him of the sincerity of my statement in having seen the document, he was astonished. He said: "If the heavenly angels had related that story I would not have believed them. But since you tell me this from your personal experience, I must accept it, and I am grateful to you for having set the matter straight and my mind at rest." In return I thanked him for his understanding and acceptance, and my peace of mind, and recounted the story to him again.

I should mention here that this person was none other

than Muḥammad-Jaʿfar Mírzá, one of the most respected members of the Baháʾí community of Tehran.

AlláhʾuʾAbhá / AlláhʾuʾAʿẓam

In those years all sorts of rumours, gossip and generally loose talk abounded in the Baháʾí communities all over Iran. Since Local Spiritual Assemblies had not yet been established on a formal and continuing basis, the trouble-makers and Covenant-breakers sat in wait for such opportunities; as soon as some news reached them they concocted all sorts of stories, spread them far and wide, and created a furor.

For example, Faezeh Khánum, a Baháʾí lady who had just returned from her pilgrimage, recounted the story that one day while she was in the presence of the Master, ʿAbduʾl-Bahá had stated that today was not a day for idleness and passivity; today was the Most Great Day [Aʿẓam] and therefore it was the time to raise the call of "AlláhʾuʾAʿẓam" [God, the Most Great]. Once the mischief-makers in Tehran heard this news, they raised the cry, "Woe betide us, calamity has befallen us," and spread the rumour that the followers of the Most Great Branch had destroyed the name of Bahá and would soon destroy the Faith of Bahá.[69]

In response to this horrible accusation, a few of the believers who were known for their hot tempers and rash behaviour actually adopted the new greeting just to spite the enemies of the Faith. Others, with cooler heads, maintained the original greeting and thus this conflict created great upheaval and disunity among the friends.

Numerous letters of protest and complaint were sent to ʿAbduʾl-Bahá. Since the individuals on both sides of the argument were among the faithful and steadfast believers, both sides therefore received ʿAbduʾl-Baháʾs bestowals of kindness and generosity. The Master explained that in the ministry of the blessed Báb four greetings had been enjoined: "AlláhʾuʾAbhá", "AlláhʾuʾAʿẓam", "AlláhʾuʾAjmal" and "AlláhʾuʾAkbar".[70] In the days of the Blessed Beauty, however, because of the Greatest Name Bahá'u'lláh the greeting "Alláh'u'Abhá" became common.

While such Tablets from the Master increased the devotion, longing and spiritual attraction of the friends, they still did not resolve the problem at hand. The faithful believers, to spite the Covenant-breakers, insisted that since "now is the time of the dawn of the beauty of the sun of the Greatest Branch, therefore Alláh'u'A'ẓam is the better and the more relevant greeting".

In short, the dispute became more and more intense with every passing day and lasted some nine months. At last, both groups together pleaded with 'Abdu'l-Bahá to confirm one greeting explicitly so that unity and joy might again return to the hearts of the friends. Praised be the Lord, a clear response affirming the use of "Alláh'u'Abhá" as a greeting was revealed from the pen of 'Abdu'l-Bahá. Peace, joy, and love returned and the gatherings and meetings of the believers were reconvened with contentment and unity.

The Covenant-breakers were defeated, rejected and mocked. The Old Hyena was utterly abased and before long became housebound. His son Ḥubb'u'lláh made a short-lived attempt to provoke conflict and trouble among the friends, but soon he too met his end and the Faith of God was finally cleansed from the corruption of such creatures; and the period of the seditious activities of the Covenant-breakers in Tehran came to an end.

The effect of the story of Áqá Mírzá Ḥasan

The very first day that I established my fireside and openly invited the public to attend, I received a Tablet from 'Abdu'l-Bahá with the following opening words:

> If thou longest to become the recipient of ceaseless divine confirmations, then array the seekers, prepare the battalions of the lovers of truth and then assault the legions of ignorance and superstition.[71]

This created a great tumult in Tehran; various groups came together with the intent of creating mischief and disrupting the meetings. For some time they camped around my house with lanterns and torches, ready to attack the house. However, the necessary steps for my safety and security had been taken.

It was in these days that the late Mírzá 'Abdu'lláh, a music teacher, sent me a message through the late Dr. Arastú Khán Hakím informing me that he had been holding fireside meetings with a distinguished Muslim cleric and felt that my presence would be of benefit. I could hardly believe that a music teacher, and a former court musician of Náṣiri'd-Dín Sháh, who obviously would have been a man of various indulgences and pleasures, could possibly have discovered the truth of the Faith and had even been teaching an erudite Muslim scholar.[72]

> *The divine secret yet undisclosed by the lover and the faithful –*
> *Whom, I wonder, did the wine seller hear it from?*

In any case, I accepted the invitation with pleasure, but felt that I should get to know the musical Mírzá better. I hastened to meet him. He was an old man with a radiant face who had accepted the Faith in his youth but had since concealed it. His acquaintance brought much excitement and delight to my heart, especially when he played a lovely tune on his instrument afterwards. We agreed to hold the fireside meeting two days later at the seeker's house.

In those days, when superstition and vain imaginings prevailed in the ranks of Islamic clerics even more than now, a young man like myself, regardless of his cleverness or zeal, could not hope to confront a veteran Muslim scholar with any degree of effectiveness. So I told myself, "Rely upon God, go and proclaim the truth."

> *Ḥáfiẓ, offering up a prayer is your duty, but no more,*
> *Not yours to wonder if He has heard it or not.*

On the appointed day Mírzá 'Abdu'lláh and I met the Áqá. He was a well-mannered, courteous and dignified man with fine features and a large turban, seated on a simple couch. We sat across from him and after some preliminary small talk and the usual drinking of tea, began to speak about the Faith.

His questions had mostly to do with the apparent conflict between the Báb's expressions of servitude on one hand, and His subsequent claim to the station of divinity and prophethood on the other, as recorded in the Bayán and others of His Tablets. Of course, responding to such questions was rather simple since similar questions and arguments raised against Islám had been answered, especially in the writings of Imám 'Alí. After we had quickly passed through this subject, discussion was focused on certain Islamic Traditions. The clergyman stated: "You Bahá'ís usually resort to four Traditions to prove your case, whereas I know some four thousand Traditions by heart, all of which disprove your claim. How can I, who wear the crown of Islám and am seated on this throne, wearing the mantle of religious authority, sacrifice four thousand Traditions which I have committed to memory with great difficulty, to just four of yours?" He expressed this sentiment with great emotional intensity.

At that moment we heard a knock at the door. The servant answered the door and we heard him disappoint the caller by informing him that the "Áqá" was not at home. At that very same moment a little child, crawling one moment and walking the next, entered the room laughing. The conversation continued, however.

In response to the Áqá I put forth this argument: "Normally evidence is offered in proof of a claim; evidence disproving it can never be conclusive. For example, in your Faith, if someone claims to have left a trust with someone and a witness affirms such a claim and another witness supports that argument, the issue is considered proven.[73] However, what could witnesses who propose to negate the argument resort to in order to prove their point? Just now, there was a knock at the door and your servant presented himself as a negative witness (that Áqá is not home). Now if this child here, who lacks the qualifications of a witness, were to call out that the Áqá is in fact at home and someone else corroborated that statement and subsequently became supported by a second witness, could the contrary view of the servant still prevail? As you know, thousands of people have sacrificed their lives to witness to the truth of those four Traditions. In Islám, Salmán was the first Persian supporting witness and many Abu'l-Ḥikams were opposing witnesses. Who was eventually proven right?"[74]

I too set forth my arguments with great fervour and emotion. The Áqá reflected for a few moments.

"Well," he said, "let us pass over these arguments, for I have heard similar contentions before, but I don't doubt your honesty or the sincerity of your beliefs. I wish to know, since you have attained the presence of the Áqá [i.e. the Master], what have you brought back with you, what did you see with your own eyes and what did you hear with your own ears?"

I was adamant. "If you expect me to talk of miracles, I have nothing further to say and I ask God for forgiveness," I replied.

But he indicated that he simply wanted to hear some of my observations and experiences. As I began to relate my recollections, I suddenly remembered the case of Áqá Mírzá Ḥasan and described the circumstances of his pilgrimage in far more detail than is narrated in these pages. Gradually, I noticed a change in Áqá's demeanour; now he listened in a state of humility and with great attention. As I told the story I noted signs of emotion in his face and before the story was completed he suddenly prostrated himself, set his forehead to the ground, said a few Arabic words in thanksgiving to the Lord, and then began to weep loudly. He wept so intensely that we began to cry too, and then he raised his head and replaced his turban – which had fallen off – and as tears rolled down his flushed face said, "I know what was in the depth of Mírzá Ḥasan's heart and the significance of the truth that he discovered." Then he gave an account of the unity and solidarity of the various far-flung Arab tribes and how at first they had asked the Prophet Muḥammad for a miracle to prove the truth of His revelation, and afterwards in a combative stance had challenged him to a *mubáhilih*.[75] The heads of the tribes had met, consulted, agreed on certain conditions and devised a plan of approach. But on the very day of the *mubáhilih* the Prophet had appeared with such power and authority that all their agreements were abandoned as they fled the scene, frightened and defeated, while some accepted the Faith of God and became believers.

This event, in fact, was far greater and much more meaningful than all the miracles that they had asked for at the beginning of the Faith. In short, he related this story in great detail and then offered his own belief and devotion to the Cause of the Blessed Beauty. Truly, this was one of the happy days of this servant's life.

That day we made appointments for future meetings, embraced each other in joy and love, and left his house. I don't know what magic was latent in that story which transformed the Áqá and infused the spirit of faith and devotion into his being – a devotion so intense that the moment he raised his head from the ground he became a fully-fledged teacher of the Cause, and while citing all of those Traditions, fables and historical accounts of past ages, reconfirmed the verities of the Faith to me.

From that day, all his hours and minutes were spent in study, reflection and contemplation of the divine verses, as well as teaching the Faith. Before long he surpassed all his colleagues in his teaching efforts. At first he began to teach the clerics, and then gradually he removed the veil, resigned his position and became the speaker at my public fireside. Soon his conversion became the talk of town and he became renowned for his devotion to the new Faith, as well as for the power and eloquence of his utterance.

The Old Hyena limped his way to him and made an attempt to mislead him. After much discussion, he was reduced to silence. To the Áqá's question as to why he had deviated from the verse "turn your faces toward Him Whom God hath purposed"[76], the Old Hyena answered that in matters of religion he had been given the freedom to act as he wished. The Áqá replied, "I have perused that particular verse in the Kitáb-i-Aqdas where it is written: 'We find some men desiring liberty and priding themselves therein. Such men are in the depths of ignorance'." And then he added, "O Shaykh, 'know ye that the embodiment of liberty and its symbol is the animal'."[77]

In brief, the Áqá had heard the call of the new Faith in Hamádán when he occupied an exalted position in the Muslim clerical hierarchy, but had not accepted it. And although Mr. Arjmand and other Bahá'í teachers had presented him with irrefutable proofs, yet he had wandered in the vales of confusion and uncertainty while in Tehran. Until suddenly the veil of ignorance was lifted and the Holy Spirit penetrated the heart of Ḥájí Áqá Ṣadru'l-'ulamá, who was later honoured by the pen of 'Abdu'l-Bahá with the title of Ṣadru's-Ṣudur. And now, to adorn these pages, and also to complete the first part of this book, one of the Tablets revealed from the miraculous pen of the Covenant in his honour is reproduced below for the honourable reader. I pray that the divine utterances of 'Abdu'l-Bahá may attract the manifold blessings of God, enabling me to complete the remaining portions of this book in such a way as may be worthy of attention in the eyes of the friends of God.

He is God!
O thou who art enkindled by the fire of the love of God that burns in the Sinai of hearts!

I convey to thee my praise and salutations from the holy vale, Mount Sinai, the blessed and snow-white spot and I say unto thee, praise be upon thee, praise be upon thee for having entered under the shadow of the divine Lote Tree which has appeared out of this Holy Land and has spread its shadows over all horizons.

Tidings of joy be upon thee for having passed through this

sanctified Spot and beheld the fire which has ignited thy being through its heat and guided thy steps through its light. Therefore, adorned with the white hand of divine knowledge, cast down the rod of celestial dominion and transform it into the serpent of power and might. Verily this hand is the hand of the power of the Compassionate One and the serpent is its clear evidence and proof. Both shall be thy aid and assistance in all the worlds and the Holy Spirit shall also confirm thee through its power and sovereignty.

Glory be upon those who art steadfast, staunch and firm and those who raise the call of God, for verily they are the true guides for the people of the world.[78]

CHAPTER TWO

He is the Most Glorious!

Departure from Tehran

When I departed the Holy Threshold, it had been my intention to stay away for no longer than three to four months. And while during that time I never ceased to contemplate a return – for I longed to be reunited with the Beloved – I never imagined that those few months could turn into several years. Attachment to the material world, however, had so dominated my existence that my life had become devoid of its spiritual dimension. I realized that physical attachments, earning a living in order to provide the necessities of everyday life, and the pleasures of the material world can deprive man of heavenly nourishment and deny him spiritual joy unless the confirmations of the Unseen and the blessings of the Divine Being rain down more generously than deserved, and the sun of good fortune rises all too unexpectedly from the horizon of grace and mercy, rather than from that of merit and true worth.

And this was what happened to this servant. As I wallowed in the ocean of busy work at the bank, totally preoccupied by the trappings of this material world, one day when I was writing busily Ḥájí Mírzá Muḥammad Afnán suddenly entered my office and handed me a telegram from 'Abdu'l-Bahá. It read: "Youness Khán is to come. 'Abbás."

I was utterly stunned by this sudden and unexpected blessing. I thought I was dreaming, for the thrill and joy of reading the telegram was nothing less than the good fortune and pleasure of attaining His presence. Instantly I saw myself in the presence of the Beloved of hearts, suddenly I found myself in a world which I am utterly unable to describe.

That day I revealed nothing of my plans. But by the next morning, when I had made up my mind and had planned the details of my journey, I announced my decision. It goes without saying that selfish and material temptations assailed me from every side, attempting to deprive me of this heavenly blessing. But the power of assistance and the inspiration of the angels of mercy and bounty proved more than adequate to overcome the enticements presented by the bank president, who offered me a large raise in salary and the opportunity to take a paid sabbatical of six to twelve months if I were willing to withhold submitting a formal resignation. However, I did submit my resignation and received a substantial sum from the bank as a sign of their gratitude for my past services, as well as a letter of recommendation expressing their deep regret at my departure.

Within ten to twelve days of receiving the telegram I was on my way. Accompanied by a fellow traveller, I departed from Tehran and set out towards Mázindarán.[79] After twelve days we arrived in Badkubih. I left my friend with Ḥájí Mírzá Ḥaydar-'Alí and then along with two others set out for Istanbul. In Tbilisi the hospitality and kindliness of the Ahmadov brothers again arrested our further progress for two days. In Istanbul we spent a week waiting for a boat at the house of my late father, who had been appointed as the representative of the Faith in that city. Having secured passage on a vessel, I travelled with great haste towards Beirut and 'Akká and at last, in early April of the year 1900, I attained the Holy Threshold.

Pilgrimage at 'Akká with an American, Mr. Hoar

When we boarded the ship in Beirut, bound for Haifa, the radiant countenance of an American traveller so attracted my attention that I concluded that either he must be a Bahá'í or deserved to become one. I longed to start a conversation and unleash my tongue. However, the stormy seas and the increasing intensity of my emotions as we approached the coast of the Holy Land prevented me from doing so until our arrival.

In Haifa, the officials of the Office of Travellers' Affairs directed us both to the house of 'Abdu'l-Bahá, and so this was the first time I had the privilege of meeting a Western believer. After lunch we proceeded to 'Akká in a carriage. The distance between the two cities was covered in about the same length of time as I remembered from a few years ago. As we journeyed on, joyful and eager, I breathed the fragrant air and with the ear of spirit listened to those same verses of praise and thanksgiving uttered by the angels of holiness that I had heard before. But this time there was a difference. Previously, I had had this experience after having tasted the sweetness of reunion with the Beloved, whereas this time I rode on with parched lips towards the sweet waters of the Euphrates of love.

In any case, this two-hour journey to the Beloved seemed longer than the journey that had brought me from Iran to the Holy Land. As it is written: "When attainment is at hand, then the burning flames of love smoulder." Furthermore, as had been done for me in my previous pilgrimage, I felt the responsibility of describing point by point the significant and interesting spots along the road until we arrived at the city gate of 'Akká where we were received. Mr. Hoar was taken to the house of 'Abdu'l-Bahá and I to the pilgrim house. Before long we were summoned to the presence of 'Abdu'l-Bahá in the *bírúní* of His house. There I tasted the sweetness of reunion and experienced once again all the emotions and feelings which had so filled my being the first time I attained His presence; His kind and loving words rejuvenated my drooping soul.

Mr. Hoar was admitted next and for the first time I had the opportunity of translating in the presence of the Beloved of the world. There was not a long exchange of questions and answers, except that 'Abdu'l-Bahá praised the American believers in loving and tender words, gave glad tidings of future victories of the Faith of God, and also spoke a few words about tests and difficulties. Afterwards He assigned us to stay in the upper guest room of the house.

From the following day Mr. Hoar began to ask questions and write down 'Abdu'l-Bahá's answers. Most of these sessions took place at the dinner table. One day the subject of Ibráhím Khayru'lláh and his disloyalty to the Covenant came up. Mr. Hoar said that although Khayru'lláh had guided many souls to the Faith, yet once he deserted the Faith all mention of him had ceased and his disloyalty had left no adverse effect on the American Bahá'í community. 'Abdu'l-Bahá agreed and added: "Since he has only recently died, his influence still endures. However, before long you will notice a foul odour emanating from him until he rots and disintegrates completely."[80] He added that any corpse follows a similar path: at first it possesses the freshness of the human body but soon it begins to exude a foul stench disgusting to any living being. As soon as 'Abdu'l-Bahá made the analogy, Mr. Hoar asked and received special instructions from 'Abdu'l-Bahá for the protection of the friends from the evil promptings of disloyalty and infidelity.

In the few days of his pilgrimage Mr. Hoar became increasingly stirred until he was on fire. By the time he left he had become, through the influence of the Master, a complete and true teacher of the Faith. Later on, when the Covenant-breakers began their seditious activities, he was the source of great accomplishments and his magnificent services were always remembered, applauded and mentioned. One such service will be presented later.

My feelings during the first days in the Holy Land

While living in Tehran in previous years, I had kept in close contact with events in the Holy Land and was fully aware of all the changes that had taken place. I knew that the Covenant-breakers had been routed and cast out forever and that the gates of reunion were again opened to the eager faces of the believers. Numerous meetings of the Eastern and Western friends had been held in both 'Akká and Haifa. The mischief had ended, and of the troublemakers, some had repented; others, defeated and alone, had lost all hope of any further activity, while a few had received their just reward for their actions. Some of them had died while others had learned their lesson. Thus the Bahá'í world had finally found peace and tranquillity. What I did not know was:

A thousand tableaux has life in store,
But not one the way we imagine before.

My first hour in the presence of the Beloved of hearts was spent in a fragmentary and disjointed attempt to translate His words, as I sat utterly intoxicated by His presence. When the meeting ended and we were all dismissed, I was summoned to His presence alone. In a hushed voice the Master confided: "You have to be here with us. Trust no one but me. Whatever is in your heart, confide it to me only. Trust no one, this land is in turmoil and the troublemakers are waiting in the wings. Be vigilant."

These words gave cause for deep reflection. I meditated on His utterances word for word and placed them in the storehouse of my memory, realizing that things had not changed as I had thought. What I did not notice then was that in addition to the Covenant-breakers, other troublemakers had also emerged and this had added to 'Abdu'l-Bahá's cares. Before long the late Ḥájí Níyáz arrived [from Egypt] in order to meet with Mr. Hoar. The Master asked me to be present at the interview and to serve as translator. We spent some time in conversation, after which I was again summoned to the presence of 'Abdu'l-Bahá, Who told me, "This man [Ḥájí Níyáz] is a trustworthy friend of mine. Do not have any concerns about him." Again, this statement added to my worries, for it emphasized the fact that the community of friends was infected by a large number of Covenant-breakers.

The condition of the pilgrims and of the pilgrim house were as before, orderly and efficient. The pilgrims and the residents visited Bahjí in horse-drawn carriages on Holy Days with the same feelings of reverence and devotion as their predecessors. The old servants were still in service; only a few details had changed, except for the addition of a number of troublemakers whom I had not seen before and who were then part of the band of servants. Amongst these was Mírzá Amín,[81] son of Mírzá Asadu'lláh-i-Iṣfáhání, a seventeen-year-old boy who was said to be related to one of the maidservants of the household of 'Abdu'l-Bahá. This young man was very agile, shrewd and intelligent and was in the service of the ladies of the holy family. Outwardly, he was quite likable and enjoyed the favour and kind attention of the household. He had established a close and friendly relationship with Mr. Hoar when he was here and at times was present at 'Abdu'l-Bahá's informal talks at the dinner table; he also used to carry messages from the ladies of the household to the American ladies.

However, I soon discovered that this young impostor had a long experience in treachery and deception. On the day that Mr. Hoar completed his pilgrimage, I received from the hand of 'Abdu'l-Bahá certain written instructions which I was to convey to Mr. Hoar to undertake once he arrived in the United States. In doing so, I was to avoid mentioning any names or handing him the actual written Tablet. Both Mírzá Amín and I were instructed to accompany Mr. Hoar to Haifa. When I explained 'Abdu'l-Bahá's instructions to Mr. Hoar, he asked me for the written instructions. It became obvious to me that Mírzá Amín had created suspicion in his mind in order to cause mischief. I had no choice but to telegraph the request to 'Abdu'l-Bahá, with whose permission I submitted the Tablet to him. Gradually I noticed that the shrewd imposter lost no opportunity to create doubt and suspicion in the hearts of all he met. However, in the House of 'Abdu'l-Bahá and among the elderly residents of 'Akká he remained a charming favourite. After the departure of Mr. Hoar we returned to 'Akká.

Description of my duties in those days

After the departure of Mr. Hoar I returned to 'Akká and to the pilgrim house, where unlike previous years I, along with other pilgrims, busied myself with the prescribed duties of translating the incoming correspondence from the West and generally enjoying some pleasant and joyful times. With the arrival of the Riḍván festivities we visited the Holy Shrine of Bahá'u'lláh, as had now become the custom, with the same ceremony and formality of past years. The gardens around the Shrine had been expanded and so the use of the Mansion's first floor reception room had been abandoned. In its place and adjacent to the Mansion had been built a small garden filled with colourful and fragrant flowers, and four rooms; this served as the resting area for the pilgrims.

To the custom of the carrying of flowerpots by the pilgrims from 'Akká to the Shrine, which had been carried out with great pomp and ceremony and in an atmosphere of complete humility and lowliness, another practice had been added. This was the transportation of water in some one hundred copper jugs by the pilgrims and residents from nearby springs to the Shrine to water the flowers while reciting divine verses and poetry. The spiritual state of the friends and the atmosphere of devotion and attraction which dominated the scene had a strange effect on any onlooker. When 'Abdu'l-Bahá held a jug of water on His shoulder as He stood before the Holy Shrine, signalling permission for the chanting of prayers, while the friends stood in reverent attention, such a heart-stirring scene was created as to cause the tears of the spectators to flow. Some even pleaded to be given jugs so that they too could share in the honour of pilgrimage by watering the flowers. In any event, after chanting of the Tablets revealed for observance of that Holy Day and completing the rites of pilgrimage for the first day of Riḍván, we all returned to 'Akká.

After the Riḍván period I was summoned one day to the presence of 'Abdu'l-Bahá. The Master asked me whether I was more fluent in French or English. I replied that although my English was limited, I was able to translate from English to Persian but not conversely. I explained that this was especially true of the sacred Tablets, which contained numerous Bahá'í expressions the English equivalents of which were unknown to me. 'Abdu'l-Bahá commanded, "You must study English; we are in great need of it. Stay in Haifa and translate the correspondence."

Next day He summoned a person called 'Abdu'lláh Bolurih from Haifa to His presence. Mírzá Amín and I were also called in. After showering 'Abdu'lláh with kindness and love, 'Abdu'l-Bahá handed the man a five-lira note in payment for him to teach us English in Haifa. Next day, the Master gave me a number of letters and Tablets to translate. He instructed me: "Rely on Bahá'u'lláh, be confident, and translate." I immediately went to Haifa where a room for my residence in the *bírúní* of 'Abdu'l-Bahá's house was arranged; 'Abdu'lláh Bolurih came daily and taught English to both Mírzá Amín and me. Shortly after, I began to translate the incoming correspondence by myself. I also took up the translation of certain original Tablets into French and, with the help of my teacher, certain other Tablets into English.

Haifa in 1900 A.D.

The *bírúní* of 'Abdu'l-Bahá's residence, also known as the pilgrim house, provided modest accommodation consisting of four rooms. One room served as the bedroom of 'Abdu'l-Bahá, while the second was used for public gatherings. The third room was the office of the late Ḥájí Siyyid Taqí Manshádí and the fourth was designated as the pilgrim house. In recent years that room had been the residence of many pilgrims from around the world. However, this year, in view of the prevailing conditions, caution had dictated a reduction in their numbers. The *andárúní* of the house was normally occupied by a number of the ladies of the Holy Family. The American pilgrim house also consisted of four bedrooms and offered Western style accommodation; over the course of the previous two years it had regularly housed assorted groups of Western pilgrims. At that time, however, in accordance with the Master's instructions, it remained unoccupied.[82]

In addition to these, a great structure was being built on the slopes of Mount Carmel to house the remains of the Blessed Báb. The Master visited Haifa periodically to supervise the construction activities; this gave the friends and non-Bahá'ís of Haifa the opportunity and the blessing of attaining His presence for a few days before He returned to 'Akká. The attraction and fervour of the friends in Haifa were no less intense than those of the residents of 'Akká.

The changes that had taken place over the previous three or four years were as follows:

First: for a short time Mírzá Áqá Ján had found shelter with the Covenant-breakers in the Mansion and had received much care and attention there. But as soon as they had determined that he had no place in their future plans, they had packed him off to the Most Holy Shrine so that under the guise of "refugee" he could continue to irritate and torment the friends by denying them the opportunity of enjoying a peaceful visit to that Holy Spot. For a short while he remained a nuisance, until the hand of Providence removed him.

Second: the late Mírzá Ḍíyá'u'lláh had remained unstable, impulsive and confused, and had followed the path envisioned by Bahá'u'lláh in one of the verses of the Hidden Words: "…bereft of the melody of the dove of heaven… return[ed] to water and clay",[83] hoping for divine mercy and blessing.

Third: The room on the lower floor of the Mansion which had formerly served as the pilgrims' reception room had been taken over by the Covenant-breakers and was now in their possession. According to 'Abdu'l-Bahá's instructions, a small garden adjoining the Holy Shrine had been purchased and established as a reception area for the pilgrims, as described above.

Fourth: the Covenant-breakers no longer accepted 'Abdu'l-Bahá's generous offerings for their expenses and therefore the financial pressures had considerably eased at 'Abdu'l-Bahá's house. Nevertheless, He often continued to support them financially on various pretexts.

Fifth: Ṭabúr Áqásí's actions against the Faith had produced the opposite effect. He had been dismissed from office and had fallen on hard times. Eventually, he came begging at 'Abdu'l-Bahá's door and received financial assistance.

Sixth: For three years, groups of friends from East and West had been arriving regularly on pilgrimage; Haifa had become the gathering place for the friends and the site of many happy and joyful meetings and assemblies. In recent times, however, the Master's instructions had limited the number of such pilgrimages.

Seventh: Due to the improved financial condition of the funds, some of the victims of greed and self-indulgence had been put to the test. One had shown a desire for position and prestige; another had sought an all-expenses-paid vacation in America; yet another, unsatisfied with his circumstances, had become an outright enemy of the Faith. In brief, the raging fire of the greed of the Covenant-breakers had also awakened the avarice of the enemies of the Faith. These new rebellions had added to the many cares of 'Abdu'l-Bahá. Yet His qualities of concealing sins and bestowing mercy and forgiveness would not allow Him to reveal the truth of the situation. A number of friends had, on their own, discovered the designs of the enemies of the Faith and yet dared not utter a word. In despair, one had lost his sanity, another had committed suicide, while a third had fled the city. For these, the distress and agony created by their knowledge of what was taking place had proved too much to bear. Such tragic circumstances had been prevalent in those years; however, since I was not in the Holy Land at the time I can present only a summary of those events.

Having been defeated in their old designs, the violators of the Covenant had found a fresh excuse to motivate the mischief-makers, and that was the construction of the Shrine of the Báb. The details of this will be covered in a future chapter.

Eighth: Two of the Covenant-breakers had resolved to assassinate the Centre of the Covenant. One had poisoned 'Abdu'l-Bahá's water jug, which had been discovered in time. The other had made an unsuccessful attempt to stab the Master. 'Abdu'l-Bahá forgave one and turned a blind eye to the other; discredited for the rest of their lives, they spent their last days in Tehran.

The morale of the believers of Haifa and 'Akká in those days

Once the rebellion of Mírzá Áqá Ján had ended and the pressures had eased, and the believers of the East and the West once again turned their attention toward the Holy Land, it soon became obvious that 'Akká did not have the capacity to accommodate such large numbers of pilgrims. The small city of Haifa became perforce the formal residence of the Master, as the House of 'Abdu'l-Bahá and the two aforementioned pilgrim houses had been completed and made ready for service.[84] Meanwhile, the friends resident in Haifa began to take on a larger share of the responsibilities and duties required at the Holy Threshold, while the friends of 'Akká continued to provide support in their many and varied services. This change of residence revived the spirits of the

Bahá'ís of Haifa and brought joy to their hearts as it revitalized their community.

The Covenant-breakers, routed, severed from the community and without hope, remained outside this centre of activity. For a time, mutiny and rebellion were replaced by peace and calm. However, a few of their loyal friends, whose greed had not been satisfied and whose many excessive desires had not been fulfilled, not unlike the Old Hyena, began to create mischief. Even so, they continued to receive their share of opportunities for service to the Cause, for 'Abdu'l-Bahá's attribute of divine concealment veiled their activities and protected them from themselves.

However, a few of the servants of the Master's household who were aware of the secrets were quite indignant about the whole affair. Accusations and backbiting were rampant. For instance, these servants used to say things – the truth of which was to emerge only some twenty years later – about Áqá Mírzá Asadu'lláh and his son, and about Áqá Siyyid 'Alí-Akbar Dahají, as well as a few others who outwardly enjoyed 'Abdu'l-Bahá's trust. This was because these servants enjoyed varied and intimate association with many and were therefore informed of matters that only time would confirm. Armed with such knowledge they would backbite to their heart's content and then repent and ask for forgiveness. When I began to hear such whisperings, I was reminded of 'Abdu'l-Bahá's advice on the first day of my arrival: "Don't trust anyone, this land is in turmoil," etc.

What was astonishing was that the very people who were the subjects of so much backbiting and rumour on the part of the intimate servants of 'Abdu'l-Bahá's household presented themselves in such a light of loyalty, constancy and humility that one felt utterly confused about the truth of such allegations. However, since four years earlier I had observed at first hand Mírzá Áqá Ján's behaviour and the crisis he had precipitated, I could not overlook the possible credibility of such whisperings. But while at the time I disregarded much of the talk, it was quite evident that some of the friends in Haifa and

'Akká were looking for opportunities for financial gain. Some travelled and wrote to 'Abdu'l-Bahá for financial help. In short, in the course of the four years of my absence, strange and bizarre changes had taken place in the general character and conduct of the friends, changes which could not have been imagined four years earlier. Praise be to God that all such people of dubious character ultimately revealed their true purpose, some after five years, others after fifteen, and yet others eventually died out and no memory of them remains.

Six months in Haifa

I have likened my six-month stay in Haifa to the life of an untrained, mute parrot who is given a cage for shelter and training in the art of speech. In my case, however, the cage was placed in the most wonderful site in the world, the divine paradise. Every few days that spiritual Teacher, that radiant and heavenly Personage, travelled to Haifa and imparted to my undeserving soul words of counsel and guidance which unveiled to my eyes sparkling vistas of the world of reality. He placed in my cage such a variety of heavenly sweets that I could not possibly desire more. At first I entertained thoughts of breaking the cage, finding a way out and soaring to 'Akká, but before long I became so acclimatized to my surroundings that when summoned to 'Akká I would go there, submit the completed documents, receive the letters and Tablets requiring translation, and return to Haifa contentedly, all within the span of a day.

One such day, while handing me a whole sheaf of Tablets to translate, 'Abdu'l-Bahá commanded, "But be careful not to translate like the Old or the New Testaments."[85] I replied that if I could translate as well as that, I would throw my hat up in the air out of pure joy. Surprised, He said, "What! You want to try to translate like the Bible was translated?" and then He recited one of the New Testament verses in Arabic and said, "Do you want to translate like this?"

"How do we know I can translate even as well as that?" I immediately answered.

He smiled again and said, "Rely on Bahá'u'lláh and you will translate well. Go, and trust in God."

I don't know what heavenly power was in those words, but it fortified my helpless soul with divine confirmation. Gradually, every undertaking and every assignment seemed well within my ability, and the act of translation, whether performed poorly or masterfully, became the simplest of tasks.

My classmate and colleague, however, was very clever and shrewd and under a variety of guises purloined some of the Tablets and translated them with the help of non-Bahá'ís. When I discovered this I began to exercise caution, and although our relationship became strained we continued our English language study sessions with 'Abdu'lláh Bolurih.

Pilgrimage by the Western friends had been suspended; and according to the servants of the Master's household the second pilgrim house and 'Abdu'l-Bahá's house in Haifa were to be closed. But the Eastern pilgrims from Iran, Egypt, India and Russia were arriving in large numbers and they usually stayed in Haifa for a few days. In the meantime, 'Abdu'l-Bahá paid special attention to Haifa and always encouraged the pilgrims to visit Mount Carmel and the future site of the Shrine of the Báb. In brief, this small town had become the promised paradise, although my only associations were limited to Ḥájí Siyyid Taqí Manshádí and the honoured Mírzá Jalál. All the friends in Haifa, especially the older ones, had a soft spot in their hearts for me. And so in the moderately warm climate of Haifa I spent six wonderfully happy months.

'Abdu'l-Bahá's visits from 'Akká to Haifa

As described before, every few days 'Abdu'l-Bahá came to Haifa to supervise the construction activities of the Shrine of the Báb, and stayed for a few days. Upon His arrival He usually visited the pilgrim house where both Bahá'ís and non-Bahá'ís who had received the news of His arrival would already have gathered in anticipation of a meeting which would last until late at night.

In the morning, the Master began the day by visiting the notables of Haifa. Visiting the poor and showering them with His love and generosity was one of His essential and customary tasks. He visited each and every indigent home, showing kindness and expressing sympathy and thus bringing happiness and joy to the hearts of the needy, who comprised people of various national and religious backgrounds. What was astonishing was that He knew the children of each household by name, and if a child or an old woman was not present, He would enquire after their health and wellbeing: "Where is so and so, how is he doing?" If there was an illness in a family, the Master expressed deep sympathy and bestowed upon them His kind and loving sentiments. He would even give complete medical instructions for the healing and recovery of the patient, and in addition offer prayers for each and every one, patting their heads and faces with His blessed hand, bestowing encouragement and wellbeing. He would then bring out from His pocket a bag of coins of every size and shape and, as dictated by the circumstances, bestow a generous sum on each, thus imparting hope and encouragement to them all. He carried on from one house to the next until the money ran out.

But in addition to visiting the friends and town dignitaries, the Master's stay in Haifa had a more significant purpose. Visiting the poor and the indigent always merited first priority. However, the task that consumed 'Abdu'l-Bahá's thoughts was the construction of the Shrine of the Báb, which will be brought to the attention of the esteemed readers in more detail below. This had given the Covenant-breakers a new excuse for mischief and sedition as they endeavoured with all their power to impede its progress.

Construction of the Shrine of the Báb

The small city of Haifa, nestling on the slopes of Mount

Carmel, could be divided into three distinct parts. The first was the old city on the lower east side where the air was warm, foul and filthy. It had a single bazaar with dark, narrow and winding alleys, similar to the one in 'Akká. The second part, on the west and the southwest side of the city, comprised the German colony, known as the German quarter. Here, the climate was moderate and the administration of civil affairs was in the hands of the Germans themselves. The third was the area of Mount Carmel and its slopes, which consisted of vineyards and were in the possession of the Germans. There were also other large tracts of land that were generally barren and unutilized. The climate of the slopes of Mount Carmel, especially on the upper southwest side, was quite temperate and mild.

Situated on the choicest segment of the slopes across from German Street, and looking out toward the sea, was a beautiful plot of land covered with tall, lively and verdant cypress trees. In the days of the Blessed Beauty this plot of land had served as a summer resort for Bahá'u'lláh. The Ancient Beauty had been so pleased with the surroundings that He had instructed that the plot should be purchased in the future and that the eternal resting place of the blessed Primal Point should be built at its heart.

At the first opportunity, 'Abdu'l-Bahá purchased a number of tracts of land in that area. It was the purchase of that plot of land and the subsequent construction of the Shrine of the Báb that again rekindled the enmity and jealousy of the Covenant-breakers. Thus began a twelve-year struggle, during which they revived and brought to the attention of the Ottoman government a variety of accusations, charges and complaints in order to destroy the edifice, extirpate the cause of God and precipitate the death of 'Abdu'l-Bahá. And so all subsequent events, the details of which will be presented later, stemmed from this land and this holy edifice.

Under 'Abdu'l-Bahá's supervision, the construction of the foundation of the Shrine of the Báb began some time before the year 1909 A.D.[86] 'Abdu'l-Bahá's attachment to that edifice was such that He made reference to it and gave descriptions of it on every possible occasion, and when He arrived in Haifa most of His time was consumed in issuing instructions for the construction and the general supervision of these activities.

Under such conditions, the friends who thirsted to attain His presence had to do so on the slopes of Mount Carmel. 'Abdu'l-Bahá's description of the future of that location and that edifice was uttered with such joy and excitement that while only the foundation work was commencing and all that could be seen was a large hole in the ground, a few dirt movers, and otherwise an expanse of rough and rugged land, nevertheless one could see with the eye of imagination the immaculate, spotless cleanliness and pristine beauty of the present structure.[87]

'Abdu'l-Bahá described in detail what portions of the work had been completed and what was planned for construction in the future. He indicated the locations of each flowerbed and the sites of various other ornamental features. The foundation of the edifice was so sound and solid that I frequently expressed my observation to 'Abdu'l-Bahá that in its strength and substance that foundation resembled the foundation of the Faith of God itself.

However, the jealousy and hatred of the Covenant-breakers and their incessant efforts to paralyse and ruin this major work were so intense that their effects brought much sadness and distress to the heart of 'Abdu'l-Bahá. In the course of twelve years, not a year, nay not a month, not even a day passed without a fresh calamity or a new treachery. One such act was the Covenant-breakers' deceiving the owner of a piece of property, land that provided access to the upper site of the construction work, to withhold its sale to 'Abdu'l-Bahá. They had assured the landowner that they would happily match any offer made by 'Abdu'l-Bahá without even taking possession of the land. They had also encouraged other owners with properties in the vicinity of the construction work to obstruct all traffic through their properties to the construction site.

Induced by the Covenant-breakers, the Germans who owned most of the land in that area began to create trouble. Anyone, whether Christian or Jew, who owned a piece of that barren and worthless land encouraged others to lay claim of ownership to a part of that ownerless wilderness and block all possible access routes to the incoming traffic hauling construction materials to the building site. All these activities gradually increased the value of the land on the slope. As soon as the edifice began to take form, the Covenant-breakers spread far and wide the rumour that the structure actually concealed an ammunition dump.

In brief, a piece of land which is now nothing but a narrow paved alley that provides access to a major thoroughfare became so valuable that although the Master offered to buy it at fifty and sixty times its fair price, the owner refused to sell. Finally things reached such a pass that 'Abdu'l-Bahá would later say, "I was put under so much pressure that one night I stayed up and recited a prayer revealed by the Primal Point that I had in my possession. After that I felt at peace. Next morning the property owner came, apologized and offered to sell the property. I told him I had no further need of the land. He insisted and explained, 'This is not my fault; your brothers deceived me and told me they would double any offer that you would make and that I should not let go of the property easily.' In any case, he pleaded and I refused until he threw himself at my feet and begged me to take the property at no cost; then I sent him to Áqá Riḍá and instructed him to pay the landowner a sum of money and complete the purchase."

This is an example of the various schemes of the Covenant-breakers. Even after this, whenever a piece of property was needed to expand the gardens, similar intrigues had to be overcome. Aside from this, the Master spent large sums for the maintenance work of the main road passing through the area, as a generous gesture towards the development and growth of the city of Haifa and towards the happiness of its citizens.

'Abdu'l-Bahá's words in those days in Haifa

Generally, whenever 'Abdu'l-Bahá came to Haifa He stayed in the pilgrim house for a day, after which His time was taken up by visits to various individuals or by supervision of the construction work. Only in the late hours of the evening would the friends find the honour and the opportunity of attaining His presence in the *bírúní* or the pilgrim house. More often than not, He had His lunch in the *bírúní* and His dinner at His residence. As before, at times His words pertained to the life stories of the troublemakers, while at other times He imparted kindly counsel to those present; yet sometimes, confidentially, He spoke about the consequences of the many intrigues perpetrated by Covenant-breakers. For example, He used to say, "The desire and the plan of the Covenant-breakers is that I should spend the rest of my life in prison and in chains. It so happens that this is also the height of my desire and my longing, since this would release me from all torment and agony and would enable me to spend my time in prayer and meditation. Nothing could bring me more happiness. Of course, for me, whatever they consider misery and agony is the apex of happiness and good fortune. Their misfortune is that whenever they lay a trap for me they get caught in it before I do. But for them the trap is hell and for me naught but paradise."

In those days, when enemies, rabble rousers and rumour-mongers abounded and were in fact wolves dressed in sheep's clothing intent on creating trouble, 'Abdu'l-Bahá especially talked about matters that were meant to reach the ear of the Arch-breaker of the Covenant, so that he might know that the Head of the Faith was not uninformed of their intrigues and that there was wisdom in His silence. For example, for a few days the theme of 'Abdu'l-Bahá's talks had been to prove through intellectual and philosophical reasoning that at times

Almighty God actually assists the actions of the non-believers and Covenant-breakers. There was wisdom in this that was unclear to man. For example, He would say, "Is it not true that as long as man's evil and sinful intentions do not translate into action he will remain free from God's punishment and retribution? Therefore, God's assistance, that may be likened to the heat of the rays of the sun, reaches all levels of existence so that the true nature of all beings may be revealed. It is only then that the wretched is distinguished from the good." And then He added, "Soon you will see the fire trap that they have set for me. The irony is that they will fall into it before I do. But for me this is happiness upon happiness and for them misery upon misery." In brief, these words of the Master created a dark picture in the minds of His audience, and yet 'Abdu'l-Bahá's face beamed with a joy and happiness that infused gladness and hope into the hearts of the friends. The general understanding was that the consequences of the actions of the Covenant-breakers would be revealed before long, but that they would not be a cause of distress or anguish for 'Abdu'l-Bahá. In fact it was expected that they would become the very cause of the progress and triumph of the Cause of God.

Another sign of 'Abdu'l-Bahá's concern with the unsettled conditions of the times was that in the previous six months no permission for pilgrimage had been issued to the Western believers. The Eastern friends, too, only rarely received permission, and so the pilgrim houses of 'Akká and Haifa were mostly unoccupied and the Western pilgrim house in Haifa was eventually closed.

Three pistol shots at 'Abdu'l-Bahá

During the Caliphate of 'Abdu'l-Ḥamíd, the Sultan of the Ottoman Empire, the central government encouraged an atmosphere of hatred and confrontation among the various peoples of the Empire in the entire region of Syria and Palestine, especially between the Muslims and the Christians. Most

THREE PISTOL SHOTS AT 'ABDU'L-BAHÁ 123

of the people ordinarily went about armed with pistols and one of their everyday pastimes was to fire their guns. At weddings and circumcision parties, firing shots in the air was quite customary and if by accident a passer-by was injured in the process, bad luck would be considered the true culprit. The smallest argument between two individuals could easily erupt into gunplay, with bullets flying back and forth between the two belligerents and at times striking innocent bystanders. According to the laws in force at that time, threatening someone with a gun, if proven in a court of law, would result in heavy punishment. However, shooting a pistol for the enjoyment of the sport was considered acceptable and allowable. Therefore, any loss of life in such circumstances was not normally taken seriously by the courts, and even a deliberate act of shooting with intent to kill could receive a suspended sentence if an adequate bribe could be raised. In short, the carrying of arms and firing of pistols were ordinary and accepted practices, and killing a man, given the conditions of the time, was a forgivable sin. A large number of the Covenant-breakers who had completely left the Faith and no longer felt any spiritual or religious attachments normally carried guns. They openly associated with the town's thugs and troublemakers and at times even threatened the life and the livelihood of the friends.

Since 'Akká was a fortress with narrow winding streets, it did not provide sufficient space for such blatant actions. However, the small city of Haifa, because of its proximity to open spaces and the sea, had become the centre of their activities, and so the sound of gunshots, whether fired for fun or to create fear, filled the nights. And since escape routes were open and unguarded, murder was rampant; under cover of night the murderer could easily flee the scene unnoticed.

This is a brief description of social conditions in Haifa. Therefore, whenever 'Abdu'l-Bahá travelled to Haifa, certain of the friends and especially the servants of the household were deeply concerned about His comings and goings at night. The *andárúní* was at some distance from the centre of town, and normally He would return from either attending to the poor and needy or visiting the notables of the town some time after midnight. He would then attend to the friends for a few minutes, either in the *bírúní* or in the Haifa pilgrim house, and then walk towards the *andárúní* by himself, a ten-minute stroll.[88] This part of town, which was in close proximity to the German district, had no street lighting and the Master did not permit anyone to accompany Him with a lamp. However, someone used to follow Him at a distance all the way to the house. When His visits were confined to areas within the city proper, He himself carried a lamp.

When 'Abdu'l-Bahá was in Haifa, those present at the pilgrim house – whether resident, pilgrim or household servant – knew that some time late at night, even if it were for no more than ten minutes, He would arrive for a visit. Therefore they waited for Him, sometimes until two in the morning. One night He arrived at one in the morning and after His customary expressions of affection to each and every one present He turned to Ustád Muḥammad-'Alí, who was quite sleepy, and said, "Chant a prayer." He immediately recited:

> O my God, my Master, the Goal of my desire! This, Thy servant, seeketh to sleep in the shelter of Thy mercy, and to repose beneath the canopy of Thy grace, imploring Thy care and Thy protection...[89]

And so one could see that 'Abdu'l-Bahá's life in Haifa was much more arduous than in 'Akká. In summer months, when nights were short, He was engaged until late at night and rose with the first light. He would then find a peaceful spot on the slopes of Mount Carmel and spend time in prayer and meditation. He never had a moment's peace. Some days He was busy all day attending to various matters, and at the setting of the sun He would return and rest for ten to fifteen minutes in His *bírúní* bedroom before setting out to take care of other matters, without anyone knowing when He might return. The lack of security in the town was a continuous burden on the minds of the friends. Walking about town where the sound of gunfire was a routine matter was not without danger, especially considering the many threats that were consistently received by the friends. It was for this reason that despite His clear instructions to the contrary, Ustád Muḥammad-'Alí, who was a builder and a shoemaker and was also considered a loyal and devoted servant, walked a few steps behind 'Abdu'l-Bahá all the way to the house.

Sometimes I assumed this secretive duty and followed 'Abdu'l-Bahá from a distance on His return to the house. Once at His door, if He was pleased with me, He would honour me with the words, "Well done! God go with you." The pride and joy of having served 'Abdu'l-Bahá made the infraction of accompanying Him admissible – nay, to my mind, commendable.

One night I began my usual walk, following a few steps behind 'Abdu'l-Bahá. We had not quite reached the midpoint when suddenly I saw three shots fired at Him from the alley to our right. At first I remained unconcerned, for I had become accustomed to the sound of gunshots at night. However, on the second shot I saw the flash of fire coming from the barrel of a gun being fired in the direction of 'Abdu'l-Bahá. I ran toward the alley. The third shot was fired before I reached the intersection but I saw someone fleeing. A second person who was halfway up the alley also ran away. Both ran toward the beach. At this moment I was but a few steps from 'Abdu'l-Bahá. The Master's gait did not change. He strolled along with the same dignity and stateliness that were the distinguishing characteristics of that radiant and heavenly Being. Unperturbed, He continued His steady strides without paying the least attention to what had just transpired. He seemed to be praying and I did not wish to disturb Him with my expressions of concern and anxiety at a time when the whole of His attention was focused on the world of the spirit.

As soon as we reached the house, He turned His blessed face around in the darkness and said, "May God go with you," granting me leave. I returned to the pilgrim house and related the story to Ustád Muḥammad-'Alí. He too became deeply distressed; he did not openly express any concern but began accompanying 'Abdu'l-Bahá from then on without missing a night. I too continued my service, as we both shared the honour of escorting 'Abdu'l-Bahá. Of course, our real concern was not due to any danger that might have threatened the Master on His short walks. It was rather in confronting those future troubles and trials that he had foretold, instigated by the Covenant-breakers.

The renewal of confinement

'Abdu'l-Bahá began in those days to disclose certain facts about the plans and strategies of His enemies, so bringing deep concern to the hearts of the friends. While He painted a rather dark picture of the future, no one had any real conception of the gravity of the emerging crisis, whose flames were to engulf first the Covenant-breakers and then 'Abdu'l-Bahá Himself. I constantly prayed and implored Almighty God to bring to realization only the first part of 'Abdu'l-Bahá's prophecy. In other words, I prayed that the Covenant-breakers might fall into the fire of their own sedition and treachery and become consumed by the flames of their own machinations and intrigues – but that the second part of the prediction ("after them, me") might not be fulfilled. But alas, His prophecy was realized to its full extent without the least mitigation of the circumstances. That Joseph of the heavenly Egypt[90] was incarcerated for eight years, until at last the Most Great Prison was dismantled and that blessed Being was able to travel, first to Egypt and then to Europe and America, to raise the call of the Kingdom in many gatherings and churches.

And we, in praise and gratitude, repeated what Na'ím has written:

> *Glad tidings to Jacob, for his beloved son*
> *Is made sovereign in the Egypt of love.*

The details of the resumption of the Most Great Prison are as follows:

Normally, a few days before 'Abdu'l-Bahá travelled to Haifa, correspondence received in that city gave tidings of His approaching journey. This provided an opportunity for the community to prepare for His arrival, and also for the construction contractors to complete their technical and financial reports for the Master's review. But this time the Master arrived in Haifa unannounced. The next day He spent in visiting certain people, while deferring to the following day a number of other invitations. His stay was only one full day and two nights. On the third day, which fell on the anniversary of the Declaration of the Báb, He rose very early, determined to visit the Shrine of Bahá'u'lláh and then return to Haifa that same night. On such a blessed day, when two great Holy Days coincided, the friends in Haifa longed to attain the presence of the Master and taste the sweetness of reunion; they therefore looked forward to the end of the day with joy and excitement.

As the Master's carriage began to pull out, Mírzá Jalál (the son of the King of the Martyrs) and this servant asked permission to visit the Shrine of Bahá'u'lláh too and return to Haifa later that evening. The request was granted and that very hour we set out for 'Akká. In the course of that one day we were able to visit the Shrine and the Riḍván Garden in a spirit of joy and elation. In the evening I presented myself at 'Abdu'l-Bahá's *bírúní* in 'Akká, to either accompany the Master to Haifa or receive permission to make the journey separately.

At this point we received a piece of news, the meaning and implication of which was beyond our comprehension. We were told that earlier in the day five or six government security agents had shown up at the Mansion of Bahjí and had taken some of the Covenant-breakers into town, and that the Master had gone to the Government House to enquire about the situation. This news created a variety of impressions in the minds of the friends. A few years earlier I had heard that the government had openly shown their dissatisfaction with the general conduct of the Covenant-breakers and had decided to transfer them to another location, which meant expulsion and exile. But the Master had prevented such an action, had explained to the authorities that they were His brothers, and had asked for leniency.

On another occasion I had heard that 'Abdu'l-Bahá had once said, "If I will it, I can tie the moustaches and beards of the Covenant-breakers together and have them exiled to the remotest place on earth." In any event, all sorts of thoughts had crossed our minds as to the nature of what was taking place, except that no-one imagined that this could turn out to be the resumption of 'Abdu'l-Bahá's incarceration in the Prison City of 'Akká.

While we were absorbed in the ocean of our thoughts 'Abdu'l-Bahá arrived, quietly and sombrely climbed the stairs, and after a few minutes summoned the two of us. We entered His presence. After about four or five minutes of ominous silence 'Abdu'l-Bahá addressed me in these words:

"Today something has happened that has brought peace and tranquillity to my mind and will bring victory to the Faith of God. But because of the love that the friends of God have for me, this will be somewhat difficult for them to bear. But the focus of the friends should be on the Faith of God and not me. Whatever has happened is for the best."

Then He said, "If you promise not to become unhappy, I will tell you what has happened."

My heart was filled with such trepidation that I could hardly collect my thoughts and answer the question.

Again He said, "It is nothing serious. Believe that whatever has taken place is for the good of the Faith and is the comfort of my heart. The friends must be happy in my happiness and should concentrate their thoughts on the Faith itself. What has happened is the cause of rejoicing for me, but a cause of grief for the unfortunate Covenant-breakers."

These words reminded me of His previous remarks on the subject. As I bowed in acknowledgement of His utterances

He continued, "I worked for forty years to turn this prison into a paradise. These individuals have worked for years and have now turned the paradise into a prison and turned ease into hardship. For me nothing untoward has happened. Wherever I am, I have to take on all the burdens and challenges and strive for the triumph of the Cause of God. But it is going to be difficult for those gentlemen who were enjoying a life of comfort and ease in the Mansion."

Then He said, "Today I heard that the government had sent officials to the Mansion and that they had taken the gentlemen into town in a state of utter misery. I went to the chief officer to enquire and noticed his embarrassment in attempting to explain the situation. I realized what had happened. He then put in my hands Sulṭán 'Abdu'l-Ḥamíd's directive to resume the state of imprisonment in 'Akká. This order had reached him some time ago, but he had not brought it to my attention and in my absence had summoned these gentlemen to inform them. I have mentioned before that soon these gentlemen…"

Starting again, He went on, "I have done my work. Only the completion of the Shrine of the Báb remains. And that too will be completed one way or another. This is comforting for me. But for those who enjoyed their freedom in the Mansion, imprisonment will not be easy. They strove for many years and spent a considerable amount of money to bring about my expulsion and exile, so that they could find peace and comfort in my absence. And this is the result of all that work."

In short, He spoke in this vein for some time, filling my heart with joy at one moment and concern and worry the next. Of course, what I recall here are not the exact words of 'Abdu'l-Bahá, but rather His intent and purpose. Yet those words seemed to have transported us to another world.

Finally He said, "You two go to Haifa straight away, bring all the friends together in the pilgrim house, and explain the situation in exactly the way I have described it. But while you relate it, beware, beware lest you bring sadness to any heart.

There is much wisdom in this imprisonment. It influences the contingent world and reinforces the power of the Covenant."

He then emphasized, "Beware, beware, lest you speak in terms that would bring sadness to any heart. May God go with you."

From the moment that we descended the steps of the *bírúní* of the House of 'Abdu'l-Bahá until we climbed the steps of the pilgrim house in Haifa, I didn't know whether I was on earth or in heaven, corporeal or spiritual. As we entered the pilgrim house I came out of my reverie, and the friends who were expecting the arrival of the Master gathered around me. I closed my eyes and haltingly began to speak, and parrot-like recounted whatever words had remained in my dazed and perplexed memory. I was utterly unaware of the effect of my words, although I saw no one sorrowful or weeping, yet all were stunned and bewildered. Mírzá Jalál, too, related the same information at the House of 'Abdu'l-Bahá.

That night was not a particularly bad one. I ate my dinner with a good deal of appetite and had a restful sleep. But I did not know whether I was asleep or awake; was I intoxicated or was I suffering from a hangover, was I drunk or sober? All I know is that I spent the whole night in the presence of 'Abdu'l-Bahá as He spoke ceaselessly to me and I, word for word, committed what He said to heart. His words filled me with such wonder that I was spellbound. Within one night, I learned the lessons of a lifetime. When morning came, I couldn't distinguish between sleep and wakefulness. At times I was overwhelmed with sorrow, when I considered the Centre of the Covenant of God imprisoned. And at other times I became full of hope, as I remembered His words about the benefits of this imprisonment and the ultimate victory of the Faith of God. Although the fulfilment of His promises took a long time, praise the Lord, they all came true, proving that the blessed words, "Only the pious will come to a good end", apply to the believer and the steadfast. My observations that fateful night, whether a dream or a vision of reality, had as its interpretation an indescribable blessing. For several years hence, in the Most Great Prison of 'Akká, I became companion and confidant to the Beloved of the world.

CHAPTER THREE

Circumstances surrounding the renewal of confinement

The Most Great Prison was reinstated. It was decreed at the outset that the rules and regulations governing the administration of the Prison City were to be similar to those established at the time of the Blessed Beauty's arrival from Adrianople at the then army barracks of 'Akká. Those regulations proscribed the holding of jobs or owning of businesses by the friends, forbade the prisoners to pass through the gates of 'Akká, and restricted all forms of commerce. All visits were to be supervised by government officials and all correspondence from the prisoners was to cease. In other words, the harshest conditions were to be enforced.

But while it had been possible to impose such severe constraints when the Holy Family arrived from Adrianople, they were no longer enforceable under the conditions now prevailing. This was because the influence and power of the creative Word of God had generated such awe in the minds of the general population, and also because 'Abdu'l-Bahá's countless acts of generosity and compassion had left such an indelible impression in their hearts, that while the issuing of such instructions by the Sublime Porte might have seemed a routine matter, enforcing them to the letter of the law was utterly impossible.

For example, how could the Governor of 'Akká dare to enforce such severe regulations? – he who had witnessed the greatness of 'Abdu'l-Bahá and had been the recipient of His

THE RENEWAL OF CONFINEMENT   133

many benevolent and charitable favours and who considered himself the servant of His servants? Even those who occupied higher positions than the Governor of 'Akká, such as the Pashas who commanded legions and armies and who owed their very lives to the Master's benevolence and untold acts of generosity, lacked the boldness to even breathe such impertinence. Their response to the new decree, therefore, was to prepare a secret report in which they assured Constantinople of their obedience to the instructions and pledged strict control over the Prison City. All the residents of 'Akká and Haifa, rich and poor, high and low, and the entire corps of government officials, had at one time or another been the recipients of 'Abdu'l-Bahá's kindness and generosity. The following is an example concerning one of the Pashas.

During the war between the Ottoman Empire and Greece[91] before 1900, the head of the Ottoman Army assigned to the frontier between Palestine and Syria was General Faríq Pá_sh_á, who was an admirer of 'Abdu'l-Bahá. When he was selected to lead his army against the Greeks, because of his personal convictions he asked 'Abdu'l-Bahá for a prayer to take with him to protect him in the forthcoming struggle. 'Abdu'l-Bahá wrote a few words and told him to tie the piece of paper, unread, to his arm and never remove it.

He did as bidden and led his army into battle. After his triumphant return, he attained the presence of 'Abdu'l-Bahá to express his gratitude. 'Abdu'l-Bahá asked him if he had removed and read the prayer. He replied that he had done only as he had been commanded and nothing more. 'Abdu'l-Bahá then told him to take it off and read it. He was utterly amazed at what he read, for 'Abdu'l-Bahá had briefly described the events of the battle and his victorious return.

The point is, all the government officials, even the judges and religious leaders, had witnessed similar wonders and received similar favours from 'Abdu'l-Bahá. Therefore, this resumption of incarceration did not entail the harsh treatment and the severe restrictions of the previous confinement. The business activities of the resident friends were not curtailed.

of these chose of their own accord not to depart from
y for a short time, but even that did not last long.
er, the Master bore the full burden and hardship of
the incarceration in the Most Great Prison. He never left the
city until 'Abdu'l-Ḥamíd was deposed from the office of
Caliph, an event which will be described in Chapter 5 of
this narrative.

Details of the renewal of confinement

The source of the substantial sums which the Covenant-breakers had used to bribe the government officials in the hope of bringing about the expulsion and exile of 'Abdu'l-Bahá was eventually discovered.

The influx of Western pilgrims into Haifa, together with the implementation of the Master's plan to acquire property for the construction of the Shrine of the Báb, had provided the Covenant-breakers with yet another opportunity to plant the seeds of dissension and discord. Supported by government secret agents and communicating assorted reports to the Sublime Porte, they had begun a new campaign of persecution against 'Abdu'l-Bahá, charging Him with the purchase of vast parcels of land overlooking Haifa, 'Akká and the sea, on behalf of neighbouring governments whose representatives travelled to and from Haifa in disguise to further their conspiracy. These properties, they alleged, were being used to build large warehouses for the storage of arms and ammunition. This story had spread far and wide, forcing the government to assign secret inspectors to investigate the situation. However, the falsehood of the claim of the Covenant-breakers was soon discovered and the issue was shelved.

But when Mírzá Áqá Ján passed away, he left a substantial inheritance to the Covenant-breakers. With these funds they bribed some of the officials and convinced the Sublime Porte at last that 'Abdu'l-Bahá's presence in Haifa was dangerous. However, weary of the Covenant-breakers' incessant intrigues and conspiracies, the government had ordered the renewal of the same conditions that had been in force during the incarceration of the Blessed Beauty and His followers. These restrictions obviously applied to the Covenant-breakers as well.

Thus the last blow inflicted on 'Abdu'l-Bahá and the Cause of God by Mírzá Áqá Ján was through the expenditure of his small fortune by the Covenant-breakers to bribe the Ottoman officials. This had resulted in their own imprisonment, as they too fell into the very firetrap they had set for 'Abdu'l-Bahá.

Release of the Covenant-breakers from prison due to the Master's intercession

The confinement of the Covenant-breakers within the Most Great Prison did not last long, for they had the Master to intercede for them. The incarceration of the believers and the Covenant-breakers was displeasing to 'Abdu'l-Bahá. He exerted much energy in negotiations with the police as well as the army officers, and intervened on their behalf to secure their freedom. The officials, who were well aware of the reality of the situation and knew that this renewal of imprisonment had been bought and paid for by the Covenant-breakers themselves, were astonished at 'Abdu'l-Bahá's efforts. Eventually the Covenant-breakers regained their freedom and the government officials witnessed the difference between truth and falsehood. As the poem by Mawlaví says:

> *Moon shines and dog barks,*
> *Each according to its nature.*

My return to 'Akká

From the day when 'Abdu'l-Bahá's visits to Haifa ceased, the horizon of that land became as dark and gloomy as the lives of the resident believers. A feeling of despair and hopelessness dominated the lives of the friends.

For a few days my duties were unclear, although I continued the task of translation, until I was summoned to 'Akká by the Master and housed in the large room of the pilgrim house. Little by little the smaller room, which was being renovated, was made ready and became my translation office.

Only a few occupied the pilgrim house. Mírzá Ḥaydar-'Alí, who was considered the "anchor" of the pilgrim house, arrived later. And while the number of residents did not exceed three, yet the presence of the heavenly Mishkín-Qalam and the honoured Zayn, who spent a considerable time there, created an atmosphere of emotional and spiritual enthusiasm and attraction. This was an especially joyful time for me, for I was inebriated by the wine of nearness to the Beloved of the world.

While living in Haifa had meant waiting many endless days to attain the presence of the Beloved, here in 'Akká I fulfilled my heart's desire freely. Morning, noon, evening and night, whenever I desired, I attained His presence. Sometimes He would stop by my office unannounced and with His usual kind and loving gestures and utterances enrapture my heart.

The volume of translation work began gradually to increase. Letters expressing loving devotion, and verses of love and longing, began to arrive in batches from America. Soon I was drowned in work. I worked from dawn to dusk. In the evenings I left the house and took long strolls towards the gate of the city. At night, along with pilgrims and residents, I attained 'Abdu'l-Bahá's presence in the reception room. Unfortunately, the long walks in the verdant fields and the strolls on the beach gazing at the waves did not bring the same pleasure and joy as in the past. In fact, they were poignant. While we were in the city, the Master's imprisonment was not noticeable. But when we stepped outside the gates of 'Akká and encountered the military guards and sentries, the reality of 'Abdu'l-Bahá's confinement became clear and tangible, and thus the pleasant verdant fields actually brought sorrow and frustration rather than pleasure and relaxation. This was especially true on Holy Days, when at the Shrine the Tablet of Visitation had customarily been chanted by 'Abdu'l-Bahá Himself. Now, as He remained incarcerated, that melodious heavenly tone no longer filled the ears and hearts of His lovers, and even on happy occasions our visits to the Shrine were devoid of those feelings of joy and excitement.

But within the city of 'Akká nothing had changed. Whoever attained 'Abdu'l-Bahá's presence became intoxicated with the joy of reunion. In 'Akká I was considered as both resident and pilgrim. Whenever the pilgrims were summoned, if work allowed the opportunity I too accompanied them, and when the residents were summoned I dashed headlong in front of the group. In addition to all this, I sometimes invented a question on a concocted issue as an excuse to be in His presence. After all, I was one of His servants and none of the servants required permission to see the Master. Little by little I became so completely accustomed to my lifestyle in 'Akká that one would have thought I had been born in 'Akká and would eventually die there.

The Covenant-breakers, shaken by the turn of events, had grown despondent over the appalling renewal of their incarceration; they kept mostly to themselves and for some time had no communication with the outside world. This had created in their midst a general state of melancholy and hopelessness. So for some time, like bats, they crept into dark corners; only at nighttime did they emerge, hastening to visit their friends so that together they could appraise the possibilities of further acts of sedition and treachery. And if by chance they encountered a loyal believer, they turned and fled. As is said: "Evil flees from those who recite the Qur'án."

At last the pilgrim house took on new life: Iranian, Indian, Egyptian and 'Ishqábádí pilgrims began to come and go. Before long a number of Western believers, too, began to arrive.

"O Breakwell, O my dear one!"

This form of address revealed by 'Abdu'l-Bahá in honour of a young Englishman after his passing is part of the Tablet of Visitation that the French believers were instructed to recite at his graveside.[92]

This young man, who had obtained permission to visit 'Abdu'l-Bahá before the renewal of His incarceration, arrived from Paris in the opening days of the imprisonment. He attained the presence of 'Abdu'l-Bahá for two days and nights and stayed at the Master's house in the midst of those dreadfully anxious times. His devotion, attraction and love were so intense that his blessed name shall endure for centuries in the annals of the Faith of God, while his wonderful life shall be retold in many accounts.

I do not know the story of his conversion,[93] but it was clear that he came from a Christian background, was endowed with spiritual sensitivity and ardour, and had accepted the Faith on the basis of the verses and prophecies of the divinely revealed scriptures of former religions, rather than a sentimental attraction to the Faith's contemporary social and philosophical principles. He would usually be seen reciting the verses of the Bible in glorification of the Kingdom of God, and while his pilgrimage was not long, yet the intensity of the fire of his love and the fervour of his longing and attraction moved the friends deeply. When in the presence of the Master he seemed enthralled by the matchless beauty of the Beloved, and as he completed his pilgrimage and received permission to depart, he evinced moving signs of deep adoration and veneration.

He did not have the opportunity of meeting the believers of 'Akká, and when he left 'Abdu'l-Bahá instructed him, "Remain in Paris." In accordance with the Master's instructions I accompanied him to Haifa and to the port of embarkation. In Haifa he was received in the home of one of the friends for about two hours. As he awaited the arrival of his transport, he gazed longingly out of the window towards 'Akká, fervently reciting prayers. All those present were overcome with emotion. Weeping, he asked my permission to correspond with me from time to time so that from my replies he might inhale the fragrance of 'Akká. At last a group of the friends tearfully bade him farewell as he embarked on his return journey.

His first letter contained, in addition to expressions of sincere devotion and faithfulness, the question: "The Master has instructed me to continue to reside in Paris and not to return to London. I am currently living here as a student and wish to know if I would be permitted to go to London for a day or two for a funeral ceremony if either one of my parents were to die." But then immediately he added: "No, please disregard the question. Christ in His first coming told His followers, 'Let the dead bury the dead'. So please do not bother to mention me in the Master's presence. However, while you are in attendance, remember me in your heart. This will bring me all the happiness and joy of both worlds."

Still, when the time was appropriate I related the story to 'Abdu'l-Bahá. The Master said with a smile, "Write to him that today the living have to bury the dead."

Some two weeks later another letter arrived. It was brief, yet so heart-rending that the mere reading of it touched the soul deeply. After expressions of gratitude he wrote: "Your response is clear. But I ask God for calamity; I desire undiminishing pain. I long for suffering without respite; I yearn for enduring agony and torment so that I may not for a moment neglect the mention of my Beloved."

Once, as the Master strolled up and down, I mentioned the letter. 'Abdu'l-Bahá said nothing. I wrote to him and acknowledged the receipt of his letter. After two weeks, another letter arrived: "My parents are asking me to go to London. I have told them that the Master's instructions are for me to remain in Paris. But, alas, my parents are old and have not recognized this supreme revelation. I ask that I may succeed in teaching them. How unworthy and undeserving I am. How did I come to merit this most supreme blessing? Please remember me in His presence."

I mentioned the matter. The Master responded briefly, "Write that he will be assisted. They will accept the Faith."

Exactly two weeks later another letter came: "My parents have come to take me back. I have taught my father. His written declaration is attached. My mother is very loving. But I long for pain and anguish so that I may become closer to God. If I were a Persian, I would have yearned for martyrdom. Please pray for me. I shall not move from Paris."

I apprised 'Abdu'l-Bahá of the contents of the letter and submitted a translated version of his elderly father's declaration of faith. 'Abdu'l-Bahá remained utterly silent. After a few days, a Tablet revealed in honour of the father was handed to me by the Master; I duly dispatched it. Two weeks later I received a strangely stirring letter: "I am ill and bedridden in the hospital for consumptives. The fire of love has well nigh consumed me. I am happy. Pray that God may not deprive me of this pain."

I informed 'Abdu'l-Bahá of the situation. He made no reply. The wisdom of silence was quite apparent.

In short, the letters continued to arrive every two weeks, and in all of them he continued to ask that he might be the recipient of the harshest torment and pain; as his illness advanced he expressed more joy and happiness. All his letters were written on small green sheets of paper, which I collected and kept with great care. Reading these letters created deep spiritual feelings. Their deep emotional impact and the dictates of my conscience obliged me to report all the details to 'Abdu'l-Bahá. Sometimes He would say, "Pass on my greetings." And at those times when He remained silent I knew that the relationship between the lover and the Beloved, the seeker and the One sought, was such as to need no intervention from any intermediary.

Then came his last letter: "I am intoxicated with the wine of suffering and pain and am prepared to receive the supreme blessing. The intensity of my torment and the magnitude of my agony have brought me infinitely closer to my Beloved. I still yearn for longer life to continue to bear this pain but my goal is obedience to His will. Remember me in His presence."

This was the content of His last letter; two weeks later no further news was received. It was clear what had happened. A few days later, as Dr. Arastú and I were accompanying the Master from the pilgrim house to His residence, the Master suddenly said, "Honoured Khán, have you heard?"

I responded negatively.

"Breakwell has ascended. I was heartbroken. I have written a moving Tablet of Visitation for him. I wrote it with such emotion that I wept as I wrote. You must translate it well so that he who reads it will not be able to hold back his tears."

I never learned who had informed 'Abdu'l-Bahá of his death. Whether the news had reached Him in English or French or whether it had been in the form of a written note or a telegram, I never discovered, although I would have been the recipient of all such correspondence.

Two days later I received the Tablet of Visitation. It was heart-rending. Several times 'Abdu'l-Bahá repeats the words: "O Breakwell, O my dear one!" My tears flowed uncontrollably. According to His instructions I translated the Tablet into two languages – French, and with the help of Mrs. Lua Getsinger into English – and dispatched them.

The deeply felt impressions left by that young man lingered in the hearts for a number of years. I received no further news concerning his parents for about a year. One day I was summoned to the presence of 'Abdu'l-Bahá to receive the incoming correspondence for translation. There were numerous envelopes from various cities, and as 'Abdu'l-Bahá reviewed each sealed envelope He suddenly selected one of them and said, "What pleasant fragrance emanates from this envelope, open it quickly and see where it comes from. Hurry up."

Since I had often experienced similar circumstances where a certain envelope was chosen by 'Abdu'l-Bahá ahead of all the others, and these invariably contained significant spiritual matters, I hastily opened the envelope. Inside was a postcard and a sealed envelope. The gold-coloured handwriting on the colourful postcard, which had a single violet attached to it, read: "He is not dead, he lives in the Abhá Kingdom." And there was the added note: "This flower was picked from Breakwell's grave."

As soon as I translated these words, 'Abdu'l-Bahá suddenly leapt from His seat, seized the postcard, placed it on His blessed forehead and wept. I too was utterly overcome. I opened the second envelope. It was from Breakwell's mother or father, expressing their deeply felt gratitude: "Praised be God, my dear son left this world having recognized the true station of 'Abdu'l-Bahá and tasted the sweetness of His love." I don't remember the details of 'Abdu'l-Bahá's reaction to the letter, but I do remember that the spiritual impact of the letter was no less than that of the postcard.

Although I have strayed from the main topic, yet I feel the need to complete this story. Three years later, when I was in Paris in the company of Monsieur Dreyfus, he told many stories about Breakwell. "When this young man was in the hospital," he related, "all the doctors, nurses and patients were overwhelmed by the intensity of his devotion and spiritual attraction, for he invited all to the divine Kingdom. Some were perplexed and moved, but some of the patients made spiteful and taunting remarks. Armed with only a few words of English, they sneered at him, pointing their fingers at him and repeating the words, 'You are dying, you are dying!' – to which he responded, laughing, 'I am not dying, I am going to the Kingdom of the heavenly Father. There, I will intercede for you.' "

In short, at his death all the nurses wept, and thus he left an enduring memory in the hearts of those who knew him in that hospital. One day M. Dreyfus and I visited his grave, and since I did not have the text of his Tablet of Visitation with me I repeated three times, "O Breakwell, O my dear one!".

The pilgrimage of Mr. Dodge's sons

We have strayed from the main theme. Let us now return to it. The friends from the East had begun to regain the oppor-

THE PILGRIMAGE OF MR. DODGE'S SONS   143

tunity of coming on pilgrimage and attaining the presence of 'Abdu'l-Bahá, albeit with extreme caution. However, there were no facilities to receive the Western friends. Despite all the caution, and because of all the mischief, adverse propaganda and political allegations which the violators of the Covenant had attributed to the Master, the government inspectors were poised to take action and the Covenant-breakers were looking for any excuse or pretext to make a move. The three houses in Haifa which had been rented by 'Abdu'l-Bahá were closed up. And the dismal fortress of 'Akká could not accommodate any visitors, nor were there any decent hotels or guest houses in that city. In addition to the residence of 'Abdu'l-Bahá there was one other house under lease to the Master, and that was the house that had been occupied by the Blessed Beauty.[94] But even that house was mostly in the possession of non-Bahá'ís, who had asked and received 'Abdu'l-Bahá's permission to occupy it temporarily. On the other hand, the American friends, who in the years of freedom had attained the presence of the Master and had tasted the sweetness of reunion, continually besought His permission on behalf of themselves and their relatives to come on pilgrimage.

It was an accepted axiom among the friends that if the degree of eagerness and longing for pilgrimage of those friends who had never seen 'Abdu'l-Bahá could be measured as equal to 1, the intensity of yearning of those who had attained, whose eyes had beheld the beauty of the Beloved of the world, was 100 times greater. And so in the days following the renewal of incarceration, numerous requests for permission to visit the Holy Land continued to pour in.

The first Westerners who were given permission to visit 'Akká after Mr. Breakwell were the sons of Mr. Dodge of New York.[95] Following the Master's instructions, these two young men arrived wearing the Ottoman-style hats, as was customary amongst the friends, and were housed in one of the upstairs rooms. They had received an adequate Bahá'í education from their father, who had attained the presence of

'Abdu'l-Bahá in Haifa two years earlier during the time of freedom. The two lads, aged eighteen and twenty, learned more about the teachings and received lessons on Bahá'í conduct and discipline from 'Abdu'l-Bahá. They usually attained the presence of the Master at the dinner table and in general did not pose too many questions. They visited a number of the Persian friends and other pilgrims with great caution and enthusiasm, and after three days they returned to their homeland happy and content.

Madame de Canavarro and Mr. Phelps

Once Mr. Dodge's sons returned home to America, they began sharing with their many visitors such glowing descriptions of 'Abdu'l-Bahá's kindliness and generosity that these too became enkindled and were encouraged to seek permission to visit Him. And so before long, group after group of such individuals submitted their humble requests for a visit. But since the conditions prevailing at the time did not allow for group pilgrimage, 'Abdu'l-Bahá cautiously gave permission to only a few individuals to make the journey.

The first to arrive were Madame de Canavarro and Mr. Phelps, who had been in the company of Dr. Arastú Khán on the last leg of their journey from Beirut to 'Akká. At the time of their arrival, the house which had been the residence of Bahá'u'lláh was fortunately unoccupied and available, and so the late doctor was taken to the pilgrim house and the two Western friends were housed in that residence.[96] The American Mme. De Canavarro had previously been attracted to the Buddhist Faith, had become one of its ardent teachers and had spent large sums over the years in propagation of her views. She had sacrificed much in order to attain mastery of the Buddhist philosophy, and in the process had won distinction and renown. Sister Sanghamitta, as she was known, was an accomplished and well-respected member of her Faith and had a long-standing acquaintance with Western philosophy and a deep knowledge of Indian mysticism. She had translated and published the book of Buddha, in both English and French, under the title *The Gospel of Buddha*,[97] and had now found the Bahá'í Faith through the Buddhist Faith. She seemed to be about forty-five or fifty years old, and although suffering from physical infirmity was yet spiritually radiant and joyful. Mr. Phelps, on the other hand might be considered to be Sister Sanghamitta's spiritual brother. He professed belief in Buddhism, had literary ability, had journeyed to 'Akká with his spiritual sister and was keeping a journal of his observations and experiences. As she entered, she humbly kissed 'Abdu'l-Bahá's hand. The Master treated her with the utmost consideration and tenderness as she was led to the *andárúní* of the Master's residence. The dinner-table discussions began next day.

This lady, unlike Mr. Breakwell and the sons of Mr. Dodge, had a multitude of questions, and as the answers came Mr. Phelps took them down rapidly. The problem, though, was that the ideas and beliefs of the sister and brother were not in harmony, and since the record of the conversation obviously had to reflect the understanding of both of them, this created undue stress on 'Abdu'l-Bahá as He had to explain matters twice. The lady asked the question, I translated it and returned the response, and Mr. Phelps swiftly recorded it. But since the enquirer and the recorder had different views, they disagreed as to the meaning of the replies, and the frequent repetition of the concepts made the task that much more arduous for 'Abdu'l-Bahá.

The part that pertained to Buddha and other prophets was reasonably straightforward. The difficulty arose with the concept of reincarnation. Here the recorder insisted on including his own views in the journal, or at least wished to reflect the discussion in such a light as to make the future publication and sale of the book of interest to those Europeans who believed in reincarnation. This problem remained unresolved for the duration of the interview.

On the second or the third day of the interview, as fresh and complicated issues began to emerge, there suddenly arose a fracas. The reason was that a subject that is considered to be one of the principal concepts of the Bahá'í Faith had proven too complex for the lady to grasp; she required repeated explanations. Suddenly, bursting out in furious objection, she addressed me angrily in harsh and unintelligible words. She was so irate that she was unable to speak clearly. At the same time, the Master kept asking, "What is she saying?" – while the lady was not giving me the opportunity to understand the cause of her distress so that I could apprise 'Abdu'l-Bahá.

At last, when the commotion subsided, what I understood from her protests, addressed directly to me was:

"Why is it that you Easterners must always be the pioneers and standard-bearers in the field of religion, although you obviously do not possess any particular qualifications or accomplishments to justify that status? In turn, we Westerners must become dependent on you to share such knowledge with us secondhand. First, you obviously have no erudition to qualify you to understand such spiritual concepts. We are the ones who introduce the subject matter and share with you the guidance to understand the issue. Then we must wait for your response. If it weren't for us Westerners, how could you hope to understand such issues? The problem is, once you comprehend the subject matter, you get the answer first and then I have to receive the answer from you. Worse still, you receive the mysteries of the Kingdom and the divine realities directly from the Master without any intermediary (meaning that you drink from the fountain head) whereas we have to obtain our knowledge from you (meaning that we drink stagnant water). Why should I focus my eyes and ears on your mouth and wait for the answer to my query?"

As soon as I understood the problem I informed 'Abdu'l-Bahá.

Yea, at such times the even-tempered, serene bearing of the Master, and His loving glances of understanding and sympathy, could transform the world. With a kindly smile He spoke:

"Tell her that the effects and influences of the mysteries of the Kingdom are spiritual, not material. Ear and tongue are material faculties. If the soul is not susceptible to receiving the divine favours, of what use are ears and tongues? These spiritual concepts are directed to your heart. I speak to you with the power of spirit and you receive these heavenly concepts with your whole being, with pure intentions and a radiant heart. The essential requirement is true, sincere and heartfelt communication. Praised be God, that spiritual connection is established. Whatever you have heard so far are the blessings of the Holy Spirit. My connection with you is direct. The tongue of the translator is only a material and physical faculty."

Then He gave further examples of those believers who had accepted and devoted their lives to the message of Christ, and demonstrated that in this wondrous age, too, people deprived of the physical faculties of hearing and sight had attained the honour of faith and reunion and become beacons of guidance to other souls.

In short, the lady was satisfied, and expressed her happiness and contentment. Peace and tranquillity were established between the two of us at last. They stayed for over a month. Many significant philosophical and religious problems were resolved, some of which Mr. Phelps recorded in his journal; others the lady committed to memory. The first part of Mr. Phelps's book,[98] which described his emotions and observations, was delightful, enchanting, and tenderly and effectively presented. The later chapters dealt with the description of Bahá'u'lláh and His family's journey in exile from Tehran to Baghdad, Adrianople, Constantinople and 'Akká. This part was written quite accurately, for the lady had received that information, properly translated into English by one of 'Abdu'l-Bahá's daughters, directly from the Greatest Holy Leaf, and then had passed it on to Mr. Phelps. But the chapter dealing with the concept of reincarnation and other similar issues contained a great many errors.

I translated half the book from English to Persian and presented it to 'Abdu'l-Bahá for His perusal. I subsequently made multiple retranslations of His comments and corrections into English or explained them verbally to Mr. Phelps. Despite all these efforts, the published book contained sections that were contrary to 'Abdu'l-Bahá's statements. Sister Sanghamitta understood the issues, but Mr. Phelps wrote as he wished.

Their happy stay came to an end at last, and they received permission to depart. For some time afterwards, letters from the Sister containing expressions of her heartfelt regard for 'Abdu'l-Bahá and a description of her many acts of service were received in the Holy Land.

Mr. Dreyfus and Miss Sanderson

During the last days of Sister Sanghamitta's stay, when 'Akká was a little more peaceful and tranquil, Mr. Dreyfus and then Miss [Edith] Sanderson arrived and were housed in the same residence where the two American travellers had stayed.

Mr. Dreyfus's knowledge of the Faith, considering his recent conversion to it, was remarkable. He spent his time in acquiring further knowledge and discussions of philosophical and spiritual subjects continued at the lunch or dinner table. The discussions were obviously in French and he frequently took notes.

At that time the celebrated case of Alfred Dreyfus still dominated the Western press.[99] One day the Master asked Mr. Dreyfus if he was related to the famous Alfred Dreyfus. He replied that he was not. 'Abdu'l-Bahá then replied, "That Dreyfus found renown in the world of politics. I desire for you even greater fame in service to the Faith of God."

This radiant young man made his first pilgrimage in 1901 at the age of thirty-one. He had become totally enkindled and attracted, longed to be of service to the Faith, and even yearned to sacrifice his life and gain a martyr's death. 'Abdu'l-Bahá granted that request, but only within the context of the spirit of the word.

He enjoyed philosophical and intellectual discussions. His

stay was about three weeks long, and in accordance with 'Abdu'l-Baha's instructions I spent a great deal of time with him. One day at the dinner table he said, "Today I inadvertently played the role of Adam and was terribly embarrassed."

Not understanding the meaning of this statement, I translated the words. The Master said, "Tell him there is no shame. Because of my great love for him I wished to behold the entirety of his physical being."

Later, I asked him [Mr. Dreyfus] about this. He said, "Don't tell anyone, but today I turned into Adam."

I asked again, and he replied, "Don't ask! I am afraid I may be driven out of paradise. You see, I always lock the bathroom door when I bathe. This time I neglected to make sure that the door was locked. When the Master knocked on the bathroom door and called my name, without thinking I asked Him to come in. He opened the door while I was naked. I was terribly embarrassed: I realized I had done what Adam did!"

Before his pilgrimage, Mr. Dreyfus had been engaged in teaching the Faith. Among others, he had spoken to an Italian lady named Di Santo Amini,[100] the author of a series of very fervent, heart-stirring prayers in Italian which Mr. Dreyfus had translated into French and which I translated into Persian. I submitted the translations to 'Abdu'l-Bahá, who was greatly pleased by them.

Mr. Dreyfus had no knowledge of the East at that time. Because of his intense devotion, and his eagerness to read the Writings, he learned Persian and Arabic and became a renowned orientalist. He attained the presence of 'Abdu'l-Bahá on one or two other occasions as a pilgrim. He travelled to Iran and China for teaching projects. After his marriage to Miss Barney, who then became well known as Mrs. Dreyfus-Barney, they continued their teaching trips to Eastern countries.

Before her marriage, Miss Barney had been a very shy young woman, the quintessence of purity and piety. She was an American citizen who during her stay in the Holy Land had been in the service of the daughters of 'Abdu'l-Bahá as a teacher. After her marriage to Mr. Dreyfus they returned to Paris. She, too, made ceaseless efforts to learn Persian.

The late Dr. Arastú Khán

The pilgrim house was now in a buzz: loyal and steadfast friends were appearing from every direction. The atmosphere of love and unity infused a spirit of joy and elation into the hearts of all the believers, washing away the bitter anguish of the renewal of incarceration. Signs of happiness and gaiety were evident in every face. At times the pilgrims from the West and the East openly associated with each other. The letters from the West brought many happy tidings; some of them were read aloud in the pilgrim house. At times the Master visited the pilgrims. Mírzá Haydar-'Alí, the anchor of the pilgrim house, shared loving and fatherly counsel with the newcomers, helping them to orient themselves in this happy paradise. Zaynu'l-Muqarrabín was the soul of the pilgrim house, while the wonderful Mishkín-Qalam brought delight and cheer to the hearts.

It was in these times that my dear old friend Dr. Arastú Khán arrived, and became a full participant in this festival of excitement, joy and pleasure. He established an intimate association with the Western believers and also became my helper in the translation work. Before long his sweet and heavenly demeanour not only endeared him to all the believers but won 'Abdu'l-Bahá's approval and praise. We were inseparable companions for about a year, after which he received his permission to return to Iran.

Mrs. Lua Getsinger

In the many years that I spent in the service of the Master there were many attracted and heavenly souls in far-off lands who longed to attain the presence of 'Abdu'l-Bahá. And had it not been for the conditions in the Most Great Prison and the difficulty of obtaining the Master's permission, the world would surely have witnessed a great movement by Westerners in demonstration of their ardent desire and loving support of the Faith of God.

However, because of the autocratic nature of the ruling government, the intrigues of the Covenant-breakers and the intense hostility of the enemies of the Faith, only those few who could adapt themselves to the conditions of the Prison City and the many challenges requiring patience and discretion, and who also had the ability to appear similar to the natives of 'Akká in dress and bearing, could receive permission to make the journey.

One of these was Mrs. Lua Getsinger, who in her intense longing to attain the Master's presence had found within herself the capacity to bear the many hardships of that environment and yet conduct herself with the wisdom and forbearance required. In the earlier years of relative freedom and tranquillity, this lady along with her husband had attained the presence of 'Abdu'l-Bahá in Haifa[101] and had left in the hearts and minds of the friends an ineffable memory of her intense devotion, passionate attraction and profound spiritual attachment to 'Abdu'l-Bahá.

Arriving in the Prison City in a state of utter humility and supplication, she now attained the presence of the Master, and for a period of a year or perhaps somewhat longer, and dressed in simple attire typical of the Christian women of 'Akká, became a member of the Bahá'í family and served as an English teacher for the ladies of 'Abdu'l-Bahá's household.

The passion of her emotional expressions and the intensity of her devotion to the Faith of God were such that her every word and deed deeply moved all those with whom she came into contact. An inextinguishable fire seemed to rage in her soul. She wished for no rest, plunging headlong into any and all forms of service to the Faith. Correspondence with friends in foreign lands, translation of sacred verses and publication of various works were among her many activities.

Aside from these, she had begun to entertain an obsession with the thought of achieving a martyr's death. Day and night she wept, appealing incessantly to the friends to pray that she might become deserving of such a blessing. Many a time she threw herself with tearful eyes at 'Abdu'l-Bahá's feet and begged to be granted her wish. Most of her nights were spent in prayer and supplication towards that end. She beseeched and entreated 'Abdu'l-Bahá for permission to journey to Iran and, like Ṭáhirih, raise the call of the Kingdom from the pulpits of mosques and monasteries [sic], so that she might become worthy of acceptance in the sight of God. 'Abdu'l-Bahá, however, would not approve. She obtained a number of prayers and invocations revealed by the blessed Báb, asking that one's wish or desire be granted, recited them all and performed their specified genuflections, but with no success.

When the upheavals of Yazd and Isfahan[102] were at their peak and the friends in those cities rushed headlong in their hundreds to the glorious field of sacrifice and martyrdom, the fire of Lua's love raged with such intensity at the receipt of the news that she lost all self-control and began to plead her case to each and every person she met. She continually wept and asked for prayers so that perchance she might attain the desire of her heart. Her state was so pitiful and the impression she made on her listeners so moving that the friends began to pray for her. Her pleas even convinced a few of the friends to recite the prayers she had found, so that she might succeed in giving her life for the Cause. As the poet says:

> *Arrow-like, I release a prayer from every side,*
> *Hoping one will find its mark and be replied.*

Both the late Dr. Arastú K͟hán and I agreed to recite this prayer at dawntide to the number of *qadír*:[103]

"Say: God sufficeth all things above all things, and nothing in the heavens or in the earth but God sufficeth. Verily, He is in Himself the Knower, the Sustainer, the Omnipotent."

We also uttered the following verse in the early morning hours:

"Is there any Remover of difficulties save God? Say: Praised be God! He is God! All are His servants and all abide by His bidding!"

In any case, Lua's constant pleading and heart-rending lamentations moved us so profoundly that we happily consented to get up at dawn just to pray for her. But even this failed to satisfy her: several times she turned directly to Ḥájí Mírzá Ḥaydar-'Alí and myself, begging us to beseech 'Abdu'l-Bahá to grant her wish of offering her life for the Faith. We, in turn, placed the matter before 'Abdu'l-Bahá several times, but He always responded in the same way:

"Tell Lua that to be slain in itself bestows neither rank nor prestige. There are many souls who, while not having experienced outward martyrdom, are considered martyrs in the path of God, and there are many who lost their lives but did not attain the reality of a martyr's rank. Martyrdom is a supremely eminent station, granted by Bahá'u'lláh to whomever He chooses. A soul may not be killed and yet can attain this station. I will pray for you to achieve this rank. The reality of martyrdom is service and you, praise the Lord, have arisen to serve. I will pray for you and will implore that you may be granted this station. Rest assured." And then He would recall the names of some of the martyrs of the Faith.

But His message to her, as I delivered it, only served to fan the fire of her love and increase the intensity of her emotions; back she would send us again to the presence of 'Abdu'l-Bahá. Meanwhile, this intense spiritual attraction gave to her words an unusual and powerful effect. Because of this, any time a curious or insincere foreign traveller or an aggressive or argumentative antagonist came to visit, his schedule included – on 'Abdu'l-Bahá's instructions – a meeting with Lua; I would serve as the translator at these meetings. On such occasions the magnetic force of her faith created in the trembling frames of her listeners such an impact that they acquiesced and withdrew, contrite and tearful.

At her own request she once confronted one of the famous Covenant-breakers of Bombay, with this servant performing the task of translation. She so utterly routed her opponent with a sudden, courageous and fearless assault that, tearful and penitent, he admitted his shame and readily acknowledged the falseness of his beliefs. I present the details of this story later on.

In brief, for nearly a year and in a state of fervent supplication and passionate devotion, Lua savoured the nearness of 'Abdu'l-Bahá and continuously contemplated sacrificing her life for the Cause, until at last the loving counsel of her Master had its desired effect, and she yielded her will to His will and gave up her own desire to His wishes. In so doing, she attained to the reality of the station of martyrdom, finally arriving at the threshold of dying in self and living in God. And in that intensely spiritual state she received her permission to depart.

One of the most astonishing things that I have ever witnessed in my service to the Cause was Lua's state when she came to say goodbye. It can never fade from my memory, nor can I find adequate words to describe it. Her face was so utterly luminous and spiritual, and her bearing so transformed, that it seemed as though an angel had been incarnated in the body of a human being. I was never more deeply moved than when I witnessed her tender and kindly disposition as we said our farewells. Never before had I beheld so wonderful and heavenly a countenance; I gazed at her in utter amazement.

Next day the Master asked, "Did you see Lua when she left? Did you notice her face and her demeanour?"

I responded that I had, and that I had been astonished by her state of spirituality.

The Master replied, "It is a pity, but she won't be able to maintain that spirit. It is impossible to remain in that state. Now consider where we find these wandering souls and how we educate them! The Covenant-breakers should educate souls similarly, if they can!"

During the first two years after her departure, Lua taught a large number of souls and attracted a great many more to the Faith. Although she was not a poet, yet because of the intensity of her emotions she composed some verses, all of which are related to the Faith. One of the poems she wrote on the boat between Haifa and Alexandria was this:

Come on this journey with me, O beloved divine,
To keep from breaking this restless heart of mine.

The world I have abandoned, Thy pleasure I would gain,
Life itself I would sacrifice should Thy leave I obtain.

Though alone I must travel on this long road
Yet Thee beside me I long to behold.

In this world, hub of sinfulness, den of sorrow,
None is there to comfort me but Thee whom I follow.

Abandon me not, my Beloved, behold my plight,
How in loneliness I pass my day and my night.

Life and soul I leave behind, without Thee I depart,
Thou art my goal, the thought of Thee the only friend of my heart.

At every moment in this broken heart of mine
The water of life, the source of grace, is every word of Thine.

Deprive not Thy servant of Thy Holy Threshold,
Hear my cry, my entreaty to my loving Lord.

While true it is I am unworthy of Thee,
I remain Thy servant, my Master Thou wilt ever be.

Behold with the glance of Thy merciful eye
My sinful life and my desperate plight.

Give ear, O my King, Thou Lord of mercy,
To my pleading day and night, to my entreaty.

Thou art my refuge wherever I go,
In my seclusion, my despair, in my loneliness too.[104]

Arrival of a Covenant-breaker from Bombay, Ḥusayn-'Alí Jahrumí, surnamed Fiṭrat

Some of the Covenant-breakers resident in distant lands considered the defiance and opposition of the Arch-breaker of the Covenant to be a superficial matter or a curable disease, and having believed his many accusations and propaganda, they entertained the futile hope of playing the role of "go-between" in order to reconcile the "sides". Their correspondence inviting a peaceful reconciliation and resolution of the disputes brought much sorrow to the heart of 'Abdu'l-Bahá.

Others, hiding behind a veil of innocent naiveté and claiming ignorance of the issues, put certain questions to the Master, compared the response with the assertions of the Arch-breaker of the Covenant, and then still maintained their inability to understand the situation.

One of these simpletons was Jahrumí, who after receiving answers to his many questions came to 'Akká so that he might – so he said – observe the situation objectively with his own eyes and judge it with his own mind.[105]

On his arrival, and to display his impartiality, he did not stay at the residence of his colleagues, nor did he appear at the pilgrim house. He took a room at a guest house in 'Akká and then asked for permission to visit 'Abdu'l-Bahá. The Master summoned the late Ḥájí Mírzá Ḥaydar-'Alí and me to His presence and instructed us to meet with him separately, acquaint him with some preliminary issues, and then report back with the results. I met him first, after which the Ḥájí had his opportunity.

The man was tall, with a husky voice, glaring eyes and a

ARRIVAL OF A COVENANT-BREAKER FROM BOMBAY 157

frightening face. He looked like someone who had just committed murder and was fleeing from justice. He spoke to me with the uneasiness and anxiety of a man running away from the law.

He asked for no proof of the authority of the Centre of the Covenant and showed no special regard for the Arch-breaker of the Covenant. He insisted that he simply wished to understand certain issues directly from the Master. After I had concluded, the Ḥájí, with that natural spiritual bearing of his, met with him but without any further success. Finally, he attained the presence of 'Abdu'l-Bahá.

I do not know what transpired in that meeting, but as soon as Lua heard about the ongoing consultations she begged 'Abdu'l-Bahá for permission to meet with him. Since the Covenant-breakers' heyday, 'Abdu'l-Bahá had forbidden everyone to exchange so much as a single word with any of them. Even if one of them asked a question, or cursed while passing in the street, no-one was permitted to utter a single word in response. But Lua at last succeeded in obtaining permission to meet with him and 'Abdu'l-Bahá instructed me to serve as translator.

The meeting took place in the *bírúní* reception room on the second floor. Lua entered the chamber with an angry demeanour and after a few cursory words of greeting began to speak about the issues. Logic and proof had no chance, since Fiṭrat was in fact an official promoter and supporter of the Arch-breaker of the Covenant and not a seeker after truth.

Suddenly Lua asked, "Is Mírzá Muḥammad-'Alí a Bahá'í or not?"

Jahrumí replied, "Surely you are aware of the nature of his kinship to the Blessed Beauty and his exalted station in the Faith of God, and that all these consultations are taking place to safeguard his rank." "I am not interested in his family connections nor is it my intention to rob him of his rank. I just wish to know if he is a believer in the station of the Blessed Beauty?" Lua retorted.

"Who is more devoted than he?" he replied.

"Then where are the fruits of his faith and devotion?" Lua enquired. "Christ said that you can recognize a tree by its fruits. So where are the fruits of his devotion? How many souls has he taught? What sort of devotion is this, that the fragrance of its breezes has not as yet been detected by any soul? I am an American woman and not sufficiently deepened in the Faith; nevertheless, since I heard the Call I have taught over fifty souls. There are thousands of women in America, better than I, the fragrance of whose love and devotion has attracted numerous souls. What has Muḥammad-'Alí done except work to weaken the devotion of the friends in America? A Bahá'í must be fair. Are these the fruits of his faith? Is creating disunity among the believers the fruits of this Branch? Is this his exalted rank in the Faith of God? Does a person like that expect to receive any attention or regard from the believers? A person like that?"

In brief, she continued in this vein with such passion and power that Jahrumí was left breathless and bewildered. At last, hanging his head in shame, his tall stature bent in defeat, he closed his terrible eyes and asked permission to leave.

"I have to recite a prayer," Lua responded. With tearful eyes, and in a state of humility and lowliness, she chanted a short Persian prayer. Jahrumí, weeping and stumbling all over himself, departed from the room. And what a departure!

Establishment of an English class

A few days after my return to 'Akká from Haifa, Mírzá Núru'd-Dín and Mírzá Munír began their English education under my tutelage, as instructed by the Master. Three times a week for one hour in the morning I was thus engaged in service. But the flood of correspondence from America hardly allowed me the three hours necessary for the proper discharge of my duties. However, the original Persian versions of the Tablets revealed in response to these letters were sent to America, where the honoured 'Alí-Qulí Khán performed the translation work. Tablets destined for Europe, however, were generally translated into French or English by this servant.

The increasing volume of translation work heightened my enthusiasm and joy – so much so that I took it upon myself to translate the poems contained in many of the incoming letters into rhymed Persian verse. All these received the Master's approval and were accordingly sent to Iran for dissemination.

One day, when I was totally absorbed in my translation work, suddenly feeling a presence I raised my head and beheld the blessed figure of the Master standing in front of my desk. I stood up and bowed.

"Jináb-i-<u>Kh</u>án, I have a favour to ask you and you have no choice but to accept," said 'Abdu'l-Bahá.

Of course, my response to such kind and loving words was more bows, broad joyful smiles, and expressions of gratitude and delight.

"One hour each day, you must teach English to the children of the friends. Áqá Mírzá Núru'd-Dín will teach them Persian and you must teach them English," He thus instructed.

From the following day, a room in the pilgrim house was allocated for this purpose. The room was prepared, benches and desks were brought in and I began the service with which I had been honoured by the Master.

There were some twenty students divided into two groups. Lessons began and before long rapid progress was achieved. The children enjoyed quite a few benefits in their training, appropriate to the prevailing conditions of austerity and hardship in the Most Great Prison. In addition to the study of Persian, English, mathematics and other lessons, they had to master a trade or vocation. Despite a rampant scarcity of all goods, each child had to have a desk.

Training in shoe-making, carpentry, and tailoring were more readily available to the children and therefore most of them were already engaged as apprentices in these trades. The Master paid a great deal of attention to all facets of education of the young. Each and every one of them, regardless of age or any other consideration, was educated under His direct and close supervision. The young men, some loyal to the Faith and some violators of the Covenant, also received the same education. And while in their childhood they had been deprived of the opportunity to study foreign languages, here they received training in Arabic, literature, calligraphy and penmanship.

The late Mishkín-Qalam taught penmanship. Even the great Zaynu'l-Muqarrabín had been assigned to teach Arabic and Bahá'í Writings. The sun of generosity shone on all, the showers of confirmation fell upon everyone. But in the midst of this some were loyal and had arisen to serve, while others were Covenant-breakers and sought every opportunity for sedition and mischief.

While I was engaged in teaching English, I noted that 'Abdu'l-Bahá's desire for the education of the children was so intense that despite the overwhelming pressures of His all-important work, to our amazement He found time to attend to the most minute details of their work.

In addition to His personal visits every few weeks, which included His enquiring into each pupil's progress in school and reviewing the results of their quarterly exams, He spoke to them at length every Friday about the significance of their education and training. The details of this will be covered in a later chapter. This method of education continued until my departure from 'Akká. For some time after that, Mírzá Núru'd-Dín continued my classes, and thus the children of the Emigrants,[106] who served the threshold of the Centre of the Covenant in that Most Great Prison where they faced great difficulty in even earning a meagre livelihood, were not deprived of the benefits of education.

News of the upheavals of Yazd and Isfahan

The smoothly proceeding affairs of the Faith in the Holy Land, its progress around the globe, the happy news flowing in from every direction, and the busy traffic of pilgrims from East and West were all cause for rejoicing and jubilation – so much so that the difficulties and trials of the Most Great Prison were gradually forgotten, the many plots and machinations of the Covenant-breakers to destroy the foundation of the Cause proved ineffective and futile, so that the friends were in good heart.

After these few happy months, events took a sudden turn. As it is written:

A new melody was heard from his lute.

The pogroms in Isfahan and Yazd came to pass.[107] Grievous, heart-rending news of the tragedies poured in ceaselessly, filling the tender heart of 'Abdu'l-Bahá with indescribable pain and sorrow. This news did not come merely from one or two sources; every day a flood of agonizing, painful letters arrived, originating from most regions of Iran, and each one was perused by the Master. In addition to these, all correspondence received by the friends (whether resident or pilgrim) containing references to the tragedies was submitted to 'Abdu'l-Bahá, which increased His sorrow and anguish.

In times past, whenever the vilification and persecution of 'Abdu'l-Bahá by His enemies brought grief and anguish to the hearts of the friends, the Master had been able to console and comfort them with His tender, heartwarming words. In fact, He always expressed His longing to experience a fuller measure of adversity and pain in the path of the Cause of God, solacing the grief-stricken friends with words of hope and encouragement and infusing a spirit of joy and enthusiasm into their beings. But alas, in this horrible tragedy, this grave calamity that had befallen the Persian friends, there was no comfort. It was through prayers and supplications that the friends beseeched God for merciful relief.

In accordance with 'Abdu'l-Bahá's instructions, Mírzá Haydar-'Alí was assigned to collect, sort and collate all incoming correspondence. Both in the pilgrim house and at 'Abdu'l-Bahá's residence, the mention of the martyrs dominated every conversation. At times the weeping and lamentation of the denizens of the kingdom of Abhá could be heard. Sometimes the ladies of 'Abdu'l-Bahá's household sent us messages asking us to resort to every possible means of distracting the Master's attention away from the painful and harrowing thoughts which must have crowded His mind. But alas, alas, no one had such power; to none was granted such a privilege. Some three hundred of the purest and most faithful believers drank from the chalice of martyrdom in the most brutal and agonizing circumstances. The details of each case, as described in a hundred different letters, a hundred assorted pieces of poetry, a hundred narratives and reports, reached the eyes and ears of 'Abdu'l-Bahá. Anyone who had either heard or witnessed any event apprised Him of the details. All this information was subsequently given to the Ḥájí to edit redundant versions, exclude exaggerated or distorted descriptions, and compile the rest into a systematic and orderly account of events. Once the compilation was completed, the resulting pamphlet[108] was translated into English on 'Abdu'l-Bahá's instructions and published in Western countries.

What was the Covenant-breakers' attitude towards these tragedies? To the same extent that news of the progress of the Faith had always rekindled the fire of their contempt and jealousy and brought disappointment and sadness to their hearts (and not unlike today's opponents of the Faith, they too denied the veracity of such news), the reports of the pogroms, on the contrary, now brought them much happiness and encouragement. They publicized the events among the non-Bahá'í populace and the enemies of the Faith, making general statements to this effect: "'Abbás Effendi's followers in Iran are so commonly despised and rejected by their own countrymen that they are being massacred with impunity in their hundreds." Thus they used these reports as the basis of their negative propaganda, to renew feelings of hatred and disgust towards the Faith in the rank and file of the opponents of the Cause.

For the faithful believers, the bitterness of the circumstances had reached such dimensions that the scorn and condemnation of the non-Bahá'ís seemed more offensive and painful than the news of the tragedies themselves.

In brief, this was one of the most difficult and agonizing periods in the lives of the resident friends. Even after the upheaval had eased somewhat, 'Abdu'l-Bahá continued to grieve. While before the renewal of His incarceration in 'Akká, and during His days of freedom in Haifa, He had found solitude for prayers in the open spaces at early dawn, or when in 'Akká had freely visited the Most Holy Shrine – now, in these days of confinement and captivity when these activities were no longer possible, 'Abdu'l-Bahá found undisturbed seclusion for prayer and meditation in a small room built entirely of wood above the *bírúní* reception area of His residence, facing the Most Holy Shrine. In the early morning hours – nay, from midnight till dawn – He spent His time in prayer and supplication.

Yes, in those days the Covenant-breakers rejoiced. Now we have to see what they are doing today and what they will do tomorrow.

The realization of one of 'Abdu'l-Bahá's predictions: Mírzá Badí'u'lláh's story concluded

Any faithful believer who surveys the eventful history of the Cause, from the inception of which some 91 years have passed,[109] knows of a certainty that each and every prediction and prophecy made by 'Abdu'l-Bahá has been entirely realized; not a single one has failed to find fulfilment. One can, then, view the future of the Faith in the mirror of its past and compare the present time with what will emerge in the future.

'Abdu'l-Bahá's promises to the friends of the triumph of the Faith, and His vision of ignominy and dishonour which He foresaw afflicting the Covenant-breakers, were revealed at a time when they were the ones who outwardly enjoyed the upper hand of power and influence both in 'Akká and outside it.

Many times I heard the Master say, "When I was giving

advice to Majdu'd-Dín and gently admonishing him: 'Do not do these things, or you will regret your actions,' I spoke with such intensity that my tears spontaneously began to flow. Suddenly I noticed that Majdu'd-Dín was laughing and thinking to himself, 'I have defeated Him completely.' I shouted at him, 'You miserable man, I am weeping for you. Did you think that these are tears of weakness?'"

On another occasion the Master had warned the late Mírzá Ḍíyá'u'lláh: "You wrote the Covenant-breaker materials and sent them out. Tell Mírzá Muḥammad-'Alí that it won't be long before you reproach yourself: 'I wish my fingers had been broken so that I might never have used my pen against the Faith.'"

It was possible to envision the realization of all these prophecies of the Master. However, His statements to some of the pilgrims regarding the misery and abasement which was to befall Mírzá Badí'u'lláh were beyond my capacity to grasp. I was therefore left with no choice but to resort to interpretation of His utterances. For four years from that moment, I kept a searching eye in all directions to perhaps discover the fulfilment of that prophecy of 'Abdu'l-Bahá. And what a discovery! The memory of that event can never fade.

As mentioned earlier, my days were usually heavy with work; I was kept continuously busy. So each evening our relaxation and recreation consisted of taking long walks outside the gate of 'Akká. In these promenades I was often accompanied by Mírzá Núru'd-Dín and Mírzá Munír, who made use of this opportunity to practise their English. After an hour, we usually returned to the *bírúní* reception area and attained the presence of the Master along with the pilgrims and residents.

However, going for walks outside the city gate had, as of late, become extremely unpleasant and difficult, for going and coming between the open, fragrant fields necessitated crossing an unpleasant area, a veritable purgatory. Just outside the gate of 'Akká, adjacent to the sentries' barracks and next to two coffee shops, there existed a dilapidated, shabby area covered with large piles of garbage and assorted heaps of refuse and trash. After a heavy rain and then under the sun's strong rays these heaps of waste generated such a stench as to sicken and disgust the passer-by – not unlike the foul odour of the writings of the Covenant-breakers. The problem was made even worse when showers of rain produced rivers of muck and slime, which ran in all directions on the public paths; once evaporated by the hot sun these made crossing that purgatory so difficult that one had to hold one's breath and run to safety. Because of this, we sometimes abandoned altogether the idea of taking walks in the countryside or on the beach – but still, at other times when the need for relaxation was too strong to resist, we prepared ourselves to endure the agony of that purgatory in order to reach the open fields.

One day, as my two companions and I were passing the purgatory in a state of utter misery and nausea, I protested angrily to my colleagues: "The people of this town and especially of this area are a pathetic and irresponsible bunch. If the town does not have a municipal administration, why don't the tenants of these coffee houses collect a few *beshliks*, dump this garbage into the sea and salvage the area? So much apathy and indifference is unbelievable."

My colleagues broke into laughter and explained that these were, in fact, not piles of garbage but an accumulation of wealth. They further informed me that this was actually the working capital of a business enterprise, a source of income. I thought they were jesting, so I jokingly added: "Yes, it must be a source of income for the Arabs."

They replied that in fact the business venture belonged to none other than Mírzá Badí'u'lláh. Still suspecting a ploy, I asked, "What does this have to do with Mírzá Badí'u'lláh?"

They explained that he and a few others had established a company transporting fertilizer from the Huron desert to this location and from here via freight vessels to Marseilles, France, earning a handsome profit. And that recently a dispute had caused a break-up of the partnership and the matter had been referred to the courts for resolution. In the meantime the fertilizer had been confiscated pending the decree of the court.

"God be praised, the Bahá'ís of this town buy wheat and barley from the Huron desert for export to Marseilles," I commented. "Why is it that Mírzá Badí'u'lláh has decided to export the very waste and refuse of that wheat and barley, especially in circumstances when the company itself is under investigation?"

Of course, the reason was obvious. This was so that the Master's words might be realized. Four years before, He had foreseen the circumstances and had predicted, "Soon you will see that Mírzá Badí'u'lláh will be content to haul manure between 'Akká and Bahjí, and even that will not be possible for him."

The return of Mírzá Badí'u'lláh to the fold

For some time a whispering of a possible return of Mírzá Badí'u'lláh to the fold of the faithful had been heard. This information was received by some with scepticism and by others with a sense of welcome and relief, and while the former group expressed concern the latter was elated.

The concern and apprehension were felt by those believers who suspected a ploy and feared a fresh mischief or plot, whereas the joy and satisfaction were expressed by the evil ones and their followers, always on the look-out for those sly and crafty Covenant-breakers who could penetrate the circle of the faithful and make an attempt to regain some degree of credibility for that outcast group.

Outwardly, this would not be without its benefits, since Badí'u'lláh had been a spendthrift who had liberally used up his wealth on utilizing all available means to oppose the Covenant, and had since tried his hand at various occupations to earn a living but without any apparent success. Trade had failed too, and so had farming. And as he had lost all he had, and had been denied the helping hand of the Covenant-breakers, he must have said to himself: where else can I turn for help except the threshold of the Centre of the Covenant? As the poet says:

> *If thou art in need, raise up thy hand to thy Lord,*
> *For he is the Beneficent, the Merciful, the Forgiving and the Loving.*

In brief, the news received a variety of interpretations. Those who were intimately acquainted with various religious scriptures likened it to the Bible story of the prodigal son who, having squandered all his inheritance on worldly pleasures and sunk to the depths of misery and poverty, eventually returns to the service of his father where his entreaty is accepted and he receives a warm welcome to the fold.

For a time such conversations and interpretations persisted, until at last the truth of the matter emerged. Mírzá Badí'u'lláh had accepted to repent, and had therefore produced a document which categorically declared his break from his wicked collaborators and his determination to rejoin the circle of his sincere well-wishers. Through the intercession of some of the friends his declaration was accepted at the sanctified threshold of the Centre of the Covenant. It was thus decided that on a certain day he would present himself at a gathering held in the *bírúní* reception room of the House of 'Abdu'l-Bahá to read his letter of repentance, and there in the presence of all the friends demonstrate his remorse and contrition.

This was in fact an unforgettable historical occasion for those who witnessed it, and a manifest loss for those who did not. Since the belief of the Covenant-breakers rested on the theory of the three-pronged alliance, the usurpation of the Caliphate and the ousting of Imám 'Alí, the letter of repentance had therefore been constructed in the format of an oath of fealty. The Centre of the Covenant, who was informed of the past, present and future, accepted that document as the ultimate confession and repentance of His unfaithful brother. As the learned poet [Rumí] says:

> *Whatever jealousies and intrigues may be hidden*
> *Are clear as the light of day in the sight of God.*

In the afternoon of that fateful day [4 February 1903] and in the presence of all of the friends gathered in the *bírúní* reception hall of the house, Mírzá Badí'u'lláh entered, and according to the prevailing custom demonstrated his sentiments of humble devotion and servitude to the Master. He read the letter of repentance and then fell at 'Abdu'l-Bahá's feet and begged forgiveness. 'Abdu'l-Bahá accepted him and showered him with loving-kindness.

The quality of the presentation of the document and the nature of its contents spoke volumes of the skill with which it had been prepared. Mírzá Muḥammad-'Alí was charged as the main culprit and held responsible for all the wrongdoing and wicked conduct, while he [Badí'u'lláh] had quite inadvertently become an innocent participant. All the major issues, including the details of the rebellion and opposition, even the deceptions, pilfering and interpolation of the divine verses and the dissemination of accusatory publications were described in detail and properly supported by documentation.

Once the formalities of penitence were happily concluded, there began the process of welcoming his return to the Faith, which included much hugging and kissing and endless chatter and laughter. In the middle of all this, those present had a variety of reactions and impressions of the true nature of what had just transpired. Suddenly I noticed that one of the resident friends, out of pure excitement and joy, was kneeling before Mírzá Badí'u'lláh and kissing his feet. Looking around with pride and self-satisfaction, Badí'u'lláh could obviously visualize the Bahá'í world humbled at his feet.

This repulsive act saddened me much, and I began to understand the intentions and desires of some of those in attendance. From that day I began to impress upon the friends our duty to pay close attention to the utterances of the Master, and to place each word before us as a guiding light, in order to remain alert to the ever-continuing machinations of the Covenant-breakers.

As to Mírzá Badí'u'lláh, he immediately gained all the comforts of life. Everything he needed for an easy and comfortable lifestyle was provided for him. On 'Abdu'l-Bahá's instructions a splendid house in the small city of 'Akká was obtained for him. All expenses and various means of comfort for himself and his family were provided; he was welcomed into the presence of 'Abdu'l-Bahá and began to accompany Him in all His outings.

Mírzá Badí'u'lláh's letter of repentance, which was in the form of a declaration, was copied and despatched to Iran. Translations of the document were sent to all the friends in America and Europe. The friends in residence, however, were ambivalent about Badí'u'lláh's return. Some viewed it favourably, but others were suspicious of his true intent. Because of this (and having detected certain intimations in 'Abdu'l-Bahá's words) they began to observe his every act, to examine his true intentions and bring the reality of the situation to light. In fact, this was quite necessary, for the purpose of 'Abdu'l-Bahá's words was to alert the friends and prepare them for all possible future developments.

Through Mírzá Badí'u'lláh's confessions as contained in his signed and sealed testimonial, the past misdeeds of the Covenant-breakers had been brought to light. Now it was time for their future aspirations and plans to be brought to the attention of the friends, so that they might become cognizant of the nature of the forthcoming events. From the day when the news of Mírzá Badí'u'lláh's repentance and return was announced, no further speculation as to the plans and strategies of the Covenant-breakers was necessary, for a past member of that group was now present among the friends, and moreover the details of their activities had been made public under his signature and seal. Now, regarding the future of the Faith, 'Abdu'l-Bahá suddenly began to continually emphasize the need for the Universal House of Justice and the significance of its establishment. In clearly defined statements,

He made us understand that the friends should not assume that after the setting of the Sun of the Covenant, the Cause of God would fall into the hands of the wicked and the corrupt. He emphasized this point repeatedly; one night He instructed us thus: "Write down My words, and communicate them to all parts of the world. Commit them to memory and mention them to anyone with whom you come into contact, so that no doubt may remain that after Me the Faith will be in the hands of the Universal House of Justice."

Since He had instructed that we should record His words, that night in the pilgrim house everyone wrote down whatever they could remember of His utterances. My notes are as follows:

The night of Monday, the 16th day of Jamádí'u'lláh, A.H. 1319 [31 August 1903] we were in the presence of 'Abdu'l-Bahá. He made certain remarks regarding the Universal House of Justice, which in accordance with His instructions are recorded as follows:

He stated: "Nothing causes me more unhappiness than disunity, and this can only be remedied by obedience to the command of the Universal House of Justice. Even before the establishment of the House of Justice, the friends must be obedient to the existing Spiritual Assemblies even if they know of a certainty that their judgement is flawed. If this were not complied with, the mighty citadel of the Faith of God would not be safeguarded. All must obey the Universal House of Justice. Obedience to it is obedience to the Cause. Opposition to it is opposition to the Blessed Beauty. Denial of it is denial of God, the True One. Renouncing any word of the House of Justice is like unto the renunciation of a word from the Kitáb-i-Aqdas. Observe, how important this matter is! The Blessed Beauty has ordained the House of Justice as the law-maker. If the votes of the members are not unanimous and there are differences of views, then the vote of the majority is the vote of the Blessed Beauty."

He then added: "Take this very moment. Should the Universal House of Justice be operating, by the one True God, beside Whom there is no God, I would have been the first to obey its decree, even if it should be against me. It is true that that Body does not possess inherent infallibility, but it is under the shadow of the protection and shelter of the Blessed Beauty.[110] Its command is the Blessed Command. Discuss this matter amongst yourselves, so that it may not be forgotten. Speak of it to one another; even, make a written note of it."

Of course, what is written here does not reflect the exact words of 'Abdu'l-Bahá. However, it does not contain any superfluous words. This sheet of paper has been kept in the files of this servant all these years.

What I do remember about the Spiritual Assembly of Tehran is that in those days the election process did not take place by the vote of the community at large. The Hands of the Cause of God, along with a few others, formed the Assembly and two or three of them stayed in Tehran at all times.

It was clear from the words of 'Abdu'l-Bahá that hidden in Mírzá Badí'u'lláh's testimonial were many devilish designs. All the friends understood the situation, but yet in accordance with the verse of the Kitáb-i-'Ahd which states: "It is incumbent upon everyone to show courtesy to, and have regard for the Aghsán, that thereby the Cause of God may be glorified,"[111] they adopted a respectful attitude towards Mírzá Badí'u'lláh, who had now returned to the fold.

But he was not content with mere respect; he expected to receive reverence and prostration. He even entertained the thought that the friends should kiss his hands and even his feet, and this expectation disgusted the friends. In those days, the Master used to emphasize, "The friends who come to me should not bow before me; the use of the greeting 'Alláh'u'Abhá' will suffice. This will bring me happiness."

'Abdu'l-Bahá used to talk mostly (in those days) about the importance of the House of Justice. One night, when He spoke on this subject again He said, "If the House of Justice had been operating in this day and pronounced my death sentence, all would have to obey."

The late Muḥammad Riḍáy-i-Qannád was disturbed at

this statement by the Master, and he asked, "Is the House of Justice of God, or is it not?"

"Of course it is," replied the Master. "How then is it possible for that which is of God to condemn He Who is of God?" asked he.

"My object", 'Abdu'l-Bahá replied, "is that you may know that on that day the House of Justice is the true one of God, for the Blessed Beauty has ordained it to be the law-maker."

In short, these words shattered the hopes of Mírzá Badí'u'lláh, frustrated his greed, and thwarted his ambitions for the future.

Conduct, manners and attitude of Mírzá Badí'u'lláh

Those friends who had not met Mírzá Badí'u'lláh imagined that because of his connection to the "Blessed and Sacred Tree" he would be endowed with heavenly talents and faculties, physical and spiritual gifts, and qualities of moral rectitude and spiritual discernment, for he had been raised and educated in the Cause of God. One would have thought him to be articulate and possessed of the power of eloquent speech. There was also much hope that once he was reconfirmed in the Covenant and had atoned for his past mistakes, he would in accordance with the command of the Exalted Pen "subdue the citadels of men's hearts with the swords of wisdom and of utterance"[112] – attract the world of humanity to the great ocean of divine wisdom.

But alas, this was not the case. Contrary to all expectations, he was utterly devoid of any knowledge of the Faith, and since he also lacked eloquence, he usually sat quietly at gatherings, and when he did participate in a conversation his choice of words were often indicative of his lack of understanding, which made his silence befitting and agreeable. As the poet has said:

> *To sit mute, quiet and silent in a corner*
> *Is better than to speak with a tongue devoid of wisdom.*

Ḥájí Mírzá Ḥaydar-'Alí of Isfahan

*Mishkín-Qalam, Mírzá Husayn of Isfahan,
Apostle of Bahá'u'lláh*

*Zaynu'l-Muqarrabín, Mullá Zaynu'l-'Ábidín,
Disciple of the Báb and Apostle of Bahá'u'lláh*

Áqá Muḥammad Riḍáy-i-Qannád of Shiraz, "a man of faith and honour", he accompanied Bahá'u'lláh from Baghdad and served both Him and 'Abdu'l-Bahá all the rest of his life.

*Áqá Ḥusayn-i-Áshchí of Káshán,
cook in the household of Bahá'u'lláh, he shared His exiles.*

The original building of the Shrine of the Báb on Mount Carmel

The Shrine of the Báb, alleged by the Covenant-breakers to be "a strong fortress"

*Dr. Youness Khán and Dr. Arastú Khán,
friends, fellow doctors, and servants of the Master*

Once he desired to study the English language, and the late Mrs. Lua Getsinger happily accepted this service in the hope that from him she would be able to gain knowledge of the Writings as well as heavenly attributes. After a few days of teaching, during which she also asked multitudes of questions in the hope of acquiring spiritual qualities, she realized that this was not the gushing fountain that she had imagined, but a bare illusion, an empty mirage incapable of quenching her thirst. And so she delicately and amiably suggested to him, "It is better that you do not learn English or study any foreign languages, so that your self-respect, and the dignity and reputation of the Faith, may not be tarnished. When crowds of Western pilgrims arrive at this spot in future, many of them may ask you questions to obtain first-hand knowledge of the Faith. Your inability to speak English would conceal your ineptitude and ignorance."

(As the poet has said: So long as a man has not spoken,/ His virtue, or lack of it, remains hidden.)

"It would be better for you to converse with the Western friends through an interpreter, so that with his help your reputation may remain unblemished."

In short, while Mírzá Badí'u'lláh lacked any quality which could attract the hearts, he nevertheless always expected to be praised and adored by the believers. And at times, when he observed how the friends of God, like moths, lovingly circled around that radiant and heavenly Candle of love and with what joyful spirits they demonstrated their readiness to sacrifice their lives in His path, he was consumed with the fires of jealousy and contempt. In accordance with the verse, "Jealousy consumeth the body and anger doth burn the liver,"[113] his jealousy and anger gradually broke down his health, weakened his body and filled his spirit with despair. Brokenhearted and depressed, he found comfort in seclusion.

Mírzá Badí'u'lláh breaks his vows of repentance

When Mírzá Badí'u'lláh's letter of repentance was published, the Covenant-breakers became silent and dejected for some time. But after a few months, the flock of the birds of night began to flutter about again. Covenant-breaker writings began to reappear, their stench filling the nostrils of friend and stranger alike. Every week, reports from Iran reflected the sadness and distress of the friends over such disturbing activities.

The Covenant-breakers publicized a variety of bizarre and far-fetched interpretations and explanations of the now famous letter of repentance, attributing to Mírzá Badí'u'lláh certain allegations. As I was told by Áqá Muḥammad Riḍáy-i-Qannád, a man of faith and honour, the Master – may our spirits be a sacrifice for Him – often urged Mírzá Badí'u'lláh, "Why don't you deny these charges?"

But he, citing a variety of excuses, refused to respond to them. While I was not told anything directly by the Master on this issue, it was rumoured that Mírzá Badí'u'lláh had begun to misbehave and demonstrate symptoms of discontent and unhappiness; that he had adopted a victimized attitude and so had secluded himself in his home refusing to go out, as a sign of his displeasure, even refusing to attend the presence of the Master. I know this much: that for a few months he was in deep seclusion and would not under any circumstances enter the presence of 'Abdu'l-Bahá. The Master, however, visited and comforted him, attended to his needs and avoided any mention of him in conversation with others. At times He even sent some of the pilgrims who had been previously acquainted with Mírzá Badí'u'lláh to visit him, offer solace and comfort, and enquire after his wellbeing. He also used to send departing pilgrims to visit him and say farewell to him.

Badí'u'lláh stayed in seclusion for three or four months. Having thus completed his secret agreement with his old collaborators, he suddenly, openly, and officially broke again from the ranks of the faithful and returned to the bosom of the violators of the Covenant, leaving the signed and sealed testimonial of his repentance behind as a memento for posterity.

Rapid progress of the Faith in East and West and the sending of the Arch-breaker of the Covenant's agent to America

The period between the years 1901 and 1903 constituted the height of the activities of the Covenant-breakers and enemies of the Faith, and the peak of the dissemination of their publications. In the closing stages of the upheavals in Yazd and Isfahan, the progress of the Faith gained such momentum as to astonish both friend and foe. The Persian divines, who had expressed contentment at the passing of the Blessed Beauty, considering the Faith to have run its course, were expressing disquiet and concern, realizing that they were utterly incapable of resisting that onrushing flood.

The upheaval of Yazd had inflamed the emotions of the friends and had increased the intensity of their faith and the audacity of their endeavours – so much so that their boundless labours generated an awakening amongst the general population, whether ignorant or heedless. This brought about a spirit of enquiry which led to major successes in the teaching work, as the effort to raise the call among the masses reached its zenith in all parts of the country.

The receipt of this news in 'Akká breathed a spirit of joy and tranquillity into the hearts of the faithful. Mírzá Badí'u'lláh's letter of repentance had one benefit. Once it was published, it brought awareness of the Covenant-breakers' secrets to those friends who lived in the far-off reaches of the globe. However, his craftiness in reentering the circle of the faithful and his subsequent dastardly return to his old ways were the cause of great sadness to the friends; everyone had discovered the nature of the greed and desire which dominated his life.

But at the last, his opposition and dissent was a blessing; it heartened and elated the friends to see the removal of such an obstacle from the path of the advancing flood of the Cause of God, and the resumption of its normal progress.

The news of these events roused the Western friends to

action. The progress of the Faith became more rapid, and many eminent, sanctified souls in America and Europe entered the Faith. Whereas previously the letters from the new believers contained only their declarations of belief and expressions of regard and devotion, now the friends published articles and books of proof. The late Abu'l-Faḍl, known as the Eastern philosopher, taught the scholars, the savants and the doctors. Teachers, both men and women, became everywhere engaged in service to the Faith; newspapers and magazines arrived in batches from America, and translations of relevant portions were forwarded to Iran on 'Abdu'l-Bahá's instructions. In every land the call of the Kingdom was powerfully raised, and was followed by a tremendous awakening and response. In India all the friends were involved in service to the Faith; in 'Ishqábád the first Bahá'í temple or Mashriqu'l-Adhkár had been built, and in Russia the call of the Cause of God had been heard by all.

During all this, the pen of the Centre of the Covenant knew no rest. According to His own words: "This pen must create the most beautiful pearls in every ocean and flood each river with clear, sweet and rejuvenating water."[114] In short, the Bahá'í world was filled with enthusiasm and joy reflecting the essence of the Master's words: "To the firm in the Covenant [these utterances] are but shining rays of light, and to those who have wavered and are wandering in the paths of delusion, flames of burning fire."[115]

The three-pronged alliance of the Covenant-breakers was utterly defeated; the evil ones were gradually crushed and discarded; and the realization of the Master's words, "They fell into disgrace" came to pass as the followers of the Centre of Sedition[116] began to cry out: Woe betide us! Woe betide us! Some of them began to entertain thoughts of repentance and return to the fold, while others remonstrated with their chief in these words: "How long must we wait for you to fulfil your deceitful pledges and empty promises? The hope of their realization has left us wandering, aimless and miserable. Every day you promised that this week we should receive news of victory, that this month the banner of triumph would be raised, that next year the rule of the Caliphate would gain ascendancy. But we near the end of our lives, as well as of our endurance and patience. The cup of forbearance is overflowing. How long are we to wait? In Tehran the Old Hyena has died in utter poverty; in Azerbaijan the exalted Khalíl[117] has experienced a miserable end; the uprising of Mírzá Áqá Ján has produced no lasting effect; no further news was received from India; and whatever happened in Egypt? In America, Khayru'lláh has not succeeded, for Anton Haddad rose in defence of the Cause. Abu'l-Faḍl was a veritable success and we, lost and dejected, still await the realization of your promises."

In short, after much debate and consultation, they decided to send two experienced men to America in the hope that these grandsons of Bahá'u'lláh would be able to penetrate the circle of the friends, spread seeds of discord, create a major obstacle to the onrushing flow of the Faith of God, muddy up this clear and pristine water, and according to their plans, begin to "bring in the fish". These two were Mírzá Shu'á'u'lláh, the son of the Centre of Sedition, and – so we heard – Ghulámu'lláh, the son of Muḥammad Javád-i-Qazvíní. These two departed – but nothing was ever heard or seen of them again.

Burdens, sorrows and labours of 'Abdu'l-Bahá

The upheavals of Isfahan and Yazd at last came to an end, yet the harrowing burdens and sorrows which assailed the Centre of the Covenant did not ease.

In all the cities of Iran the friends of God were encountering a variety of cruelties and injustices; each believer sought relief from his pain and anguish at the threshold of his loving Master. No day passed without letters bursting with the heart-rending sighs and groans of the Persian friends reaching Him, and no night saw the first light of dawn yet failed to find 'Abdu'l-Bahá in that small wooden cabin on the upper floor, engaged in supplication, or to hear His lamentations.

The return of Mírzá Badí'u'lláh to the fold did not in fact lessen the weight of 'Abdu'l-Bahá's burdens; rather, it increased His anxiety. The subsequent breaking of his pledge simply broke His heart, a heart already overflowing with sorrow. All this took its toll on His health, weakening His body with every passing day. And all the while the pressures and stresses of His manifold occupations continued to mount.

The reaction to the injustices and cruelties in Iran generated a new awakening among friends and strangers alike, and expanded the frontiers of the Faith of God. It created new occupations; it brought about new challenges which defied solution – and it was the Interpreter of the Book, the Centre of the Covenant, the Solver of all problems, who had to prescribe the remedy for all the ills.

From Iran and around the world, scientific questions, spiritual queries and abstruse religious problems poured in, and comprehensive answers were given to each one. Many of these were in His own hand; some were dictated to Núru'd-Dín-i-Zayn, a number of others to Mírzá Munír, the son of the late Mírzá Muḥammad-Qulí, and still others to a few other friends who were blessed with this privilege.

Mírzá Munír-i-Zayn and this servant were the last to attain the honour of this service. The increased number of secretaries, however, did not lessen the problem, since 'Abdu'l-Bahá had to dictate the contents, then review and correct the draft, and then again read and correct the revised version.

It was 'Abdu'l-Bahá's habit to find relief from one tiring occupation by engaging Himself in another. For example, whenever He grew tired of writing, He would turn to the dictation of Tablets, and when He grew weary of this, He would summon the pilgrims and impart to them words of counsel and admonition. Once He felt tired out by writing, dictation or speaking, He would take long walks in the narrow winding streets of the Most Great Prison, and if in the process He encountered a believer or a non-believer, friend or foe, He would stop and spend a few minutes talking to him of matters of interest to that person. Thus, as He simply strolled down the streets of 'Akká, 'Abdu'l-Bahá actually performed the important task of attending to a great many side issues.

If He felt any weariness, He visited the sick and the poor. The sick received His prayers and blessings, and the needy the contents of His moneybag. As soon as the famous moneybag emerged from His pocket, the whole household would circle around that heavenly Personage like moths. The older ones received *majídís* and *beshliks* and the younger ones a few *metliks*.

As soon as the moneybag was empty He would return home. If there was any daylight left, He would summon Mírzá Núru'd-Dín and pick up where He had left off. If it was early evening, and the chanter of the Qur'án was already in the *bírúní* reception area, He would listen to the chant and permit some of the friends and certain others to attain His presence at the same time. If it were late at night, He would visit those pilgrims and residents who were gathered in the *bírúní* area waiting for Him to come, and bestow upon them the expressions of His loving-kindness. He would then ask someone to chant a prayer, and afterwards he would retire to the *andárúní* where He busied Himself with managing the affairs of the house and attending to the education of each member of the blessed household.

After a short rest, He would be up before the first light of dawn and engaged in prayer and the revelation of divine verses until sunrise, when He would begin His busy day. Thus the only temporary respite and comfort for 'Abdu'l-Bahá was the time He spent at the dinner table – and even that time was taken up by the many questions of the Western friends. These required a variety of answers ranging from philosophical explanations to logical proofs, from abstract and traditional references to theological topics. Mr. Phelps's book, *Some Answered Questions*, and many others were revealed at the dinner table.

Happy is the one who reads these books and marvels at the way the days and nights of 'Abdu'l-Bahá were spent.

Hardship fills my days and anguish my nights –
O, what days and nights do I pass without you!

The effect of difficulties and sorrows on 'Abdu'l-Bahá

Although the sorrow and pain which afflicted the body of that heavenly Personage caused a degree of anxiety and distress, yet the sanctified manifestations of the Divine Being, like the luminous heavenly sun, always dominate circumstances and influence the lives of all earthly creatures while remaining unaffected themselves by the upheavals and convulsions of the material world. They affect and remain unaffected; they generate change but remain unchanged. Therefore, while seemingly in the grasp of the fire of Nimrod and assailed by the hatred of His enemies, the reality of 'Abdu'l-Bahá's being remained cheerful and happy; at the emergence of adversity and tribulation, He even desired more. This is attested by the fact that all the most captivating verses and exhilarating Tablets, those which revive and rejuvenate melancholy souls, were revealed at such times.

Whenever the lamentation of that dearly Beloved could be heard, it was due to His tender feelings for the weak and the helpless. As He once had told Mírzá Majdu'd-Dín: "You misguided man, My tears are for you, not that you have rendered me weak and powerless." He frequently sent messages to the Centre of Sedition, informing him: "Neither are you that 'Umar who can raise aloft the banner of this great Faith, nor am I that 'Alí who because of your disloyalty would weep in the palm groves."[118]

I could give many examples to show that the pain and sorrow that afflicted 'Abdu'l-Bahá, while weakening His body, had no effect on His heavenly powers; and that it was precisely at such times that the emanations of His pen infused a fresh spirit in the hearts of the devoted souls. Each Tablet or prayer revealed in this time of sorrow brought great happiness to the hearts of the friends; while His utterances generated feelings of hope and joy in His audience.

If we review the Tablets revealed in the honour of certain souls during that period, and consider the nature of the prevailing circumstances, then 'Abdu'l-Bahá's mental and spiritual state as He revealed these Tablets becomes clear. For example, during the rebellion of Mírzá Áqá Ján, when "the wine of calamity overflowed", His words awakened the soul and raised one's spirit to the loftiest paradise. And during the upheavals of Isfahan and Yazd, when 'Abdu'l-Bahá's eyes were always tearful, every word that left His pen or His lips bestowed a spirit of hope and inspiration. And if faithful servants beseeched 'Abdu'l-Bahá for relief from the calamities, and a renewal of calm and tranquillity, He would with a gesture and a word create such feelings in the hearts that one found oneself afire with the desire for more calamity and a longing for more adversity.

For instance, during the period of the tragedies I made several pleas in a state of humility and lowliness for some degree of relief from the intensity of the horrors. Despite receiving convincing answers, I continued to persist. One day, while I was accompanying 'Abdu'l-Bahá in the unfrequented alleyways of 'Akká, I took advantage of the opportunity to entreat Him further. Expressing my deep sorrow, I made several remarks in the hope that He might at last be persuaded to intercede, or that He might seek from the depths of His own heart an end to this cup of tribulation.

No matter what I said, His response was clear and convincing – yet although convinced, I could find no peace. And so, employing the most persuasive and heart-rending language that I could muster, and with tears of grief and pain streaming down, I cast at His feet my case. I felt certain that my words of supplication had been effective, that the arrow of my prayerful entreaty had finally struck its target. But now hear what I was told. Turning His blessed face towards mine, and with a smile that melted the heart, He explained, "Jináb-i-Khán, this is what is intended. If it were not for this, the friends would lose their fire and the Cause of God would cease to progress. Now what do you want me to do? Do you want me to pray that the cup of calamity may not overflow?" And then He uttered words which filled my heart with such happiness and contentment that I longed to be in Yazd so that I could take a single gulp from that elixir of sacrifice.

On returning to the pilgrim house I told Hájí Mírzá Haydar-'Alí what had happened and reiterated my concern over the terrible effect of the news of tragedies on 'Abdu'l-Bahá's wellbeing. He promised to follow up another time, and with more eloquent and effective words, so that perchance 'Abdu'l-Bahá's will might incline towards a mitigation of the intensity of the tragedies. One day, when a tremendous storm had brought heavy rain, he was summoned to the presence of 'Abdu'l-Bahá to accompany Him in a walk through the streets of 'Akká.

Taking advantage of the opportunity, the Hájí opened the subject and humbly communicated, in some detail, his appeal to the Master. 'Abdu'l-Bahá replied, "Jináb-i-Mírzá, have you noticed the intensity of the rain?"

"Yes, Beloved, I have," replied Mírzá.

"Have you seen how much water flooded the area? Now, even with all this water, if you dig into the ground to the depth of one finger-joint, you will find it dry. We are the same way; these storms of tribulations have no effect on the reality of our existence."

Mírzá became convinced and did not bring up the issue again. And indeed, while all such calamities and tragedies had no effect on the reality of 'Abdu'l-Bahá's being, whenever He observed any trace of sorrow or distress in the friends He spoke about happy things and told delightfully humorous stories, changing their mood. The spiritual humour of that sanctified and heavenly Being demonstrates those sentiments expressed by Bahá'u'lláh in His Tablet which opens with humour and ends in such a way as to fill the heart with delight and joy.[119] The following story is an example, which I offer as a memento to my dear readers.

A story

Once, when the stones of allegations and calumnies were ceaselessly raining down from the war engines of the enemies, when acts of sedition and treachery were at their peak, a particularly painful spear of accusation struck the heart of that quintessence of gentleness. Its nature was unknown to me. His distress and sorrow were so intense that for some days He hardly visited the *bírúní* reception room at all to meet the many pilgrims.

The more intimate of the resident believers were aware of the facts of the problem, but did not disclose them to anyone, for the incident was disturbing and disruptive. While I had received no intimation from anyone about it, yet sensing the significance of the issue I did not permit myself to make any enquiries.

In short, the friends were upset and subdued; it was as though they were in mourning. On the surface, it brought back memories of the time of Mírzá Áqá Ján's rebellion when 'Abdu'l-Bahá had been entirely absorbed in dealing with endless problems. Then, the friends had been deprived of the heavenly pleasure of His presence, until He received this servant's few verses of poetry, which again inclined His attention towards the believers.

This situation continued for a few days. One night the Master was present in the *bírúní* reception room as the friends, somewhat subdued, waited longingly for Him to break the dark shadow of silence with the heavenly melody of His utterance. Áqá Ridáy-i-Qannád, one of the old and experienced believers who had been one of the original prisoners and emigrants, knew the source of the problem. No longer able to bear the pain, he suddenly broke the wall of silence. Tearing down the veil of meditation and reflection, he spoke out boldly: "Beloved, we cannot endure this any longer.

Patience and forbearance are fine. But till when? Why is it that the ocean of divine wrath has not surged? Why is it that the avenging sword of God has not left its scabbard? Why does the Master show so much forbearance? Why is this happening?"

He continued in this vein until his inner fire blazed so fiercely that his tears began to flow uncontrollably, so easing the intensity of his emotions. The Master, who had serenely and attentively listened to this emotional plea, broke His silence at last and with a heartwarming smile said, "Yes, in the path of the Blessed Beauty one must drink heartily from the overflowing cup of difficulties and afflictions in order to experience its consummate intoxicating effect. One type of adversity only does not have the same effect; it does not bestow that inebriating pleasure. Wines of diverse flavours must be consumed in this divine banquet, until one is utterly intoxicated."

He uttered these words with such joy and ardour that every atom of our beings soared with a sense of ecstasy and rapture. Then He added, "But you have never attended a drinking party. To get completely drunk and ultimately lose all sense of himself, a drinker mixes his drinks. For instance, in one round they drink wine; in the following round they drink *araq*; this is then followed by a round of cognac, then by rounds of rum, whisky and champagne until they drink themselves into a stupor. We, too, must drink various tastes from the cup of tribulation." Suddenly, in a booming voice He asked, "Jináb-i-Khán, is that not so?"

All eyes were focused on me. And I without a moment's hesitation replied, "Yes, Beloved, that is so. By the way, they drink something else too."

"What is that, then?" asked 'Abdu'l-Bahá.

"They mix wine and whisky and say, we are drinking 'wineky'!"[120]

Suddenly His laughter rang out, His tearful eyes looked heavenward, and with a smile He said, "We, too, as the Khán says, drink wineky, drink wineky!"

In short, for some time that night He shared with us glad

tidings of the future of the Faith, the ascendancy of the believers and the abasement of the Covenant-breakers. Since that time many – and possibly all – of those promises have been fulfilled.

And so this has been a brief account of the life of 'Abdu'l-Bahá at this time, an example of His sweet utterances at a time of test and difficulty. And now we must read a sample of His writings, revealed in a spirit of hope and reassurance and in honour of the friends at a time when opposition was at its peak.

> He is God!
> O servant of God, arise and gird up the loins of endeavour and aspire to a rank loftier than the heavens. O servant of God, the fleet-footed stallion is at the ready, the vast arena beckoning, the ball of good fortune in play and the bat of divine confirmation at hand. It is the time of action and winning the ball from the field of play. I say unto you what it behoveth you to know. Hasten, hasten, for the time is short and the music of the minstrel about to end. If in such a feast, you don't clap your hands, play the tambourine and raise your voice in song, when then will you know true rapture and heavenly intoxication?
> The Glory of God be upon thee.[121]

One task does not distract Him from another

However generously a person is endowed with willpower and faith, however abundantly he possesses the capacity to dominate circumstances, and however great his outward means of control and authority, yet once he confronts the onrushing flood of events and is faced with assorted and unexpected difficulties and predicaments – and if it also falls to him to shoulder grave and at times conflicting responsibilities while facing great odds in fulfilling them – he will perforce experience such feelings of apprehension and anxiety as to render the attainment of a composed and tranquil mind an impossibility.

Such a condition may lead to occasions of over-indulgence or conversely lack of effort, errors of judgement in the conduct of affairs, and at times an excess of harshness or severity in pursuing his goal.

In the many years of my residence at the threshold of the Master's presence, I often wondered how and by what means was that blessed Personage able to solve the manifold problems created by the raging storms of adversity and hardship? How was He able, in matters large and small, to act with such dignity, composure and unwavering focus as to appear as though He had absolutely nothing else to do?

At such a time, when the onrushing flood of destiny was fast approaching, when the tempestuous storm of adversity threatened, when the battered Ark of the Cause of God seemed to be overwhelmed by surging waves, and when even the very life of that heavenly Beloved was in danger, I was utterly perplexed, longing to understand the strategy – aside from the innate powers which distinguished His every act – that enabled Him to master every situation and overcome every hardship. And one day He solved the puzzle in His own wonderful way and shared with me the answer to this longstanding enigma. That explanation, for which I had thirsted for so many years, was so significant and precious that if I were to write a hundred books from the utterances of 'Abdu'l-Bahá, this one response would stand out as the highlight of His words. I now present it to my honoured readers in the same manner that He granted it to me – as a priceless gift.

One dark night, as 'Abdu'l-Bahá paced up and down the long front hallway of the reception room, relaxing and easing the stresses of a busy day, He asked me the following question. I was the only one in His presence at the time, and for a span of one hour had the sole honour of listening to His heavenly utterances.

"Do you know how I administer this Faith?"

(I said to myself: that is exactly what I have been longing to know.)

Then He said, "I pull the sails of the ship firmly and fasten the ropes tight. I locate my destination and then by the power of My will I hold the wheel and head out. No matter how strong the storm, no matter how dangerous the threat to the safety of the ship, I do not change course. I do not become agitated or disheartened; I persevere until I reach my goal. If I were to hesitate or change direction at the sight of every danger, the Ark of the Cause of God would surely fail to reach its destination."

I had discovered a new principle and had understood the ways of the Master. I realized that the sails of the Ark of God were tightly bound and the helm was in powerful hands.

What need we fear when You are defending the fortress?
None fear the ocean waves with Noah at the helm.

Then and there I resolved never to allow myself to become overwhelmed by undue worry or sorrow, but to put my reliance in the Beloved of the hearts, and to consider all future incidents or accidents as occasions of joy and contentment, for by their very nature they would aid the progress of the Cause.

And yet, whenever I beheld 'Abdu'l-Bahá sorrowful, broken-hearted or dispirited, my ever-present joy faded into melancholy. In His presence I became a lifeless statue, and at home I was downhearted and sad, until I could detect the signs of happiness in His face once again.

One evening, both pilgrims and residents were in His presence in the front hallway of the reception room. It was one of those difficult days when due to various events 'Abdu'l-Bahá was deeply grieved and quiet. His words were stern and severe, and all present were despondent and silent. A feeling of shame and remorse pervaded the room, for His state of sorrow was caused not only by the acts of enemies of the Faith and the Covenant-breakers. The misconduct and ill behaviour of some faithful believers had added to the problem. At this point one of the most respected believers, who was the subject of general regard and veneration, stepped out of the crowd and asked a meaningless, pointless and irrelevant question.

Having received a dignified and convincing reply, he walked back to where he had stood. But I, being the youngest and least experienced member of the group, became furious at this untimely intrusion. Beside myself with indignation, as silence dominated the room and the Centre of the Covenant continued to pace the floor, I slowly found my way to where that man was standing. Impolitely and boldly, yet in a subdued tone, I reproached him: "Sir, this was no time to ask a question like that! Did you not see how upset the Master was? Considering His condition, why did you not show some consideration?"

He, in contrast, gave me a reply which not only silenced me but also generated in me feelings of shame and regret for my bad manners as I realized that he knew 'Abdu'l-Bahá better than I did. His response, accompanied by a loving glance and a mirthful smile, was, "One task does not distract Him from another."

Ka*sh*kúl or pumpkin bowl?

After the ascension of Bahá'u'lláh one of the Covenant-breakers' stratagems – as has been described in the first chapter of this book – was on one hand to burden 'Abdu'l-Bahá with exorbitant expense, and on the other to claim indigence, misery, starvation, privation and terrible hardship. At the same time, they had spread the rumour that the incoming Ḥuqúqu'lláh funds were being embezzled by the Master's close associates, and that having stolen His seal they were stamping the receipts and cashing them. As 'Abdu'l-Bahá frequently noted, their aim in spreading all these rumours was to dissuade the believers from sending in their Ḥuqúqu'lláh, and thus upset 'Abdu'l-Bahá's financial affairs.

Their well-publicized claims of poverty and misery, especially from the time they refused to accept their expenses from the Master, rejecting subsequent deliveries of their daily provisions and supplies, became so grave that their cries of seeming anguish and suffering could be heard from all quarters. Before long they adopted the appearance of paupers, begging their livelihood from anyone who would have pity on them, and hoping that such melodramatics would strike a blow against the dignity and reputation of the Cause of God.

This reminded me of the beggar who told his son, "Beg as hard as you can, so that you won't have to be obligated to anyone." In the days following their decision to reject their daily expenses from the Master, 'Abdu'l-Bahá would from time to time send them certain sums of money on various pretexts. I even remember an occasion when He sent an amount of one hundred French francs to Mírzá Ḍíyá'u'lláh on the pretext that He owed him that sum. But as these acts of charity became more frequent, they increased their complaints of poverty and misery to non-Bahá'ís, which filled 'Abdu'l-Bahá's heart with aversion and disgust. News of this type used to reach 'Abdu'l-Bahá's ears regularly, and added to his pain and sorrow.

One afternoon, when both pilgrims and residents were in His presence in the outer reception room, one of the respected Shaykhs of the area, whose name I have since forgotten, arrived. This person enjoyed the favour and blessings of the Master and had an important position in the Syrian and Palestinian communities. Formerly one of the most successful merchants of the area, he had since become renowned for piety and godliness, and had been appointed as the Muftí of 'Akká for several years now, enjoying the respect and regard of the community. This person entered and took his seat at the head of the room near 'Abdu'l-Bahá; after the exchange of the customary greetings he began to whisper to the Master. The room was now quiet, all eyes on the Master, whose face reflected a variety of moods – now angry, now astonished, now smiling. When the Muftí had completed his report, 'Abdu'l-Bahá turned to those present and said, "Áqá Shaykh has a strange tale to tell, and I would like all of you to hear it from his own lips." Then, turning to the Shaykh, He said, "Tell the story for our friends either in Turkish or Arabic, whichever you prefer, so that they may hear it too."

"I can oblige in whichever language you prefer," replied he. The honoured Muḥammad-Riḍá volunteered to translate from Arabic into Persian. The Sha<u>y</u><u>kh</u> accepted this offer and began his story:

* * *

"This morning I was in my office busy with work when a respected member of the community walked in for a visit. I saw that he was unduly upset and unhappy, for his face betrayed his chagrin.

'You seem agitated ?' I asked.

'I don't rightly know what to say,' he replied.

I thought he might be upset with me, so I enquired, 'You are not your usual self. What has upset you?'

'I just do not know what to say,' he repeated.

'Then what was your purpose in coming here?' I asked.

'Where else could I go? With such people where can one go and what can one do?' he complained.

I realized he was very upset, and so I persisted and told him that if he was upset with me he should tell me so that I could apologize.

'It is not you. I have no expectations of you. It is about someone whom I considered to be an Imám, the true guardian and a righteous Caliph. Not only that, I even considered him equal to the Prophet. Today I found out ...' he agonized.

But at this hesitation I lost my temper. So I closed my books, removed my glasses and expressed my true feelings: 'Friend, have you gone mad, using heretical words like "equal to the Prophet"? Why are you concealing the matter?' I protested.

'I have sworn not to confide in anyone or reveal the secret of one of God's creatures. But I can no longer bear this. Praise be to God. What a world. You cannot really know anyone.' Having said this, he sighed.

Urged on by a strong sense of curiosity, I began to press

him for more. But he was not about to reveal the secret of his heart. At last I said, 'Whatever you have sworn to, I also swear that I shall not reveal the matter to anyone.'

'Whether you do or not will depend on the purity of your devotion,' he retorted. 'Today I was with Muḥammad-'Alí Effendi. He complained a great deal about his brother, 'Abbás Effendi, and told me stories about Him which astonished me. He wept and lamented and then swore me to silence on the Holy Qur'án. These poor people have fallen into the abyss of misery and misfortune. "Things have gotten so bad that – there is no point concealing it from you – we are in need of daily bread but we cannot provide it. This morning the children were crying and asking for bread, but there was none to be found in the house. Bread, bread! This is what we have come to. And we cannot trust this matter to anyone," he told me. In short, I was so upset that I wanted to offer to lend him a sum, but I was too embarrassed to do it. Now I am wondering how I can send them some wheat without hurting their sensitivities.'"

The Shaykh then went on, "I continued to listen to the story with admirable patience. When he reached the words 'Bread, bread', I wanted to interrupt him, but his intensity would not have allowed my interruption and so I waited until he had finished. And then I said, 'You don't need to send any wheat. Go there right now and tell him that the Shaykh says that any time you need money, from one *lira* to one thousand *liras*, just send me a note and I will honour it.' Since it is contrary to customary financial practice, I did not wish to reveal the fact that Muḥammad-'Alí actually had an account with me and that his money was in my safe-deposit box. I just said, 'Tell him to instruct me and I will pay the sum.'

But my friend did not grasp my meaning, and retorted, 'O Shaykh, this man has integrity and cannot borrow money without collateral.'

'Excuse me,' I said, 'but in fact what he does have is money and what he is devoid of is integrity.' He shook his head and said, 'Maybe it is better to talk about something else.'

'Let's do something else,' I replied. 'Go and tell him that the <u>Sh</u>ay<u>kh</u> says, change into coins one *lira* of the sixty *liras* I sent you only two days ago, and with the coins go and buy bread for the children.' 'What sort of talk is this?' he replied. 'If this man had even just enough to barely keep alive, he could not talk to me with that degree of desperation and sorrow.'"

"In short," the <u>Sh</u>ay<u>kh</u> concluded, "I realized I had no alternative but to remove the veil and reveal the truth, and so I opened my safe-deposit box and extracted the note he had cashed the day before and showed it to him. I showed him the handwriting and the signature and told him, 'Now go to Muḥammad-'Alí and tell him to stop his begging, for no one will pay him the least attention.'

Once he saw the note he sighed and his face lost all colour. After a few minutes silence he said, 'May God be praised. I have made a terrible error of judgement. I was deceived by that devil and cursed my Master. Now what am I supposed to do?'

Weeping, he asked me to come here and make apologies on his behalf. He promised to present himself at a later time to kiss the hem of the Master's robe and personally ask forgiveness."

After that, the <u>Sh</u>ay<u>kh</u> added, "I have come to apologize on his behalf, and later he will come himself. But, Beloved, you should know that in this world you have only one enemy, and that is none other than your own brother."

* * *

The <u>Sh</u>ay<u>kh</u> drank his sweet coffee and took his leave. The Master then uttered some words about the lengths to which the Covenant-breakers were prepared to go to destroy the Faith. But as soon as He saw that the friends were becoming saddened, He spoke about other things and gave glad tidings of the future of the Faith. For example, He said, "Before long these difficulties will be solved and the Covenant-breakers' schemes will be thwarted. Be assured. The Faith of God will not become the plaything of the ignorant. These unfortunate people wish to go to such lengths and endure such suffering and pain just to oppose me. They struggle so much, they wear the garb of beggary and hold out the *kashkúl* towards anyone and everyone, and what have they gained from it all except 'Verily, this misery and beggary causes them injury'? Each of them might as well follow his leader, carry a *kashkúl* and make the rounds." And then He joked with a smile, "If I could find a *kashkúl*, I would send it to Mírzá Muḥammad-'Alí as a gift, so that he could walk the streets officially as a dervish and beg."

"Beloved," I said, "a *kashkúl* would be wasted on him, for it is something rare and precious. They are normally carried by selfless dervishes who have not the least intention of begging. While they walk around praising the Lord, anyone according to his own desire may voluntarily drop some coins in it. The word *kashkúl* is a misnomer, for a real dervish who wears the proper robe and carries the *kashkúl* does not beg, nor does he make any demands. But the begging bowl carried by real beggars is made out of a half-pumpkin."

'Abdu'l-Bahá asked, "How does that work?"

"They pierce the dried skin", I explained, "on both sides of the pumpkin, pass a string through each hole and tie a knot on each side, and then carry it on their arm and walk about in the streets and bazaars harassing people and persisting until they receive a *derham* or a *dinar*."

The Master said, "A pumpkin bowl! What a good idea." And then He stood up and left the room smiling. From then on the friends used to remark to each other, "A pumpkin bowl for the beggar – what a good idea!"

The effect on the pilgrims of meeting 'Abdu'l-Bahá

The talents and capacities of all those who entered the shores of this Most Great Ocean differed, of course, each profiting according to his own potential. For example, one who was devoid of any depth of spiritual understanding would find it sufficient to merely behold this boundless Ocean and marvel at its beauty. Another, who came with a small cup, would receive his cupful; while he who possessed a chalice would partake of a larger share. But true contentment and joy belonged to the one who ventured further, who was able to tread the deeper waters and acquire the hidden and priceless pearls and precious gems. It is then clear that capacity, worthiness, volition and effort were the first requirements. And so these were the conditions of those who besought 'Abdu'l-Bahá's heavenly blessings.

But the blessings of this Most Great Ocean, as ordained by its very nature, did not emanate with any uniform or predictable consistency. This boundless Ocean was sometimes calm; at other times it would surge; and at yet other times it was turbulent, leaving a variety of impressions in the minds of His listeners.

When calm and tranquil, He filled every observer's heart and soul with joy, breathed into them the spirit of faith, and bestowed upon them visions of the world of spirit. At other times, He brought out in them feelings of wonder and astonishment. Sometimes the wine of the love of God was so intoxicating that, utterly unaware of self, a person's entire being was transformed into a pair of eyes fixed on the exalted beauty of the Beloved.

Moreover, this state of selflessness and evanescence at the time of attaining His presence was the invariable, unchanging attitude of every believer, none of whom had any desire save His pleasure. It is said that a philosopher was asked, "What do you desire from God?" "I desire that I desire nothing," was His response.

And while the effect of His words and blessings bestowed on the hearers wings to soar into the heavenly, sanctified worlds of the spirit, it was not infrequent that, as He spoke, their prayers were answered, their deepest hopes and longings were realized, and their perplexing problems found solutions.

However, the essence of happiness and virtue was gained

by those who attained to the station of absolute nothingness and complete evanescence, as described in the revealed verse: "We are but drops which have hastened to join thy billowing ocean",[122] and who like drops entered the heaven of reunion and attained to the truth of: "Verily we are of God, and to Him shall we return".[123]

The manner of revealing verses

Various accounts have been left by pilgrims of the way in which verses were revealed. One says that "during the revelation of the verses, my limbs trembled", another says "my spirit soared", or "I found myself in another world". One says, "I saw the Master speaking Turkish while serving His Bahá'í and non-Bahá'í guests and simultaneously revealing verses in Arabic, as the secretary in attendance recorded them"; another says, "I saw with my own eyes that with His blessed hand He wrote down Arabic verses while conversing in Turkish." Still another says, "I saw Him writing in Persian and yet dictating Arabic verses to the secretary." In short, one speaks about the speed of His pen while another recounts His awesome power while revealing verses. Although some of these claims may seem exaggerated or distorted, they are in fact true, with due allowance for the fact that each pilgrim has expressed the truth according to the depth of his own understanding; none, however, has trodden the path of exaggeration and fancy.

For example, the one whose limbs trembled, or the one whose spirit soared, or who saw himself in another world, were obviously under the influence of the prevailing atmosphere of divine outpouring, as described in a previous chapter. And the one who observed the simultaneous performance of multiple tasks had witnessed yet another heavenly power possessed by that radiant Being, described earlier under the title, "One task does not distract Him from another".

Of course, there are many matters that nobody can adequately explain. I give the following story as an example, and afterwards I shall recount the manner of the revelation of verses, so far as my limited understanding permits.

Four years ago, two pilgrims returned from the holy threshold of the beloved Guardian of the Faith of God. One was endowed with the gift of eloquence, while the other was devoid thereof. In our meeting with the first one, he related to us in clear language the beloved Guardian's emphatic reminders regarding the maintenance of an up-to-date register of enrolment of the believers. As he continued his report, he quoted the Guardian: "Do not be overly concerned with the numerical size of the community. Do not enrol those who are not willing to declare their beliefs. One sincere, courageous believer is better than ten inactive weaklings."

In the same manner, we met with the second pilgrim and enquired about the news from the Holy Threshold. After a pause he said, "The beloved Guardian stated something to the effect that 'a hundred souls are more than a thousand souls; ten souls are more than a hundred souls, and one soul is more than ten souls.'" Now, it is clear that this person was not treading the path of exaggeration, but was expressing, however inadequately, his understanding of the same issue.

And now, regarding the effect of the revelation of divine verses on those present: it was often more powerful than the effect of the reunion itself. Once 'Abdu'l-Bahá was freed from His many daily engagements, He would call Áqá Mírzá Núru'd-Dín and begin dictating divine verses. At the same time, previously revealed Tablets were presented to 'Abdu'l-Bahá for His review, correction and signature. Here, He wrote in His own hand while simultaneously dictating verses, for He was the essential reality of the phrase "One task does not distract Him from another"; mental confusion had no meaning at that threshold.

However, it was also necessary at this hour for the many pilgrims – who were scattered all over 'Akká, some at the pilgrim house, some in the reception room downstairs and yet others in the streets and bazaars, all longingly waiting – to be given the opportunity of attaining the presence of 'Abdu'l-

Bahá. In this way, while relishing the joys of reunion they could also benefit from the wisdom of His words revealed in response to various complex questions.

Having been summoned to His presence, they would arrive and take their seats. After bestowing on each His expressions of love and greeting, He would again begin to reveal divine verses, at times uttering the words simply and distinctly in a powerful and commanding voice, at other times chanting the verses in that same melodious and heavenly tone which He used to chant Bahá'u'lláh's Tablet of Visitation.

Those in attendance were utterly overwhelmed as they listened. Yet at the same time they perceived, either explicitly or implicitly, answers to many of their own deep-seated personal questions. Some of the pilgrims considered the Master's words to be admonitions directed specifically to them. The atmosphere became charged with an indefinable emotional intensity, as spirits became attracted to the Abhá Kingdom. But alas, this warm and tender gathering, this retreat of love, was often disrupted by the arrival of non-Bahá'ís, for the door of 'Abdu'l-Bahá's house was open to all: no doorkeeper or watchman blocked the way to any guest.

Suddenly two or more guests would enter. If they were not enemies of the Cause, they would be received warmly by the Master with the words, "Welcome, welcome. How are you?" After imparting His expressions of love and greeting to each, the revelation of verses would begin again and that spiritual state would return. However, if they were not worthy, or if the number of people exceeded the capacity of the room, then with the words, "Go in the care of God," 'Abdu'l-Bahá would give permission for the friends to leave and would then return to His work. This is how Tablets were revealed when dictated to a secretary.

But more often than not, the Tablets were revealed in 'Abdu'l-Bahá's own hand and under the circumstances already described. When He found some free time and a private setting, He would take up the pen and begin to write. Yet He did not wish to abandon the pilgrims to themselves, or to leave them in a state of expectation, anticipation and weariness, and so when He brought out batches of incoming letters from His pocket and began to read them and write replies, He also remembered the pilgrims. Some of them might have been the originators of some of the letters, while a number of others might have been the couriers of these letters on behalf of other friends from various Eastern countries. In any case, when the Pen of 'Abdu'l-Bahá was in motion and no guests were in attendance, it was a good time for them to come in, sit down and be enraptured by the pleasure of nearness to Him.

As soon as they had been summoned and entered His presence they were greeted by His loving words, "Welcome, welcome, welcome". But while His words of loving greeting flowed uninterruptedly, His pen was in motion all the time. Sometimes He would enunciate the revealed words as He wrote them; at other times, silence dominated the room. Sometimes He would break the silence and urge the friends, "Go ahead and talk, I can hear you." Of course, they were helpless to utter a word, utterly overwhelmed and bedazzled as they were by that magical, wondrous countenance. However, the arrival of uninvited guests usually broke the wall of silence. Whether an Arab Sh̲ay̲kh or an Ottoman dignitary, one or several would arrive. Now the proper courtesies would be observed according to custom and as appropriate to the rank of the arriving guest. After a formal exchange of greetings, the pen would recommence its dash across the paper while the words flowed from His lips. If no one spoke, He would address the Arabs in Arabic, "O Sh̲ay̲kh, how are you?", or if the guests were Turks and remained quiet out of respect, He, with that radiant face and enchanting smile, would repeatedly urge them in Turkish to open the conversation. And if the silence persisted and no other sound save the scratching of the pen could be heard, He would repeat His request in Turkish so that perhaps someone would break the silence; as others gave their attention to the conversation, 'Abdu'l-Bahá too could participate in it.

Of course, such sessions did not always pass peacefully. At times, while 'Abdu'l-Bahá was absorbed in His work, certain individuals would come in and bring up various topics for discussion; these sometimes led to arguments, shouting and even altercation. Above all the clamour and uproar, undisturbed, 'Abdu'l-Bahá's pen continued its pace across the paper.

Lává Páshá was a case in point. He used to enter the Master's house through the back yard, shouting, "Hey, hey, Ismá'íl Áqá! Make me a delicious sweet cup of coffee". With his military boots and spurs clanking, he would climb the stairs rapidly and enter the room. Tall and lean, once inside he would bow before the Master and take 'Abdu'l-Bahá's hand in his with the intention of kissing it. When 'Abdu'l-Bahá refused the gesture by withdrawing His hand, Lává Páshá would humbly kiss his own fingertips as a sign of reverence and devotion; then he would immediately sit down and engage in conversation. Before long his ringing laughter would fill the room. Then without notice he would introduce a topic and enter into a heated debate, invariably asking 'Abdu'l-Bahá to endorse his views. During all this time the flow of divine revelation was neither interrupted nor suspended, until the work at hand was completed and Ismá'íl Áqá's sweet coffee was about to be served.

O my dear reader, the purpose of this lengthy description is so that we may understand the circumstances surrounding the revelation of all of these Writings, Tablets and prayers which enrapture our souls and transport us to the Abhá paradise, while at the same time enabling us to appreciate the many obstacles that were encountered and had to be overcome.

It is also interesting that while the act of witnessing the revelation of divine verses enthralled the devoted believers, it generated in non-believers and even those mischief-makers who might be present a state of humility and lowliness. The following story is presented as an example.

Two high-ranking Muslim divines, returning to Iran from their pilgrimage to Mecca, stopped in 'Akká for a visit. Outwardly, they were Muslims, but inwardly they inclined somewhat toward Yaḥyá or somewhere in between. Like all other pilgrims they were welcomed at the pilgrim house, and every day along with the rest of the pilgrims, and without receiving the slightest favour due to either background or rank, they too attained the Master's presence and left with the others. The visits to the Most Holy Shrine took place in similar fashion.

One day, the Master told Mírzá Ḥaydar-'Alí and myself, "These people are not here to seek the truth. Establish a warm, friendly relationship with them. Suspend all other work for a while, spend some time with them, and treat them with affection and kindness, so that they may return to their homes content and happy." We therefore deferred all normal duties and attended to them constantly. During the daytime we usually took them for long walks outside the gates of 'Akká, until word came of their permission to depart for Istanbul on a certain day and on a certain vessel.

One night we were in the presence of 'Abdu'l-Bahá along with the rest of the pilgrims. While busy writing, the Centre of the Covenant was also attending to all the incoming guests, both Bahá'ís and non-Bahá'ís. A few hours after sunset, the non-Bahá'ís were granted permission to take their leave, after which 'Abdu'l-Bahá addressed the friends. Gradually, signs of weariness began to appear in His blessed face; He dismissed everyone with the words, "Go in God's care." When all stood up, the Muslim Shaykh humbly put forward a request: "I beg that a Tablet may be revealed in the honour of Shaykh Hádí so that I may carry it to him."

(The late Áqá Shaykh Hádí was the most erudite and highest-ranking Muslim divine in Iran. He had a peculiar creed. Some suspected that he was secretly a Bahá'í and some believed him to be a Bábí; in any case, he had a large and devoted following.)

'Abdu'l-Bahá replied, "I have written to him recently; that should suffice."

But the Shaykh insisted, "I wish to be granted the honour of carrying to him such a gift."

'Abdu'l-Bahá then consented, "Very well, I shall write it." As we all began to leave the room, the Master said to Áqá Mírzá Núru'd-Dín, "I am very busy, but I do not want to put this off. I may as well write it now, or I won't have another opportunity to do so. So come and sit down and I will dictate a few words." Pen in hand, Áqá Mírzá Núru'd-Dín complied immediately.

The melodious chant of the Master filled the air, as divine verses in the Arabic tongue, indescribably eloquent and sublime, and with the rapidity of copious rain, flowed from His lips. God be praised, the atmosphere that dominated the hearts and the minds of those present is beyond description. The awesome power of that long, eloquent Tablet so overwhelmed every faculty of my being that neither pen nor tongue can describe it. As the poet says:

> *As in a dream, yet indescribable,*
> *Nor is the world ready to hear it.*

At last the Tablet was completed; at His command, "Go in God's care," we left the room, unconscious of ourselves and of each other and removed from this world as each of us sought our separate ways back to the pilgrim house. Darkness had enveloped the city, and I found myself walking in a very dark, narrow alleyway. Suddenly and quite unexpectedly I heard the voices of two men speaking Persian.

One was saying, "It certainly was a strange phenomenon. It affected me deeply."

The other agreed, "Yes, the words were not His; yet He who spoke them spoke the truth."

They continued in this vein, to the effect that the words had been revealed through divine inspiration from the unseen world. These were the same two individuals who had asked to handcarry Mírzá Hádí's Tablet to Tehran. That night at the dinner table they seemed intoxicated, as though they had just awakened from a trance. Next day, having received their instructions to depart, they began their return journey utterly transformed, carrying with them Mírzá Hádí's Tablet. It is thus clear that the magnetic attraction of the divine utterance enraptured not only the spirits of the believers, but also stole the unyielding hearts of the non-believers.

Fridays

Friday morning was a time of joy for the poor of 'Akká; a time of praise and reward for the schoolchildren; and a time of soul-searching, discovery and often astonishment for the pilgrims to the Holy Land. One part of this festivity of the poor and the disabled, which greatly resembled Jesus Christ's charity to the poor and needy, was observed one Friday morning by the above-mentioned Mr. Phelps from his window overlooking the front courtyard, and is exquisitely described in his book.[124] Other parts, namely the opening and closing ceremonies of this happy day, left lasting impressions and were recorded in the memories of those believers who observed and experienced these events.

It is Friday morning, and in the area in front of the *bírúní* of 'Abdu'l-Bahá's house there is a commotion. Crowds of hopeful poor and disabled people from neighbouring villages have come to town and have filled every available inch of space in the courtyard. Young, old, children, adults, men, women – all in a variety of worn-out clothes, all disabled and sickly, downtrodden, helpless and downcast, sighing and lamenting, await the return of the Master of the house. Having had their breakfasts, the pilgrims too have come to view the spectacle. The small children, the pupils of a modest school in 'Akká, each carrying their notebooks, their completed writing exercises, and their pens and ink pots, enter the area and run to the front yard. The servants have already swept the yard and watered the lawns and are busy with other things. But all impatiently await the arrival of the Master.

No one knows where He might have gone so early on a Friday morning, before the rising of the sun. Unlike Haifa, the fortress of 'Akká is devoid of open spaces and wide beaches where He might have repaired for prayer and meditation. Possibly, He has gone to visit those of the poor who rise early to perform their obligatory prayers and await the coming of their beneficent and noble guest. Anyone who has ever accompanied 'Abdu'l-Bahá on such days to the humble dwellings of this group of the needy, knows that these are people who have encountered misfortune in their lives and have fallen from a position of wealth to the depths of poverty. And since they have never asked for a helping hand, they have gained a special place in 'Abdu'l-Bahá's heart. It is related that the Prophet Muḥammad counselled: "Have pity on the wealthy who have fallen on hard times."

Now, in those homes, the Master is caring for the needy: giving counsel to one, praying for another, offering hope of material success to a third, prescribing medical remedies for yet another, and giving glad tidings of the confirmations of the Holy Spirit to all. Then, as He begins to take His leave, with a radiant and happy face He hands each a sum of money that will cover his expenses for the week.

On His return He enters through the front gate. The waiting poor press forward to reach Him, extending their hands; each according to his own beliefs begins to praise and glorify the name of the Lord. These poor people, usually numbering around sixty to seventy souls, have not come here only for money. One wants a prayer, one implores healing, one desires success in earning a livelihood. In short, whatever ails them, they confide in 'Abdu'l-Bahá and ask for a remedy. The crowd is unruly and troublesome as they press forward. With kind words, He consoles all and as He begins to disburse money, since there is no particular order or queue some stand up twice, and some pry out more than they deserve. 'Abdu'l-Bahá's command, therefore, is firm and loud: "Sit down, everyone sit down. Whoever refuses to sit down will miss out and whoever rises out of turn will not receive a share."

Some semblance of order returns. Now they are seated in two rows with a narrow space between them. And so, in an orderly fashion, from one side He begins to hand out money.

After receiving it, no-one has the right to move, so that the Master may not confuse the one already rewarded with a newcomer.

He sends away unrewarded the strong-bodied, lazy individuals. He refuses the children so that they may not develop the habit of begging. To those who are disabled, with whom He is better acquainted, He is more generous. In the meantime the pilgrims, standing around in corners leaning against the wall with their arms crossed on their chests, observe the proceedings with wonder and receive a lesson in true service, learning the meaning of kindliness and compassion.

Biting a finger in astonishment, Wisdom gazes
As it contemplates that incomparable being that amazes

My longing for you consumes me to the core
Like a candle that burns until it is no more

If on resurrection day any desired wish I am given
I take the Beloved and leave for you earth and heaven

The festival of the poor has come to an end. The friends follow 'Abdu'l-Bahá into the outer yard. Here, a more delightful festival takes place. The festival of the poor ended, now is time for the celebration of the Bahá'í children. But 'Abdu'l-Bahá has not as yet found an opportunity to rest.

The schoolchildren are standing in line according to their height, holding their completed handwriting exercises and waiting for 'Abdu'l-Bahá's arrival so that they too may receive His heart-warming attention, His generous favours and gifts, and His spiritual teachings. First, 'Abdu'l-Bahá walks quickly to the nearby sink to wash away the effects of the many blemishes and marks left on His hands by the hasty assaults of the poor, eager to extract their share from His hands. Then He prepares to meet the children.

Here, some twenty-two or -three children are standing in line. After bestowing upon them words of affection and love,

He first enquires from their teacher after their manner of conduct and behaviour. Then, He takes the completed exercise sheet from an older child and reviews it. The reed pen, already cut to a suitable tip, is ready in the hand of the student, who gives it to the Master. "This must be written this way. This letter should be written somewhat higher. The straight lines have not been adhered to." In short, He reviews each one, praising some and giving proper instruction to others. "This time you have written better," or "Your handwriting has got worse!" When He reaches the younger children He treats them with special affection and shares with them a few humorous words. Then at random, He takes their English homework and asks some of the students a few questions. He paces up and down the line, paying attention to the details of their lessons. He even examines the cleanliness of their hands. Finally, He offers some advice regarding certain general topics such as one's manners and conduct, then He talks about turning to God and about the nature of religion. Gradually His words gain momentum, and the pilgrims and residents who are standing some distance away move closer. As He paces up and down, 'Abdu'l-Bahá's words become so moving that one feels transformed, finding oneself in a different world. The effect is so intense that while soaring in the world of spirit one becomes aware of one's past and future shortcomings. Each according to his capacity and understanding clearly discerns that reality which is sanctified beyond any word or mention. On the one hand he forgets the world of being and all that is therein, and on the other he beholds the invisible and recognizes the unrecognizable. On the wings of spirit he soars to such heights that he would refuse the possession of this world were it to be offered to him.

God be praised, for the sake of these children the bounty of utterance has surged to such lofty heights, carrying His listeners to heavenly worlds beyond. It is to be hoped that through this bounty, worldly listeners may receive spiritual perfections and His earth-bound devotees may discover heavenly virtues.

As soon as the talk ends, out comes the moneybag. There are plenty of quarter-*majídí* and two-*qurushi* pieces to go around. He starts with the top student and works down to the smaller children. What makes it more wonderful is that as He passes out the coins He continues to entertain the children with humorous remarks and funny stories. Having completed the task, He takes a seat in the *bírúní* reception room, and along with the rest of the friends enjoys a round of sweet coffee. He spends a few more minutes attending to the pilgrims. Suddenly He notices that His pockets are heavy. It is the letters from the friends that are as yet unanswered. He rises immediately, summons one of His secretaries and climbs the stairs to the upper floor. But Friday is a public holiday, and non-Bahá'ís, too, wish to see Him. They come in groups. And so the dictation of Tablets will have to wait for another time. In the afternoon, the pilgrims and residents arrive together to visit 'Abdu'l-Bahá and visit Bahjí in accordance with His command, some on foot and others using carriages.

So this is Friday's schedule. On Sundays, however, which is a Christian holiday, most of the visitors are Christians. On Sunday mornings 'Abdu'l-Bahá visits only the Christian poor, and in the evenings the Christian dignitaries come to visit Him.

My dear reader, in this third chapter of the book the pen has run wild and the story grown long. But alas, alas, not even this overly-long presentation can truly depict a drop from the ocean of what I can remember observing. What I experienced at that threshold requires another than I, a different pen than my inadequate one. Therefore, to comfort the minds and gladden the hearts of the friends, I present below one of 'Abdu'l-Bahá's short prayers revealed at a time of difficulties and troubles, to bring this chapter to a happy conclusion; and through the power of these transforming words I entreat Him for heavenly confirmations for you and for myself.

O Thou Pure and Omnipotent God! O Thou my kind Lord! Grant me such power as to enable me to withstand the onslaught of the peoples and kindreds of the world, and give me such might as to cause the waves of my endeavours, like unto the Pacific Ocean, to reach the shores of both East and West.[125]

CHAPTER FOUR

He is the Glory of the Most Glorious!

The Prison City again – one year later

In the days following the first anniversary of the renewal of confinement in the Most Great Prison, Eastern pilgrims would arrive to visit the Master, either separately or in small groups, so keeping the pilgrim house lively.

The resident friends thought that in the absence of any further mischief, the time had come to gradually lift the restrictions calling for confinement within the Prison City of 'Akká. This idea was reinforced by the fact that the Governor of 'Akká, as well as other officials, considered it a shameful act to imprison a blessed personage such as 'Abdu'l-Bahá, who was an advocate of spiritual values and a promoter of the principles of love and humanity. Sometimes the Governor himself, while in the Master's presence, would entreat Him to feel free to leave the town and take his walks in the open countryside outside the city walls, but 'Abdu'l-Bahá would not accept this.

The friends also felt that the Covenant-breakers, having failed in their seditious activities and having lost all hope of carrying out any further mischief, should feel grateful to have regained their freedom through the Master's intercession. They had succeeded in their efforts to acquire the government order for the reincarceration of the Beloved of the world, and yet owed their own freedom to His compassion and benevolence. Doing evil, they had received goodness in return; unfaithful themselves, yet they had witnessed love and fidelity. Having regained their freedom, they had returned to their happy lives in the Mansion of Bahjí. It was to be hoped that they felt ashamed of what they had done, that they would now cease their mischief-making and having learned their lesson would choose peaceful coexistence. But alas, alas, the truth was quite otherwise. Not only were they free of remorse, but their hostility was now even greater, demonstrating their true nature even more clearly than before. As the poet says:

Moon shines and dog barks,
Each according to its nature.

Yes, they had misused their freedom, sending their agents to various cities to sow more seeds of mischief. They had been in communication with the governors of various provinces to submit their allegations and charges; all this now resulted in new restrictions and hardships afflicting 'Abdu'l-Bahá, closing the gates of reunion to the faces of the pilgrims. The pilgrim house was now empty, and more important, it was no longer possible to use the city of Haifa as the centre for all correspondence, for secret agents of the Government were assigned to confiscate all incoming communications there. Even the letters which arrived in Haifa in care of the late Ḥájí Siyyid Táqí Manshádí – who was also responsible for forwarding 'Abdu'l-Bahá's Tablets – were no longer safe, and so the centre for correspondence was shifted to Port Said in accordance with 'Abdu'l-Bahá's instructions.

Áqá Aḥmad Yazdí was appointed at that location to receive all correspondence from both East and West and to transmit it to 'Akká by all means available. Similarly, he was to receive and dispatch the Tablets revealed in response so that they might be kept safe from being opened and confiscated by government officials, and from the Covenant-breakers' hostile schemes.

The progress of the construction work on the Shrine of the Báb on Mount Carmel was very slow at this time, but thank God, it never slowed to a halt. Only, for a long period of time permission for pilgrimage was denied to all applicants and so in the second year of the renewal of confinement, the city of 'Akká did not witness the busy traffic of pilgrims coming and going; for a time Mírzá Ḥaydar-'Alí was even sent by 'Abdu'l-Bahá to other cities to teach the Faith, which for all practical purposes left the pilgrim house deserted. However, the flood of correspondence from East and West continued to pour into 'Akká. 'Abdu'l-Bahá's time was totally occupied; meanwhile no one was granted permission to travel to 'Akká and thus every applicant privately cursed the Covenant-breakers for having precipitated this situation.

But this renewal of confinement, with all its resulting hardships, gave new lustre to the Cause of God around the world. Although the city of 'Akká was quiet, every corner of the world was abuzz with activity. The friends in various parts of the globe began to take action, sending heart-rending letters to 'Akká. Several letters from the Western friends, signed by seven hundred to eight hundred individuals, expressed their readiness to sacrifice their lives so that the decree of imprisonment might be lifted. In short, as the hardships increased, so did the intensity of the attention and attraction of the friends around the world; the more pressure was applied at the centre, the stronger became the eruption of heavenly light from every nook and cranny. In fact, like the power of pressurized steam, which when confined in a closed space will begin to spew out at the sides, this power, too, began to erupt from various parts of the globe. They tried to impede the flow of its uncontrollable energy, but its abundance flooded the world.

When these letters from the West arrived and I could see the progress of the Faith, I was reminded of 'Abdu'l-Bahá's words when He had sent me to Haifa bearing the frightful news of the renewal of His incarceration within the walls of 'Akká. He had said, "This imprisonment will lead to the advancement of the Cause and is the comfort of my heart." And therefore, when the friends were facing the onslaught of the harshest tests and difficulties in 'Akká, and suffering pangs of melancholy and despair, 'Abdu'l-Bahá's joyful demeanour and encouraging attitude transformed that sadness into gladness, that despair into hope. At the same time the rapid progress of the Cause increased their wonder and astonishment. This was especially true of me, for I was the translator of these letters, and at times I became so overcome with joy and delight at the incoming glad tidings that I lost all sense of reality.

Sometimes the contents of the letters were verses of love; sometimes, religious and philosophical issues; and at other times, scientific questions that I was incapable of understanding and for which, therefore, I could prepare only a literal translation. However, I derived a great deal of knowledge from reading the replies to them.

In accordance with 'Abdu'l-Bahá's instructions many of these translations were sent to Tehran so that Áqá Mírzá 'Alí-Akbar Khán Rawhání, the Secretary of the Assembly, could copy and distribute them to the community. Verses either in the lyrical[126] or laudatory[127] style, and their translations into Persian verse, received 'Abdu'l-Bahá's commendation. Sometimes He particularly wished English verse to be translated into Persian verse, and of course whatever He particularly wished acquired heavenly confirmation, so that the resulting translation received His approval.

And now I give some of the poems that were received and translated. Here is one written by Mr. Walter George of New York and entitled "The Star of 'Akká".[128] Here are the first few lines of the poem:

Above the darkened earth, in God's heavenly throne
The Star of Bethlehem once again has shone.
Peace, love and brotherhood have found true meaning,
Loss and hardship no more – victory's light is beaming.
He is the All Glorious!

This is the translation of the poem written by Margaret Kern, which appears in her book proving the truth of the Cause.[129] These soul-stirring verses were written for 'Abdu'l-Bahá.

> *Of Throne of Glory Thou art King,*
> *O Master, to serve Thee is my calling.*
> *I long to sacrifice in Thy path*
> *My heart and soul, my life's last breath.*

Among the famed poets who wrote beautiful lyric verses for the Master was Mrs. Louisa Spencer.[130] Here is a sample of her poetry:

> *His glorious Sun has risen, to set for us no more;*
> *The echo of His praises now rings from shore to shore;*
> *He came to banish darkness, to show the perfect way.*
> *This is the radiant morning of the millenial day!*
>
> *Go tell the joyous tidings: His Kingdom now hath come!*
> *Wherein all pain and sorrow, and every doubt succumb;*
> *Established here on earth it is, and "whosoever will"*
> *May enter in, and love divine and peace his heart shall fill.*
>
> *He came and dwelt among us, with all His wondrous Powers;*
> *His Love embraced all nature – the birds, the trees, the flowers;*
> *King of a Royal Kingdom, we praise Thy Holy name;*
> *The glorious Sun has risen, its Light no more to wane!*

Numerous wonderful verses full of meaning were speedily translated, and in accordance with 'Abdu'l-Bahá's instructions recited aloud in the presence of the friends and also sent to Iran.

There were also certain letters which possessed a special quality. They came from gnostics and Sufi mystics and contained certain subtle terminology and mystical concepts which no one but 'Abdu'l-Bahá could understand. But as I translated His replies, the hidden meanings were revealed.

One such correspondent, who seemed to live in a trance-like state of dreams and spiritual discovery, was none other than Amatu'lláh Miss Sarah Farmer, the founder of Green Acre Bahá'í School. Many of her visions and prognostications came true. Her approach to the discovery and understanding of truth, her method of reasoning and her logical arguments not only closely resembled those of the early Bábís, but also served to elucidate their many mystical and obscure concepts.

There were many such believers, both men and women, at that time; some of them posed substantial and abstruse questions and received cogent replies, which I sent to Iran along with their respective translations.

The believers in the Millenium, those who awaited the impending return of Jesus Christ and expected His reign to last no less than a thousand years, showed great interest and submitted a number of enquiries. In addition to the correspondence from the believers, there were many newspaper articles containing favourable references to the Faith. The dissemination of these in Iran by Mírzá 'Alí-Akbar Khán Rawhání, who was responsible for such proclamation efforts, served to awaken and admonish the heedless.

Many of the American believers, whose efforts to visit 'Abdu'l-Bahá had been frustrated by His imprisonment, spent much time in prayer and wrote heart-rending letters imploring 'Abdu'l-Bahá for the reopening of the doors of reunion. In short, the second year of imprisonment, more than any other period, brings to mind the painful sighs and lamentations of the believers of the West.

The arrival of certain Western believers wearing the *fez* in the Ottoman style

At this time, not unlike the period of the incarceration of Bahá'u'lláh, those friends who desperately longed to attain the presence of 'Abdu'l-Bahá would have been satisfied to travel long distances from far-off lands so that, standing outside the gates of the city, they too could gaze unwaveringly at the wall of the prison fortress and focus their adoring glances on the window of His cell which overlooked the open fields and the moat circling the fortress, that perchance they might steal one glimpse of the Beloved and then return to their homes.

But praise be to God, hardship had not as yet reached that level of intensity. The grandeur and glory of the Head of the Cause was intact and the gates of 'Akká were open to all; no one expressed any discourtesy towards the followers of 'Abbás Effendi unless they were foreigners, or unless the Covenant-breakers had discovered their identity and informed the authorities at Beirut or the government headquarters at Istanbul. Therefore, if rarely one of the Western friends arrived in an Ottoman-style *fez*[131] and stayed only briefly, the time would be too short for the Covenant-breakers to initiate any mischief. And so, every so often one of the Western friends, having fervently implored 'Abdu'l-Bahá to attain His presence, and having applied endlessly and persistently for that precious opportunity, would be granted permission to make the journey. Once at Port Said, he would receive proper instructions and a report on the situation in 'Akká; armed with that information and a *fez* in the Ottoman style, he would arrive at Haifa, and avoiding contact with foreign guests at any of the hotels, he would cautiously travel directly to 'Akká.

For a period of one or two days he would attain the presence of the Master without meeting anyone else. After that, happy and contented, and with great caution, he would return to Port Said. Thus rejuvenated and filled with heavenly joy, he would become the bearer of glad-tidings of the well-being of 'Abdu'l-Bahá to the friends of the West.

But the journey of the ladies was uncomplicated. Firstly, these visitors were dressed in the habit of the Christian women of 'Akká; secondly, they never left the Master's House unless accompanied by the ladies of the household, and then only to visit the Most Holy Shrine; third, if someone recognized them, the position of English teacher was an obvious and acceptable explanation to justify their presence. Examples of these were Mrs. Lua Getsinger, Mrs. Jackson, Amatu'l-Bahá Miss Barney, and others who in recent years had come quite frequently and stayed in 'Abdu'l-Bahá's residence for long periods.

But the men were not received in this manner, since at the Covenant-breakers' instigation they could easily become objects of suspicion. Spying and political conspiracy were the most frequent charges on which they could be accused. These suspicions and accusations had grown to such far-fetched levels that they [the Covenant-breakers] had tried to convince the Ottoman authorities that the Shrine of the Báb was in fact a storehouse for military arms.

Mr. and Mrs. Winterburn

Two of the visitors to the exalted threshold during that time of turmoil and suffering, and in the midst of the harshest onslaught of tests and difficulties, were Mr. and Mrs. Winterburn. It had been a year since this couple had received their permission to visit 'Abdu'l-Bahá. Suspending the normal course of their lives, they had embarked on their journey. Once in Paris, because of the outbreak of fresh crises and the subsequent onset of restrictions and hardships in 'Akká, they had received a telegram instructing them to postpone their travel plans until further notice. They had spent several months in a state of anxiety and prayer, until they received permission to travel to Port Said. But again, further unrest – the gales of fresh test and trials – halted their journey; on 'Abdu'l-Bahá's instructions they stayed in Egypt for some time, bewildered and disconcerted.

At last, after a full year, permission was granted for them to travel. Practising much caution and prudence, they arrived at 'Akká and attained the presence of 'Abdu'l-Bahá at His residence. This was at a time when the pilgrim house was totally deserted. Even Ḥájí Mírzá Ḥaydar-'Alí had been sent to 'Ishqábád by the Master. There remained only an old

Zoroastrian Bahá'í from Bombay with his ten-year-old child, who for some reason were unable to secure transportation to depart. At that time, the hardships were so intense that even the daily comings and goings of the friends were carried out with extreme caution. Even the nightly gatherings at 'Abdu'l-Bahá's *bírúní* reception room had been suspended.

The arrival of these two guests was so secret that not even the resident Bahá'ís were aware of it. Mrs. Winterburn was housed with the ladies of the household and Mr. Winterburn was given a small room. A pilgrim who had endured so much pain and agony to achieve his heart's desire obviously had great appreciation for the blessing granted to him. He hardly ever left his room and spent much time in prayer and meditation. He committed to memory everything he observed and wrote down all that he heard. In the presence of 'Abdu'l-Bahá, he sat in a state of utter awe and wonderment while beholding the countenance of the Beloved, and since he had endured much suffering in his year-long odyssey in Europe and Egypt, he became the recipient of much love and compassion. One day he asked me, "Is it possible for me to meet one of my Persian brothers?"

I was quite moved by this request and gave him a not too definitive response. It just so happened that the old Zoroastrian Bahá'í expressed the same desire to meet Mr. Winterburn. I left the issue open pending 'Abdu'l-Bahá's permission. Happily, having secured the permission and with great caution and care, the meeting between the old man and his son and the Winterburns took place the next day.

As soon as the old man, in his long, faded *'abá* and dome-like hat, his black beard unkempt, reached the entrance of the room along with his child and was greeted by the American couple, there was an indescribable outburst of feelings; cries of joy filled the room. Mr. Winterburn ran to meet the old man and embraced him, while his wife took the child in her arms, as tears of happiness flowed and the meaning of the phrase, "East shall embrace the West", was truly demonstrated. In such a meeting the social conventions and the ceremonies of introduction had no meaning or application, for in addition to the effects of their warm handshakes and loving embraces, their spirits were so united and their hearts so attracted that any words spoken by the introducer and translator would have been superfluous. There was no need to talk or translate. The one, in pure Persian[132] and with a Pársí accent repeated, "May my life be a sacrifice for you," while the other, in English and with an American accent, returned the sentiments with words of love and affection. So I had nothing to do. I just stood there and shared in this outburst of intense emotion, until at last each wiped away the other's tears from his own face and they sat down.

I asked Mr. Winterburn the reason for so much tearful emotion. He said, the Pársís are the lost brothers, as mentioned in the Holy Scriptures,[133] and now they have been found. Having said this, he looked at his brother again, rose and joyfully shook his hand, and then returned to his seat.

There was not much else to say. Whatever was necessary had already been said in a way which is sanctified above words and letters. After a few more minutes and further expressions of salutations and best wishes, the meeting ended. But for me, the memory of it shall endure forever, and the account of it in these pages shall, I hope, bring joy and inspiration to many hearts.

Mr. Frank Frank

Another of the American friends who visited 'Abdu'l-Bahá in the midst of these restrictions and hardships was Mr. Frank Frank. His first and last names were an indication of his honesty and sincerity – truly befitting, for he was characterized by truthfulness and simplicity of conduct. Having accepted the Cause, and filled with love and anticipation, he had decided to visit the Holy Land. In Port Said he had received a message detaining him until further notice. The local believers had pleaded in his behalf, beseeching 'Abdu'l-Bahá for permission, and it had been decided that he could come, but with great caution and vigilance.

On his arrival in Haifa, one of the Christian troublemakers, an enemy of the Faith who was a translator and guide for foreign travellers, deceived him by claiming devotion to the Faith and firmness in the Covenant and accompanied him to 'Akká, functioning as his translator. When Mírzá Núru'd-Dín and I were in 'Abdu'l-Bahá's presence, the news was brought of this American pilgrim by the name of Frank who had just arrived accompanied by that deceitful spy.

'Abdu'l-Bahá was quite annoyed. He instructed me to "go and attend to that traveller downstairs and send the troublemaker to me". I immediately found Mr. Frank, and after the exchange of loving greetings I asked him, "When you were in Port Said, did you receive any instructions regarding observance of caution when travelling from Haifa to 'Akká?"

"Yes, I travelled with extreme care and prudence," he answered.

"Where did you get to know this rascal?" I asked.

"This man came to me as soon as I got here and greeted me with the Bahá'í greeting of Alláh'u'Abhá. He told me the latest news of the Cause and asked after the health of many of the American believers by name and background. He even claimed that he had been awaiting my arrival for some time. Then he declared his devotion and obedience to 'Abdu'l-Bahá, expressed his gratitude to Him for having sent his children to school abroad, and added, 'We owe our whole existence to 'Abdu'l-Bahá.' I asked him if he had any occupation other than his translation work and he explained, 'Here, there is no freedom of the press. So with the help of 'Abdu'l-Bahá I have started a small manual print shop where I print business cards.' And so I promised to help him and brought him here with me."

"Everything that he has said is true, except that he has just left out one detail: he happens to be a deceitful man, a collaborator of the Covenant-breakers and an associate of the enemies of the Faith," I informed him. In brief, I advised him of the situation in the Holy Land and explained the verse: "Do not believe everything you hear and do not trust all who approach you." Indirectly, I awakened him to the fact that, as the poet says,

So often does Satan appear in human form,
Do not shake just any hand that is offered.

Once Mr. Frank realized what had happened, he was very taken aback but remained quiet. At this point we were summoned to the presence of 'Abdu'l-Bahá, just as the deceitful guide was being dismissed from His presence. Once in the Master's presence, and while Mr. Frank was expressing his sentiments of humble devotion and servitude, I wondered by what heavenly strategy and celestial skill had 'Abdu'l-Bahá got rid of that insidious character.

As soon as we left His presence I found Mírzá Núru'd-Dín and asked him, "How was Mr. Guide thrown out?"

"Whatever it was," he said, "it was heaven-sent, because he repented and promised never to approach any of the friends of God again. Here are the details: as he entered the room, 'Abdu'l-Bahá spoke to him sternly and warned him: 'What sort of deception and hypocrisy is this that you commit against your own religion? You are a Christian and receive an income from the Protestant Society, and yet you betray your own Faith by bringing American travellers to me so that I may invite them into the Bahá'í Faith? To them you say negative things about me and you receive a salary for teaching your Faith. But by guiding them to me you betray your own conscience. Do you want me to write a few words which would cause your dismissal?' – and other words in this vein. The guide was taken aback. He began to tremble, grasped 'Abdu'l-Bahá's *'abá* and said, 'O my Master, I repent. I did wrong. Please don't take away my livelihood!' 'Very well, I forgive you this time. But if you commit such an act of betrayal again, I will acquaint the Christian Mission with the details of your activities,' responded 'Abdu'l-Bahá. Then the guide swore that he would never again meet with any American Bahá'í pilgrims or even approach them. So he was dismissed, and ran all the way back to Haifa."

Mr. Frank was given the small room upstairs and was offered hospitality at the dinner table of 'Abdu'l-Bahá. He had had no idea that he would be treated as a guest and receive so much kindness and attention. He whispered to me, "I imagined that I would have to prostrate myself from afar, like visiting the Pope, approach on my knees and be dismissed after a short visit. And now I see that we eat at the same table! Since I never considered myself worthy of such a station, please ask if I may be excused."

When I communicated his request, 'Abdu'l-Bahá showed him even more kindness and bestowed on him an even larger measure of His heart-warming attention and regard.

In addition to the dinner table, which was the customary place and time of meetings, 'Abdu'l-Bahá summoned him on other occasions as well. Yet while expressing himself with utter simplicity and without any preconceived design, he used to say curious things and ask for odd favours. For example, he had purchased a small Egyptian silk rug to offer as a gift to 'Abdu'l-Bahá. As he presented it, he remarked, "I wish to make You a gift of this rug, but with the condition that whoever may in the future be the recipient of this gift from the hand of the Master must be a Bahá'í. I would not be happy if a non-Bahá'í were to step on it."

'Abdu'l-Bahá smiled lovingly, agreeing to the condition. "Rest assured, I will find a good place for it so that no non-Bahá'í may tread on it," the Master assured him. I thought that it would be earmarked for the Most Holy Shrine, but later I discovered that the station of that rug was even loftier than what I had imagined. This rug became the site before which thousands of sincere believers would prostrate themselves in worship: it draped the bench upon which the two or three photographs of Bahá'u'lláh and the Primal Point were placed.

From that time on and for many years, when the pilgrims came to behold these pictures, it was this rug that they kissed in reverence as they prostrated themselves, and perhaps it still remains so. In any case, the utter simplicity and true sincerity of this man brought joy to 'Abdu'l-Bahá. His words created a happy atmosphere. After two full days, he received permission to depart and for some time the friends continued to mention his name.

One night, when the Master was remembering this man and praising his simplicity and inner purity, the late Áqá Riḍáy-i-Qannád said, "I see that the American friends have overtaken us Persian believers and have surpassed us in every service."

'Abdu'l-Bahá remarked, "From America, I await the appearance of a few people. Soon they will appear. And then you will behold unprecedented victories for the Cause." And then He brought up a matter which He had repeatedly mentioned before. He said,

"The Persian friends have been tested and therefore they are firmly established. This will not happen in other places. The Persian friends have witnessed tests the like of which will not be seen again in the world. I am not saying that the Western friends will not experience tests and difficulties; they may, indeed, experience the harshest tests and in the realm of sacrifice and self-consecration, like the Persian friends, be subjected to much hardship and agony, since faith without test is not possible. However, the tests that the Persian friends have endured, others in the world will not experience their like. But tests are not of just one or two kinds and therefore they will somehow be tested and you will witness their triumph in enduring and overcoming those tests. And yet, the like of those tests experienced by the Persian Bahá'ís will not be witnessed again. For example, one of those tests was the rebellion of Mírzá Yaḥyá. The world will not witness another Mírzá Yaḥyá rising against the Cause. But you will see how they will overcome their own tests. That is why I say that the Persian friends have established themselves. For example, was the uprising of the Covenant-breakers a small matter? This type of rebellion will not take place again in the world. Yes, the Persian friends have been subjected to this type of tests and that is why they have become confirmed. Obviously the Western friends will witness grave tests, but the tests of the Persian friends were a different thing." And again He added, "I await the emergence of those few; they will soon appear."

It is clear that after some thirty-two years, the words and expressions used in these accounts cannot be the exact words of the Master. However, this was His theme, and He had frequently made these remarks before, emphasizing the fact that the Persian Bahá'ís were most firmly established, in such a way that is not forgettable. After these words, He once again praised the sincerity and honesty of Mr. Frank.

Further progress of the Faith in the East; construction of the Mashriqu'l-Adhkár in 'Ishqábád

In the years 1902 and 1903 the progress of the Faith in Iran, India and Russia was very rapid. The increased restrictions in 'Akká brought about a swift expansion of the frontiers of the Faith around the globe. While the actions of the Covenant-breakers elicited in reaction feelings of aversion and disgust in the friends, the receipt of news from abroad brought comfort, joy and hope in similar measure. Bahá'í institutions began to be formed. Local Spiritual Assemblies were established in major cities. The foundation of the Cause of God gained strength and power. As sorrow and distress increased at the centre, joy and solace poured in from abroad.

We all waited impatiently to receive glad tidings from far-away lands, to heal the wounds and relieve the pain. And praised be God, we were never disappointed or discouraged. And while the Post Office in 'Akká was controlled by the enemies of the Cause, life-giving news and glad-tidings from the East reached the friends every week and infused a spirit of joy in their hearts. The crisis of Yazd passed, yielding its expected fruits. The blood shed in the path of God produced marvellous results; the gatherings and meetings which had been held in secret became open and free; the Government adopted a more conciliatory approach; the injustices of the clergy were cut short; the Covenant-breakers failed in their plots to sow further seeds of doubt, as the more they wrote, the more disgrace they brought upon themselves; and so the vision of 'Abdu'l-Bahá slowly began to find its fulfilment.

There appeared an especially great movement in 'Ishqábád. The sanctified blood of Mírzá Riḍá the martyr[134] left its effect, in that the friends were able to begin the construction of the first Bahá'í House of Worship (Mashriqu'l-Adhkár) in the world. This happy news brought much joy to the friends in 'Akká and much pain and disappointment to the violators of the Covenant. The news was announced to the friends by 'Abdu'l-Bahá in a wonderful and happy meeting.

One night, when all the resident believers were gathered in the *bírúní* reception area, 'Abdu'l-Bahá made an announcement: "Although the scope of Jináb-i-Ḥájí Vakílu'd-Dawlih's business activities has become severely restricted, nevertheless, having estimated the total worth of his wealth to be some twenty thousand *tumans*, he has decided to consecrate the whole sum to the construction of the Mashriqu'l-Adhkár. Moreover, despite his state of health and weakened condition, he has taken it upon himself to begin the construction activities and has therefore started on the excavation work. I have written to him that the construction of this type of public Bahá'í institution requires the participation of the entire Bahá'í community."[135]

After this, He bestowed on him many blessings and again explained the importance and necessity of universal participation in such projects; that a single individual should not undertake alone the construction of a great edifice, but that everyone should participate, no matter how modestly. He repeated that universal participation was necessary and required.

Thus He concluded his remarks: "Since all the friends will

participate in this sacred undertaking, it will be befitting that the believers who reside at this sanctified Threshold collect and dispatch a sum, as a gesture of love and sacrifice, to attract divine confirmations." Then again He added, "It is obvious that the friends here possess no wealth. However, regardless of the size of their contribution, it will still have a vital impact on erecting such a divinely ordained institution. I myself have sent a certain sum, and anyone who wishes to make a pledge can remit the equivalent amount to Áqá Riḍá; once all the pledges are collected the sum will be sent."

He uttered these words in such a state of heavenly delight that all spirits soared with transports of joy. It should be obvious how intense were the emotions of joy and ecstasy of a people who had been wronged, who had suffered subjugation and imprisonment in the Prison City of 'Akká, and who over the course of many years had received no news but reports of suffering, anguish, and accusations, both from within the prison fortress and abroad – when suddenly they receive so explicitly from the lips of the Beloved of the world such tidings of success and victory as to discover that the foundation stone of the first Bahá'í temple in the world has been laid!

Utterly enthralled and oblivious of self, as he drank heartily from the intoxicating wine of 'Abdu'l-Bahá's words, was Áqá Ḥabíb Mesgar (coppersmith), one of the indigent friends among the emigrants.[136] Rising, he walked up to 'Abdu'l-Bahá, then knelt and prostrated himself in thanksgiving and said, "Beloved, I ask that nine *liras* be written in my name."

"Come now, you don't have the means to contribute nine *liras*," replied 'Abdu'l-Bahá.

At this, Áqá Ḥabíb began to weep loudly.

"Very well, very well," said 'Abdu'l-Bahá, "whatever you want. My purpose is that a small contribution from the Most Great Prison may be made in order to attract divine blessings." With this, He rose and left the room.

The friends, each according to his own means, informed

Áqá Riḍá of their pledges and the following week the contributions were collected and sent off. In the meantime, Áqá Riḍá wished to make a clear record of each contribution from 'Akká and Haifa as well as the overall amount transmitted, so that later no question regarding the correct amounts contributed might arise. Such a record would clearly protect all contributors against any lapses of memory or possible errors in arithmetic, and at the same time prevent the enemies from spreading false rumours. He therefore decided to request that 'Abdu'l-Bahá seal and sign the receipt of each sum contributed.

But as soon as this was done and news of it reached the ears of the friends in 'Ishqábád, they too asked for the Master's seal and signature. Soon this news spread to all regions of Qafqaz, and the friends there too requested signed and stamped receipts.

In brief, the assorted difficulties and hardships associated with the administration of the project fell squarely on the shoulders of the peerless person of 'Abdu'l-Bahá. And so the construction of the Mashriqu'l-Adhkár created numerous problems for the Master. Neither were the Iranian Bahá'ís who participated in this undertaking exempt from the rule. All the friends in the provinces and villages, whether man, woman or child, who were by in large poor in the material world and rich in the eternal one, needed stamped and signed receipts for each penny contribution in order to attract divine blessings and worldly prosperity. And so for a period of two years they added another care to 'Abdu'l-Bahá's already backbreaking tasks. Every week several stacks of receipts, issued locally, were received for signature. Each and every one of them was signed by 'Abdu'l-Bahá with joy and pleasure.

One afternoon, as I walked up the stairs to attain His presence, the Master was just stepping out of the *bírúní* reception room. Standing at the doorway, He leaned against the wall looking exhausted. Addressing me He said, "Jináb-i-Khán, I am very tired. I wish to take a short walk. They sent me several stacks of the Mashriqu'l-Adhkár receipts to endorse. I have finished them all, but it tired me out to sign so many. The amounts were negligible. Today I realized the truth of something they have frequently written to me from 'I_shqábád. They wrote that the construction of the Ma_shriqu'l-A_dhkár has become a real test. Those from whom much was expected have not assisted at all, or contributed very little, while on the contrary, those from whom nothing was expected have truly sacrificed everything they had, especially the poor and the downtrodden. They have truly done their utmost. Even the very poor gave a few *shahi* or a few *qeran*. I sign their receipts with pleasure and joy."

Since the signs of fatigue were quite apparent in 'Abdu'l-Bahá's blessed face, I decided not to present the matter which had brought me to Him, so that I might not add to His many cares. In support of His remarks, I began to tell corroborating stories and for some time droned on with my endless chatter. I commented, "Yes, Beloved, I have seen a story told in pictures in the Bible, that one day as Jesus was seated on the ground leaning against the wall of the Temple with His disciples, He noticed a charity box hanging on the wall, into which everyone dropped some coins as they passed by. A strongly built and wealthy Jew, quite pleased with himself, dropped a handful of gold coins in the box. Another Jew followed, adding a handful of silver pieces. Then a poor, disabled old woman, in ragged clothes and with trembling hands and feet, dropped a single *nehas* in the box. Jesus said, 'This woman has given the most.' One of the disciples replied, 'Beloved, you did not notice, but I saw the large man with the broad neck put in a handful of *liras*.' Another disciple said, 'This woman only put in a single *sahtoot*, while I saw that young man put in a handful of yellow and white coins.' Jesus replied, 'This woman has given the most, because that proud, wealthy Jew who contributed a handful of *liras* gave only a fraction of his wealth, and the other who gave a handful of yellow and white coins did the same, whereas that woman gave all she had, and it is in that light that she will be accepted in the Kingdom of God.' "

As I told the story, 'Abdu'l-Bahá affirmed my words: "Yes, that has always been the way."

And so, one should be aware that this Ma<u>sh</u>riqu'l-A<u>dh</u>kár of the land of love ('I<u>sh</u>qábád), constructed in the midst of much hardship and pain, was an added ordeal in the everyday life of 'Abdu'l-Bahá. Happy is he who hastens to this Ma<u>sh</u>riqu'l-A<u>dh</u>kár at the hour of dawn.

Rapid progress of the Cause of God in the West

Generally, whenever new crises arose and harsher restrictions were imposed, 'Abdu'l-Bahá's promises of success and victory became more explicit and emphatic and were fulfilled before long. He specifically and repeatedly referred to the Battle of <u>Kh</u>andaq,[37] where some faint-hearted followers of the Prophet Muḥammad could not believe that they would soon achieve great victories. But once they had conquered Persia and seized such abundance of unexpected riches, they all confessed, "This is what was promised to us by the Prophet of God."

Here too, the pernicious activities of the Government's secret inspectors, induced by the Covenant-breakers, which had brought about the suspension of all travel to and from 'Akká and led to the search for and seizure of all incoming Bahá'í correspondence, resulted in a major crusade by the Persian Bahá'ís to teach and spread the Word of God. Soon the Faith grew in strength and stature, the clergy were pacified, and the Government became more agreeable in its treatment of the friends.

The friends in India also arose in great numbers and eradicated all vestiges of Covenant-breaking in Bombay. In its place they planted the seeds of the love of God, and also made great strides in teaching the Faith. In Turkmenistan, too, the friends raised the banner of the Faith: the Ma<u>sh</u>riqu'l-A<u>dh</u>kár was completed and the Cause of God was firmly established in Russia. This is a brief account of the situation in the East.

In the West, however, the news was overwhelming. My connection with the Western believers was through the flood of their correspondence. Two things stood out: on the one hand the reports of the progress of the teaching work, and on the other the deeply moving sentiments of tenderness and sympathy that the friends felt for the Master because of His subjugation and mistreatment at the hands of His enemies. One of the teachers of the Cause at that time was Amatu'lláh[138] Mrs. Brittingham. Arriving in the midst of all the troubles and difficulties, she stayed for a few days, witnessed 'Abdu'l-Bahá's forbearance and serenity, and returned home. When she departed she was so transformed that she began inviting people to the Faith in groups. Every week she sent letters of declaration from a number of new believers. One of her distinguished converts was Amatu'lláh Dr. Moody, whose service and sacrifice are world-renowned. In any case, Mrs. Brittingham taught the Faith so energetically that one day, when I submitted a translation of a letter from her, together with the letters of declaration of those she had taught, the Master remarked, "The Blessed Beauty named S͟hayk͟h Salmán a 'Bábí-maker', for whenever he returned from a journey to Iran he used to submit a long list of newly declared believers and ask that Tablets might be revealed in their honour. Now Mrs. Brittingham has turned out to be our 'Bahá'í-maker'. No one has taught so much."

This is a brief account of the teaching work. But the new believers' intensity of feeling was something to behold. The fame of 'Abdu'l-Bahá and His suffering called for urgent action, for their love for Him had generated fresh enthusiasm in their hearts.

Some entertained thoughts of freeing 'Abdu'l-Bahá from the clutches of His enemies. They wrote Him a string of letters and prayed constantly for His release. They sent letters signed by a thousand individuals who expressed their desire to sacrifice property and life in order to acquire His release. Mme. Jackson and the late M. Dreyfus and two others collected a large sum of money with the intention of travelling to Istanbul to do whatever necessary to bring 'Abdu'l-Bahá's imprisonment to an end.

Káẓim Páshá, the Governor of Beirut, stood to profit handsomely from such a venture, based on the influence he could exert. However, as soon as 'Abdu'l-Bahá heard the news He cabled instructions to put a stop to the notion. As a result, the Covenant-breakers found a new excuse to rekindle the fires of the hatred and enmity of the Ottoman officials and enemies of the Faith towards 'Abdu'l-Bahá. In fact, one day the Master remarked to me, "My freedom is in the hands of God. No other attempt should be made. But as soon as I telegraphed Paris to stop further attempts to bring about my freedom, the Covenant-breakers discovered the matter, found a new excuse and wrote to Káẓim Páshá saying that if the Effendi had not prevented the undertaking, you would have stood to gain a minimum of thirty thousand *liras*, and that was done out of contempt for you. In return, Káẓim Páshá arose against Us."

In brief, in various cities of the West there appeared tremendous movements. The opposition of the enemies galvanized and spurred the friends into the arena of service. The clergy began to whisper words of opposition and the friends unhesitatingly accepted the challenge; the renown of the Faith of God reached the far corners of the globe; the newspapers widely reported relevant stories, published strange and unusual pictures, and described Abu'l-Faḍl as the "Eastern philosopher" wherever he went. Scholars and thinkers arose in opposition to the Faith and the arena of teaching became so vast that its clamour and commotion were heard everywhere.

All this news, as described in letters and newspapers, reached 'Akká and was rapidly translated; some of it was sent to Iran. It was these reports that brought delight to the hearts of the resident believers and imbued their spirits with joy. Nevertheless, the confinement and utter submission of the Beloved of the world filled the hearts with sorrow and pain.

At the beginning of spring, after our daily work was over

we used to take restful walks in the open fields outside the gates of 'Akká. On our return, 'Abdu'l-Bahá would sometimes ask, "Are the fields green? How tall is the grass on Tel Fa<u>kh</u><u>kh</u>ár?"[139] Have the anemones of 'Akká blossomed yet?" In short, the incarceration of 'Abdu'l-Bahá was so difficult to bear that the resident believers, who were free to go where they pleased, stopped going for a stroll in the gardens and green fields. But the Master was always concerned about the happiness of the friends. Visiting the Most Holy Shrine twice a week was one of the requirements of their lives. Whenever there was some relaxation of the rules and a measure of freedom could be enjoyed, He would decide that a feast should be held in the Garden of Riḍván, so that the friends would not become deprived of the beauties of nature and suffer melancholy or despair. Moreover, with the power of His utterances and glad tidings, He kept their hopes high and their spirits cheerful.

Many of the translated letters or newspaper articles were read aloud in the *bírúní* reception room. And at the same time, 'Abdu'l-Bahá's Tablets to the American friends were revealed with the frequency of spring rain. In these He praised them, encouraged them and inspired them liberally, so that they too might not be distraught or depressed at His imprisonment and the resulting impossibility of reunion.

As a result of such encouragement, the friends arose to establish Bahá'í institutions. In the land of liberty and freedom of conscience, such rapid progress was possible that they climbed the ladder of success and achievement two (and sometimes three) steps at a time. Their success reached such dizzying heights that, as farmers say: "Before reaching the bitterness of the unripe grape they achieved the sweetness of the raisin, and before experiencing the life of a chick they fulfilled the promise of an eagle." They established and expanded their organizations, and in 1902 they formally elected a body of believers in Chicago and called it the "House of Justice"; it performed great service. Once the Faith was established there and the friends became thoroughly acquainted with the tenets of the Faith, they modified the name of the elected body to "House of Spirituality".

The essence of the above is that all the pressures and restrictions brought about these victories for the Faith of God. This brilliant Light could not be concealed behind the veil of accusations and calumnies of the Covenant-breakers, but continued to illumine the horizons of the world. That was our yesterday; this is our today. Happy are they who will witness our tomorrow.

The condition of the Covenant-breakers

It has already been noted that after Mírzá Badí'u'lláh broke the divine Covenant as well as his repentance, he spent some time at home in idleness. Then, reunited with his brother, together they renewed a bold agreement with the various enemies of the Faith. Thus united, they hoped for ultimate success. Mírzá Shu'á'u'lláh was sent to America to aid Ibráhím Khayru'lláh (Kheiralla) in his attempt to counter the work of Mírzá Abu'l-Faḍl. Mírzá Ghulámu'lláh received the assignment to go to Europe to prepare the way for their evil, mischievous plots.

Once the means required to misrepresent the Faith and instil doubt and suspicion in the minds of the believers were in place, all the violators of the Covenant, both within and without, began suddenly to put their plans into action. They began, little by little, to deny even the most obvious, self-evident issues. And at such a time – when the intense restrictions of the Prison City had brought the feelings of the Eastern and Western friends to a boil and sapped their patience and endurance – at such a time, they denied everything.

They told the Westerners that no trace of the Faith was left in the East, and informed the Easterners that no sign of the Cause could be detected in the West. One day they claimed that the 'Ishqábád Mashriqu'l-Adhkár did not really exist but was only a figment of the imagination, saying, "How can one determine the truth or fallacy of such fantasies?" They complained to some that the people of America were too proud to accept the Faith, and told others that the friends in Iran were too divided to make any progress in the teaching work.

At times they spread the rumour that the Master had advanced a claim [to the station of Manifestation] "which has resulted in separation of the people of Bahá from us", and at other times they recommended: "Read the verse 'Whoso layeth claim to a Revelation direct from God...'", or "and see the verse, 'We have chosen...'"[140] Sometimes it was the fundamental principles they objected to, while at other times they resorted to interpreting allegorical verses.[141]

And so for some time they manufactured all sorts of rumours, buzzing about like flies and making a great deal of noise, all in order to influence the believers. It was not long before they received their answer: "It has been said: 'O, fly, the heavens where the Phoenix soars is not your field of play.'"[142] Defeated at last on all sides, they gradually curtailed the scope of their propaganda as well as their plans to undermine the devotion and firmness of the believers. In Tehran the Old Hyena met with eternal damnation. The two mischief-makers of Tabriz[143] received their due reward: one died and the other found sanctuary with the Protestants. And in Bombay, Jahrumí failed miserably.

Of the 'Akká Covenant-breakers, some returned to the fold while others found themselves cast out and beyond redemption. Those notorious traitors who had appeased both sides in pursuance of their own interests were abandoned and forgotten. About the year 1904, the Centre of Sedition and a few of his helpers crawled back like spiders into their den of seclusion and wove webs of vain imaginings, superstition and deception, biding their time for the opportunity to trap any naïve, simple-minded individual and fill his heart and mind with doubt and suspicion – as they had managed to do with the naïve Ottoman official whose story, along with that of the money-changing Shaykh, has been told under the title 'Kashkúl or pumpkin bowl'.

RAPID PROGRESS IN THE WEST 233

However, even this inactivity did not signal the end of their struggle: like the germs of infectious diseases such as anthrax and diphtheria they concealed themselves, while continuing to inject their poison into the bloodstream of the sublime temple of the Faith of God in the hope of injuring and eventually disabling it.

They lay hidden in this way for some time while their poison circulated. In 1906 it resulted in the arrival of the Government's Commission of Enquiry, a committee bent on dispensing pain and grief for the community. Now they emerged once again from their seclusion and asserted themselves, like horrible viruses entering the circulatory system, but at that point, in the words of 'Abdu'l-Bahá, "the cannon blast of divine confirmation was heard". The details of this story will be told in the last chapter.

Visits by non-Bahá'í Westerners

As soon as the Western believers, making use of all means at their disposal, began their efforts to proclaim the name and fame of the Faith of God, many American and European scholars began to examine the Cause. Reaching various conclusions about the Faith, they hastened to 'Akká to visit 'Abdu'l-Bahá.

Some came to visit a Persian prophet who had a vision of the future. They understood the term "prophet" to mean a visionary, a prophesier, as referred to in the Old Testament. Others came to visit an erudite philosopher who had shaken the very foundation of the creeds and religions of the world. They came, and spurred by curiosity and an urge to discover future events, brought with them a list of questions. Since the war between Russia and Japan was going on, the date of the end of the war and the identity of the victor were at the top of their list.[144] These people were not readily admitted into the presence of 'Abdu'l-Bahá; the same restrictions which limited the visits of the believers applied to them too. Any such visit could have provided ammunition for the enemies of the Faith and consequently might have led to more restrictions and hardships.

More often than not, I suspected that some of these visitors were government spies sent by the Sublime Porte[145] for its own purposes. In any case, 'Abdu'l-Bahá's response to these people was simple and direct: "We are a prisoner of the Government and are not allowed to meet visitors freely. If you wish to investigate the truth and learn the tenets of the Bahá'í Faith, there are special centres in America that you may contact." However, many of the visitors did not give up that easily, and insisted on attaining His presence and asking their questions. At times, they came wearing an Ottoman *fez*, although they were Europeans or Americans.

Some came bearing their hateful prejudices. It was not clear what their intentions were in mind and heart. They would bring with them a translator of the kind who had accompanied Mr. Frank, mentioned earlier. But it was extraordinary that despite their feelings of contempt and bias, however onerous their questions, and however demanding they appeared in the course of the interview, they left His presence contented, convinced, grateful and even in humility.

One day when we were in His presence in the reception room on the second floor, news came that a few European men and women were asking to be permitted to attain 'Abdu'l-Bahá's presence. He said, "Tell them that we are prisoners and under the surveillance of the Ottoman government, and therefore a meeting is not possible." Word was brought back again to the effect that, "We are from America and have travelled two thousand miles, and beg to be granted a five-minute audience." And so at last they attained the presence of 'Abdu'l-Bahá, accompanied by a Christian translator of the type who had accompanied Mr. Frank.

After a few perfunctory words of greeting devoid of any genuine regard, the young translator, speaking on behalf of the other three, asked, "We wish to ask, for what purpose have you come to the world and what is it you teach?"

'Abdu'l-Bahá replied, "First, my own translator is present and our conversation should be through him."

The visitors said, "We have brought our own special translator to translate our words."

"I do not wish your translator to be our intermediary. My translator knows both English and French," 'Abdu'l-Bahá repeated.

"Since you have granted us permission for this meeting, we ask that you permit our translator to be our intermediary."

"Very well then," 'Abdu'l-Bahá agreed, "but I will ask my translator to pay close attention to the conversation so that he can tell me whenever your translator commits an error."

Then the Master told me, "Listen closely, and if he fails to translate properly, let me know."

After that, the Western translator began the conversation, asking again, "What is your mission and purpose?"

'Abdu'l-Bahá replied, "We have no purpose other than the promotion of love and unity in the world of humanity and the establishment of world peace."

"By what authority do you promote these teachings?" he asked.

"I have no title except servitude at the threshold of the Blessed Beauty," was the Master's reply.

"Who is the Blessed Beauty?" he asked.

'Abdu'l-Bahá replied, "The supreme Manifestation of God, Bahá'u'lláh, is the Promised One of all the Holy Books and scriptures."

Here, the conversation began to gain momentum as religious proofs were presented. The translator could not countenance the arguments, lost his concentration, and either deliberately or inadvertently mistranslated. The visitors asked for clarification; the translator, speaking his own mind, offered an incorrect interpretation. I immediately interrupted his elaboration and described the details to 'Abdu'l-Bahá.

"Tell them, now you see that your translator is not equal to the task," He remarked.

The translator presented an excuse worse than the original error, but then expressed his apologies on behalf of the listeners and yielded. And so I began to translate and the interview began again. At this point the gardener of the Riḍván Garden came in, bringing a bouquet of flowers for 'Abdu'l-Bahá. Indicating one of the guests, the Master told him, "Give the flowers to that elderly lady."

As she was handed the flowers, the four visitors gave each other meaningful glances as if they were secretly relieved to have got rid of the sorry translator.

And now the true purpose of the interview had been realized; an attitude of humility and reverence replaced the objections and protests. They lowered their heads and acknowledged the truth of 'Abdu'l-Bahá's words. I don't remember exactly which part of His utterances affected them most. It reminded me of the Egyptian, Mírzá Ḥasan, who was mentioned in Chapter 1. I said to myself: Ḥájí Ṣadr should have been here.

Soon a state of utter devotion replaced the sentiments of humility and reverence. And then 'Abdu'l-Bahá reminded them that they had asked for only five minutes and had taken two hours. While they expressed their apologies, it came to light that the speaker was a Frenchman and the other man and the two ladies were Americans. They explained that they were the leaders of a sect which believed the intellect to be the master and ruler of the world of existence. As they said their farewells, the Frenchman said, "We came here with preconceived notions and perceptions which were unworthy of your exalted rank. Now we realize that the universal intellect speaks through you."

Since they were to sail next day for America, they asked for addresses of Bahá'í centres there. They were referred to Áqá Aḥmad Yazdí in Port Said for details of these. As they said their goodbyes, they asked to kiss 'Abdu'l-Bahá's hand, and when the Master declined the gesture, the two ladies suddenly knelt and kissed the hem of His robe, then rose and departed.

Many individuals of this kind were admitted to His presence, received their fill according to their capacity, and left. Most of them wished to know the outcome of the war between Russia and Japan, and asked about a possible world war. They even enquired about the ultimate destiny of Palestine, wishing to know whether or not the day was coming when the power and sovereignty of the Jewish people would be established in this land.

I particularly remember that on several occasions the American believers asked if in the future the lands comprising Palestine would fall into the hands of the Jews and that 'Abdu'l-Bahá gave an affirmative answer. They asked if this ascendancy would come about as a result of their favourable response to the Bahá'í Faith – in other words, if their return to the Holy Land would take place subsequent to their acceptance of the Cause. 'Abdu'l-Bahá responded, "No. Their control will not be the result of their acceptance of the Faith. These lands will come into the possession of these very Jews." This view was expressed at a time when the Ottoman Empire was at the height of its power, and when a world war was unthinkable to anyone at that time. In any case, non-Bahá'ís were not the only ones asking such questions. One day several European visitors arrived and attained the presence of 'Abdu'l-Bahá as described previously, with much insistence and stubbornness. First they asked about political questions, to which 'Abdu'l-Bahá refused to reply. "We have no involvement in the world of politics," He said.

So they approached the question from a religious point of view, adopting a more civil attitude in their questioning and enquiring about the future political outlook. To the question of future domination by the Jews, they received an affirmative response. Then they remarked, "All the politicians are of the view that a world war will envelop the earth," and asked if the Bahá'ís shared such a view.

"Yes," replied 'Abdu'l-Bahá.

"When will it happen?" they enquired.

"It is near," replied the Master.

The youngest member of the group asked, "Will I be a witness to it?"

"You will all witness it," 'Abdu'l-Bahá replied.

Then they said, "Many politicians feel that the war between Russia and Japan will lead to the major world conflict."

"No," was 'Abdu'l-Bahá's answer.

"Who will win the war?" they asked.

As 'Abdu'l-Bahá remained silent, they realized that they had trespassed the bounds of courtesy, and so they modified the political nature of the issues, adopted a moral approach, and asked, "Of course, we know that Japan was the instigator and invader, but could Russia have avoided engaging the Japanese in the conflict?"

The Master replied, "Yes, they could have, since they were the ones who initiated the declaration of world peace and were the spearhead in motivating other governments in the establishment of the World Peace Conference at The Hague.[146] It would have been better had they not gone to war, but had adopted a defensive position. Then, in collaboration with other governments, they could have issued an ultimatum to Japan." 'Abdu'l-Bahá continued in this vein, uttering astonishing concepts which left His stunned listeners overwhelmed.

Using a world map, He pointed out the frontiers of Russia, gave the number of their warships and categorized them in groups, indicating the role of each group in battle. He then explained how Russia could have effected a general retreat, in the meantime communicating with neighbouring governments and inviting their participation in the issuing of an ultimatum for a ceasefire. Then He elaborated on the design and execution of a comprehensive peace plan. 'Abdu'l-Bahá's descriptions were so clear and lucid that His listeners were beside themselves with astonishment and delight. One of them said, "I wish the politicians of the world were aware of these possibilities."

As they appeared to be receptive to spiritual matters, 'Abdu'l-Bahá spoke to them about the Faith for a few minutes. As they took their leave they exhibited a wonderful attitude.

Their thoughts and ideas had been completely transformed and were contrary to those with which they had arrived. They had thought to visit a visionary, or an astrologer, or at least a Jewish prophet, one who could prophesy future political events. But once the sound of spiritual melodies reached their ears, their attitudes changed and their hearts were transformed. They realized that they had met the educator of the world of humanity, the well-wisher of the human race. And so at the moment of departure, after expressing their inability to give adequate thanks, they asked for blessing and confirmation for themselves and their people.

Account of the conversion of an American lady in 'Abdu'l-Bahá's presence

Another of the anti-religious visitors who entered the House of 'Abdu'l-Bahá as an implacable adversary of the whole concept of spirituality, and yet left it after having declared her belief in the Cause of God, was an American lady who arrived quite suddenly, and accepting no excuse almost forced her way to the *bírúní* reception room on the upper floor. In her arms she held a dog of an unsightly colour and with a hideous snout, which she petted incessantly.

Her first question to 'Abdu'l-Bahá was this: "I have heard a lot in America about your greatness. They tell stories about you, but I really have not understood the reality of the situation and I want to know what the truth of the matter is."

Of course, I do not recall the opening questions and answers, I just remember that 'Abdu'l-Bahá, using Bahá'í terminology, uttered a few words regarding the unity of God and gave proof of His existence with great eloquence. Suddenly she laughed and said, "I am astonished that you can compose so spontaneously, and with such eloquence and fluency, such sophisticated verses of poetry in proof of an imaginary thing. What does 'God' mean? It is truly a pity."

I immediately realized what she meant by the words "eloquence and fluency" and "sophisticated verses of poetry".

'Abdu'l-Bahá had not spoken in the simple vernacular of this woman, but had used the literary expressions of the Faith; moreover, I had not shown any understanding of the situation and had translated the words parrot-like in the same manner. As the poet says,

I was taught the parrot's art by the Master divine,
Parrot-like I repeat His words, yet none that is mine.

And so this woman, being unfamiliar with these expressions, had thought the eloquent utterances of 'Abdu'l-Bahá to be merely verses of high-flown poetry.

I explained the matter to the Master. He broke into a broad smile but made no change in the manner of His speech as He presented additional proofs. At this point the woman remarked, "I am not capable of understanding such concepts; moreoever, I am in no way willing to lose my freedom; and furthermore, I have no attachment to any imaginary being. But I do wonder what purpose all this knowledge, wisdom and philosophy serve? If you only knew what high-ranking scientists and scholars have written books refuting all such thoughts! And now your followers in America walk in your path. But if you come to my home town of Boston in America, you will see that this kind of talk enjoys no support. The atheists of Boston are world-renowned."

'Abdu'l-Bahá smiled again and then uttered some words of counsel and guidance, but without any apparent result. She wished to take more of 'Abdu'l-Bahá's time, but fortunately that wretched dog began to show signs of restlessness like a spoiled brat, and so she rose to take her leave. Her parting words were, "If your God is the true God, then ask Him to guide me as He has guided your followers, otherwise I…"

She stopped, then went on: "Tomorrow, I intend to leave 'Akká and visit the nearby towns; I am returning in five days time. Let's see what this God of yours will do for me." But no sooner than she had stepped outside than she turned around and said, "But you have a God to whom you look for guidance; where can I look, who have no such beliefs?"

'Abdu'l-Bahá replied, "Very well, leave that to me too. Go in God's care."

It was interesting that despite her many discourtesies 'Abdu'l-Bahá did not show the slightest hint of displeasure, and treated her with extreme gentleness and compassion. In the afternoon of the next day she returned from Haifa, and again presented herself to 'Abdu'l-Bahá unannounced. Confessing her feelings, she said, "I spent a restless night and so missed my planned trip this morning. Before I came here I was quite confident in my beliefs, but now I am anxious and unsure. Please, either grant me guidance or confirm me in my original belief."

This time she observed all the requirements of courtesy, as she listened to 'Abdu'l-Bahá for almost an hour. At times she questioned and argued, and at other times she acknowledged His utterances. At last she said, "I now realize that there is something of substance here. There are realities, the understanding of which is beyond my capability." As she left, she asked 'Abdu'l-Bahá for His blessing.

Next day nothing was heard from her. We thought she had left Haifa. But back she came, weary and distressed, and was taken to the presence of 'Abdu'l-Bahá. She asked a few questions and then admitted that she had been able to see a glimpse of hope. She left revived and happy. For four or five days there was no news of her. And then I heard that she had arrived from Haifa, had taken refuge in the *andárúní* of the Master's House and had vowed her intention not to leave until she could recover her peace of mind. When 'Abdu'l-Bahá summoned me to translate, I saw her walking out of the *andárúní* in a state of humility and reverence, without her constant companion in her arms.

Reverently and with 'Abdu'l-Bahá's permission she took her seat, listened to the Master's words, and in a state of lowliness and selflessness demonstrated her submission and obedience. For a few days she was in the company of the ladies of the household, and then she returned to America contented and joyful; the heavenly fragrances of her faith and certitude spread to every part of that land.

Servitude

From the day when the contents of the Kitáb-i-'Ahd were disclosed and other Tablets and verses revealed by the Most Exalted Pen came to light (as contained in various other writings) in praise of "Him round Whom all names revolve",[147] those of the friends who had no desire for position or rank in the Faith considered the rank of 'Abdu'l-Bahá to be coequal with that of Bahá'u'lláh and the Primal Point, based on these verses and their own observations and experience. They viewed the rising of this Sun of Truth as a movement of the original Sun from the most exalted point on the horizon of revelation to the ultimate and concluding point. And their firm and indisputable proof was this: that whatever they had witnessed in the revelation of the Supreme Manifestation of God which had guided them to accept the Cause, they now witnessed without the slightest difference in the Person of the Centre of the Covenant. Furthermore, due to the changing requirements of time and place, the nature of revelation, and the appearance of various signs and evidences, they considered the first to be the Herald, the second the Supreme Manifestation of God, and the third the Interpreter and the Branch sprung forth from the Ancient Root.

This was the understanding of the generality of the true believers. Of course, above and beyond this, each individual had formed his own opinion reflecting his corresponding mode of conduct and manners, just as one's outward appearance is governed by one's thoughts, beliefs and disposition, and of course no two people are the same. In their understanding of the divine verse, "We have chosen the 'Greater' after the 'Most Great' ",[148] the friends considered the Greater Branch [Mírzá Muḥammad-'Alí] to be the future successor to 'Abdu'l-Bahá; they interpreted the word 'after' in the above verse in the context of time (rather than rank), totally unaware of its veiled and hidden meaning as well as its implications for the future of the Faith. They regarded all the Branches after the manner of the sanctified Imáms of Shí'í Islám – as the successive spiritual rulers of the Faith of God, to whom all unanimously and unitedly had pledged their allegiance and obedience in their service to the Cause.

However, those who were contemplating the attainment of a position of leadership in the Faith regarded the setting of the Sun of Truth as an opportunity for the rise of the darkness of waywardness; like bats of the night they came to life again. First they declared the major principles of the Faith to be "null and void", then they resorted to allegorical and mystical references and through misinterpretation spread doubt and suspicion, as has been described in the first chapter of this book. Unitedly, they arose against the Faith of God and brought a variety of accusations against it. And yet, for four long years the Centre of the Covenant of God counselled and guided them without disclosing any of their actions – until the Covenant-breakers at last, openly and under their own seal and signature, declared and spread the news of their opposition.

It should be said that in the course of those four years, concealing their opposition and contempt was not without its problems, for the pilgrims, resident pioneers and local believers wished to communicate to Iran their observations of the Covenant-breakers' actions in order to alert the friends and keep them informed of the latest developments. At the same time, out of their intense love for and attachment to 'Abdu'l-Bahá, the friends had begun to regard the Master in the same light as the Abhá Beauty, praising and venerating Him with the same expressions. However, both were contrary to 'Abdu'l-Bahá's wishes. During those years, therefore, all letters to Iran written by the friends had to be reviewed and corrected by the Master and receive His stamp of approval, so that no one could communicate even a whisper of the disunity among the Aghṣán or exaggerate and magnify the position of 'Abdu'l-Bahá as His lovers were wont to do. These concerns are reflected in all the Tablets revealed at that time.

But when the self-incriminating correspondence of the Covenant-breakers was disseminated, the secret was divulged, their identity was exposed, and the friends of God recognized those who had renounced and violated the Faith of God. Also, those pilgrims who had observed the injustices of the Covenant-breakers but had remained silent in accordance with 'Abdu'l-Bahá's instructions were now free to tell what needed to be told.

I was one of those pilgrims who had witnessed Mírzá Áqá Ján's rebellion, as well as other acts of opposition, in the fifth year after the ascension of the Blessed Beauty. As soon as I returned to Tehran I had therefore revealed all that I had seen. As described in the first chapter of this book, when I returned to Tehran from 'Akká things had come to such a pass that one day 'Abdu'l-Bahá remarked to me, "You see what they are doing to me? Go to Iran and recount whatever you have seen here. Whatever I have refused to disclose, you reveal fully. Whatever I cannot reveal, you expose." Because of this emphasis on "you tell all", I did tell all at that time, and I still consider it relevant to repeat it.

In brief, the intense opposition and hostility of the enemies in those years emblazoned the fire of the love of God and generated an atmosphere of great enthusiasm and excitement among the friends. If the Covenant-breakers misinterpreted the blessed verse: "Turn..."[149] in accordance with their own whim and fancy, and not unlike the Sunnís in the early years of Islám adopted the verse: "The book of God shall be sufficient unto us" as their justification for breaking away from the body of the Faith, some of the Bahá'ís out of their intense love and devotion for 'Abdu'l-Bahá now became Nuṣayrí.[150] They extended the interpretation of the verse "Turn...." to the furthest extremes of its meaning, interpreting the word "after" in accordance with the verse: "after God there is naught but utter darkness".

I had heard the word Alíyu'lláhí[151] from the lips of

'Abdu'l-Bahá numerous times. He frequently stated: "All the friends know how I have emphasized my rank of servitude and lowliness, with both heart and tongue, both inwardly and outwardly. Now if one of the friends against my wishes treads the path of exaggeration, what fault can be ascribed to me? Once I even heard that when Yúsuf Khán-i-Vujdání was in 'Akká he had once faced the *darb-khánih*[152] while performing his obligatory prayer. I rebuked him and expressed my disapproval of his action. He was about to resort to the verse: 'Turn…'. I asked him, 'Where is the Point of Adoration according to the Text?' and as soon as he began to quote the verse: 'Wherever thou art, there is the face of God'[153] – I told him, 'You are wrong, don't you know where my Point of Adoration is?' At this, he immediately repented his action." In brief, however much the Covenant-breakers denigrated 'Abdu'l-Bahá, many of the believers just as intensely exaggerated His station out of their boundless love and devotion for Him. However, His emphasis on His station of servitude was so marked that if someone composed an ode in praise of that station, he received 'Abdu'l-Bahá's approval and praise, while on the contrary, any statement which glorified His being met with absolute rejection. He would even say: "Repent, repent."

The only rank that the Master assumed exclusively for Himself was the position of Interpreter of the Book. And the reason for this was that if anyone, based on the divine utterances and Tablets revealed in praise of the one "Who had branched from the Ancient Root" tried to glorify 'Abdu'l-Bahá, He would respond: "I am the Interpreter of the Book and all these appellations mean 'Abdu'l-Bahá." And if someone made reference to the verse: "Servitude is the quintessence of divinity," He would reply: "This interpretation is wrong. My servitude is clearly established beyond all such stations." And when the dispute was raging about the two greetings "Alláh'u'A'ẓam" and "Alláh'u'Abhá"[154] thousands of prayers and Tablets regarding His station of servitude were revealed. Among them was this particular prayer, above which the following words of 'Abdu'l-Bahá appear:

"Whoever recites this prayer with lowliness and fervour will bring gladness and joy to the heart of this Servant; it will be even as meeting Him face to face." This prayer, as He ordained, is observed as the Tablet of Visitation[55] for that Beloved of the world; for the last thirty years or so, we Persian Bahá'ís recite it every morning after our obligatory prayer. Here, He takes the station of servitude and selflessness to the loftiest heights: "Lord, give me to drink from the chalice of selflessness; with its robe clothe me, and in its ocean immerse me. Make me as dust in the pathway of Thy loved ones and grant that I may offer up my soul for the earth ennobled by the footsteps of Thy chosen ones in Thy path, O Lord of Glory in the Highest."

O my dear reader: since most of the friends know this prayer by heart and recite it every morning, I have not reproduced it here. However, I ask that if you also know it by heart, recite it now; then you can continue with the rest of the story.

A bittersweet story

In the days when the friends in Iran were on fire with the love of 'Abdu'l-Bahá and yet patiently enduring the fires of jealousy ignited by the enemies of the Faith and the slander of the Covenant-breakers, poets and scholars were composing beautiful odes in praise and glorification of 'Abdu'l-Bahá, lauding the greatness of His station without any misgivings. But we, the residents of 'Akká and the servants of the Most Holy Threshold, committed no such errors. We whispered not a word about His divinely ordained station and His holiness, for He had frequently counselled His eulogizers to compose, instead, words of praise about His station of servitude and self-effacement.

It was during these days that a letter containing some verses of poetry arrived in care of this servant, composed by one of the handmaidens of God, Ṭáhirih Khánum. The verses had been constructed in the form of a prayer to the sanctified threshold of the Divine Being.

At a suitable time, I handed the letter to 'Abdu'l-Bahá as He came down the steps of His house by the sea. As soon as He had read one or two verses He turned His blessed face to me and said with profound sadness and indignation, "You, too, hand me this kind of letter? Don't you know how sad these appellations make me? Is it possible that even you do not know me yet? If you don't know this, then who can be expected to know? Don't you see everything I do and everything I write, day and night? I swear by God, beside Whom there is no other God, I consider myself more insignificant than all the lovers of the Blessed Beauty. This is my belief. If I have misunderstood the point, then tell me I have misunderstood. This is my longing. I don't claim even this, for I am weary of all claims." Then He turned in the direction of the Most Holy Shrine and said, "O, Blessed Beauty, assist me to attain this station."

He uttered these words with such passion that my heart almost stopped beating. My breath was arrested in my chest; all movement ceased. Life itself seemed suspended. I lost the strength to speak, nay, even to breathe. I longed for the earth to open up and swallow me whole so that I might never again behold such sorrow in the face of my Master.

For a moment I was not in this world. As He resumed His descent, the creaking of His boots on the marble stairs under the rain brought me back to reality. I immediately followed Him down the stairs and heard Him say, "I told the Covenant-breakers: the more you persecute me, the more the friends will glorify my station…"

Since this statement seemed to exonerate the friends and place the blame squarely on the shoulders of the Covenant-breakers, I began to recover my senses and energy. I tried to listen carefully to His words but, having lost my concentration, my thoughts were elsewhere. I realized that it was in reaction to the harassment and torment inflicted by the Covenant-breakers on the person of 'Abdu'l-Bahá that the believers felt an uncontrollable urge to respond. Now that the Covenant-breakers had emerged as the true culprits, the worst part of this bitter experience of mine was over.

I could hear 'Abdu'l-Bahá talking as He paced the floor in the vast hall, but I had lost my sense of concentration and my ability to understand His words. I was blaming myself in this wise: Would that I had died before bringing so much distress to my Beloved. I was confused and upset. Suddenly, I heard 'Abdu'l-Bahá say, "This is not the fault of the friends. They say what they say out of love, dedication and steadfastness." Again my thoughts drifted away, and then again I heard His words, "You who are so dear to me…"

This statement brought back to me the fact that the deeds and actions of 'Abdu'l-Bahá were the same as His words: "Beware, beware lest thou offend any heart."[156] And now was the time for giving consolation and comfort.

At His words, my heart melted, the lump in my throat exploded, and my tears began to flow uncontrollably. I tried to pay closer attention to what He was saying, but His heart-warming utterances and kindly words went far beyond the bounds of consolation, to such an extent that when I measured those loving words against my utter unworthiness I could no longer endure such tenderness and compassion, and therefore did not allow myself to commit any part of it to memory.

However, I was overtaken by such feelings of joy and bliss, and felt such intense devotion and ecstasy, that I wished the heavens would open so that I could soar up to the kingdom of reunion. In brief, once I was dismissed from His presence I was so intoxicated by happiness that, having taken the wrong street, I found myself wandering around lost in the city of 'Akká.

And now, my dear reader, you can see how my bitter story found such a sweet ending, and came to a happy conclusion. Neither earth nor heavens opened up, whether to swallow me up or to draw me into the Abhá kingdom, so that I am now able to present to you these memories of bygone years, and in remembrance of that radiant and holy Countenance, may extend to you the greeting, "Alláh'u'Abhá".

Medicine

I had frequently heard the Master speak about the practice of medicine. On a number of occasions He talked about Jináb-i-Kalím[157] and his skills in the medicine of the old days, and how he used to treat those who came to him with medical problems. 'Abdu'l-Bahá Himself had formerly prescribed medicine for those who sought His advice. However, Bahá'u'lláh had told them that such medical practices should cease, so that the believers might not develop the habit of consulting anyone but actual physicians, or of receiving medical advice from anyone except qualified practitioners. The intention was that the verse: "Resort ye, in times of sickness, to competent physicians"[158] might be understood and applied.

Despite this, and while we all knew that because of this blessed verse, the Healer of all spiritual infirmities would not interfere in cases of physical disorder, nevertheless whenever anyone had fallen ill and had at last lost all hope of recovery through the conventional means practised by the physicians, he would seek a cure at the threshold of 'Abdu'l-Bahá, imploring, "O Thou panacea of our every incurable pain, and O Healer of all of our maladies and afflictions." And since to disregard a plea or refuse an appeal had no place in the ocean of compassion and loving-kindness of that quintessence of generosity, and none had ever come away empty-handed or disappointed, so through the use of some material means or approach He would impart healing to the supplicant. What was even more astonishing was that non-Bahá'ís too, who had no knowledge of the principles and beliefs of the Faith, applied even more than the believers for the healing balm of the Master, never losing hope in the eventual effectiveness of the prescribed cure.

One of the remedies readily available to 'Abdu'l-Bahá, and one that could be freely prescribed for anybody, was a heavenly mixture with a delicious taste. It was nothing but a sauce made of pomegranates from the Garden of Riḍván. The Master would prescribe it for the patient, saying, "This sauce is prepared from pomegranates picked from trees in the Garden of Riḍván which have been blessed by the gaze of the Blessed Beauty."

Whether its efficacy was due to the patient himself, or to the medicine, or to the will of 'Abdu'l-Bahá, I cannot say. All I know is that experience showed that this heavenly and tasty panacea cured many a suffering patient.

This subject had become a frequent topic of conversation in the pilgrim house. Another of 'Abdu'l-Bahá's methods of healing was through diet, or a simple reduction in the amount of food consumed; this, of course, is in line with today's scientific knowledge. But the third approach to healing on the part of that Physician of the souls was a specific method; no psychologist can ever comprehend or discover its mystery unless he is one of those true and sincere believers who understand the power of the supernatural and possess pure and radiant hearts. I will now tell the stories of two people, one a believer and the other a non-believer. One was healed through material means, the other without the use of such means. The believer, who was healed without resorting to any physical means, was none other than myself, and the story is as follows.

In the days when the late Dr. Arastú Khán resided in the pilgrim house, I suffered over the course of three to four weeks from a disease which caused the appearance of numerous boils and abscesses all over my body. Although the disease persisted and the excruciating pain increased, I still refused as long as I could to ask 'Abdu'l-Bahá for a cure. The doctor called upon his whole range of skills, based on his long experience, but without success. The older men of the community came to his aid, even suggesting remedies, but the pain persisted.

One night the pain grew intense and my incessant moaning and groaning so disturbed and annoyed the pilgrims that at two in the morning we finally agreed to send Áqá Muḥammad Ḥasan, the servant of the pilgrim house, to the House of 'Abdu'l-Bahá and beg His assistance on my behalf.

Whether 'Abdu'l-Bahá was asleep or awake at that hour of the morning I cannot say, for by the time Muḥammad Ḥasan returned I had fallen asleep.

The next day I awoke around noon, feeling free of pain. By late afternoon I realized that I could move about without much trouble. And since during the previous twenty-five or -six days, when I had been ailing, and the few days that I had actually been bedridden, I had not attained the presence of 'Abdu'l-Bahá, I decided to walk ever so slowly toward the *darb-khánih*.

In the front entrance hall I found myself in His presence. He asked after my health and imparted to me words of kindness and sympathy. I decided it was a good time to ask for a definitive cure. He remarked, "Very well, but you must submit to bleeding."[159]

The word "bleeding" scared me half to death, and so like a spoiled child I raised my shoulders and began to mumble something to the effect that I could not bear the idea of the blade and the letting of blood, especially mine. The Master replied, "Well, well, I want to send you to face swords, and you are afraid of losing a few drops of blood?"

Remaining true to my nature as a reckless blabbermouth, I rejoined, "Until that time comes, God is most merciful. Besides, if I wanted to be cured through the torture of bloodletting, why would I have pleaded my case before the Master?"

'Abdu'l-Bahá smiled, began to pace the floor, and continued talking. Thus my last definitive cure took place in this fashion, and did not involve any material means.

Now, the story of healing with material means is as follows: Shaykh Ṣáliḥ,[160] a wealthy and well known leader of the Druze community, and who at the time was 80 or 90 years old, was the Persian Consul in 'Akká. He had a son, Shaykh Maḥmúd, about 60 years old and one of the leading Druze clerics, who lived some distance from 'Akká. Having been taken ill with sciatica, Shaykh Maḥmúd had been taken to 'Akká, but all the doctors there had failed to produce a cure.

The pain, however, which stemmed from the irritation of the sciatic nerve, increased daily.

We heard that Shaykh Ṣáliḥ had already appealed to 'Abdu'l-Bahá for a cure for his son, but that he had not received a response from the Master. This time, he knelt down, seized 'Abdu'l-Bahá's robe and weeping aloud, pleaded, "I beg from you the recovery of my son." So greatly did he weep and lament that at last 'Abdu'l-Bahá accepted his appeal and summoned me to His presence. At that time there had been no mention or thought regarding my possible future study of medicine, or that one day I might actually become a practising doctor. As I entered His presence, 'Abdu'l-Bahá said, "Shaykh Maḥmúd, son of Shaykh Ṣáliḥ, is seriously ill, you must cure him."

The thought of the famous pomegranate sauce came to mind. I asked the Master what I should do. He told me, "Take a piece of mustard plaster, sprinkle some essence of opium onto it and place it on the painful spot." I did not know what "essence of opium" was, but assumed that the pharmacist would be familiar with it, so I rushed over to the pharmacy of Áqá Ḥusayn-i-Áshchí. Shaykh Ṣáliḥ followed me briskly, albeit with a pronounced limp and praying all the way.

The mustard plaster was easily identified and purchased, but the essence of opium remained an unsolvable mystery. I was perplexed. Then, after some consultation and as a last resort, and relying wholly on God, I put nineteen drops of liquid laudanum onto the plaster, rushed to the patient's house and placed it on the sore spot. Since I had no other instructions, I did not wait to evaluate the results. The next day I heard that the patient had had a comfortable night, and the following morning he ate a big breakfast. Two days later I saw him in the presence of 'Abdu'l-Bahá expressing his gratitude and receiving permission to depart for his home. At the time, 'Abdu'l-Bahá was explaining to him that the frequently used expression *"erqu'l-nesa"* (sciatic nerve) was incorrect and that the original and correct term was *"erqu'l-nes"*.

Trusting the road to the highwayman

Any friend who had spent years in the service of 'Abdu'l-Bahá and become familiar with His way of doing things knew that that dawning-place of heavenly wisdom accomplished many a task in a way seemingly contrary to logic and human reason. The angel of blessing and confirmation accompanied His every act, while the demon of failure had no access to that threshold.

For instance, to leave the goat in the care of the wolf, or to entrust the calf to the protective claws of the leopard, or to assign the cat to watch over the sparrow, or to keep the fragile glass next to the solid rock – all of which are signs of the Day of Revelation[161] – were among the routine accomplishments of that Beloved Being.

Many a secret locked in the memory of the Ottoman government's spies and informers, or of the Covenant-breakers' secret detectives – the disclosure of any one of which might have led to major disasters – remained unrevealed because of the force of His will. 'Abdu'l-Bahá's will was so dominant that if He appointed a highwayman to keep a road safe, the brigand would perform his task with heart and soul. This was but one manifestation of the power and influence of His blessed word. I have witnessed examples of it many times and present one such case here.

One of the second-generation Bahá'ís of that community was a man whose childhood had passed without the benefit of proper training and discipline. Encouraged by the Covenant-breakers, with whom he had established an intimate relationship, his youth had been spent in pursuit of worldly pleasures. He was so captivated by their fancy lifestyle that he kept aloof from the friends, gradually withdrew from the Faith and became a willing tool of the Covenant-breakers.

However, because of his close relationship with a number of the most faithful and steadfast friends he was not formally rejected or severed from the Faith. But, as far as possible, 'Abdu'l-Bahá prohibited the young people from associating with him, because he was, according to the Arabs, a hoodlum, and according to us Persians, a profligate and a thug. He carried assorted weapons; typically a dagger hung from his belt. He got drunk and was vociferous in public. Whenever there was any trouble he was a willing tool of the Covenant-breakers, and routinely reported to them any local Bahá'í news which he received from his relatives.

When the Commission of Enquiry arrived in 'Akká from the Sublime Porte, they instituted a variety of restrictions and took over the Post and Telegraph Offices as well as other important buildings. Moreover, they installed a number of their public inspectors and informers just outside of the front door of the House of 'Abdu'l-Bahá. The details of this have already been covered briefly and will be further described in Chapter 5.

In these days, the entire group of the resident friends was fearful of the trouble and mischief that this young man might cause. What if he stole some Tablets, or pilfered certain letters and handed them over to the Covenant-breakers to provide ammunition for their many accusations? Although the gates of reunion were closed to all, yet in the event of a sudden arrival by a Western pilgrim it would be a daunting task to shield him from the clutches of this person, since he had access to the community of the believers and would inform the opposition of the arrival of such a guest. So this added another dilemma to the many other cares that confronted the community of believers.

Now, this very thing that the resident Bahá'í community feared the most came to pass unexpectedly. A recently declared Western believer, innocent, unsuspecting and sporting an Ottoman *fez*, arrived in 'Akká. While the Commission of Enquiry's informers were engaged in their investigations and harassment, this believer, with or without permission, attained the presence of 'Abdu'l-Bahá in the *bírúní* reception room of His residence.

If, like Mr. Winterburn, he had been deepened in the Faith, he might perhaps have been able to spend a few cautious but happy days in 'Abdu'l-Bahá's house before returning to his home. But he wanted to visit all the Holy Places, and also to quench his spiritual thirst with the crystal waters of the Master's blessings and confirmations – and be able to complete all this and depart in the early evening. And so, after a one-hour meeting with 'Abdu'l-Bahá, the Master sent someone out to summon that wilful troublemaker.

As soon as he arrived, 'Abdu'l-Bahá gave him the following instructions, addressing him by name: "This person is one of our friends and an American. His name is 'such and such', his last name is 'such and such', and tonight he must depart on the ship 'such and such'. Take him in the carriage to all the Holy Places: first, the Most Holy Shrine, then 'Akká, then the Firdaws Garden, and then the Garden of Riḍván. You must tell him the name of each place and describe it properly, so that he may perform the rites of pilgrimage. But as you know, the inspectors are lying in wait, so be very careful that no one learns about this. Don't even mention to any of the friends that such a guest has arrived. Beware, beware, lest anyone find out. Bring him back here before sunset for another visit before he leaves. Go in God's care."

This service was completed in fine fashion, and two or three hours later the troublemaker – now friendly – arrived, bowed, delivered the precious guest, and left with the words "Go in God's care" in his ears. That night the pilgrim left for Haifa and from there departed for Europe, happy and grateful. Even after the event, nothing further was heard from any quarter. This was the effect of 'Abdu'l-Bahá's words on His listeners. This power was not exclusive to His utterances, but was also inherent to the highest degree in His Writings and even in His messages. It was not infrequent that when the friends complained about an action of the enemies, He issued instructions that the enemies themselves should be solicited for help. The following story is presented as an example.

Jináb-i-Áqá Mírzá Músá, entitled "the Immortal Letter" [Ḥarf-i-Baqá], to whom reference was made in the first chapter of this book, possessed great wealth including assorted properties and real estate holdings in Baghdad. These had been seized from him by a court judgement and awarded to his enemies. The legal battle to recover the fortune had gone on for many years without success. Mírzá Músá had never uttered a single word about material and worldly matters to 'Abdu'l-Bahá. However, now that he was over 80 years of age and his life had entered its twilight season, and the fragrant breezes of the immortal Kingdom were being inhaled by the "Immortal Letter", he realized that while his debts had mounted, none of his properties had been recovered. In utter helplessness, he therefore briefly mentioned the matter to 'Abdu'l-Bahá.

The answer came that he should solicit the help of the same troublesome judge [who had rewarded the properties to others]. As soon as he received the Tablet, summoning his courage and determination he sought out the judge and boldly asked for a just consideration of his rights and recovery of his properties. The judge, who did not expect such a strong and unequivocal petition and was therefore utterly taken aback, asked, "How can you expect a helping hand from me?" Mírzá Músá replied, "It is the command of my Master."

At this the judge was visibly shaken. He asked to see the written command. Mírzá handed him 'Abdu'l-Bahá's Tablet. The judge was contrite. Humbly, he picked up his pen and wrote the order for the release and return of the properties, appointing the Governor of Baghdad as the executor of the order. In a short time the properties were recovered and subsequently sold and, according to his [Mírzá Músá's] wishes, the funds collected were kept under the jurisdiction of the court.

All his creditors were summoned by public announcement to the court and were paid in full, both principal and interest. A few days after the settlement of all of his debts, the Immortal Letter ascended to the immortal Kingdom, and was buried with all due pomp and ceremony. The mercy of God be upon him, and upon him be the Glory of Glories.

CHAPTER FIVE

He is the Most Glorious!

Various Miscellaneous Events

"The triumph of the Cause of God is in his hands"

The first event to be described in this chapter pertains to glad tidings shared with us by 'Abdu'l-Bahá, as evidence of divine blessings and mercy, at a time when He was besieged by a whole host of difficulties and beset by untold hardships. When the heavy clouds of sedition and insurrection had darkened the firmament of the Faith of God, suddenly one day I received a letter from America addressed to this servant, in which the writer requested that I should ask a question of 'Abdu'l-Bahá and advise him directly of the reply.

While the question seemed simple enough, yet to a Persian Bahá'í like myself its implications were unimaginable. Making the enquiry was not without its difficulties either. Just as it would be impossible to be convinced that bright day is in fact darkest night, so it was equally unimaginable that a future day without 'Abdu'l-Bahá could prove to be more glorious than the one that had passed in His presence. And besides, when a beloved father is generously providing the means of a happy and joyful life for his loving children, how can one ask him about their future prospects once he has departed this transitory life, or about the identity of the one who is to provide their future livelihood?

However, since every question deserves an answer and

each request calls for a reply, I had no choice but to face up to the task. And so, when 'Abdu'l-Bahá was walking in front of the _khán_ I approached and told Him, "Someone has written to me from America that we have heard the Master has said that the one whose appearance will follow me has recently been born and is in this world. If this is so we are answered, but if this is not so then…?"

After waiting a moment, with a look full of meaning and secret exaltation, He said, "Yes, this is true." Hearing these glad tidings my soul rejoiced; I felt assured that the Covenant-breaking would come to naught and the Cause of God would triumph throughout the world, and this world become the mirror of the heavenly world. However, to understand what He meant by "appearance", as we Bahá'ís conceive its meaning, was very difficult for me, and remained in my mind a mystery; seeking further information I therefore asked Him, "Does this mean a revelation?" If He had replied with "yes" or "no" this would have created more complications and aroused more questions, but fortunately His answer was conclusive and such as to silence any questioner, and in even clearer words He said, "The triumph of the Cause of God is in his hands!"[162]

In short, I wrote the reply to America accordingly but did not mention the matter to anyone in 'Akká. I did not even allow myself to wonder whether this child was in 'Akká or in another part of the world. The matter was resolved some five years later, when wondrous moral virtues and manifest marks of greatness were readily observable in the childhood and early youth of the Guardian of the Cause of God.

One day, quite confidentially, I related the matter to the late Mírzá Ḥaydar-'Alí, while at the same time keeping the focus of my heart and mind on nothing else but the threshold of the One "round Whom all names revolve".[163] Some years later at a meeting of the Spiritual Assembly of Tehran, while reading a newly received Tablet from the Holy Threshold, I unwittingly disclosed a part of the story. Fortunately it did not arouse undue attention until the assumption of that august office by that scion[164] after the ascension of 'Abdu'l-Bahá and the reading of His Will and Testament in the Spiritual Assembly. As the reading was completed, the late Báqiroff, expressing his sentiments of obedience, acceptance and affirmation, spontaneously exclaimed, "Praised be God, the Faith has become young!"

This reminded me of the poet who, after the king's death and the prince's accession to the throne, expressed in a single verse his feelings of mourning and bereavement on one hand and his heartfelt sentiments of joy and delight on the other:

> *Why should I not shed tears of blood?*
> *Why should I not burst out laughing aloud?*
> *As the surging ocean recedes*
> *While the priceless pearl is revealed.*

And so the promise was fulfilled and 'Abdu'l-Bahá's utterance that "The triumph of the Cause of God is in his hands" was realized; the Faith was formally recognized; National Spiritual Assemblies were formed and victory followed victory.

While all this was taking place, I was puzzled by a mystery, the solution of which became an all-consuming task. The mystery was that letter from America containing the information that "'Abdu'l-Bahá has said that 'the one whose appearance will follow me has recently been born and is in this world'." I wondered about the basis of this statement and which particular document contained it.

This was constantly on my mind until once, on my way to Europe, I stopped off in Alexandria to meet the honoured Ḥájí Muḥammad Yazdí. As we reminisced about past times, he said, "Yes, this matter was the subject of discussion and speculation until the Tablet revealed in honour of an American believer reached us. I have a copy of it." I was given a copy, which I immediately sent to Iran; I now reproduce it below in order to grace the completion of this section.

He is God!

New York
Miss F.———

O Maidservant of God!
Verily, that child is born and is alive and from him will appear wondrous things that thou shalt hear of in the future. Thou shalt behold him endowed with the most perfect appearance, supreme capacity, absolute perfection, consummate power and unsurpassed might. His face will shine with a radiance that illumines all the horizons of the world; therefore forget this not as long as thou dost live inasmuch as ages and centuries will bear traces of him.

Upon thee be greetings and praise
'Abdu'l-Bahá 'Abbás[165]

The definitive date for the end of the Covenant-breaking period

Ever since the advent of the Cause, and throughout the course of its growth and progress up to the present day, the believers have always been beset by a variety of tests and difficulties. One of their spiritual delights, and a true cause of joy and happiness to them, has always been the fulfilment of 'Abdu'l-Bahá's prophecies, the realization of their hopes and longings. Praise be to God, in no case was there ever a breach of those promises. Even the assurance of the exaltation of the believers and the abasement of the Covenant-breakers came to pass on the exact day specified by the Master.

In fact, if we consider the profound implications of 'Abdu'l-Bahá's words and meditate on His utterances with a discerning heart, we note that none of them ever failed to come true. The story of Mírzá Badí'u'lláh and his fragrant business venture, as well as other examples presented in Chapters 1 and 3 of this book, corroborate this claim.

One such example is as follows. One day at the dinner table and in the presence of two Western lady believers, the Master spoke about the injustices, misdeeds and cruelties of the Covenant-breakers and their intrigues and mischief in their hope of arresting the progress of the Faith. Everything we already knew of their activities 'Abdu'l-Bahá recounted to us, and also things He had concealed up to that time. The information was so saddening that all those present were moved to the core of their beings. Suddenly and spontaneously I asked, "Beloved, will they continue to thrive?"

With a meaningful glance, 'Abdu'l-Bahá replied, "What are you saying, Khán? In four years they will be finished. They will cease to exist, although the followers of Yaḥyá will continue to endure in the world. However, no trace of these Covenant-breakers shall remain. Mírzá Badí'u'lláh once told me, 'Master, we are finished.'" The term "four years" stuck in my mind and I decided not to multiply it by ten or a hundred in order to somehow interpret or justify its fulfilment. I considered it to be a full period of four solar years. And then, in Istanbul, the "cannon blast of God's grace" sounded, the banner of Covenant-breaking was torn down forever, and the promised four years was fulfilled. The details of the "firing of the blast" will be presented in Chapter 7.

Collapse of the domes

At the outset of the Constitutional Revolution in Iran, one segment of the clerical class was for the new system while another was against it. Charging one another with heresy, the two contending groups arose to vanquish each other. Eventually, as a compromise, they decided to transform an inauspicious and ill-understood constitutional system into a legitimate and religiously lawful representative government. They agreed to place the final review and approval of all the laws passed by the *majlis* [parliament] under the jurisdictional authority of the two white and black domes, and included this requirement as a permanent and inviolable part of the country's Constitution.[166] However, since in the second or third year of the Constitutional era these multi-coloured "domes" collapsed by the force of nature, other "domes" too began to weaken and flounder, paving the way briefly for the development and progress of the country and the happiness of the people. But we had been unaware that under protection and regular financial support from the last monarch of the House of Qájár,[167] these public parasites had, like annoying and obnoxious insects, already laid their eggs in various nooks and crannies of the sacred institution of the National House of Representatives, as well as in the heart of every other significant national organization. And so it was not long before every crevice yielded a turban; these resolved collectively to take control of the minds of the people, and in so doing they again transformed society's happiness and prosperity into abasement and abomination, and reduced the overall health of the society into a variety of ills.

Once again, and for a few years more, the friends of God became the objects of the injustice and cruelty of these fanatical *mullás*, until the prophecies of 'Abdu'l-Bahá began to be fulfilled. The powerful hand of God emerged from the unseen realm and extirpated the very roots of that Qájár dynasty which had subsidized and supported the institution of the clergy, and consigned it to the bin of oblivion. At this time all heaven-sent helpers were given brooms to sweep out of every nook and cranny of the land the last traces of their existence, and flood out and destroy all vestiges of their miserable lives. After this, the Lord's command for the establishment of a uniform type of headdress freed the heads and filled the hearts with joy.[168]

In the midst of all the commotion many domes collapsed; only a few survived. Four years later another decree called for the removal of all types of headdress altogether, and the replacement of the Eastern garb with the Western mode of dress. Thus the malevolent and the wicked experienced such fear that the remaining domes were also discarded. All this happened so that the truth of the promises of the beloved

Master of this gentle Faith might be demonstrated. He had promised that "these white and black domes" would ultimately collapse.

"Once I was embarrassed"

'Abdu'l-Bahá's admonitions typically included the necessity of shunning the dangers of moral corruption inherent in any association with the violators of the Covenant. He would say, "Covenant-breaking has an adverse effect on public morals. The result of sowing such seeds of corruption will incline the people of the world towards ungodliness and atheism. The friends must therefore evince such heavenly character and attributes as to remove the foul smell of Covenant-breaking from the world of being. The friends must also be alert lest the Covenant-breakers sway public opinion to their advantage, for their loathsome stench renders people's nostrils incapable of inhaling the heavenly fragrances, and blinds their eyes from beholding the divine light."

In this vein, He would offer examples supported by verses from the Qur'án, presenting logical proofs and reminding the friends of their unequivocal duty to prevent the Covenant-breakers from penetrating the Bahá'í community. He would give the same examples that the Blessed Beauty used to offer about the followers of Yaḥyá. One of these stressed the fact that in whatever city a follower of Yaḥyá had lived, his foul odour would persist for a long time, slowing down the teaching work. Bahá'u'lláh had offered as an example the city of Kirmán[169] to demonstrate that the whisperings of the Covenant-breakers were worse than the temptations of Satan.

Of course, the truth of these utterances was clear to us, for we had observed at first hand the effects of the Covenant-breakers' intrigues on the people of Syria and Palestine. It was plain to see that at least three-quarters of them would have accepted the Faith without the least effort in teaching them, had their minds not been poisoned by the machinations of the Covenant-breakers.

One morning in the *bírúní* reception room, 'Abdu'l-Bahá was addressing me on this very subject, only two other people being present. I was reminded of a certain story which I wished to tell in support of 'Abdu'l-Bahá's words, and at the same time demonstrate the extent of my own services to the Cause as well as the service of certain others. So I remarked, "In Tehran, a school was established and Ḥubbu'lláh, the son of the Old Hyena, was a candidate for a teaching position there. As soon as we heard the news, the Hands of the Cause, along with two others and myself, met and consulted on ways to block his acceptance by the school. Finally, it was decided that Mr…….. should meet with the school authorities and persuade them to reject Ḥubbu'lláh."

I expected to receive 'Abdu'l-Bahá's praise and encouragement confirming our great service, but even before I had completed my remarks, He interrupted: "What! You consulted on how to prevent a Covenant-breaker from earning a living? This is not how the Faith is served. In matters of earning a livelihood there is no difference between a believer and a Covenant-breaker. The friends must be the signs of God's generosity and charity. They should shine like the sun and be as bounteous as the spring rain. They should not consider the capacity or merit of a person."

In short, He continued in this vein for some time, while I felt deep pangs of shame and remorse for my actions and words. I lowered my head, realizing that in my attempt to please the Master I had been too much of a meddler, and for once I was embarrassed.

The sweet fragrance of some of the letters

When 'Abdu'l-Bahá handed me the batches of incoming mail, He often selected one or two of the letters and instructed me to "translate these first". It was obvious that certain qualities were attached to those letters which could not be detected outwardly. One day, as I approached the House of 'Abdu'l-Bahá, I noticed from a distance Ḥájí Siyyid

Táqí Manshádí handing the Master a batch of recently arrived mail. As I arrived and bowed, 'Abdu'l-Bahá selected one of the letters and remarked, "This letter has such sweet fragrance. See what it contains."

Since He had used the words "sweet fragrance", I spontaneously raised the letter to my nose and sniffed it, but did not detect any scent. Suddenly 'Abdu'l-Bahá said, "Hurry up and read it."

I opened the letter immediately, following 'Abdu'l-Bahá outside. The envelope contained two pieces of paper, one blue and one white. With haste and anticipation I unfolded the blue paper. Again He asked, "What does it say?"

Feeling somewhat confused and anxious at 'Abdu'l-Bahá's haste, I went over the blue sheet quickly without grasping much of its meaning. From the subject and the power and authority of the words I concluded that it had to be a translation of one of the Tablets of the Blessed Beauty. I then unfolded the white sheet. It was a letter from Mr. Hoar, whose pilgrimage has been described in Chapter 2. As we walked, I read the letter aloud line by line and translated it for 'Abdu'l-Bahá.

The letter reported that Muẓaffaru'd-Dín Sháh (since deceased) was in Europe and that he had written him a letter informing him of the Western Bahá'ís' love and affection for the sacred land of Iran (a copy of the letter was in the envelope), and so implored him to treat the Persian Bahá'ís with justice and fairness. Now that the subject of the letter was clear, I reread the blue paper, the contents of which I had not originally understood. It was a copy of the letter to the Sháh. This time I read the letter and translated its contents. 'Abdu'l-Bahá then handed me a few other envelopes, and told me to go back to the pilgrim house, translate these two letters quickly and bring the translation to Him forthwith.

The letter addressed to the Sháh was so eloquent and powerful that on the first reading I had imagined it to be from the Writings of Bahá'u'lláh. On the following day, when I attained the presence of 'Abdu'l-Bahá, a Tablet in response to the letter was revealed. I discovered that my original impression had not been all that wide of the mark when I heard the Master's words of profound praise for Mr Hoar's initiative. The contents of his letter had proven to be so pleasing and praiseworthy that these words were contained in the Tablet revealed in his honour: "I swear by God, it seems as though I dictated that letter and you wrote it down." Clearly, he had been truly inspired. At that very moment I was reminded of the letter from Breakwell's father, mentioned in Chapter 2, about which 'Abdu'l-Bahá had used the same words before it was opened: "It has such sweet fragrance," and had told me to translate it straight away.

So it is clear that purity of heart and selfless devotion on the part of the believers can result in divine inspiration. The sweet fragrance of some of the letters was an indication of those heavenly attributes.

You conquered my heart before I ever existed

In all my years of residence at that sanctified and radiant threshold, I read many strange and unusual statements in the letters from the Western believers to the Master; however, I never felt at liberty to reveal any of them, except those for which I had explicit permission from 'Abdu'l-Bahá. In those times, my emotional sensitivity was so acute that the news of the joyful devotion and all-consuming love of the friends, who lived thousands of miles from the shores of nearness, and the anxious and anguished expressions of longing which filled their letters, moved me so intensely that at times I could not help but weep and ask God's confirmations on their behalf. I also tried, to the extent possible, to make mention of them while in the presence of 'Abdu'l-Bahá, and prayed and implored God that they too might one day become intoxicated with the wine of reunion.

An example of this was a letter from an American believer who had declared his faith in Baha'u'llah at the ripe old age of 108. This old man had been filled with such child-like joy and delight that it seemed as if he had been born into a new world and had just begun his growth and development anew. Despite trembling hands and feeble eyesight – as evidenced by the size of his handwriting, each page containing no more than four or five words – he had used thirty to forty pages to express his pent-up longing. His words were so moving that they deeply touched the reader. He wrote that he had belonged to the Millerite group[170] and that on the night of the Declaration of the Báb and birth of 'Abdu'l-Bahá he had awaited the second coming of the promised Messiah on the roof of his house; gazing up at the movements of the heavens he had beheld the dawning of the star of a new revelation, as well as changes in the configuration of other stars. These fulfilled the requirements of their beliefs, yet they had not grasped the significance or the true meaning of the descent of the Messiah in the form of the human temple. Since that time, however, he had remained true to his beliefs, telling himself, "Tonight the Messiah did assuredly descend from the heavens; while He did not appear to my physical eyes yet He filled my heart and soul with His presence." In fact, that fateful night in 1844, when all the astronomical transformations and shooting stars appeared to the Millerites, coincides with the 5th day of Jamádí of the lunar year 1260[171] and on that very night in the skies of Isfahan, as described by ......, a new star did appear.

However, this newly declared 108-year-old Bahá'í was with enthusiasm and erudition setting forth proofs: "On that very day I was convinced of the dawning of the Sun of Truth, and if my physical senses failed in recognizing the divine light, my spiritual consciousness failed nary a moment, for as soon as I heard the call from a Bahá'í, a vision of the Most Great Prison appeared before the eyes of my spirit and I beheld the very thing that had so completely penetrated my heart. And so I ask and implore you to accept my belief and devotion from that very day of my acknowledging the Faith of God and consider me to have been a true believer from the days of my youth, so that the youthful spirit of this worn-out body may experience true delight and happiness."

In short, he wrote with great eloquence and beauty, expressing his intense spiritual attraction and tender feelings. The reading of it touched the very depth of one's heart. He reiterated his request: "Fifty-eight years ago, before I found everlasting life through the spirit of faith, my heart continually yearned to become a throne worthy to receive the promised Messiah when He descended, and now that I have found a new life and am intoxicated with the wine of joy and delight, I ask that I may be accepted as a true believer from that time."

I was able to read the letter at last, though with much difficulty, and completed its translation with much care. However, since I always used to write a few words in red as a summary at the top of the page of every letter to facilitate 'Abdu'l-Bahá's subsequent reply, I wondered what brief words I could use to describe the gist of that letter. Then the blessings released by the purity of motive of that youth of the spirit brought to mind the opening verse of a love poem by the Nightingale of Shíráz [Sa'dí], a poem which had once been received with great acclaim by Tehran's Society of Poets, and so I wrote:

> *Never shall I abandon this intoxicating bliss*
> *Since you conquered my heart before I ever existed.*

The name of the first Japanese Bahá'í was Yamamoto

While the identification and recognition of the first believer in any revelation encourages and motivates other believers, so too the recognition of the first believer of each country is naturally of much interest to the future believers of that land. But true felicity belongs to the soul who is the cause of the guidance of the first believer of any country. In the Far East, this honour belonged to Mrs. Helen Goodall of California,[172] who taught her Japanese servant. In her letter to 'Abdu'l-

Thomas Breakwell.
"Thy Lord hath verily singled thee out for His love"
('Abdu'l-Bahá, Selections, *p. 188)*

*Hippolyte Dreyfus,
Disciple of 'Abdu'l-Bahá*

*Lua Getsinger,
Herald of the Covenant*

*Disciples of 'Abdu'l-Bahá:
William Hoar and
Isabella Brittingham*

The Master's carriage, driven by his faithful servant Isfandyár

The Bahá'ís of 'Ishqábád, carrying materials for the construction of the Mashriqu'l-Adhkár. Vakílu'd-Dawlih (Ḥájí Mírzá Muḥammad-Taqí Afnán, cousin of the Báb) who was instrumental in carrying out the project, is the turbaned figure in the front row, right.

The ‘Ishqábád House of Worship under construction

Above, the streets of 'Akká: a view down Saladin Street; below, Bahá'ís in front of Tel-i-Fakhkhár, with the Mansion of Bahjí in the distance on the left. (Getsinger, 1900)

Bahá she wrote, "I have taught the Faith to my manservant, Yamamoto. I ask for divine confirmations to enable him to spread the glad tidings in his country."

Praised be God, that supplication was answered, and later on Jináb-i-Yamamoto arose to serve the Faith. Here is the story: When I received the letter from this new believer declaring his faith, along with the letter from his spiritual teacher, the only word I could read was his signature in English, and so I submitted the letter, just as it was, with a translation of Mrs. Goodall's letter, to the attention of 'Abdu'l-Bahá. The Master mused, "Well now, you do not know Japanese."

"No, Beloved," I volunteered. "I hardly know English."

"So, what are we to do with this letter?" He remarked, smiling.

I bowed, and in my heart proposed, "The same thing you do with other letters."

"Very well, then," He said, "We will rely on the Blessed Beauty and will write him a reply."

Next day two Tablets were revealed in reply. I translated and sent them. Some time later other letters expressing gratitude arrived; these confirmed Jináb-i-Yamamoto's determination to arise and serve the Faith. 'Abdu'l-Bahá's Tablet[173] is reprinted below:

Care of Amat'u'lláh Helen Goodall
– the Glory of God be Upon Her – California
To Kanichi Yamamoto of Japan

He is God!

O thou who art the single one of Japan and the unique one of the extreme Orient!

That country hath been deprived of the divine breath until this time; now, God be praised! thou art initiated in the mysteries and conscious of the secrets of the lights.

Thou hast been earthly, I hope that thou wilt become

heavenly; thou hast been gloomy, I desire that thou wilt become luminous. Thou wert wandering in the wilderness, thou hast found a way to the abode of the Beloved One; thou wert a thirsty fish, thou hast attained to the endless Ocean; thou wert a roving bird, thou hast reached the divine Rose Garden; thou wert spiritually sick and thou hast found real health!

Now is the time that thou shouldst entirely abandon the comfort, ease, enjoyment and the life of this transient world, and wholly arise to guide the people of Japan, illuminating faces, perfuming nostrils and conquering, through the heavenly hosts and divine reinforcements, the hearts of the people of that region.

Do not wonder at the favour and bounty of the Lord. By the favour of God, how often a drop hath become undulating like a sea, and an atom become shining like the sun!

The Sun of Truth hath enlightened the divine world and illumined the universe. The rays of His grace have shone upon the East and West, and His heat hath caused vegetation in all countries. So the lights and the heat of the Sun of Truth being help and assistance, what more dost thou need?

Thou must warble, like the nightingale of significances, in the rose garden so that thou mayest inspire all the birds of the meadow to chant and to sing. Upon thee be greetings.

'Abdu'l-Bahá 'Abbás

His gait and bearing defy words

The best and happiest hours for one who has remained remote from the threshold of nearness for thirty years are those spent in remembering those bygone days, bringing to the mind's eye the Beloved of the world, that dawning-place of divine light – and reminiscing about His disposition, His manners, His gait and bearing.

In this respect, this unworthy servant considers himself the most fortunate of all the people of Bahá, since despite suffering the ravages of a feeble memory and the lack of adequate notes, whenever I pick up the pen to write these memoirs, suddenly that radiant, heavenly countenance, that glorious figure, emerges in my memory with such lucidity and intensity that the hazy, disoriented faculties of my mind are suddenly transformed into shining mirrors reflecting ever so brightly that celestial Light, that embodiment of heavenly attributes. Many a detail of which I was either unaware or had lost all recollection manifests itself with bright clarity.

While I feel utterly powerless to ever express the depth of my gratitude for these divine gifts, I also feel a measure of embarrassment at my inability to express what is in my heart and mind. And while many features of the Master's manner and bearing clearly appear before my mind's eye, yet their description defies words; the pen is rendered powerless to leave a meaningful mark.

I have already mentioned, albeit briefly, the Master's busy schedule and have described, so far as I am able, the effect of the revelation of Tablets and utterances. I hope that in so doing I have been able to share with the reader a drop of the ocean of my experiences and observations. However, 'Abdu'l-Bahá's bearing and gait were not something that pen or tongue can describe. For example, His way of walking – the simplest of physical movements – did not in any shape or form resemble the walk of any other human being. This had become an established fact; the resident believers bore witness to having heard the Blessed Beauty remark, "Look how the Master walks. No one in the world has a more sublime gait."

The friends in those days used to say that when the Blessed Beauty resided in the Mansion of Bahjí, He used to gaze at the fields from the balcony of the building and as soon as the blessed figure of the Master appeared, approaching the Mansion, Bahá'u'lláh would invite all who were in His presence, saying, "Come and see the Master walking."

In brief, the same applied to His eating, drinking, sitting and rising, all of which were in their way unique and matchless. And of course whatever quality or virtue that could merit Bahá'u'lláh's approval and praise is obviously beyond His servants' ability to adequately describe.

While 'Abdu'l-Bahá's manner of speaking was ever pleasant and delightful, yet when it came to humour His anecdotes left such an effect in the hearts that His listeners were beside themselves with joy and delight, especially when He told a story to illustrate a point. And however commonplace such a story might be, His manner of presentation was such that it seemed as though a sublime and holy Tablet was being revealed. This is why stories told by 'Abdu'l-Bahá cannot have the same effect when repeated by anyone else.

And now I present below, in simple language, two or three stories which I have heard from the lips of 'Abdu'l-Bahá.

A story to illustrate a point

In Chapter 3, as well as in the account in this book of the intense hardships and restrictions, it was related that 'Abdu'l-Bahá's heavy responsibilities were so time-consuming that He hardly found the opportunity at the dinner table to eat a full meal, or even the chance to take a bath. At these times, Mírzá Ḥaydar-'Alí and I collaborated on some ways to provide a respite for the Master.

It was decided that he would invite 'Abdu'l-Bahá one day to a public bathhouse. Fortunately the invitation received His acceptance. The Master, however, wished both of us participate in the festivity too. We fulfilled our duty by sitting outside the bath, biding our time until He came out. However, things did not go well, and even in the cloakroom much was left to be desired, as just out of spite the required services were not properly provided.

This facility, known as the Great Bathhouse, was the cleanest and best organised Turkish bath at that time.[174] When I visited it some four years ago, the building had completely deteriorated and had therefore been abandoned. In any case, the invitation to the bathhouse did not lead to a regular once-a-week or twice-a-month event, and so after further consultation with the Ḥájí we agreed that the architect Áqá Bálá, who was in 'Akká on pilgrimage at the time, should beg

'Abdu'l-Bahá's permission to build a small bath in His house. And so he submitted his request. Since he was one of the pure in heart, his request was granted. He immediately obtained the required construction materials and set out to build the facility under the stairs of the *bírúní* area. He also wrote to the Bahá'ís in Beirut asking them to purchase a metal bathtub, as well as the other materials required, and to ship them as soon as possible.

One night, only three days after work had started, when all the friends were in the presence of the Master, 'Abdu'l-Bahá suddenly said, "Jináb-i-Ustád Áqá Bálá, is the bath completed?"

The architect anxiously replied, "No, Beloved, I am working on it, but there is no news from Beirut yet."

"Well then, when will it be finished?" 'Abdu'l-Bahá enquired.

I cannot quite remember how Áqá Bálá responded to that question, but suddenly 'Abdu'l-Bahá smiled broadly and remarked, "The story of you and I resembles the story of an Arab who went about without a hat for three years. In the streets and marketplace, in cold weather or hot, in rain or snow, he was without a head covering. A philanthropist, feeling sorry for him, decided to buy him a turban and so he took the Arab to a shop to buy the fabric. As soon as the salesman brought out the fabric roll to measure the length required, the bareheaded Arab suddenly grabbed the end of the fabric and began to wrap it around his head, without allowing the salesman to cut the proper length.

"'Wait, let me measure the material,' complained the salesman.

"'How long am I supposed to wait? If I wait any longer I will catch my death of cold!' protested the Arab."

The Master on health

'Abdu'l-Bahá often spoke about health. The scientific aspects of what He said have not remained with me, for at that time

I was not yet a physician, but I could understand the practical aspects emphasized by the Master.

The harmful effects of eating meat and the benefits of vegetarianism were made clear by the Master; He offered a variety of natural, physical and rational proofs. He would explicitly show how the human body was predisposed towards the digestion of fruits, grains and vegetables, and that eating meat was a habit that had afflicted man over the course of time and generated dependence on the consumption of animal products. In fact, it was man's need and dependency that had prevented God's Manifestations from officially forbidding its use.

The Master Himself rarely ate animal products. One of the English friends had asked me to present a question to 'Abdu'l-Bahá about the Society of Vegetarians, and to advise him of the Master's response. 'Abdu'l-Bahá replied, "The truth is that it is not befitting for man to be carnivorous. However, man has accustomed himself to such a life and now it has become routine and acceptable. That is why its prohibition is not advisable at present."[175]

When there were no guests, there were no particular arrangements for 'Abdu'l-Bahá's meals. However, washing the hands before eating and brushing the teeth afterwards were customary and definite practices. Small portions of food, and regular change in the type of food served at each meal, were customary. For example, bread and cheese, or bread and olives, or merely bread, were at times quite usual. Sometimes He would take a small serving of kebab and would explain at the dinner table the reason for His choice.

The one bounty which was invariably available, whether in the *andárúní* or in the presence of guests in the *bírúní*, was a most delicious bread baked by Ismá'íl Áqá, who performed this duty out of pure love and devotion. One or two loaves were always ready. And if there were guests around the table, the Master would divide the bread among them. The bread was so delicious that it was possible to forego other dishes in its favour.

Whenever 'Abdu'l-Bahá sat at the dinner table He spoke of happy things, and if Western believers were present the answers to their questions were also presented in a state of joy and gaiety. In such cases dinnertime would last a long time.

When served in the *andárúní*, 'Abdu'l-Bahá's meals were very simple. The expenses of His lunch and dinner, if guests were not present, were much less than one could possibly imagine. Cleanliness and purity prevailed at all times. The Master would take some water with His meals. This was generally the arrangement of meals served to 'Abdu'l-Bahá.

The raiment that clothed that beloved body was abundantly soft and delicate, light and free-flowing, and while the air of 'Akká was not as laden with smoke and other pollutants as that of the cities of Europe, and a gentle breeze always cleared the air, yet the Master changed his shirt twice daily. This did not take much time, for it was not difficult to remove the *'abá* and *qábá*[176] and then put them on again, for they were comfortably loose and conveniently devoid of any superfluous buttons. The brightness and delicacy of 'Abdu'l-Bahá's shirts and headgear dazzled the eyes. Most of the Master's clothes were made of cotton and quite inexpensive, and since the clothes were loose, His blessed body was always free. The shawl that He wore around His waist was soft and loosely held in place. The colour of His clothes was generally beige or a bit darker. I never saw 'Abdu'l-Bahá in black or other dark colours.

In brief, the Master's good health, maintained through eating little and adhering to absolute cleanliness and simplicity, complied perfectly with the requirements of nature. After I had become a physician and was spending my vacation at 'Akká, I once checked 'Abdu'l-Bahá's pulse at His request. While at that time the signs of age were quite apparent in the Master's eyes and face, yet there was no sign of hardening of the arteries. I shall write more about this in the final chapter of this book.

'Abdu'l-Bahá was hardly ever ill. He used to say that after the passing of the Blessed Beauty and the onset of the Covenant-breakers' activities, He had been afflicted with *duláb* disease[177] for a few days; this was diagnosed as diabetes caused by a nervous disorder and lasted no more than a few days, after which He regained perfect health. In my last days in His presence, He sometimes caught a cold and ran a slight fever. However, that mighty will, that innate and heavenly power, always maintained His delicate, precious and celestial body in perfect balance and health.

When in 1909 A.D. I was given permission to return to Iran, 'Abdu'l-Bahá was in the sixty-fifth year of His life. His body was straight as an arrow and He enjoyed perfect health. He was the very embodiment of joy and cheerfulness.

Another illustrative story: "Six years of hard work did not go to waste!"

One of 'Akká's famous physicians, who held a deep-seated resentment towards the Faith, was once called upon to pay a professional visit at 'Abdu'l-Bahá's residence. He performed his duties with great enthusiasm and sacrifice, even visiting the patient two or three times daily, well beyond normal requirements. In the end, however, he submitted a bill which was so exorbitant that it astonished everyone. 'Abdu'l-Bahá paid the bill in full and then told the following story to illustrate a point.

"From the actions, facial features and general disposition of this doctor, it was quite obvious to what an extent the hatred and disgust prompted by religious prejudice had penetrated his every limb, and how strongly the signs of animosity showed on his face. We referred three patients to him. He applied himself with such a happy face and amiable disposition that I was amazed. I told myself, 'I know this person and how spiteful and malevolent he is, so how can this much care and service be possible?' However, when his work was finished and he sent in his bill I realized he had charged ten times the true worth of the services rendered. I paid the bill immediately, and I am happy that in this way I came to know him well!

"There was once a young *mullá* who wished to become specialized in the evaluation of human character through the study of physiognomy. Leaving his home, he travelled to Egypt and for six years studied the science of facial features. After a great deal of the hardship which is the lot of any foreigner in a strange land, he passed his tests in both theory and practice, and having been granted the required certificates he mounted his mule and happily headed back towards his homeland.

"On the way, he made it a point to study the face of anyone who crossed his path; through practising his science he was able to discover many truths about that individual. One day in the distance he saw a person whose face betrayed signs of meanness, jealousy, selfishness, greed and stinginess. He said to himself, 'Lord God, I take refuge in God from His anger, but this is a face the like of which I have never seen before. A person with such a sinister face and such terrible qualities is well worth knowing, so that I may test my scientific knowledge and observations.'

"As the *mullá* was deep in thought, the stranger approached and with a happy smile and a humble disposition greeted him warmly, took hold of the bridle of his mule and said, 'Honourable sir, where are you coming from and where are you bound for?'

"'I am coming from Egypt and returning to my native town; tonight I plan to stop in such-and-such a village,' the *mullá* replied.

"'But sir,' advised the stranger, 'the village is quite far away, it is late and my house is very near. It would be better if you honoured my house with your kind presence and filled our home with pride and joy.' As the poet says:

Though the house is unworthy and bleak,
Yet thy noble presence I seek.
Enter it then and banish the dark
By the light that shines forth from thine eyes.

"The *mullá* noted that the stranger's words and behaviour were in complete contrast to his evaluation of the man's facial features and gestures, and he began to have second thoughts about his technical competency. So in order to further test his true ability, he accepted the invitation and proceeded to the stranger's house.

"With joy and pleasure the host provided every possible comfort. Tea, coffee, sherbet, and the water pipe were served one after another, as he constantly and persistently invited his guest to partake of all manner of food and drink. Each time the host made a kind and affectionate remark while serving his guest, the *mullá* sighed deeply and said to himself, 'I worked for six futile years specializing in a science which has ultimately proved false and useless.'

"When the time came for dinner to be served the *mullá* took a look at the variety of food before him and sighed again, thinking, 'I have made a huge mistake in not distinguishing a great and generous man from a contemptible one.' Hardly touching his meal, he spent the night in a state of misery. Next day before dawn he arose and prepared to take his leave. But the host expressed his dismay at losing the companionship of such a friend, and insisted that he should at least remain for lunch, immediately providing all the means of comfort and pleasure.

"In short, after three days of this warm and kindly reception, this generous and even persistent hospitality, the guest finally persuaded his host of his decision to leave. The host groomed his guest's mule and prepared it for the journey, and with great courtesy helped him mount. As he held the reins fast for the *mullá* to mount, he handed him an envelope. The *mullá* thought it was a gift to help him on his journey and exclaimed, 'You should not have done this. What is it anyway?'

"'This is your bill,' replied the host.

"'Bill for what?' asked the astonished *mullá*.

"The host, dropping his mask of deceit, frowned and replied, 'You thought all this was for free?'

"The *mullá*, having come to his senses, opened the envelope and gazed with horror at an itemized price list of what he had eaten and some of what he had not, totalling some one hundred times the real worth of the services he had received. Of course, he had no such funds available, and so he placed the bridle of the mule, with his saddle bag and his other belongings, in the hands of his host and began to walk home, frequently kneeling down and praising the Lord thus: 'Praised be God, those six years of hard work did not go to waste!'"

Charity devoid of hypocrisy

'Abdu'l-Bahá frequently spoke about charity, noble conduct, kindliness towards all and serving the cause of humanity. He especially emphasized the fact that showing kindness and performing a service is acceptable, laudable and worthy to be considered an act of devotion, only if it is sincere and devoid of any hint of hypocrisy. Otherwise, if an ulterior motive or intent prompt the act, even if that purpose and intent is in itself praiseworthy and sacred, the act of charity will be tainted with hypocrisy; it will be unacceptable as a goodly act in the path of God, and will have little effect in the world of being.

"Rays of sunlight, the heat of the sun, or the falling rain of divine bounty are bestowed unconditionally and without any ulterior motive. In the same manner, a Bahá'í must be the manifestation of divine generosity and charity. Like the sun, he must shine on all and bestow his light on every land. You see that the infinite mercy of God embraces the whole of creation and knows no bias. The people of Bahá must be the manifestations of this mercy and perform their charity similarly without any condition or intent.

"Indeed, it is this charity that educates the world of humanity; it is this charity that turns nature green and beautiful. I wish that you, the people of Bahá, may attain this great blessing, so that from the bounteous outpourings of each one of you this world of nature may be transformed into the most glorious paradise. If you look to the Abhá Kingdom and behold the outpouring mercy and divine blessings which are vouchsafed equally to the obedient and the rebellious, then you will learn how you can become the signs of divine mercy and how, while bestowing your gifts, you can remain free of all conditions and motives, even if that condition is for the sake of God.

"For example, it is clear that no intent or act is more praiseworthy than teaching the Faith of God, no act is more sacred than guiding the nations. Yet if you show someone kindliness and use this as a means to disarm and convert him, this, too, is hypocrisy and deceit. If you serve someone, do not allow this hypocrisy to enter your heart, so that your service and your charity may be true to God, and its effects more enduring. As far as you can, you must be charitable without the slightest hint of hypocrisy and without any expectation of result or reward. Only then will the heavenly blessings attained through your acts of generosity transform this contingent world into a reflection of the Abhá Kingdom."

In short, the Master spoke a great deal on this subject, presenting many logical proofs which have been perused by the friends in a thousand Tablets. However, the many stories, proverbs and anecdotes which accompanied these admonitions and not only added humour but offered a deeper understanding of His utterances, are so indescribable that a thousand eloquent tongues and brilliant orators would fail in their attempt to recount them, much less the stammering tongue, trembling fingers and chaotic thoughts of this servant, who is even incapable of describing any particular feature and quality related to one such as himself.

One night, 'Abdu'l-Bahá spoke about consecrating one's possessions and the pleasure of giving generously. Explaining the meaning of the verse of the Blessed Perfection that, "To give and be generous are attributes of Mine; well is it with him that adornest himself with My virtues,"[178] He spoke with fervour, citing some interesting points regarding the evils of greed and miserliness. Quoting this verse: "Woe betide every slanderer and defamer, him that layeth up riches and counteth them,"[179] He went on to explain, "Whoever, out of miserliness, selfishness and frugality, amasses great wealth for unlawful purposes, will certainly not succeed, and ultimately that wealth will be used for purposes contrary to his wishes." He then gave some examples, citing several of the wealthy men of 'Akká in the past who were well known to the resident Bahá'ís, described their intentions in amassing their fortunes, and how all that wealth was spent in ways contrary to their purposes when they eventually left this world.

One of the resident friends then made a remark, in response to which 'Abdu'l-Bahá related the following story: "Once a poor Arab was weeping and wailing in the wilderness while tending to his dying dog. A passerby asked the reason for his grief. The Arab replied: 'This animal has always been my companion; whether at home or on the road he has faithfully guarded me against danger, and now he is dying of starvation in this barren wilderness and I am left utterly powerless to save his life.'

"The passerby, who himself lacked provisions for his own journey, felt pity for the poor Arab, and wishing to be of some help began to console him: 'It is not right that you should shed so many tears, moaning and groaning over this dying animal.'

"The Arab's lament grew louder: 'But this is not an animal, this is a trained dog who has been my constant companion, accompanying me on all my travels. It has performed good and faithful service and has rescued me many a time from life-threatening danger.'

"In short, he enumerated a list of extraordinary qualities to describe his loving companion. These expressions were so moving that the passerby too began to weep. After about an hour the traveller prepared to take his leave. As he stood up, he leaned his hand against the Arab's travelling bag. As he pressed on the bag he heard a crackling noise, so he asked the Arab what he had in the bag. The Arab replied, 'It is dried bread for my journey.'

"'Why do you not give some of it to this dying animal?' asked the traveller. Insulted, the Arab stared at him and exclaimed, 'I said I loved the dog, but not enough to share my own bread with him!'"

Infiltrating the Faith of God

'Abdu'l-Bahá spoke a great deal about the future of the Faith, giving glad tidings of the complete and final triumph of the Cause. Regarding the firmness of the structure and objectives of the institution of the Universal House of Justice, and the necessity of avoiding any condition that might lead to instability or division in the Faith of God, He spoke in emphatic language. He would explain the reasons behind the instability and division in the different existing religions, and how certain capricious characters had infiltrated the Faith of God, formed various groups and beliefs, and thus destroyed the very spirit of the Cause. And furthermore, how these leaders had made their worldly and selfish desires appear to be heavenly aims, deceiving the naive and simple-minded in the name of following the Law of God. In so doing they had created disunity among the believers and weakened the pillars of the Faith. The strength of the Universal House of Justice, however, would prevent this division and weakness. For now, the Spiritual Assemblies are responsible for the affairs of the Cause until the Universal House of Justice is established.

In short, from the utterances of the Master it could be gleaned that nothing could be more harmful and destructive than division and disunity. And that while the Faith of God was protected against such afflictions, the friends of God must still be alert and aware, so that the circumstances besetting the fortunes of other religions did not repeat themselves. They should beware lest someone generate a following based on a personal interpretation of a divine verse, form a group similar to the dervishes, and thus deviate from the straight path of the Cause of God. The following warnings were specifically and repeatedly emphasized by the Master:

"Whenever you see anyone who deviates to the extent of a needle's eye from the straight path of the Cause of God, who in the name of service or the practice of self-discipline or any other name tries to impress his own views on others, beware; for his purpose is to instil doubt and cause departure from the divine path so that he may acquire a following and form his own group. This departure from the straight path, though negligible at first, will lead after a time to remoteness from the path of guidance. And so from the very beginning any such deviation must be prevented.

"Of course, anyone who wants to gain a following and create division among the friends will at first resort to one of the divine verses and make himself appear to be sincere and deeply attached to the Faith. Words of humility and sacrifice flow from his tongue so that he may deceive the simple and the naive. For example, we repeat the Greatest Name ninety-five times a day. If someone proposes, 'What harm is there in repeating it ninety-six times?' – just once more, or 'We should repeat it twice ninety-five times,' you should know that his purpose is to infiltrate the Cause of God.

"In this Faith there are no hidden mysteries or esoteric allusions. The path of the Cause is straight. I too, in the position of Interpreter, have explained and written whatever was necessary. But the friends must be aware and alert, and eschew the company of such masters of deceit, and if they see someone who has supporters and followers, they must exercise great care and find out what plans are in his heart and what ambitions motivate his mind, since these people have no motive but to infiltrate the Faith."

The meaning of generosity

In the Islamic world His Holiness 'Alí, may peace be upon him, is considered a symbol of generosity, the quintessence of charity and magnanimity.[180] The record of his many acts of benevolence is ample proof of the veracity of this claim by the Muslims, and of the high regard in which he is held. The generosity of Ḥátem-i-Ṭá'í, too, is now a byword among the people of the East, to such an extent that any act of boundless giving is referred to as Ḥátem-giving.[181] This is absolute magnanimity, the gold standard by which acts of charity are measured.

However, 'Abdu'l-Bahá's counsels and admonitions to the people were as described in the section entitled "Charity devoid of hypocrisy". 'Abdu'l-Bahá would offer the example of nature's greatest gifts such as the sun, the moon, the heavenly rain and the celestial breeze, and express His desire that the friends should learn from nature, bestowing boundless favour upon all and under no circumstances allowing the slightest hint of partiality to influence their judgement, never considering merit or worthiness; in this way they would become signs of divine generosity.

These were the Master's teachings. And it could be observed from His own actions that His own boundless charity knew no limits, even given the prevalent circumstances and the lack of material means. The highest pillars of greed and avarice of the most self-serving individual could not reach the loftiness of the edifice of His generosity and munificence.

Now, the meaning of generosity must be understood. First, helping the poor, caring for the downtrodden and receiving and serving the beggars and paupers of 'Akká on Fridays, as described earlier, cannot in my view be considered signs of generosity, for they were 'Abdu'l-Bahá's expressions of mercy and kindness to those who were in need of those blessings. Even if He refused monetary help to a few ablebodied men, that too was a form of mercy and affection, in the hope that they might come to their senses, take on the hardships of labour, and earn an honest living.

Secondly, if on a cold rainy day in the streets of 'Akká, 'Abdu'l-Bahá gave His *'abá* to a needy person and returned home in only His *qábá*, this too could not be considered an act of generosity but rather an act of kindness and compassion towards the poor. Rochefoucauld, the French scholar, says:

"Witnessing the hardship of the poor stimulates the sense of pity and compassion, and therefore giving up one's material possessions alleviates these feelings."[182] Therefore, such an act cannot be defined as generosity either. So what is the true meaning of generosity?

In the opinion of this servant, true generosity is the greatest divine virtue and is utterly unrelated to the feelings of satisfaction and pleasure that are derived from attending to people's needs and wants. The station of 'Abdu'l-Bahá's generosity was the very embodiment of the divine verse contained in a prayer by the Abhá Beauty: "From the billows of the ocean of Thy generosity the seas of eagerness and enthusiasm were revealed."[183] In truth, from the billowing ocean of this manifestation of generosity, this source of charity, oceans of desire and greed were ever-present, for whoever was acquainted with that beloved personage longed with his whole being to be the recipient of His limitless blessings and charity, whether he was from the class of the poor or from the ranks of the affluent.

What was unusual was that regardless of the size of His gift, He Himself was never satisfied with the offering and would increase it. All the non-Bahá'ís, therefore, had noticed that in 'Abdu'l-Bahá's charitable hands material means and wealth had no value, regardless of their worth. And so the greedy and the avaricious – especially the ever-acquisitive Arabs – were always drifting around 'Abdu'l-Bahá. The story of one such man is presented here.

One day, one of the Shaykhs of Súr and Seydá[184] who had frequently been the recipient of 'Abdu'l-Bahá's acts of charity was in the presence of the Master. I too was summoned, and as He went on writing He told me, "Help the Shaykh to put on this 'abá." The 'abá was a fine garment made in the city of Ná'ín (famed for that industry) and every year a few were shipped to 'Abdu'l-Bahá from Iran to give away. I unfolded the 'abá from its package, shook the wrinkles out, and with both hands placed it over the tall shoulders of the Shaykh; then I stood next to him and awaited permission to sit down.

The S͟hayk͟h seemed distracted and pensive; with rapid hand movements he kept rubbing his fingers along the surface of the *abá* and muttering something. 'Abdu'l-Bahá raised His head and said, "O S͟hayk͟h, what is the matter?" But the S͟hayk͟h just stood there mumbling. The Master asked, "What do you wish to say?"

"But Effendi, this is cotton," He replied. In other words, this *abá* is made of cotton and is not worthy of my social rank.

'Abdu'l-Bahá's patience was wearing thin. He stood up and remarked, "This is not cotton. It is one of the best *abás* of Persia, it was made in the famous city of Ná'ín and arrived just yesterday, and I am offering it to you today. My own *abá* is made of cotton and I purchased it for two *majídí*, but your *abá* was purchased in Persia for ten *majídí*, not including the cost of shipping and customs." In making these remarks, 'Abdu'l-Bahá spoke with such an air of humility and melancholy that I was deeply moved. Again He spoke: "You know I am not the one to wear the better *abá* and hand you the inferior one. Now come, let us make a test." He then walked out of His small office and over to the adjoining room and stood near the window where He had the best light, and asked for a match. Then with much patience He removed some material from the surface of the fabric of the S͟hayk͟h's *abá* and made it into a small ball. He then put the flame to it and held the rising smoke under the S͟hayk͟h's wretched nose. Then the Master held the burnt woollen ball in front of his eyes until he was convinced. Next, He removed some lint from his own *abá*, burned it, and placed the smoke under the nose of the S͟hayk͟h until he agreed that 'Abdu'l-Bahá's *abá* was of cotton.

When the test was over, the Master uttered a few more words which touched my heart to its very core. I don't know what you, the readers, might have done had you been the ones listening to His words. He said, "O S͟hayk͟h, if I had worn the good *abá* and offered you the ordinary one, then you would have had the right to protest, but now you see that I gave you the better *'abá* and kept the cheaper, the two-*majídí 'abá*, for myself. But even if I had given you the cotton *'abá*, it would have been more worthy of you to have accepted the gift and not offended me. You could then have asked me for another *'abá* rather than breaking my heart by rejecting my gift."

As soon as the Shaykh lowered his head 'Abdu'l-Bahá, not wishing to witness his shame, said, "Don't be sad, I will give you the price of another *'abá* in cash." He then told me, "Go downstairs, find Áqá Riḍá and ask him to give fifteen *majídí* to the Shaykh."

I ran down the stairs, passed on 'Abdu'l-Bahá's instructions and returned. The Shaykh was receiving permission to leave. Afterwards the Master told me, "You see what I have to put up with?" Then He added, "These are not my real concerns, my real worry is that this news might reach the ears of the Covenant-breakers who would then find the poor man and fill his head with doubt and untruth, just to add to my cares."

In fact, the matter did not end there, for what 'Abdu'l-Bahá had envisioned came true. The Shaykh received the *'abá* and the fifteen *majídí* and took his leave. But the Covenant-breakers did discover the matter; they found him and filled his head with stories, the nature of which I am unaware. The next day he returned the *'abá* and the money to Áqá Riḍáy-i-Qannád. Áqá Riḍá reported the matter to 'Abdu'l-Bahá. The Master remarked, "That is not a problem. Keep his trust for him. The Shaykh will regret his action and will return for them."

After a time the Shaykh did in fact return contrite and regretful, and confidentially took back his trust from Áqá Riḍá. Later on, whenever he attained the presence of 'Abdu'l-Bahá, he would always receive his share of 'Abdu'l-Bahá's charity and generosity. This is the true meaning of generosity.

"Eat the bread, but don't drink the wine"

Those who lived within the precincts of the Holy Threshold bear witness that whoever attained the presence of the

Beloved, drank from the wine of nearness and became intoxicated by the ecstasy of such reunion, would lose control of his faculties, forget all the requirements of custom and convention, and fail to distinguish between the sublime and the unsightly.

I was one of these: I had become so inebriated with the wine of His favour and bounty that I was beside myself with joy and had lost the capacity to distinguish right from wrong. This was because I had recognized in my loving Master the tendency to consider the unworthy actions of human weaklings as true service, and their sins and shortcomings as non-existent.

Where Thy mercy abounds,
The undone is considered done,
The done undone.

I had no thought or concern about anything except that I constantly tried to do something – good or bad – in order to avoid the effects of idleness and sloth.

A way into the Friend's heart I must win,
If virtue should fail me, then through sin.

Peace and calm had no place in my life, and inactivity was abhorrent to me. I considered action and motion to be the very essence of the life of the spirit and – as I have described in Chapter 1 under the title "My duties on this pilgrimage" – through the intense devotion that burned in my heart I knew that the mercy and favour of my Master would cover my shortcomings and conceal my sins, and that while aware of the error of my ways He would respond with benevolence and forgiveness.

It so happened that none of the pilgrims who arrived at that time were any wiser than I, especially those who had been rescued from the tragedy of Yazd or had fled the calamity of Isfahan, or those who had escaped the sneering and taunting of the enemies and had at last found tranquillity and safety under the protective shadow of the Beloved of the world. They were all intoxicated with the wine of the eternal Covenant and lived in the paradise of nearness in utter joy and peace. One of these pilgrims, who stayed for quite some time, was the honoured 'Alí-Muḥammad Khán, known as Khán-i-Bahá'í. He had formerly been a close associate of Jalálu'd-Dawlih, the Governor of Yazd, the man who was the instigator of the holocaust and responsible for the murder of a large number of the martyrs who gave up their lives in the path of God.[185]

Khán-i-Bahá'í, of course, had witnessed all those dreadful, horrific events, and agonizing memories of the atrocities of Yazd were constantly in his mind. From the advent of the era of the Covenant [1892] he was held in such high regard by the Master that a Tablet was revealed in his honour every week or at least every month during a period of four years.

During his pilgrimage in 'Akká he was a constant recipient of 'Abdu'l-Bahá's blessings; while in His presence he received much of His attention. He was also called "Jináb-i-Khán" by the Master, and because of the abundance of His loving attention and kind favours, he, like me, had become spoiled and pampered. However, he was more deserving of 'Abdu'l-Bahá's blessings than I was, for he was weak and in ill health. He constantly complained of indigestion problems, consuming every day a handful of strange pills, herbs and seeds prescribed by Persian physicians. At that time he was less than 50 and more than 40, but the signs of age were quite apparent in his manners and behaviour, and while he was spiritually strong, his body was weak and feeble. However, now that he is over 80 years old he walks the fields and goes hunting, chasing his prey on foot. Furthermore, he never fails in his constant service to the Cause, and his only sign of age is a slight deafness which was discovered in his youth and which has stayed with him ever since. So the source of his physical health and energy should be clear. Rumour had it that he had asked 'Abdu'l-Bahá for healing and recovery of his powers. I do not know what instructions he received from 'Abdu'l-Bahá, but the Master had prescribed for his indigestion that he should take nothing but pure milk for a time, and had told the servant of the pilgrim house to provide him with an abundance of fresh milk every day.

For the first two days he was quite committed to his diet. On the third and fourth days he had to force the liquid down with distaste, and so once in the presence of the Master he begged to be relieved from drinking any more milk. 'Abdu'l-Bahá, however, re-emphasized the diet and so by the fifth and sixth day he could hardly move and was unable to leave the pilgrim house. On the seventh day, which was the day for visiting the Most Holy Shrine, I suggested accompanying him to the House of 'Abdu'l-Bahá where we could board a carriage. But then I realized that not only was he unable to walk, but that he even lacked the strength to talk.

Feeling sorry for him, I told him, "Just a piece of bread and a cup of tea should not be harmful."

"If I eat bread, what will I say to the Master?" he replied. "Didn't you see how adamantly He forbade me to consume anything but milk?"

I thought I could lovingly persuade him to eat, and then in the presence of 'Abdu'l-Bahá take the blame for his disobedience on myself. I was about to say, "Don't you know the saying of the Holy Imáms about the believers in this Dispensation: 'May my life be sacrificed for your sins', which makes the whole idea of disobedience non-existent?" But I realized that he could not appreciate such profound wisdom on an empty stomach, and so I said, "Why are you worrying about disobedience so much? Answering 'Abdu'l-Bahá won't be all that difficult."

"What should I do then?" he asked.

"Eat the bread and think of it as though you have drunk wine, and then repent immediately," I replied. This answer was as spiritual food to his soul. He got up straight away, hastily ate some bread and drank half a cup of lukewarm tea, and got his old energy back. So we set out towards the Master's House.

On the way, he kept me amused by his threats to disclose my part in the story and show me up as the real culprit. That day we visited the Most Holy Shrine and on our return we attained the presence of the Master. K͟hán-i-Bahá'í waited anxiously for 'Abdu'l-Bahá to ask after his health so that he might throw the responsibility off his own shoulders and onto mine. But as it happened, 'Abdu'l-Bahá did not even mention the subject, and so at dinner time in the pilgrim house he had himself a full serving of *abgusht* which he ate with great relish, and the next morning he felt no shame in putting away a good size breakfast either, after which he hastened to the *darb-k͟hánih*.

An hour later he came running back to the pilgrim house and found me. "I really had to cook your goose in order to get my release to eat bread," he shouted with joy.

"So what did you do?" I enquired.

"I attained 'Abdu'l-Bahá's presence in the *bírúní* and received so much kind attention and loving words that in my shame, I began to cry. He asked me, 'You are not eating any bread, are you?' 'Yes, Beloved, I am,' I replied. 'What had I told you?' asked 'Abdu'l-Bahá. 'Beloved, Youness tempted me. He told me to eat the bread and think of it as though I had drunk wine and repent immediately,' I responded. 'Abdu'l-Bahá's laughter rang out as He laid His hand on my shoulder and remarked, 'Very well, very well. Eat the bread but don't drink the wine!'"

Having said this, he attacked the bread basket once more and put away as much of the bread as he could hold, whispering all the while, "Very well, very well. Eat the bread but don't drink the wine."

What sort of place was 'Akká?

The walled and fortified citadel of 'Akká had served in the past as the central site for the storage of heavy military artillery and ammunition, as well as the garrison headquarters for the

Ottoman army. Frequently coveted by the great conquerors of Europe, it had known bloody battles in the Napoleonic wars, when the Ottoman army gained ultimate victory.

The city's climate was so ghastly that it was used as a place of exile for murderers and other criminals who had been given the death sentence. And because of the foul stench of the fumes emanating from a variety of filth and sludge, infectious diseases were rampant. Even when the Blessed Beauty and other prisoners were brought here under the agreement between the Persian and Ottoman governments, the Persian ambassador had written to Náṣiri'd-Dín S͟háh, "The climate of the selected place of exile, namely the fort of 'Akká, is so terrible that if birds were to fly over it they would surely die."

In this dilapidated fortress there are structures several thousand years old. The ancestors of the inhabitants of 'Akká were either prisoners themselves, or military officials, or border guards of the citadel, and it was said that they were a physically feeble and frail people. It was frequently mentioned by 'Abdu'l-Bahá and acknowledged by all the resident believers that all the water from the city wells contained salt and was unpalatable, and that the only well which produced marginally drinkable water was the 'Aynu'l-Baqar well[186] located some two kilometres outside the city. All the residents of the town received their water from this well, carried into town on wagons drawn by oxen.

There are many Traditions about the exalted nature of this fortress. An example is the Tradition: "Blessed is the one that hath drunk from the Spring of the Cow", which recognizes the station of the well.[187]

From the day that this fortress became the place of exile of the Beloved of the world [Bahá'u'lláh], the climate gradually began to improve, the pollution of the atmosphere by those odious fumes ceased, the air quality improved and even the water from the city well turned fresh and drinkable. The change in the quality of water was so dramatic that the use of the famous 'Aynu'l-Baqar well was abandoned; it became a historical site about which elderly citizens of 'Akká told stories to the young. Furthermore, the once-rampant infectious and contagious diseases vanished. I frequently heard from 'Abdu'l-Bahá – and was once a witness to it myself – that in the forty-year period of the Most Great Prison plague and cholera epidemics several times engulfed many cities in the Holy Land but did not enter the gates of 'Akká, nor did they descend on the city from the air, despite the fact that the two most important agents for the spreading of these diseases, namely rats and flies, abounded in the area to such an extent that their numbers were beyond estimation.

In this period, in addition to the climate changes, many municipal developments were undertaken due to the encouragement and persuasion of the Blessed Beauty. For example, an aqueduct was established and drinking water was piped to homes. And since the inhabitants of 'Akká had seen little of parks or gardens, through 'Abdu'l-Bahá's generous gifts and contributions a city park called Baladieh was built just outside 'Akká, although it has been abandoned of late. Also at the command of the Blessed Beauty the Gardens of Riḍván and Firdaws, which were used by the public at large, were built.[188]

In short, due to the blessed presence of Bahá'u'lláh the dilapidated fortress of 'Akká was renovated and its environs developed into green fields and gardens bringing to mind the verdant gardens of Paradise itself. The villages and hamlets around 'Akká used to produce only dates, except in a few areas where citrus fruits and olives were grown. But after the change in the climate, summer and winter fruits such as dates, pecans, apples, pomegranates, figs and others became abundant. They used to say that the air of 'Akká was still and stagnant, but now a fresh breeze blows from all four sides. Some are of the belief that the reason for this air current is the opening of the Suez canal, which guides the current from Port Said, and that in summertime it brings with it the rain clouds of the Indian peninsula.

In any event, the people of 'Akká attributed these miraculous changes to the auspicious presence of Bahá'u'lláh; they were in no doubt about it. However, despite all these improvements in the climate and urban conditions, there still existed other difficulties and hardships in 'Akká. The resident believers used to recall that Bahá'u'lláh referred to these as "effulgences of the Most Great Prison". A few of these "effulgences" (*ishráqát*) had disappeared with the passage of time, but some remained. I will now describe one such "effulgence"!

One "effulgence" of the Prison, the thirty-day fast

The resident believers used to say that the phrase "effulgences of the Prison" was a term which had been revealed by the Tongue of Glory[189] to characterize the hardships and tribulations associated with life in 'Akká; it had endured among the friends through word of mouth.

At the beginning these hardships were numerous, but many of them disappeared little by little, mainly because of the changes to the environment. Others still persisted. The various deadly epidemics, which during the time of Bahá'u'lláh's imprisonment in the barracks had annihilated a large number of the inhabitants, had disappeared leaving no trace, as had the foul-smelling fumes which had caused and spread infectious diseases.

Still, one of those "effulgences of the Prison" which the passing of time and change in the climate had failed to overcome was the assault of the fleas, mosquitoes, flies and ants, which confirmed the expression, "Blessed the one who is bitten by the insects of 'Akká". Another was the thirty-day fast, which according to the command of Bahá'u'lláh was to be observed until the end of the period of incarceration to commemorate the Islamic holy month. Every sincere and devoted believer was expected to observe it gladly and of his own free will.

This thirty-day fast, which according to the Islamic calendar is observed in the month of Ramaḍán, continued to be kept until the end of the period of imprisonment in 1909 A.D. For the pilgrims and resident believers, who led relatively comfortable and peaceful lives, observing the thirty-day fast was not a difficult undertaking. But for the blessed person of the Centre of the Covenant, whose life was filled with numerous occupations and hardships (as described in Chapter 3 of this chronicle), it can be imagined how arduous and exhausting such an observance was. This was especially true when in the month of Ramadán the Muslims of 'Akká, including all the government officials, switched their nights and days and conveniently slept during the daytime, while at night, after breaking the fast and observing the obligatory prayers, they crowded 'Abdu'l-Bahá's *bírúní* to while away the night and disturb the Master until dawn.

But that spiritual and heavenly Being had to begin His many tasks before the rising of the sun, as has been described in previous chapters. And so in the month of Ramadán no comfort was possible for 'Abdu'l-Bahá; at times even the opportunity to partake of the meals did not present itself, and therefore His fast began without any breakfast and ended without any dinner. Thus the "effulgences of the Most Great Prison" sapped His strength and weakened His body. Many times during these days of fasting I saw the Master in such a state of exhaustion that I was deeply shaken.

On one such day He summoned me to His presence in the *bírúní* area. As He spoke, signs of melancholy and weariness were apparent in His voice. He slowly paced the floor and then began to climb the stairs with difficulty. The symptoms of fatigue gave way to expressions of displeasure and weariness: "I don't feel well. Yesterday I did not eat any breakfast and when the time came to break the fast I had no appetite. Now I need a bit of rest." As He spoke, His face was so ashen that I became alarmed for His wellbeing. So I boldly exclaimed, "It is better for the Master to break the fast."

"No, it is not proper," was 'Abdu'l-Bahá's reply.

I persisted. "With the way the Master feels, fasting itself is not proper either."

"It is not important, I will rest a while," responded 'Abdu'l-Bahá.

"The believers cannot endure to see the Master in such a

state of physical weakness and exhaustion," I remained unyielding.

'Abdu'l-Bahá gave an effective and moving explanation in the hope of convincing me to relent. It did not work. In fact, it increased my ardour, and I continued to try to persuade Him to break the fast. As He would not yield, my words became mixed with tears and lamentations. But He would not let up.

Suddenly I realized that I had found a new quality in myself which did not allow me to give in, despite all the reasons that 'Abdu'l-Bahá had offered. And so, stubbornly holding my ground, I told myself, "Regardless of what may come of this, I will continue to beg, plead and implore until I achieve my purpose, for I can no longer behold the Beloved of the world in such a condition."

While begging and supplicating, strange thoughts crowded my mind. It was as if I wished to discover in what light my servitude and devotion to that Threshold was regarded in the sight of God. As such, I would consider success in this to be a good omen. And so from the very depths of my heart I entreated the Most Holy Shrine for assistance. Spontaneously these words flowed from my lips, "So may I make a suggestion?"

"What do you want me to do?" 'Abdu'l-Bahá replied.

Tears streaming from my eyes, I begged Him, "Come and for this once break your fast, to bring happiness to the heart of a sinful servant of Bahá'u'lláh."

God be praised, I know not where those words came from, but they brought such joy to the heart of that quintessence of kindness and love that quite loudly He exclaimed, "Of course, of course, of course."

Immediately He called for Náṣir and told him, "Put some water in the pot and boil it and make a cup of tea for me." And then He put His blessed hand on my shoulder and said, "Are you pleased with me now? If you wish, you can go back to your tasks now and I will drink the tea and pray for you."

Such feelings of joy and ecstasy flooded my being at that

moment that I was rendered incapable of a reasonable response. Looking at me, 'Abdu'l-Bahá remarked, "Do you want to be present to see with your own eyes when I break my fast? Very well, come and sit down." He then withdrew to His small office, took up the pen and began to write, as I watched. Áqá Ridá now came into the presence of the Master for some particular purpose. 'Abdu'l-Bahá remarked, "Today I do not feel well and in response to the request of one of the loved ones of God I want to break my fast." As Áqá Ridá left the room, the teapot with a single glass and a bowl of sugar were brought in. Addressing me, 'Abdu'l-Bahá said, "Jináb-i-Khán, you have performed a praiseworthy service. May God bless you. If I had not broken the fast now, I would surely have fallen ill and would have been forced to break the fast." And with every sip of the tea, He bestowed on me other kind and loving words. After that He arose and said, "Now that I feel better, I will go after my work and will continue to pray for you."

And then He started down the stairs. In the *bírúní* reception room there was no one except the late Áqá Siyyid Ahmad-i-Afnán (the same Afnán upon whom the rank of martyr was bestowed posthumously). Addressing him, 'Abdu'l-Bahá said, "Jináb-i-Afnán, today I was not feeling well and intended to rest, but at the request of a beloved friend I have broken my fast. I am happy to have done so, for otherwise I would have fallen ill. But now I feel well and can continue the work of the Cause." Having said this, He walked out of the room. Jináb-i-Afnán, his eyes shining with the light of pure joy and delight, said, "God Almighty, who was that 'beloved friend', so that I can sacrifice my life for him?" And I, drunk with manifest victory, exclaimed, "It was I, it was I."

In brief, rather than any attempt at sacrifice of life, and filled with heavenly joy, we embraced each other as our spirits soared. As we did so, I placed in the storehouse of my memory the fact that the thirty-day fast truly was an "effulgence of the Most Great Prison".

"My wellbeing and its opposite are in the hands of the friends"

In certain chapters of this book I have presented short accounts of 'Abdu'l-Bahá's feelings and emotions during periods of hardship and suffering, and also in the section entitled "One thought cannot divert Him from another" I have briefly described His powers of endurance and perseverance in the face of a multitude of crises and predicaments. Now I wish to describe those types of hardship and calamity which caused Him the most pain and sorrow, and conversely, those conditions which brought joy and delight to His heart.

While I have already touched upon this issue as far as my failing memory can recall in some of the previous chapters, yet to elucidate the point I present the following account. And in this wondrous era, when the Sun of the Most Great Covenant of Bahá'u'lláh is shining from the horizon of the Guardianship of the Faith of God, I beseech God to help me succeed in bringing some measure of joy and happiness to the heart of the beloved Guardian. At the top of the list, the very first thing that distressed 'Abdu'l-Bahá and brought sadness to His blessed heart was disunity in the Cause of God. Compared to this, the breaking of the Covenant by the Covenant-breakers, the sedition of Mírzá Áqá Ján, and the wickedness and mischief of the trouble-makers and enemies of the Faith paled into insignificance. I had heard frequently from the lips of 'Abdu'l-Bahá: "I forgave Mírzá Áqá Ján and overlooked his many transgressions against me. However, forgiving him for the wounds he inflicted upon the Cause of the Blessed Beauty is not up to me."

Indeed, neither the opposition of the detractors, nor the refutation of the unbelievers, nor the infidelity of the Covenant-breakers displeased Him as much as the slightest odour of disunity detected in whatever quarter [among the Bahá'ís]. This was further demonstrated by the fact that while some of the Covenant-breakers were so brazen and impertinent that at times in the presence of the Master they were blatantly discourteous and even used slanderous words, none of this had the smallest effect on 'Abdu'l-Bahá. I heard the Master remark many times, "I have no complaints against Muḥammad Javád-i-Qazvíní, since he is openly and admittedly my enemy. I know where I stand with him. My complaint is against the unfaithful sceptics who create disunity."

So it was quite clear that there was nothing worse than creating disunity. Even the disunity created over the adoption of the Bahá'í greeting "Alláh'u'Abhá" compared to "Alláh'u'A'ẓam", which was described in the closing paragraphs of Chapter 1 of this book, was a source of great sadness to 'Abdu'l-Bahá. As soon as that storm was dissipated and the dark clouds of disunity were lifted, and the light of love and fellowship illumined the hearts, the Master's happiness and joy knew no bounds.

Secondly, what truly caused sadness and grief for the Master was the injustice of the enemies and the utter submissiveness of the friends – so much so that whenever the Persian friends suffered injury at the hands of their enemies, signs of deep sorrow could be detected on His blessed face for a long time. The account in Chapter 3 of this narrative of the holocausts in Yazd and Isfahan demonstrates the truth of this matter.

Thirdly, what really caused 'Abdu'l-Bahá much pain and sorrow was the misconduct and misdeeds of those who claimed attachment to the Faith. And conversely, the good deeds of any of the friends were a source of joy and happiness to the Master. The following story is presented as an example.

'Abdu'l-Bahá's health, as I witnessed it over the nine-year period of my stay, was such that He never took to bed when He was unwell; whenever He developed a fever He would simply endure the discomfort, not disclosing the matter to anyone; by adopting certain diets He was usually able to cure himself. Only by the way He ate and drank at the dinner table with the Western pilgrims – or abstained from food and drink – could we tell that He was not feeling well.

One day we heard that the Master was ill in bed and had not left the *andárúní*. Since an illness that would confine Him to bed was unprecedented, the resident friends became quite alarmed and for a few days whenever we enquired after His health we were given glad tidings of His recovery. But the Master did not appear in the *bírúní* area. After a while we began to lose patience and could no longer endure the situation. Every morning, every night, and at various other times we would show up at the *bírúní* area and enquire after His health from any relative or servant who came down the stairs. But since they all gave hopeful replies, it was clear that they were obeying 'Abdu'l-Bahá's instructions to impart only good news, lest the friends become unhappy and worried.

After some eight or nine days I presented myself at the Master's House very early one morning, before the rising of the sun. For a while I walked around the flower beds waiting for one of the servants to come down the stairs so that I could enquire about His health. Suddenly I heard the sound of 'Abdu'l-Bahá's finger rapping on the windowpane of His study. I raised my face and looking up beheld the blessed countenance of 'Abdu'l-Bahá in the first light of dawn. I was benumbed by the intensity of joy which flooded my whole being. With a movement of His finger, He beckoned me. Taking long jumps, I scaled the stairs and entered His presence. There stood the luminous figure of 'Abdu'l-Bahá. The Master seemed quite happy and fresh. I bowed.

"So you are here to enquire after my health? Praise God, I am quite well," He said. Then He told me to take a seat. As He began to write, the following utterances were revealed: "Nothing affects me more than the actions and conduct of the friends. The main reason I was ill over the last few days was a letter I had received from Persia describing the misdeeds and misconduct of one of the believers. The news brought me such pain and sorrow that I fell ill and had to stay in bed until last night, when Mírzá Haydar-'Alí delivered a letter from 'Ishqábád bearing news of the good deeds of one of the friends. It made me so happy that I became well. So if the believers wish for my happiness, they must adorn themselves with heavenly character and conduct." He continued in this vein with further admonitions, until He said, "It is because of this that I have always said that my wellbeing and its opposite are in the hands of the friends."

A grand feast

From the dawn of the advent of the Cause down to the present day, all the feasts and gatherings held in either Haifa or 'Akká have possessed a particular grandeur and splendour which in their own way have remained unrivalled. This was especially true when such feasts were hosted by none other than the noble person of 'Abdu'l-Bahá.

We had heard that one or two years before the renewal of confinement, in 1898 and 1899, the grandest feasts were held in Haifa; travellers of different faiths and from various far-off lands of East and West all attended, attired in their diverse native dress. But since confinement in the Most Great Prison had resumed and the holding of gatherings and assemblies had been prohibited, this type of feast was no longer held, and thus the longing of the friends to experience such meetings went unfulfilled.

Until one day, when the hardships and restrictions caused mainly by the intrigues of the Covenant-breakers were at their peak, such a feast came to be held quite unexpectedly. At a time when the doors of ease and comfort were closed on all sides, Mrs. Jackson, one of the renowned American believers, was visiting 'Abdu'l-Bahá at His residence along with another visitor. Other Eastern pilgrims, practising extreme caution and prudence, had been able to arrive unnoticed from various directions and had gathered in the pilgrim house. 'Abdu'l-Bahá decided that these assorted people should meet each other at a feast, and although none of them understood each other's language, the dinner table was set and prepared in 'Abdu'l-Bahá's House and the guests came together and occupied the seats around the table. Everyone was utterly enamoured of the matchless beauty of the Master's countenance and captivated by His every act.

Praised be God, the various religions and creeds were represented by at least one person, uniquely dressed as each came from a different background: Muslim, Christian, Jew, Zoroastrian, Hindu, and Buddhist, all of whom regarded each other as brothers, nay, as loved ones. Each was attired in his native dress and hat. Seeing the Persian hat, the Egyptian *fez*, the Indian turban, or the long Zoroastrian *qábá*, in contrast to the physical features and dress of the American pilgrims, all in one place, all so utterly different in appearance and yet united in their views, their convictions and ideals, gave the onlooker a special feeling. As instructed by the Master before the start of the meal, I stood at one end of the table while He stood at the other end and spoke for about ten minutes. As He spoke, the eyes of the participants were fastened on Him, their souls soaring in the loftiest paradise. Each person beheld his own Beloved, the object of the desire of his own Faith, clothed in the garment of humility. The simple words of the Master brought such joy to the hearts and delight to the souls that everyone became oblivious of the contingent world and soared in the kingdom of the spirit. I translated His words into English, but not all those twenty individuals knew Persian or English, and so an English-speaking doctor took notes for the others.

The theme of His brief talk was as follows: "Meetings, celebrations and feasts where the participants come from diverse nations and backgrounds have been witnessed before, but that spirit of love and unity which brings the hearts and souls together has not been seen in this world except at this feast and under the shadow of the Word of God." Then He added: "Magnificent and splendid celebrations and feasts abound in this world, yet in this prison with all its hardships and restrictions, the like of such a lively and happy gathering has never been and never will be witnessed."

Love

The heavenly qualities manifested by 'Abdu'l-Bahá are beyond the power of description; their exalted station is outside the realm of understanding and comparison. None of these qualities could be appraised by the intellectual faculties, for they were an integral part of His being and His person was the quintessence of such qualities.

This was especially true of the quality of love. Like a flame, it radiated from the core of His being, igniting the fire of the love of God in the hearts of men. All that has existed in the past, and all that exists now in the contingent world, as well as in the divine Kingdom, is due to this love that has illumined the world of being.

Of course, if the light of such a love had not emanated from the heart of 'Abdu'l-Bahá, it could in no way have penetrated the pure hearts of the devoted servants, and thousands of eager souls would not have rushed to the arena of sacrifice. His own words bear witness to this assertion – words that have filled the ears, eyes and spirits of thousands of souls, that endure in the deepest recesses of the hearts, and are recorded in unnumbered chronicles.

When He says:

Unless ye must,
Bruise not the serpent in the dust,
How much less wound a man.
And if ye can,
No ant should ye alarm,
Much less a brother harm[190]

any man of understanding and discernment will testify that the fruits of such a love – namely, kindliness, compassion and mercy – can rescue mankind from the horrors of hatred, enmity and savagery.

In a previous section I presented a short account of 'Abdu'l-Bahá's generosity and had intended to write a few words concerning the love of that manifestation of mercy and blessing. But the pen was rendered helpless to reach such a threshold, and was unworthy to enter such an arena. And so I now present a brief account of the effects of this love emanating from the horizon of mercy and compassion.

One of the Covenant-breakers of old had raised his expressions of hatred and enmity to such a level that the pen is ashamed to make mention of it and the heart is chagrined to recall it. When his enmity and intrigues failed to bring any results, he wrote a letter to 'Abdu'l-Bahá. One afternoon, as the Master was pacing up and down in the front entrance of the *bírúní*, talking on various subjects, He made mention of that person with love and sympathy, although in the past the man's flagrant misdeeds had become a byword among the friends. His conduct had been so disgraceful and outrageous that in the field of wickedness I considered him first and Muḥammad Javád-i-Qazvíní a close second. In any case, from the sympathetic nature of the Master's utterances I thought that he must have repented and that the depth of his abasement and degradation had moved the ocean of divine compassion. So I asked 'Abdu'l-Bahá, "Has he repented?"

"You have no idea what has befallen that unfortunate man," He replied. "I feel very sorry for him."

Again I thought that he must have been afflicted by some horrible calamity and fallen into the depths of misery. So I asked, "What has happened?"

"He has fallen into disgrace and expressed his repentance," replied 'Abdu'l-Bahá. Then He added, "Come, I will show you his letter."

We climbed the steps and entered the small and rather dark room situated on one side of the *andárúní* area. There He took the letter from His pocket and began to read. But the more I listened the less I detected any words of repentance and contrition. He simply attributed all the flagrant violations to Mírzá Muḥammad-'Alí and presented himself as guiltless. He also described his own miserable condition – how he had experienced great loss in business ventures and had not done much better in farming either, and how furthermore, none of the promises of the Arch-breaker of the Covenant, who had foretold great triumphs and glory, had been fulfilled. And now in the face of all this misery and misfortune he expressed great longing to rise to the heights of success, and hoped that his investments in commerce and agriculture might prove to be profitable.

During the reading of the letter, 'Abdu'l-Bahá expressed such tender, kind sentiments that I was deeply moved. At the same time, I recalled that man's many flagrant misdeeds, and wept over the tender heart of my beloved Master. At last 'Abdu'l-Bahá said, "I shall pray for him, and will write him a favourable reply." I don't know what the Master wrote him, but later I found out that while his business had improved, he had not abandoned his resentment and malice towards the Faith. Over the years I would think about him every so often. Eventually, after seven or eight years, I heard that he had repented. However, I could not believe he was sincere until I saw with my own eyes that he had not only expressed contrition but with all his strength of conscience, both outwardly and inwardly, and with all his words and actions, he had arisen to serve the Faith.

Another characteristic of the loving heart of the beloved Master was that He could never allow anyone either to think of or mention the misdeeds of anyone else in His presence, or utter any words of criticism, lest the pure stream of love become sullied. It frequently happened that under the influence of His love and compassion disagreements between friends melted away.

Yet another quality of His love was that whoever evinced a more hostile attitude received a larger measure of His attention and love. Among the fanatical Protestant missionaries was an old woman known as Mrs. Ramsey, who was consumed with the fire of religious prejudice and hatred. The Covenant-breakers found out about her and fanned her flames of rancour until she became a true enemy of the Faith. It just so happened that she had to pass 'Abdu'l-Bahá's house several times a day on her way to the American Protestant doctor who has been mentioned in Chapter 1 of this book. Each time, as her glance fell on the blessed person of 'Abdu'l-Bahá, she would writhe in agony, grimace and lower her head while quickening her pace to a run. Several times 'Abdu'l-Bahá remarked to the friends, "You see how much Mrs. Ramsey dislikes me, and yet I love her very much."

One day as she passed, looking upset and perturbed, the Master called her over and remarked to her,

"Mrs. Ramsey, do you know how much I love you?"

"How much?" she asked.

"As much as you dislike me," He responded.

Stunned by the answer, she began to stammer, and hurried away. I don't know what became of her. I just know that the magnetic power of 'Abdu'l-Bahá's love attracted any cold-hearted person who came into contact with Him and in turn made his heart a magnet attracting other cold hearts. I have made implicit references to this point in some of the stories presented in this book.

And now I must put down the pen and open the heart and soul to the utterances of that noble Beloved, who some thirty years ago addressed an American friend in these words:

> He is God!
>
> O thou who art attracted by the fragrant breezes of God,
>
> I have received thy recent letter, bearing thy sentiments of fervent love for 'Abdu'l-Bahá, thy trust in God and the purity and sincerity of thy purpose in service to the Cause of God. Thou hast well stated in thy noble letter the great need in those regions for love and fellowship between hearts and souls. This is but manifest truth, beyond which there is naught but error and perdition.
>
> Know thou of a certainty that Love is the secret of God's holy Dispensation, the manifestation of the All-Merciful, the fountain of spiritual outpourings. Love is heaven's kindly light, the Holy Spirit's eternal breath that vivifieth the human soul. Love is the cause of God's revelation unto man, the vital bond

inherent, in accordance with divine creation, in the realities of things. Love is the one means that ensureth true felicity both in this world and the next. Love is the light that guideth in darkness, the living link that uniteth God with man, that assureth the progress of every illumined soul. Love is the most great law that ruleth this mighty and heavenly cycle, the unique power that bindeth together the divers elements of this material world, the supreme magnetic force that directeth the movements of the spheres in the celestial realms. Love revealeth with unfailing and limitless power the mysteries latent in the universe. Love is the spirit of life unto the adorned body of mankind, the establisher of true civilization in this mortal world, and the shedder of imperishable glory upon every high-aiming race and nation.

Whatsoever people is graciously favoured therewith by God, its name shall surely be magnified and extolled by the Concourse from on high, by the company of angels, and the denizens of the Abhá Kingdom. And whatsoever people turneth its heart away from this Divine Love – the revelation of the Merciful – shall err grievously, shall fall into despair, and be utterly destroyed. That people shall be denied all refuge, shall become even as the vilest creatures of the earth, victims of degradation and shame.

O ye beloved of the Lord! Strive to become the manifestations of the love of God, the lamps of divine guidance shining amongst the kindreds of the earth with the light of love and concord.

All hail to the revealers of this glorious light![191]

CHAPTER SIX

Again, never-ending tasks and severe hardships

In the course of the year 1904, when the victories of the Faith of God were on the rise in both the East and the West, the jealousy and rancour of the Covenant-breakers increased in intensity by the same proportion. Although outwardly they had kept themselves in seclusion, yet the wicked, malicious plans they had made in the past, and the seeds of sedition and corruption they had sown previously, began to bear fruit.

The pressures and restrictions on the prisoners increased. Lies and accusations spread far and wide. Things reached such a point that an actual assault by the enemies and hate-mongers became a real possibility. In the streets of Haifa and 'Akká assorted rumours spread and a variety of false reports travelled from mouth to mouth. Sometimes it was rumoured that an Ottoman warship was on its way from Istanbul to 'Akká to take the Effendi into banishment. At other times it was heard that the police had made plans to take definitive and final action.

In the meantime, a flood of letters from East and West was pouring in and so 'Abdu'l-Bahá's occupations grew to levels in excess even of those described in Chapter 3 under the title "Burdens, sorrows and labours of 'Abdu'l-Bahá". Comfort and peace had become impossible; the few hours of rest and relaxation that had previously been available to Him now became completely out of the question. Many a night passed into day as He wrote uninterruptedly, and endless days turned into nights as He stood guard over the interests of the

Faith and the wellbeing of the friends. The pressures of work had grown to such intolerable levels that Mírzá Ḥaydar-'Alí and I both begged the Master to reduce His workload and implored Him to take a few days of rest by decreasing His work hours. But this was not accepted.

And now I present below a Tablet revealed in these times of enormous pressure and increasing problems, so that you may discover how He uses the language of humour and love to apologize for being late in His response to a letter:

He is God!

Tehran
Jináb-i-Muḥammad Mihdí Khán,
upon him be the Glory of God, the Most Glorious

O confidant of the heart,

It is dawn, and the fingertips, the eyes, the back, the knees and arms, even every strand of hair, are so exhausted and weary as to be beyond description. From sunset till now this pen has been in motion, and therefore consider and judge with fairness the intensity of love with which 'Abdu'l-Bahá's heart is connected with those of the friends of God. Thus, if there has been a delay in response, or if the handwriting resembles the intertwined strands of curly hair, it is not my fault but the fault of the overly long and darksome night.

An excessive volume of work has left only enough time for brief letters. Surely the friends will pardon me, as each word thereof is but a wave of the great ocean of love, and evidence of the attachment of the spirit. God willing, that honoured friend will, with the power of spiritual attraction and in all haste, cause all those who thirst to drink from the cup which bestoweth life everlasting.

'Abdu'l-Bahá 'Abbás[192]

'Abdu'l-Bahá's utterances in these days

In the nine-year period I spent in His service – either in 'Akká or in its proximity, but ever in close contact with that luminous spot – times of hardship alternated with times of relative comfort. One day the storm of misfortune and suffering would be so intense that the Ark of the Cause of God seemed lost beneath the overpowering surge of the waves of adversity, and yet the next day peace and tranquillity reigned and the affairs of the Faith would progress favourably. And so all these evil whisperings, like the buzzing of flies, had little effect on the friends unless such warnings of upheaval and turmoil were heard from the lips of 'Abdu'l-Bahá. Unfortunately, in these days His intimations of such events were frequent. For example, He used to remark repeatedly, "If they banish me to the Desert of Fezzan[193] or cast me into the depths of the sea, or hang me by the neck in full public view, the friends should not become distressed and troubled; they should rely on the teachings of the Faith of God. When Jesus Christ was crucified, He had only eleven disciples, but the lovers of the Blessed Beauty, praise be to God, have conquered the world, therefore why fear? Why worry? Praise be to God, the Cause of God is well established. I have done what I had to do. Rest assured." The words, "I have done what I had to do" obviously referred to 'Abdu'l-Bahá's Will and Testament,[194] of whose existence we were at that time unaware, since the age of the beloved Guardian at that point was no more than 7 or 8, and the signs of power and authority in him did not reveal themselves until he was 11, and even then the recognition of such signs was a blessing with which only a few were endowed, a blessing of which the generality of the friends remained deprived.

In any case, these utterances bore portents of troubled times ahead. On occasion 'Abdu'l-Bahá instructed that all Writings of the Faith be gathered up, which signalled the possibility that government officials might unexpectedly force their way into homes where such Writings and Tablets were kept. The room of Mírzá Núru'd-Dín, who was responsible for transcription of the Tablets, and my room where I was engaged in translation, were both of particular interest to the foes and subject to rumours and allegations by the troublemakers. As described previously, the enemies and the Covenant-breakers portrayed the spiritual association of the Western world with 'Akká as a political relationship, and had generated an atmosphere of fear and suspicion in the minds of government officials.

And so 'Abdu'l-Bahá's utterances in those days on the one hand gave glad tidings of the triumphs of the Cause of God, and on the other indicated that major changes were to take place. These became apparent a year later, and details will be presented in Chapter 7.

My own circumstances at this time

In these times, that air of enthusiasm and joy which had animated the hearts of the friends in previous years had all but vanished; a strange silence and stillness overshadowed their lives. The pilgrim traffic had also ceased. The *bírúní* area of the House of 'Abdu'l-Bahá was utterly deserted. Only the reciter of the Qur'án presented himself at night and earned his wages by chanting Quránic verses for a few minutes, in Egyptian style.

The Master would arrive later than before and leave earlier. He spoke less, and His utterances mostly emphasized these points: "This land is in turmoil. The officials are engaged in various secret activities and have given the government ample reason to be in fear of us. Of course, whatever happens will eventually be of benefit to the Cause, but it would be helpful if the friends would not remain in 'Akká and would instead disperse to destinations elsewhere. This would give me the freedom to protect and guard the Cause of God."

In brief, the same utterances that He had imparted to us after the rebellion of Mírzá Áqá Ján a few years earlier (briefly described in Chapter 1 in the section "Dismissal"), He now repeated, encouraging the friends to take their leave and depart from 'Akká. The only difference was that at that time the fame of the Cause of God had only just reached America, and so the volume of incoming correspondence was quite moderate. Now, however, 'Abdu'l-Bahá's workload had grown a hundred-fold and the flood of letters and messages could not even be properly evaluated. As already quoted in the first part of this chapter, in a Tablet to Muḥammad Mihdí <u>Kh</u>án 'Abdu'l-Bahá reveals the following: "... the fingertips, the eyes, the back, the knees and arms, even every strand of hair, are so exhausted and weary as to be beyond description." Such was the effect of 'Abdu'l-Bahá's workload.

Meanwhile, His compassion and bounty to me were such that only a small drop of that endless ocean of work was entrusted to me. I was responsible for the translation of the incoming letters and the daily supervision of the lessons given to the youth. However, gone were those feelings of intoxication, enthusiasm and joy that we had felt before. There were no pilgrims to share experiences with, no companions to enjoy socializing with, and no time for such fellowship. Loneliness and excessive work brought boredom, fatigue and raw nerves. The noise from the caravanserai of the pilgrim house, formerly hardly noticeable, now hurt my eardrums, while the incessant commotion of the square just outside the west window of my room was so raucous and loud that it hardly allowed me a tranquil moment for my translation work. So on occasion I occupied the room in the pilgrim house, or at times I found a restful haven for an hour or so in the front garden of the House of 'Abdu'l-Bahá.

But there were also those nights when the bellowing of the camels and the shouts of the Arab camel drivers from early evening hours until late at night were quite deafening. The reason for this was that lately great quantities of corn and grain had been shipped to 'Akká from the Huron desert to be later exported to Marseilles. And since the narrow streets and bazaars of 'Akká could not accommodate the two-way traffic of thousands of camels to and from the Huron, the evening hours had therefore been designated for the arrival of the products, and the daylight hours for shipping them out. Thus their entry into 'Akká was made through the land gate at night, and in the morning the loaded ships sailed through the sea gate.

In brief, all this noise and racket day and night made for sleeplessness and shattered nerves. One funny thing was that the voice of the *muezzin*[195] at the local mosque was so jarring and discordant that in comparison all other noises seemed pleasant and even musical. Every dawn the first sounds of "Alláh'u'Akbar" made me jump, and as the poet says:

> *The shrill noise of your axe grinding on granite*
> *Fails to match the rasp of your call grating on my heart.*

Things finally reached such a point that once, when the Master was referring to the harshness of a certain *muezzin*'s chant, I too began to complain about this one. The Master remarked, "You are talking about him? Let me tell you a little about him. Some time ago, the French Consul used to live right across from the Mosque, and decided that he could no longer tolerate that hideous voice. So he summoned him and asked, 'How much are you earning for chanting the *adhán*?' 'Three *majídí* a month,' he replied. The Consul proposed, 'I will give you four *majídí*. Take the money and don't chant any more.' And so while the Consul was in residence he kept silent. But as soon as the Consul took a trip abroad the offensive chant filled the air again."

Weary and irritated, I put up with the situation for a few months until on the Master's instructions I moved my office to the Persian Consulate building.

The Persian Consulate building

In those times most Persian Consuls were unpaid clerks who had no interest in extending a helping hand or support to the Persian residents in times of need. Both 'Akká and Haifa had a Consul and a Vice-Consul. The Haifa Vice-Consul was an Italian businessman who represented Italian shipping concerns. The Consul in 'Akká was that same Shaykh Ṣáliḥ whose son Shaykh Maḥmúd had recovered from a very painful case of sciatica as a result of medical advice given by 'Abdu'l-Bahá. Shaykh Ṣáliḥ was a landowner and hardly ever ventured into town.

The term "Consulate" was therefore a misnomer since the building was mostly unoccupied; on occasion it was the neighbours who raised the flag over the building. So these Consulate buildings were of no practical use until on 'Abdu'l-Bahá's instructions one of them became my residence for a time; thus, under the flag of Iran the Bahá'í Faith's translation office received, at least outwardly, some measure of protection from the secret government inspectors.

This small house was comprised of three small rooms and a hall, and was isolated from all the noise and clamour. While the rooms were not as airy as those in the pilgrim house, the silence and tranquillity they afforded was a natural sedative. So this servant was rescued at last from the deafening howl of the camel-drivers. Since summer had arrived and I had begun to frequent the beach, soon the problems related to my nerves, and my sleeplessness, which had been caused by the excessively loud noises of man and beast, were completely cured and I regained my ability to perform my daily tasks.

Miss Barney and *Some Answered Questions*

Miss Barney, who after marrying Monsieur Hippolyte Dreyfus earned renown as Madame Dreyfus-Barney, was endowed with an avid enthusiasm for acquiring spiritual qualities and heavenly attributes, and 'Abdu'l-Bahá therefore honoured her with the title of Amatu'l-Bahá.[196] During my stay, she visited the Master three times.

On her last visit, she brought with her the maidservant of God Miss Rosenberg, a Londoner, as her secretary and amanuensis, and stayed for about a year immersing herself in the ocean of divine knowledge, where she discovered many a precious pearl. In her eagerness to grasp the realities of the teachings, she considered the Prison City of 'Akká and the small house of the Beloved of the world preferable to the most splendid mansions of Western countries. And although she was both wealthy and young, she had an intense affinity for life in her present surroundings. She spent much time with the ladies of the Holy Family helping them practise their English. In the heat and confusion of 'Akká, she joyfully pursued her solitary task of collecting the Writings of the Master. And as she meditated and soared in the realms of spirit, she beheld the light of the celestial flame in the Sinai of her heart and discovered many divine realities.

Because of her intense piety, she was greatly favoured by 'Abdu'l-Bahá. Sometimes, in jest, the Master would remark to her, "In the heat of this summer season you should be living in the beautiful mountains of Switzerland in a palace or a mansion. What are you doing in this dilapidated city of 'Akká spending time with us prisoners?" In brief, she was the recipient of many a light-hearted loving comment such as this, which only served to increase her devotion and zeal.

During her one-year stay, she not only became familiar with the fundamental principles and mysteries of the Cause of God but also emerged as a source for the diffusion of these divine blessings among the people. In her service to the Cause she left as a memento for future generations a significant book from the utterances of 'Abdu'l-Bahá. She compiled this precious divine philosophy in both Persian and English under the title *Mufavidhat-i-'Abdu'l-Bahá*.[197] The manner of the compilation of the work was as follows.

Like the other Western friends, this lady received her share of spiritual education at the dinner table. As described in previous chapters, the Master's excessive workload only allowed time allotted for such question and answer sessions at the dinner table and then only at lunch time, at about 1 p.m. 'Abdu'l-Bahá usually did not eat more than one meal a day. During the days of the Fast the evening meal which broke the Fast replaced the daily lunch for these sessions. These "table talks" – the actual title of the book – served the auspicious purpose of setting a definite time for 'Abdu'l-Bahá to sit down at the table and enjoy a properly cooked meal, unlike those occasions when He simply made do with bread and a few olives, or bread and cheese. Unfortunately, the time He spent in explaining the concepts and delineating the issues left Him practically no time to eat, and so instead of receiving sustenance of body, He wound up imparting nourishment of the spirit. In any case, 'Abdu'l-Bahá was not annoyed by this inconvenience, nor did He complain of the fatigue that such an activity entailed.

One day as He rose from the table, while expressing a bit of weariness, He happily remarked, "It is encouraging that after all this labour, at least she understands the concepts. This is refreshing. What would I have done if after all this effort she still failed to comprehend the issues?" – the point being that the Master was content and happy to oblige this lady despite the burden of the work.

The seating order around the table which was observed most of the time placed 'Abdu'l-Bahá at the head of the table, with Miss Barney on His immediate left and Miss Rosenberg next to her; after this eight or nine of the pilgrims and resident friends were seated. This servant usually sat on 'Abdu'l-Bahá's right, opposite Miss Barney, and translated her questions from English into Persian; then I translated the Master's replies from Persian into English, while Miss Rosenberg swiftly recorded both. It must be said that things did not proceed smoothly or at all easily, for Miss Barney had first to explain the question to the translator; he then had to interpret his understanding of the concept to the Master and then again translate the response as accurately as possible into English – albeit with a Persian accent and using Bahá'í terminology, as Miss Rosenberg rapidly took down what she heard.

If the explanation was unconvincing to the enquirer, the issues had to be discussed again; this repetition lengthened the session so that eating was delayed or even suspended altogether. Fortunately, unlike Amatu'lláh Madame de Canavarro, who has been mentioned in Chapter 3 of this book and who was a newly declared Bahá'í, this lady was not similarly uninformed of Bahá'í expressions and entertained no feelings of jealousy or envy towards the translator. Thus there were no protests, such as, "It is through the bounty of my knowledge that you have become the recipient of such great blessings and acquainted with such truths," and she never made any complaint against this servant. Furthermore, the recorder of the account was a well-known Bahá'í; unlike Mr. Phelps, she did not include in the record of the discussion any personal philosophical views. She was also perfectly familiar with Bahá'í terminology and Eastern expressions and so the discussions were concluded in an atmosphere of joy and amity. However, the matter of partaking of food and drink usually remained unresolved, as eating and drinking were interrupted and discontinued, since the nourishing of the soul took precedence over the feeding of the body.

As He explained and delineated the issues, 'Abdu'l-Bahá's manner of expression and utterance utterly enchanted and enraptured the listener. At times He Himself would raise the question or objection before the enquirer had posed them, and would then offer the answer. Once, as He spoke on the subject of "the nonexistence of evil", He suddenly remarked to me with a smile, "Now she will ask why, then, did God create the scorpion?" Hardly a minute had passed when the Amatu'l-Bahá asked the question. 'Abdu'l-Baha said: "What did I tell you? Now in response tell her that this is in the nature of things. It is true that the scorpion is evil, however it is only evil in relation to us; in relation to its own environment it is not evil. This poison is its means of defence; with its stinger it protects itself. But since the nature of the poison is not conducive to our wellbeing we consider it evil."[198] Numerous similar references were made which generated a light-hearted and joyful atmosphere. Sometimes the Master was concerned that I did not take a fuller share of the variety of food spread before us, and would often say, "Now eat your food and talk later." But I was so completely immersed in the ocean of utterance, so intoxicated by the wine of His nearness, that physical food offered no true pleasure, especially when with that smiling and joyful countenance which was characteristic of His hospitality, He introduced humour into the discussion, transforming this material food into heavenly nourishment and celestial sustenance.

Once as He was encouraging me to eat first and talk later, while I was deeply involved in the discussion at hand, He suddenly asked Miss Barney, "How do you translate the word '*motarjim*' into English?"

"Interpreter," she responded.

Then He asked, "What is '*gorosneh*' in English?"

"Hungry," she replied.

Then with His blessed finger He pointed at me and exclaimed, "Hungry interpreter, hungry interpreter."

I was deeply pleased with the Master's term. I wonder how someone else would have reacted, but afterwards I had a stamp made of it, so that this royal title stuck! I did not, however, relinquish my permanent title of "Jináb-i-Khán" granted to me by 'Abdu'l-Bahá.

So the table talks continued in this vein for some time, until the members of 'Abdu'l-Bahá's family and other relatives who heard His words realized that if Miss Barney had not immersed herself in the depths of this divine Ocean, those precious gems would have remained undiscovered forever; those heavenly jewels would have been left concealed in the depths of the storehouse of meanings. And now that these hidden gems had come to light, what could be better than to record them in the Persian language so that they might remain intact and inviolate for posterity in the annals of the Faith. So they asked 'Abdu'l-Bahá to assign an amanuensis to attend the meetings and take down in Persian each and every gem-like word.

Praise be to God, the request received His consent and Mírzá Munír, son of the departed Mírzá Muḥammad-Qulí, was assigned the task. Every day he sat next to 'Abdu'l-Bahá and recorded His words. This approach, however, was not without its difficulties for the Master either, for the review and correction of the transcripts was an additional burden on Him. Moreover, compiling the texts of the earlier table talks from their English translation, and their subsequent correction and orderly arrangement, was also added work for 'Abdu'l-Bahá. This compilation of His previous talks from their English translated versions proved lengthy, and for Miss Barney, fraught with much difficulty. In any case, when some two thirds of the book was transcribed, my journey to Europe intervened and therefore the Master's daughters were assigned to take over the work of translation. In the meantime the Amatu'l-Bahá had become quite fluent in Persian from her continual practice of it, as well as her study of the Holy Writings, and so she was able to complete the work and present this great service to the Bahá'í world, a gift that will cause her to be remembered eternally.

A change in conditions: The arrival of biased officials

In the first months of Amatu'l-Bahá Miss Barney's work in compiling her book, the situation in 'Akká had eased somewhat. Several pilgrims arrived from Iran attained the presence of the Master, among them the now departed Adíb.[199] News of the passing of my father reached me at that time. On 'Abdu'l-Bahá's instructions a splendid memorial service was held in his honour in the presence of the Master and was attended by many of the friends; this turned out to be the last grand assemblage of Bahá'ís to be convened in those years.

Before long, evil whisperings were renewed, and nonsensical, absurd allegations began to spread. 'Abdu'l-Bahá's utterances gradually began to hint at major changes signalling the onset of fresh calamities. Not unlike the time of Mírzá Áqá Ján's rebellion, He encouraged the Bahá'ís of 'Akká and Haifa to leave the cities. He would often say, "I can weather the difficulties better if I am afforded some measure of solitude. Also, the resident friends and pilgrims can easily take their leave now, for at present there are no restrictions to prevent their departure and no one can be held accountable. However, events may transpire which could result in a tightening of restrictions on travel and cause the onset of greater calamities. Whoever leaves now will have made it easier for himself and for me."

He repeated these admonitions frequently. Shortly afterwards the pilgrims received notice to depart, and gradually, not unlike the time of crisis over Mírzá Áqá Ján some seven years earlier, the pilgrim house became deserted. Incoming mail was reduced and then completely suspended. A strange silence enveloped all. The comings and goings of the friends as well as of non-Bahá'ís ceased. The inhabitants of 'Akká, both high and low, Christian and Muslim, had been frightened by the false rumours and allegations and no longer visited the House of 'Abdu'l-Bahá. Moreover, major changes were made in the government offices. Two of the senior officers, namely Faríq Páshá and Lává Páshá, both of whom had been devoted friends of 'Abdu'l-Bahá, were accused by the scheming evilmongers of open defiance and rebellion and were summarily dismissed from their posts in 'Akká, later being reassigned elsewhere. These two were replaced by a hateful, deceitful and crafty man also named Lává Páshá. This man's expressions of malice and rancour were instinctive; unlike his predecessors, he continually plotted and planned to bring disgrace upon 'Abdu'l-Bahá. He hardly ever visited the Master, and when 'Abdu'l-Bahá would repay a visit He was received coldly and inhospitably.

I once accompanied 'Abdu'l-Bahá on a visit to his house. He received us in a manner so utterly devoid of the simple rules of civility and hospitality that on our way out I spontaneously and boldly expressed my feelings to the Master.

"How can such a discourteous person become the recipient of 'Abdu'l-Bahá's blessings?"

"You have no idea", replied 'Abdu'l-Bahá, "how many

problems I have to deal with and how carefully I must protect and safeguard the lives of the friends of this realm. Within one or two years some of the Bahá'í youth will reach the age of military service and the Ottoman government could lay claim on them. I must treat people like this with love and affection so that when the time comes I will be able to safeguard the youth."

Problems such as these were many, and since the government of Iran did not have an able Consul in 'Akká, Iranian citizens were at the mercy of the Ottoman government and were the victims of its injustices and tyranny. In addition, there was assigned to 'Akká at that time a judge who treated the friends harshly and rudely, unlike the judges of previous years. When he attained the presence of 'Abdu'l-Bahá he would have his servant carry his two- to three-metre-long pipe about with him. At each and every opportunity he would ask for it, taking one end of it in his mouth as the other end was placed somewhere in the middle of the room with smoke rising from it to the ceiling. In the meantime, smoke would issue from his miserable throat like a chimney. To wit, in order to showcase his knowledge and erudition he would speak Arabic but with a Turkish accent, and talk incessantly of piety and godliness. For example, when the chanter of the Qur'án was reciting verses in the *bírúní* area, he would make uncalled-for remarks. At the end of each verse he would say, "At this point an act of prostration must be performed," or "Why don't you cover the floors with carpets and prayer rugs so that Islamic traditions are properly observed?" It was obvious that he coveted owning a Persian carpet or two. And since he had heard of 'Abdu'l-Bahá's generous habits, his greed was running rampant. In the meantime, he had instructions from Istanbul to employ a discourteous and irreverent attitude and conduct towards 'Abdu'l-Bahá in the hope of exposing a weakness or flaw in the Master. However, praise the Lord, 'Abdu'l-Bahá's dignified bearing and behaviour defeated him at his own game. This, then, was the condition and conduct of the officials of that time.

My journey to Europe

When government officials from Istanbul came to 'Akká with hostile intentions and plans against the Faith of God, 'Abdu'l-Bahá dismissed the entire company of pilgrims. Furthermore, He issued the instruction to stop the flow of incoming mail from Port Said, so as to prevent it from falling into the hands of the officials and inspectors. These actions were taken in order to establish some measure of peace and tranquillity.

And so, not unlike the closing days of the fifth year after the ascension of Bahá'u'lláh [1897] as described in Chapter 1, although things were outwardly calm and quiet, yet the smouldering embers of turmoil and sedition lay dormant, only waiting for the winds of defiance and dissension to blow and fan them into the blazing inferno of hatred and enmity. All visits to the house of 'Abdu'l-Bahá ceased. Even at night the chanter of the Qur'án could not attract an audience and so became his own solitary listener.

Whenever and wherever the friends did attain the presence of 'Abdu'l-Bahá, the conversation usually revolved around the activities of the enemies of the Faith. The Master frequently emphasized that whoever was able to save himself from this veritable danger would contribute to His peace of mind. Yet the resident Bahá'ís, most of whom had businesses and to whom 'Akká and Haifa were home, found it not easy to abandon such established lives. So although they lived in an environment of fear and trepidation, they continued to procrastinate in making a move from one day to the next, without ever budging an inch.

I, however, who had no involvement in business affairs and owned no property, decided to comply with 'Abdu'l-Bahá's command before anyone else did, so that haply others might follow. But deciding on a destination was very difficult: I considered a return to Iran to be out of the question, for any thought of remoteness from the threshold of 'Abdu'l-Bahá was deeply distressing to me. After much reflection I at last determined on Marseilles as more suitable than any other city, since it was not too distant from 'Akká. Moreover, I had previously established a good working relationship with a number of branches of the International Bank of Moscow, and so I felt it would be easy to find a position with the Marseilles branch of that bank. I planned to establish my residence there and then, as I had done in Tehran, organize a teaching campaign and attract the hosts of divine bounty as promised in 'Abdu'l-Bahá's Tablet to me when I had lived in Tehran: "If thou longest to become the recipient of ceaseless divine confirmations, then array the seekers, prepare the battalions of the lovers of truth and then assault the legions of ignorance and superstition."[200]

And so I thought out the details of my plan and at a time which seemed suitable presented it to 'Abdu'l-Bahá. Every part of the plan was received favourably by the Master. He then added, "However short your journey turns out to be, it is necessary." Then He spoke a great deal about Paris, emphasizing the importance of meeting the friends and teaching souls in that city, and promising the definite bestowal of divine confirmations.

Since 'Abdu'l-Bahá had brought up the subject of Paris, the significance of that city began to dawn upon me, and I realized that the idea of Marseilles might have been only a product of my imagination and that possibly I should disregard Marseilles and consider Paris as my destination. Then the Master added, "You are not going there on your own. I am sending you there. And whenever you wish to return, this remains your own home." In short, 'Abdu'l-Bahá's utterances filled my feeble being with hope.

And so I prepared the necessities of the journey. Next day I was summoned to the presence of 'Abdu'l-Bahá. He enquired about the state of my finances. I reported the status of all that I owned. Immediately He handed me 27 gold liras, which I accepted with mixed feelings of embarrassment, apprehension and gratitude. Next day, the day of my departure for Port Said, I received my permission to leave.

On the day of departure, my spirits resembled the emotions I had experienced on the occasion of my return to Iran a few years before. Of course, 'Abdu'l-Bahá entrusted me with certain special tasks and some minor assignments to be accomplished in Port Said. So I left with a heart filled with joy and happiness. But once we were about an hour outside 'Akká I suddenly began to see the world in a different light. My four-year stay in 'Akká seemed but a dream, as I reconstructed in my mind's eye and within the space of a fleeting moment the minutes, the hours and the days of those bygone years. But no matter how intensely I trained the telescope of my frail and helpless mind toward the future, I could see nothing. I compared the bright horizon of the past with the dark outlook of the future and was overcome with sorrow and remorse. I reproached myself, "My God, what have I done? All the resident believers kept their own counsel, but I had to show off and play the leader, and now have lost the nearness of the Beloved of the world."

In short, as such thoughts flooded my whole being, life itself began to appear worthless and absurd. I could find no relief but through the flow of tears which streamed down copiously as I wept myself breathless:

> *Tears are the cure for the incurable pain,*
> *A weeping eye is the fountain of God's grace.*

Such was my plight until the angel of bounty flew overhead and whispered in my ear the words of the Beloved: (1) However short your journey may turn out to be, it is necessary; (2) You are not going on your own – I am sending you; (3) Whenever you wish to return, this shall remain your own home. As soon as I heard these words I jumped up like a happy child and laughed at my own foolish thoughts.

Once in Port Said, I spent one night with Áqá Aḥmad Yazdí and on the second day continued towards Marseilles.

Arrival at Marseilles

On the way to Marseilles I almost succeeded in teaching the Faith to a Dutch citizen and when we arrived in the city we spent two days together. After his departure, however, I could find no one else to teach. On the second day of my arrival the very first thing I did was to go to the bank. I discovered that that branch had been closed and so I immediately wrote a letter to the central bank in Moscow with which I had formerly established a favourable working relationship. The response was that the International Bank of that name had been dissolved and that the bank had been restructured under a different name, and so the directors of the main bank as well as all the branches had been replaced.

The five or six days that I spent in that city, therefore, were among the bleakest and grimmest of my life. Observing the life of the city – its inhabitants' incessant striving after material and physical pleasures and their deprivation of the bounty of the spirit – filled me with such fury that many a time I was tempted to raise my voice in public in a cry of "Woe betide this people!", while at the same time I recalled the disciples of Jesus, who endured similar tribulations in order to raise the banner of Christ in strange lands stricken with ignorance and heedlessness.

But since I could not find in myself such capabilities, I penned a long article expressly for the newspaper *Matin* in order to relieve my agitation and find peace of mind. In this article I expressed all that was in my heart, unburdening myself of a load that bore heavy on my conscience and my spirit. Some years back I had sent a similar article to the newspaper *Débats* in response to certain published reports containing false accusations against the people of Bahá on the occasion of the assassination of Náṣiri'd-Dín Sháh.[201] While that effort had borne no encouraging results, yet the force of my convictions now forced me to write what I was unable to speak. Once I had penned what needed to be said I took it to the offices of the newspaper, and having regained my peace of mind fled that city and proceeded to Paris.

Arrival in Paris

However dark the horizon of Marseilles had appeared, and however intensely I had detested that city, yet by the same measure the horizon of Paris appeared bright and radiant, for the believers there at the time were most sincerely on fire with the love of God, and once there I became the recipient of the inebriating wine of their love.

At that time the fire of the love of God had only recently been ignited and the light of faith and devotion had illumined the hearts of only a handful of individuals. The centre and essence of this fire and attraction was the revered person of Hippolyte Dreyfus, whose visit to 'Abdu'l-Bahá has been described in Chapter 3. He had taught the Faith to a few of his relatives, one of whom had formerly been a Mormon.

Coincidentally, a number of recently declared American Bahá'ís were living in Paris at that time, and the Bahá'í population of the city was around fifty or sixty souls. In addition to this, some ten or twenty others had begun to investigate the principles of the Faith; some of them were sympathetic, others critical, and a few confused and perplexed. In short, Paris seemed to be longingly awaiting the arrival of someone bearing glad tidings from 'Akká. Now I realized why 'Abdu'l-Bahá had so emphasized the wisdom of my journey when He had said, "However short it may turn out to be, your journey is necessary." He had then specifically emphasized the friends of Paris, whereas my chosen destination had been Marseilles, and outwardly no news of the general receptivity and spiritual maturity of the people of Paris had been received in 'Akká.

In any case, after Marseilles Paris was a veritable paradise. My nights and days were arranged on an hourly basis, morning, noon, afternoon and evening, and each segment provided me with the opportunity of attending a Bahá'í meeting where an enthusiastic audience eagerly awaited news and glad tidings from the Holy Threshold. Since the majority of the American friends could not speak French, but still gathered with the French believers in one place, arrangements were made whereby the friends sat in two groups and in this way each person received the heavenly glad tidings in his own language. Meanwhile, those who understood both languages received the glad tidings of the Kingdom of mysteries twice, gave praise twice, and experienced the joy and elation a thousand times over.

Late one night I met a few seekers whose sympathetic response and subsequent acceptance were astonishing. One of them was Monsieur Engleman, who had composed some verses of poetry in praise of the Cause which I translated and dispatched to 'Akká forthwith, and also included in the book *Irtibat-i-Sharq va Gharb*.[202] Another seeker, a lady who was hard of hearing, presented many objections but once she accepted the Faith her heart was transformed and she arose to make up for lost time. The son of Áqá Riḍá Qannád, Mírzá Ḥabíb entitled 'Aynu'l-Mulk [Eye of the Nation], who in his later years became over-ambitious and for the sake of title and position forsook his service to the Faith, was at that time zealously active and would not accept a moment's rest. His nights and days were spent in service to the Cause and in assisting Monsieur Dreyfus to proclaim the teachings to the inhabitants of Paris. In short, with his help I was able to meet and speak with a number of important individuals. I spent a month in great joy and contentment, and yet the memory of my days in 'Akká and the unhappy events in that land were forever before my eyes. Once I considered attending one of the night schools whose notices I had seen everywhere in the city. I thought about studying philosophy in order to facilitate the translation of the Tablets, which called for the use of special terminology. But I lacked the financial means for that; all I owned at the time was a voucher issued by the State Bank of Russia which had to be sold in Moscow by the French bank. This delayed my final decision as to what I should do next. The idea of studying medicine presented other problems. In short, surrounded by multiple obstacles and difficulties, the decision to return to 'Akká became inevitable.

Return to 'Akká

While my stay in Paris was not without its charm and excitement, and meeting the friends had generated a heightened spirit of joy and delight, yet remoteness from the Holy Threshold and lack of news caused me such concern that after five or six weeks I decided to return, despite the friends' insistence that I should tarry longer. Leaving Paris, I reached 'Akká after seven days. On my arrival I proceeded directly to the House of 'Abdu'l-Bahá and attained His presence straight away. After receiving the blessings and bounty of that peerless Beloved I went to the pilgrim house. Here there was only one other believer, apart from Mírzá Ḥaydar-'Alí. This was Áqá Shaykh Muḥammad-'Alí Nabílí, who later received his permission to depart the next day.

A quiet and deadly calm dominated all quarters of the city. At night the only sound was the melody of the chanter of the Qur'án in the *bírúní* area. The resident friends seldom showed up for a visit, and just like two or three months before, the utterances of 'Abdu'l-Bahá concerned the approach of turmoil and upheaval and therefore no permission was granted to anyone to enter 'Akká. Miss Barney hardly ever left the House of 'Abdu'l-Bahá except on certain occasions to visit the Shrine of Bahá'u'lláh, which was undertaken with great care and caution. In my absence, the task of translation had fallen on the shoulders of the daughters of 'Abdu'l-Bahá. On my arrival the Master conferred upon me many loving words of praise and welcome, and in the evening summoned me to His presence once more. I was in His presence for a long time as He paced up and down in the front area of the *bírúní*.

I presented a detailed report of my journey, conveying to Him the various expressions of utter servitude and evanescence of the Paris friends, as well as their many entreaties and supplications. Despite the fact that these were days of extreme distress and difficulties in 'Akká, 'Abdu'l-Bahá appeared serene and joyful. His kind and loving utterances to this servant were beyond measure. I was so overwhelmed with feelings of pure joy and ecstasy that I no longer knew what I was saying. Once, acknowledging my gratitude and expressing my feelings of thanksgiving, I recounted how I had been the recipient of such unexpected bounty and divine grace on this journey that whenever I spoke, the friends whether English or French responded so warmly and enthusiastically and heaped upon me such words of praise as to make me feel unworthy and embarrassed. Suddenly 'Abdu'l-Bahá halted, and turning His blessed face to me asked, "How many years have you been with us?"

"Four years," I replied.

"In these four years you don't know what I have given you; you have no idea what you have absorbed from me. Let's leave this until the proper time."

These words of 'Abdu'l-Bahá ring in my ear always, and at times I witness their truth with my own eyes and find them realized in my own heart. O 'Abdu'l-Bahá, You are the source of all truth!

The next day at the dinner table I was summoned to translate. That day I attained the Master's presence several times and described the sentiments of the Paris Bahá'ís in detail. I told Him of their deep devotion and enthusiasm. One day I again recounted the many acts of kindness they had shown me and my feelings of unworthiness and embarrassment. The Master said, "Yes, this is the result of service to 'Abdu'l-Bahá."

In any case, I spent a few days like this at a time when the doors of all correspondence were completely closed. There were no incoming letters to deal with and so no Tablets were being revealed in reply, for secret agents were everywhere and all sorts of rumours were being spread near and far. 'Abdu'l-Bahá reacted to all this with patience, tranquillity and dignity. At the same time He spoke to us of the absolute certainty of disagreeable events to come.

One very early morning I was summoned to the presence

of the Master. After imparting many expressions of kindness He said, "Last night I was thinking about you. I came up with a good plan for you. You must study."

When He said that, I thought He meant me to study philosophy, the plan I had considered pursuing in Paris and of which I had apprised Him in detail. "What should I study?" I asked.

"Whatever will be of benefit," He responded.

"Where?" I asked.

"In Beirut," He replied. "Go to Beirut and investigate the matter, and come back. Then I will tell you."

"Are there classes in literature and philosophy in Beirut?" I enquired.

"Something that will be of more benefit," He hinted.

The more I thought what could be of more benefit, the less I succeeded in finding an answer. Suddenly I said, "Should I study medicine?"

"Yes, yes, that is very good," was His response. "The Catholics have a very good medical school. The Americans have one too. Go and find out which one is right for you." He then talked about the seditious activities of the Covenant-breakers and the upheavals to be expected in 'Akká, and how beneficial it would be for the friends in residence to disperse.

These instructions from 'Abdu'l-Bahá, which I had not expected, left a marked effect on my being. All day long I was immersed in an ocean of thoughts. Giant obstacles presented themselves. How could I succeed in the study of medicine? How would I provide the necessary means? And how could I complete such studies in an unhappy condition, being so far from 'Akká and the threshold of 'Abdu'l-Bahá? Aside from all this, how was I to provide the financial means for such an enterprise?

I spent that day and the following night engrossed in these agitated thoughts. At times a ray of hope would emerge from the depths of my sombre ruminations and transform the darkness of ignorance into the light of understanding. I told myself: since this decision has emerged from the will of the

Beloved, it will obviously be accompanied by divine confirmations. In short, I spent that night filled with anxiety and apprehension and in a state of prayer.

Next morning I was again summoned to the presence of 'Abdu'l-Bahá. As He walked the dark narrow alleys of 'Akká on His usual visits to the poor and the downtrodden, He continued with the theme He had begun to expound the previous day. He repeated the necessity of the dispersion of the resident believers, and then explained the importance of education, and the secrets which would lead to success. He considered success and progress in any field conditional first on divine confirmation and then on wholehearted perseverance. He also gave some astonishing examples of the power that is generated from focusing one's mental faculties on a single goal. He gave the example of the heat that is created through the concentration of light at one point, and the pressure that is generated by the concentration of steam in an enclosed space, and other similar examples.

These words of 'Abdu'l-Bahá again kindled the light of hope in my heart, and I suddenly discovered a newfound confidence. I felt that since the success of any enterprise is conditional upon divine bounty, I would therefore receive my share of that bounty, for this matter had emerged from the will of 'Abdu'l-Bahá and that sacred will would attract divine confirmations. As this feeling of assurance penetrated my heart I asked, "When should I leave for Beirut?"

'Abdu'l-Bahá expressed delight at my acceptance of and enthusiasm for His plan and since the arrival of the next ship was scheduled for three days hence, He told me, "Leave on such-and-such a day. Stay in Beirut for three or four days, complete your investigations and then return to 'Akká."

And so for two days I awaited the arrival of the ship. Despite my new-born confidence in my eventual success in the study of medicine, my nights were filled with agitated thoughts and worry at my remoteness from 'Akká.

A brief visit to Beirut

When I arrived in Beirut I found the friends of that land distressed and upset. Those same rumours that had troubled the friends in 'Akká and Haifa were being circulated a hundredfold by the government officials. Many of 'Abdu'l-Bahá's non-Bahá'í friends were constantly making enquiries of the believers, and this added to their general concern and distress. In the newspapers of Beirut and Egypt, certain intimations had been published which although devoid of truth brought sorrow and anguish to the friends.[203]

Praised be God, my four or five days' stay served to allay their fears. In that time I made an adequate study of the schools, and then returned to 'Akká to find the Amatu'l-Bahá still persevering at 'Abdu'l-Bahá's dinner table with her question-and-answer sessions.

'Abdu'l-Bahá's teachings on how to attract divine confirmations

On my return to 'Akká I reported my findings to the Master. This served to finalize 'Abdu'l-Bahá's decision and made my departure certain. Yet to prepare for such a journey and to nourish the soul for such an expedition required heavenly provisions and divine guidance. This was especially true since despite His many counsels and promises of heavenly confirmations, the flame of confidence had not yet illumined my heart. At times I saw a glimmer of hope, and yet whenever I considered my utter unworthiness that glimmer disappeared and the darkness of hopelessness overshadowed every faculty of my being.

It was unimaginable that at that stage of my life, with all the pain and anguish which remoteness from the threshold of the Beloved would entail, I could muster enough strength and energy to begin and complete the study of a science in which I had no background. In any case, I spent three or four more days in 'Akká, and on every one of those I gained admittance to the threshold of the Beloved and was honoured by His words of encouragement. Every day bestowed a fresh bounty and every hour was endowed with a unique blessing. The words of the Beloved Master, each a priceless jewel uttered to fortify and comfort my despairing and melancholy heart, were so plenteous that their sheer abundance concealed their true value, and yet some of these gem-like utterances continue to ring in my ear and will eternally remain in my memory. For example, one day when strolling through the streets of 'Akká the Master made this specific remark: "Regard not thyself. Look to the Abhá Kingdom so that the confirmations may reach thee. Education requires absolute concentration and wholehearted commitment so as to attract divine confirmations. Do not consider the attraction of divine bounty to be proportionate to your capabilities and talents. Rely upon the heaven of mercy and generosity and be confident. Be confident."

In short, as these loving utterances flowed from the lips of 'Abdu'l-Bahá, bewildering thoughts and strange visions filled my mind. Suddenly the story of Abraham and His communion with God as He was being entrusted with His prophetic mission came to mind. He had found Himself reluctant to believe God's promise that His progeny would number more abundantly than the stars in the heavens; for entertaining such doubts, He had been reprimanded by God until His heart had at last gained assurance and confidence.[204] As soon as this story crossed my mind, 'Abdu'l-Bahá suddenly turned His face towards me and asked, "Do you feel confident now?"

However, after such spiritual reprimand I lacked the power of speech to make a reply and so I bowed my head and heard, with the ear of spirit, the voice of my heart as it exclaimed rather loudly, "Yes, I am confident, quite confident." As soon as this call came from the depths of my heart, the agitation of my mind subsided and the anxiety of my heart gave way to confidence. I knew of a certainty that I had succeeded in the study of medicine and in fact had already become a skilled physician, and all apprehension thus left me, and the only question that remained was the day that I was to leave for Beirut.

Although my agitation had disappeared, 'Abdu'l-Bahá's utterances continued unabated. As He continued to walk the streets of 'Akká the Master expounded His approach and began to give specific instructions on how to attract divine confirmations and strengthen the powers of perseverance.

Regarding the power created by the concentration of forces on a single point and the application of a single idea uncluttered by any other, He gave wonderful examples which I now find myself incapable of remembering. However, regarding the importance of perseverance in the performance of any task, I heard Him reiterate an exhortation which I had heard frequently from His lips; now again, as a reminder, He repeated those words, reviving and awakening me.

"In any and all endeavours, divine confirmation is wholly dependent on action. Persevere, so that the hosts of divine bounty may assist you," were His words. I even remember that once in the course of His utterances, taking God as witness He said, "The hosts of divine blessings are poised behind this very window waiting for you to act. If you do not enter the arena of service, of what use are the hosts of heavenly confirmation? If the commander of the army remains idle and passive, how can the army achieve victory?"

In short, He spoke on this subject a great deal, but I have now forgotten most of it. Only one point has stayed with me, and this continued to guide my way throughout my studies: "Divine confirmation is dependent on action."

In any case, as soon as He noticed that I had become utterly enraptured by the wine of His love and tenderness, He dismissed me with the words, "May God go with you," and on the very next day and at the same hour again summoned me to His presence.

Moving to Beirut

This time when I attained His presence, my sense of trust and confidence was so strong that I was about to ask about the date of my departure and settle it, when 'Abdu'l-Bahá's utterances began to flow. He issued further instructions concerning the strengthening of one's faith, some of which I am able to recall. He gave a detailed explanation of the virtue of piety and the benefits of the fear of God. Then He deliberated on the necessity of perseverance in studies and that one should not become discouraged at the emergence of difficulties and obstacles. And then He spoke on a matter which troubled me so deeply that I could not bear to listen. I was then unaware that that guidance would preserve me from a tremendous danger. Here is the story.

In the days when the rumours of the arrival of the Commission of Enquiry had filled the thoughts of friend and foe, the Covenant-breakers had deceived some of the Iranian residents of Beirut, and had generated an atmosphere of scepticism and apprehension about the Cause. Moreover, having been joined by an Azalí collaborator,[205] they had gradually begun to infiltrate the schools and poison the minds of the students. As a result, all the Iranians in those Syrian lands, who used to bow in reverence at the name of 'Abdu'l-Bahá, had in these days become highly critical, derogatory and offensive, and like the Covenant-breakers were looking for opportunities to create trouble.

It was at such a time that I received my instructions to depart for Beirut, and since schools there were attended by a few Bahá'í students, it was essential that they too should receive 'Abdu'l-Bahá's counsels and instructions for their own protection. The Master spoke about the virtue of perseverance, then He made reference to the qualities of patience and forbearance, and then He said, "Put love for all the Persians in your heart; never express any displeasure or aversion towards anyone. The more they express enmity, respond with an added measure of kindness. It is not necessary to teach them the Faith in any formal way. Do what you can so that they may develop true sympathy towards the Faith of God. If you wish to succeed in your work, do not forget these counsels. Loving the friends is of no major merit. In this journey you must become a lover of your enemies, so that the purity of your love may attract the hearts."

In short, as He strolled through the narrow dark streets of 'Akká, these were the words that flowed from His lips. Little by little 'Abdu'l-Bahá's utterances gained in intensity until He said, "Never allow the enmity of the Persians in that city to make you unhappy. Confront them with a joyful face. Even if you see with your own eyes and hear with your own ears that they curse my name, smile at them, do not display displeasure, and take no offence. If you follow this you will succeed, but if you are unable to do this, tell me now and I will not send you, because I have a purpose in sending you there."

These words of the Master broke my heart and depressed me so utterly that my legs lost the strength to move, for I could not find in myself such tolerance and patience. At this, 'Abdu'l-Bahá turned His face towards me and said, "This is not a difficult thing to do. Come, I will tell you how. You must put this thought into your heart, that that poor individual does not know me. How can he be held responsible? You must pray for him. He who knows me as you do, and he who does not know me at all, are not the same. Let's assume you quarrel with him or allow yourself to hate him. Of what benefit is that to you, or to the Faith, or to me? However, if your heart is free from rancour and responds with kindness, it is possible that you may touch his heart. For the sake of God and for His pleasure as well as mine, you must not on this journey allow the hatred of anyone to enter your heart; so you may succeed in your purpose. On the other hand, consider: what damage can the calumny of the foolish inflict on my work? What difference can such words make to me? I pray for all of them. You must look at me and strive to gain my good pleasure. And my wish is that you do not take offence at anyone. When I am happy with you, how can you be unhappy?" In short, He continued with such utterances until tears began to stream uncontrollably down my face. In my heart I repeated a poem that says,

> *If my death a thousand foes pursue,*
> *I fear not, for I have a Friend in you.*

While that day's utterances complemented His previous words, they contained many fine points which served to warn me of future events, the realization of which, I was sure, was not too far off. In fact, each episode came to pass as the Master had predicted. I shall present the detail of this in later chapters.

As I have described earlier, these days the Master did not appear to be overworked, in contrast with previous years, for the portals of reunion were closed to all and the pilgrim house was completely deserted. Also, there was no correspondence to deal with and therefore no response was required. Non-Bahá'ís, who had formerly come in groups to visit the Master, did not dare to approach lest they be accused of friendship with 'Abdu'l-Bahá and one day become the subject of a legal investigation.

At nights, the reciter of the Qur'án chanted for about half an hour, mostly for himself and one or two of the household servants. During the days, the *bírúní* area was deserted and the Master spent His time mostly in building flowerbeds and planting trees in the front garden. At times He took long walks in the narrow streets of 'Akká, visiting the city's poor and downtrodden and bestowing on them His loving attention and encouraging words. At such times, He would take along any of the friends whom He wished to accompany Him, and I was one of these who in these last days was called upon regularly and was granted the honour of listening to His words of guidance.

The lessons He taught me in those three or four days became my constant guide for the rest of my life. All my scientific and medical achievements, nay, the very development and progress of my spiritual and physical existence, owe their success, both outwardly and inwardly, to those loving counsels. And now, after some thirty-two years, any time I envision them my memory presents me with such a clear, lucid picture of those events that it seems as though they took place just yesterday. Even the very face of 'Abdu'l-Bahá appears before my tearful eyes, and His words ring in my ears so distinctly and clearly that I become convinced that over eighty per cent of those exalted utterances of His that I have reported in these last pages are in exactly His own exalted words.

And if I did not write those words on paper for the record, praised be God, I have written them in the pages of my memory as though etched in stone. Now, with the help of the angel of bounty, I have been able to reproduce them on paper so that they may endure the passage of time. It is to be hoped that those who long to receive heavenly confirmations in their material and spiritual affairs may take these words of guidance to heart and make of them a permanent pattern for their lives.

Let us return to the story. The last time 'Abdu'l-Bahá outlined those words of wisdom, He also imparted certain instructions specifically for Bahá'í youth, whether attending the schools of Beirut or not, in order to attract and kindle their hearts. He then added, "Whoever of the Persians whom you perceive as sympathetic to the Cause, you may, if you consider it prudent, send to me. And although I give nobody permission to come here, yet if you consider it prudent I will accept anyone you send to me."

The intention of the Master was that any of the Persians who were sympathetic towards the Cause of God might travel to 'Akká and receive His blessings. He even remarked, "Whoever you introduce with a few words and send to me, or whoever you bring to me yourself, I will receive as a very dear guest, and you yourself can come any time without a second permission. This is your own home. Whoever you send is your guest as well as mine."

'Abdu'l-Bahá wished to make me aware that in Beirut

there were those who were destined to achieve important positions in the future and that if these were to accept the Faith formally, their words about the Faith would be considered as merely subjective and thus be discredited. Moreover, they would become fearful and try to conceal their belief. But if they were not formally Bahá'ís and yet became sympathetic towards the Cause, they could serve the Faith fearlessly and their views would be generally received more objectively. As He spoke, He repeated His advice again about firmness and perseverance in studies, and then I heard from His lips some words which included the following: "Some of the teachers may show harshness. You must tolerate this in order to achieve your end." I quickly perceived that I might become the object of enmity on the part of the professors, and this would require patience and tolerance. Like His other advice, I took this to heart and wondered when it would come to pass.

The sailing date of the ship from Haifa to Beirut was set by this time and it was decided that I should receive my permission to leave the next day. On the day of departure, I again received another series of encouraging and hopeful utterances. As words of prayer for the attraction of blessings and confirmation began to flow from the lips of the Master, I bowed and kissed His hand and the hem of His 'abá. He drew me to Him, placed my head on His chest and conferred upon me His blessing and bounty.

With tearful eyes and a burning heart I left 'Akká. In the course of those four or five hours as I sailed towards Beirut there passed before my mind's eye with the speed of light all the events of the past four years. One by one I mentally paraded the many acts of love and kindness that 'Abdu'l-Bahá had shown me. I recalled that personification of supreme sacrifice, remembered His patience, serenity, tranquillity and dignity, and His bearing and demeanour in the face of all those unpleasant events and the wicked actions of the Covenant-breakers. I had no concerns about my own future, for the bounty of assurance bestowed upon me by His heavenly promises filled my whole being. Then, I considered all those events as a prolonged dream, leaving the interpretation of it to the future.

Having recalled the memories of the past with such clarity, I began to think about future events in 'Akká. But I realized that I had no access to that domain any more, and thus helpless, I resorted to chanting a prayer that I knew by heart until I reached the object of my desire. This prayer has always had, and continues to have, a happy and spiritual effect on my mortal existence which is beyond my power to describe. And so I reproduce it below to illumine the hearts of my dear readers.[206]

He is the Most Glorious!
Make firm our steps, O Lord, in Thy path and strengthen Thou our hearts in thine obedience. Turn our faces toward the beauty of Thy oneness, and gladden our bosoms with the signs of Thy divine unity. Adorn our bodies with the robe of Thy bounty, and remove from our eyes the veil of sinfulness, and give us the chalice of Thy grace; that the essence of all beings may sing Thy praise before the vision of Thy grandeur. Reveal then Thyself, O Lord, by Thy merciful utterance and the mystery of Thy divine being, that the holy ecstasy of prayer may fill our souls – a prayer that shall rise above words and letters and transcend the murmur of syllables and sounds – that all things may be merged into nothingness before the revelation of Thy splendour.

Lord! These are servants that have remained fast and firm in Thy Covenant and Thy Testament, that have held fast unto the cord of constancy in Thy Cause and clung unto the hem of the robe of Thy grandeur. Assist them, O Lord, with Thy grace, confirm with Thy power and strengthen their loins in obedience to Thee.

Thou art the Pardoner, the Gracious.

'Abdu'l-Bahá

CHAPTER SEVEN

He is the Most Glorious!

This compilation of nine years of memories was prepared several years ago. The first six chapters were then submitted in six booklets to the sanctified threshold of the beloved Guardian of the Cause of God. Later, in order to collect additional information and supporting documentation covering events after my departure from 'Akká, I decided to ask the help of some of the devoted souls resident in that city at the time.

I therefore sent a letter to Áqá Mírzá Hadí Afnán,[207] a request to Áqá Mírzá Núru'd-Dín and a petition to Amatu'l-Bahá Madame Dreyfus-Barney, asking them to provide descriptions of the events they had witnessed during my absence from 'Akká, so that these might be properly documented here. The honourable Afnán's reply was quite brief. The events of that period were so many and varied that he could not be expected to remember the details regarding which I had solicited his help. And so I eagerly awaited an answer from the Amatu'l-Bahá. I even sent her those extracts from the book that pertained to her rôle in the story. Since she had left 'Akká some time after I had, I hoped that she might have witnessed the heart-rending events that had followed, and that she might be able to provide an account of what she could recall, so as to confirm the accuracy of the information presented in this narrative.

Several letters were sent to her, and at last one reached her. Her reply took two years to arrive. This caused a long delay in completing this account, as over the course of time I lost track of the story altogether. Several years then passed in idleness as I made no further attempt to continue the work. However, many of the friends who knew about the first part were expecting to see the remaining portion, and they persistently urged me to complete the work in view of its historical value. And so after this lengthy sabbatical I again took up the pen, in accordance with the wishes of the spiritual friends.

Here follows the reply[208] from Amatu'l-Bahá – the Glory of God be upon her:

Aug. 7th, 1937
Dr. Youness Khán, care of Mr. Samímí, Tehran, Iran

Dear Dr. Youness Khán,
Your December letter and its attachments reached me only last week after a lengthy journey. Of course, the book that you have undertaken to write will be of much benefit, and I was delighted with what you had written about me. It was truly a great bounty for us to have spent such an extended time in the Holy Land and seen and heard 'Abdu'l-Bahá. If it is not too late, I wish to bring to your attention certain facts that will enable you to modify the pages that you have sent me.

In line 17 of the first page where reference is made to Miss Rosenberg, who had transcribed the English translation of the book [*Some Answered Questions*], no further explanation is provided and people may think that the published English version of the book reflects the exact words she recorded. However, this is not the case; the published English and French versions are translated directly from the Persian rendering which had been corrected by the Master. Also, in the middle of the third page, the following is stated: "Lately it was decided that the utterances of the Master should also be recorded in Persian." While I desired from the very beginning that the Master's utterances be recorded in Persian, it was only when the Master mentioned that at some time these transcripts would have to be reviewed and corrected, that He made the decision that His utterances be also recorded in Persian. Of course you know that the Master not only corrected Mírzá Munír's first draft, but after the corrections were incorporated 'Abdu'l-Bahá again reviewed the corrected version and signed each corrected subject. Last winter I had Mrs. Angiz <u>Kh</u>ánum Tabrízí deliver to Shoghi Effendi the final draft of the book as corrected and signed by 'Abdu'l-Bahá. I do not think that when the Commission of Enquiry arrived in 'Akká, any more than two thirds of the book had been completed.

I thank you for having asked me to write a few pages concerning the events during your absence from 'Akká. I do not think this would be of much benefit for the sort of book that you have in mind, however I do recommend that you study the Preface that I wrote for the book in 1907.[269] I cannot remember now whether the Preface written and published for the English and French versions is the same as the one for the Persian version, so may I refer you to either of the two copies. There are some points there which will be of benefit to your work. The first subject which the Master revealed is presented in the initial chapter of the book. I think this is the same chapter which was originally written in English. Also, much of the third section and some of the fifth are those which were recorded in English only.

As you know, it was on my third visit to 'Akká that I arrived with Miss Rosenberg. I spent the winter of 1904 there. I visited Egypt briefly and in the spring of 1905 paid a visit to my mother, after which we both returned to the Holy Land. I left again in the midsummer of 1905, returning to 'Akká in the fall of that year. I spent a part of that winter in Cairo and returned to 'Akká and Haifa by the end of spring. After that summer, I journeyed to Iran and then came back to Europe, and in the fall returned to 'Akká. On my return, *Some Answered Questions* had been corrected and permission had been granted for its publication.

The following year, the Persian version as well as the English and French versions of the book were published and distributed. In the second edition of the book two additional subjects were added.[210] In 1908 I returned to Haifa, and when the Master visited Europe I again gained admittance to His presence. In the United States I had the honour of attaining His presence again, and after the War, in 1918, my husband and I travelled to 'Akká on pilgrimage. The last time I visited 'Abdu'l-Bahá was in 1921 when we were on our way to the Far East. In Rangoon, Burma, we heard of His passing. On my last visit, I had ample time to report a number of social issues to the Master, which today have come to pass and have revolutionized the present social order. I have many notes which, God willing, I will compile and send to Shoghi Effendi before publication and distribution.

Dear Youness Khán, please inform me of the progress of your book and call on me if I can be of any service.

Yours truly,
L. Dreyfus-Barney

This was Amatu'lláh Mrs. Dreyfus-Barney's response to my letter written in the summer of 1935. While acknowledging her comments, I wish to note that in Chapter 6 of this book these matters have been covered in the section on "Miss Barney and *Some Answered Questions*", although I was not aware that Miss Barney had desired a Persian compilation of the book from the outset. It was also quite clear that the notes taken by Miss Rosenberg could not possibly have been used exactly as they were and compiled into a properly sequenced book. Not unlike Mr. Phelps's book referred to in Chapter 3 above, under the title "Madame de Canavarro and Mr. Phelps", they would have required multiple revisions before formal approval could be granted. Although Madame de Canavarro was a devoted believer, since Mr. Phelps's heart had not been illumined by the light of faith he, while employing all his literary talents and a distinct flair for writing in compiling the book, had incorporated in it his own thoughts and thus had deviated from the real issues. But the Amatu'l-Bahá, due to her strong faith and intense devotion, was able to compile her book properly and thus receive 'Abdu'l-Bahá's approval. It is certain that the English and French versions are both from her own pen[211] and not from the pen which hurriedly took the notes at the dinner table. Therefore, each word and line of that book should be considered as the revealed Word. Happy is the one who reads those words, who ponders their meaning and contemplates their significance.

The response from Jináb-i-Núru'd-Dín-i-Zayn, dated the 17th of Sháhru'l 'Ilm, 92 B.E. – equivalent to November of 1935 – was written after those treacherous activities of the Covenant-breakers of which I was aware. This letter is reproduced in its entirety at the end of this chapter for my gentle readers.

Multiple investigators, both secret and open

In the blessed days of 'Abdu'l-Bahá, secret agents and official investigators played their part in the story from a year after the ascension of the Abhá Beauty, when the Covenant-breakers established their evil organization and began to disseminate their seditious literature in all directions, inciting both the government and the people against the Cause of God. As described in Chapter 1, their secret agents were exposed at the time of the rebellion of Mírzá Áqá Ján, when the incident concerning Tábúr Áqásí and the upheaval in 'Akká came to pass.

From that time forward, the birds of night[212] flew in all directions, especially to Beirut, Istanbul, and cities in Egypt, as Ottoman secret agents began to arrive in 'Akká from Istanbul. It was the policy of the Ottoman courts at that time to give credence to the words of any mischief-maker and accuser whenever a voice of dissent was heard from any direction. Sedition and rebellion were rampant in all parts of the Ottoman Empire, and the Covenant-breakers took advantage of the fear and apprehension at the court of the

Sultan; every day they brought a new allegation and made fresh efforts to undermine and damage the Faith.

Because of these activities, there was always a group of secret agents in 'Akká. At times a commission would arrive to conduct open enquiries. An example was the sudden arrival of the Commission of Enquiry in 1902 or 1903 [*sic*, actually 1904], which conducted an investigation and then departed. After that, rumours began to be spread in 'Akká and there was real fear that the Master could be taken prisoner; the newspapers in Egypt and Syria made frequent references to this issue. At the House of 'Abdu'l-Bahá all written materials were being collected as an Ottoman warship dropped anchor alternately at the Ports of 'Akká and Haifa and awaited the return of the inspectors. 'Akká was beset by turmoil and chaos. The resident friends were fearful and distressed, and some of the citizens of Haifa and 'Akká made innuendoes and intimations to the friends indicating their conviction that the Master would be taken prisoner. It is thought that the Will and Testament of 'Abdu'l-Bahá was revealed at this time.[213]

At dangerous times such as this, Escobino, the Italian Consul in Haifa who was devoted to 'Abdu'l-Bahá and who was the official representative of the Italian shipping lines, several times invited 'Abdu'l-Bahá to board one of his ships and depart for whatever destination He wished.[214] This time, when he arrived in 'Akká and extended this offer he received a negative response. The rumour was circulating that 'Abdu'l-Bahá was to be exiled to the Fezzan desert of Western Libya. 'Abdu'l-Bahá had frequently mentioned the dreadful climate of that region and used to remark, "These people are heedless, for if God wills it, the climate of that place will change just as that of 'Akká did, and that desert too will be transformed into paradise."

On another occasion, one day when the friends were besieged by fear and agitation, 'Abdu'l-Bahá, with a bearing dignified and serene, slowly began to stroll towards the port. He walked out of the gate of the city to take a look at the sea. He threw a glance at the warship anchored at some distance from the shore and then came back. A few hours later, the ship pulled anchor and departed. It was not clear what had happened in Istanbul to bring about a recall of the inspectors. The matter was now dropped. This was two years before the events which necessitated my journey to Europe and subsequently to Beirut. In this connection I am reminded of a story which I present below.

Interpretation of Mírzá Núru'd-Dín's dream

Mírzá Asadu'lláh, a teacher of the Faith who ultimately went astray and turned Covenant-breaker, had been blessed by Bahá'u'lláh with the ability to interpret dreams. Bahá'ís and non-Bahá'ís alike, therefore, came to him to discover the meaning of their dreams, and his interpretations were invariably realized before long.

In the course of my stay almost every one of the friends sought his services two or three times, and later witnessed the accuracy of his interpretation. I myself had only one dream during my stay, and this was interpreted by the Master Himself, the truth of which has only recently been realized. I shall recount the details of that dream later at a more opportune moment.

Mírzá Núru'd-Dín, who during the recent crisis was assigned the task of gathering up both the voided and the authorized copies of the Holy Writings accumulated over the years in various secret locations, had had a dream one night. When he saw Mírzá Asadu'lláh he asked him to interpret it. He described his dream in these words: "A few nights ago I dreamt that a large jug of attar of rose (which at that time came from Istanbul and cost one gold lira per *mithqál*) broke and the fragrant contents were splashed all over the floor. I was labouring feverishly to recover all I could by picking up handfuls of the liquid and pouring it into a large drum. There seemed to be no end to the expensive fluid, and I was whispering to myself that every few drops that fell from my fingers was worth one gold lira, and so how precious must be the value of this much perfume."

Mírzá Asadu'lláh responded, "You will be instructed to gather up the rough drafts and the obsolete copies of the divine verses revealed in recent years and put them in a safe place!" And indeed, that dream was realized that very night.

The moral of this story is, first, to demonstrate the gift that was granted to Mírzá Asadu'lláh despite his subsequent heedlessness and infidelity and the unfortunate end that awaited him, and secondly, to show that the government agents were active both covertly and openly, and generally on permanent assignment, which called for constant vigilance. Once or twice things became so critical that the Master gathered together all written materials, and I too collected all my papers and dispatched them to a safe place. In the meantime the Ottoman warship was making preparations to take the Master away, and so the friends were deeply agitated and distressed. On previous similar occasions, unexpected events in Istanbul creating a general state of fear and anxiety had prompted the government to abandon the idea of arresting 'Abdu'l-Bahá. The most recent occasion had been the one which had precipitated my departure from 'Akká.

As I reviewed my recollection of these events some thirty years after my return to Tehran, I found my memory incapable of differentiating between these various episodes, and my pen unable to describe each case independently and accurately. Therefore, I had to seek help from the above-mentioned honourable souls, and it took several years before Mrs. Barney's response was received. In the meantime sloth and apathy had won me over for a time and I lost track of the story. In any event, I have already commented on Amatu'l-Bahá's letter, and will write my remarks concerning Jináb-i-Núru'd-Dín-i-Zayn's letter in the last part of this chapter.

Intrigues of the Covenant-breakers

Many of these events, as covered in Chapter 4, took place at a time when the upheavals and hardships were at their peak, and yet significantly this period of time, i.e. 1902 until 1905, saw the beginning of the great services that would be rendered during the period of the Covenant. Many of 'Abdu'l-Bahá's plans for the Western countries began to be put into action when He visited those countries, and many a prophecy made by Him during His years of imprisonment was fulfilled.

The details of the seditious activities of the Covenant-breakers are as follows:

The Governor of 'Akká, that same pasha who due to 'Abdu'l-Bahá's intercession had freed the Covenant-breakers from their confinement in the Prison City of 'Akká, insisted that 'Abdu'l-Bahá should not consider Himself a prisoner and that He should feel free to move about as He wished. This insistence, of course, stemmed from his own devotion and attachment to 'Abdu'l-Bahá, and the fact that he could not tolerate such an injustice as the imprisonment of the obviously exalted personage of the Master during the period of his administration. However, he certainly had received no official permission from the Sublime Porte approving such an instruction, and yet he continued to identify himself as a supporter and defender of 'Abdu'l-Bahá. But his many appeals and entreaties to the Master to move about freely failed to persuade 'Abdu'l-Bahá, until he devised a plan which he felt would produce the desired result. He officially asked for permission to visit the Shrine of Bahá'u'lláh, on condition that such pilgrimage should take place in the presence of the Master. His request was granted, and one day he visited the Shrine in the presence of 'Abdu'l-Bahá, performing all the required and customary rites of pilgrimage.

The Governor was hopeful that from that day on the Centre of the Covenant, in accordance with the same terms which He had presented to intercede on behalf of the Covenant-breakers, would consider Himself at liberty to re-establish His normal practice of visiting Bahjí and Haifa as He had done in earlier years. As this hope was not realized, he again requested 'Abdu'l-Bahá's presence in yet another visit to the Shrine of Bahá'u'lláh, this time with certain prominent members of the government. Again they made their pilgrimage and performed the required rites in the same manner as the believers, without the slightest deviation. Reportedly, that day proved to be one of the most disappointing and difficult days that the Covenant-breakers had experienced in their earthly lives. When the noise of the carriages arriving reverberated through the area as they came to a halt behind the Mansion, the Covenant-breakers rushed to the windows to watch. The sight of 'Abdu'l-Bahá leading prominent people, including the Governor of 'Akká, Faríq Páshá, Lává Páshá and Badrí Big, who humbly walked behind Him, bowed themselves before the Shrine of Bahá'u'lláh and emulated 'Abdu'l-Bahá in kissing the Threshold as they entered the Shrine itself, must have been utterly frustrating and intolerable. All their attempts to renew 'Abdu'l-Bahá's incarceration, including the expenditure of the wealth left to them after the passing of Mírzá Áqá Ján, had come to naught. They had witnessed with their own eyes the greatness of the Faith of God and its triumph. But once again these dormant germs came to life again, gathered together, summoned their colleagues from within and without, and after much consultation resolved to attack the very foundation of the Faith and try to extirpate the Cause of God altogether.

So they decided to bring together the means for the destruction of the Master, or at least cause His banishment from 'Akká. However, they were unable to decide on an effective strategy, until at last they saw their salvation in denouncing the representatives of the nation and the government officials. Bringing charges against the very Governor who had freed them from imprisonment, as well as against some of the high-ranking military officers who had brought honour and esteem to the Faith, and even discrediting the Mufti of 'Akká who had always viewed the Faith in a favourable light, was the approach they chose in order to implement their devious plan.

This was of course easy, for in the despotic reign of Sulṭán 'Abdu'l-Ḥamíd the law allowed citizens to bring charges against anyone. Even if the charges were proved false, the accuser was not held responsible and was liable for no penalty or censure for slander. In this way, the royalists held absolute power and were able to remain in control. Anyone who held a grudge against another could destroy his opponent by bringing against him a well-thought-out allegation. In this way thousands of innocent people lost their lives, thrown into the sea without benefit of trial, while those who could get a hearing and prove their innocence became, by the end of such proceedings, totally discredited and disgraced without their accusers being held accountable in the slightest. This, then, was the policy of that Caliph who possessed the highest rank in Islám at that time.

When the Covenant-breakers, well practised in sedition and deception, perceived the favourable attitude of the government officials towards the Faith, they brought together a group of mischief-makers and drew up a document, signed by them all, which declared that 'Abdu'l-Bahá had captured the devotion and obedience of 'Akka's highest-ranking officers, had formed an army of some thirty thousand troops and aimed to soon raise the banner of revolt and usurp the very foundation of the Ottoman reign. This is a summary of the document attached to the report prepared by the government's chief investigator and sent to the Court of the Ottoman Sulṭán. The Covenant-breakers, however, far from being satisfied with this series of actions, intensified their efforts by entering another avenue as follows. Shaykh Abu'l-Húdá, the Shaykh'u'l-Islám of the Ottoman Court, was the spiritual leader of the realm and regent to the Caliphate. He was a man who in the field of gnosticism [spiritual insight] was mentor and counsellor to the Sultan, and he enjoyed tremendous influence at the Sublime Porte. The devotion and esteem of the Sultan for the Shaykh was similar to Muḥammad Sháh's veneration of Ḥájí Mírzá Áqásí. The Shaykh had great influence even in political matters, reminiscent of Mullá Baqír Májlisí's power at the court of Sháh Sulṭán Ḥusayn Safáví.[215] Abu'l-Húdá possessed pre-eminent authority and leadership in spreading the principles of various Sunní schools of Islám, until some two thirds of the Ottoman nations had adopted Mawlaví or Yektai religious orders as well as other similar sects.[216]

It was reported that Shaykh Abu'l-Húdá had some knowledge of the Faith, but because of his religious standing and elevated rank in the mystical and spiritual fields he did not openly display any opposition to it. However, on the prompting and provocation of the Covenant-breakers he now arose against the Cause. On the day when in response to the persistent entreaties of those prominent personages of 'Akká, 'Abdu'l-Bahá led the procession to visit the sanctified Shrine of Bahá'u'lláh as pilgrims, and directed them to circumambulate that holy Spot, the jealousy and hatred of the Covenant-breakers boiled over. With renewed energy they strove night and day to muddy the water at its source, and ultimately found a way to make the acquaintance of the above-mentioned Shaykh. Having provoked concern and fear in his mind, they brought a series of flagrant charges against the Centre of God's Covenant. Reportedly, they wrote that Bahá'u'lláh had been a dervish who in His spiritual visions had spread the teachings of Islám, but that 'Abdu'l-Bahá had elevated his Father to the rank of divinity and was worshipping him as the Godhead; that he identified himself as the very religion of God and the manifestation of the Messiah and considered that he had the personal right to world sovereignty; that he had brought into his camp many Western Christians whom he was inviting to 'Akká in large numbers; that furthermore, he was planning to conquer Syria and Palestine and had been promised the cooperation of the high-ranking members of the Army; and that ·before long he intended to usurp the Ottoman Caliphate and destroy the Empire.[217] They had even written that various pieces of incriminating evidence were in their hands, that witnesses were readily available to testify, and that they only awaited the arrival of the Commission of Enquiry to present their case. In short, they published a variety of absurd and preposterous allegations and lies and spread them far and wide; they now awaited the arrival of the Commission of Enquiry in confident expectation.

The situation in 'Akká as the Covenant-breakers awaited the impending chaos

Whenever certain acts of mischief or dissent were about to take place in 'Akká, the Master would usually inform the believers, first implicitly and then openly, so that the friends would not become apprehensive and lose sight of caution and prudence, but at the same time would understand the future outlook of various affairs. And since most of the friends were familiar with the Master's tone, they immediately understood from His implied words that another major upheaval was in the offing. 'Abdu'l-Bahá's utterances in these days were not unlike those at the time of Mírzá Áqá Ján's rebellion as described in Chapter 1 under the title "Dismissal", as well as those in Chapter 2 in the section about 'Abdu'l-Bahá's utterances in Haifa. In short, the Master reminded us all of the approaching upheaval in 'Akká, and openly expressed His eagerness to endure whatever suffering and tribulations were in store for Him; yet at times He created before our minds' eyes a vision of the confirmations of the unseen paradise and the triumph of the Cause.

The situation in 'Akká had become generally chaotic. The enemies of the Faith had become openly hostile and overtly belligerent. From every corner one could hear whisperings, hints and allusions, while theft and slander had become rampant. The shopkeepers in the bazaar openly harassed their Bahá'í neighbours. In Haifa, the Arabs had become quarrelsome and vilified the friends. The reason for this maltreatment was that the Covenant-breakers had secretly informed them that before long the Ottoman officials would arrest and exile these same Bahá'ís, and in return would bestow manifold favours upon the Covenant-breakers who had delivered the Ottoman nation from the menace of these foreigners.

The Covenant-breakers were so completely confident of their imminent success and final victory that they spread these rumours undaunted, until the friends too heard of their intentions. However, the utterances of 'Abdu'l-Bahá at this time revolved around the necessity of patience, calmness and perseverance, so that unseen confirmations and divine mercy might reach us. And then He would add, "Now the friends are free to go wherever they wish. They will encounter no obstacles and provoke no opposition. If the resident friends would take their leave, it would serve to ease my mind and would bring them much comfort. So while there is yet time, let whoever is able begin his journey, so that 'Akká may become quieter." Because of this, and before the matter became urgent, the Master dismissed all the pilgrims. It was at that time that Ḥájí Mírzá Ḥaydar-'Alí went to 'Ishqábád.[218]

Because of 'Abdu'l-Bahá's emphatic and persistent requests, some of the friends prepared to leave. Of that group only a few departed, while others procrastinated until they were arrested, although all were released later by various means.

The arrival of Sulṭán 'Abdu'l-Ḥamíd's officials, and their departure due to the cannon blast of divine confirmation

Now that these rumours had spread all over the country, an Ottoman ship suddenly dropped anchor in Haifa, landing four or five pashas with the full authority of the Commission of Enquiry. Their first act was to seize the Post and Telegraph buildings in 'Akká and Haifa and to assign special officials, accountable to them only, at both sites. Next, as is customary in a *coup d'état*, they replaced the Governor of 'Akká with his deputy, the vilest of men; dismissed the senior military officers such as Fariq Páshá, Lává Páshá and Badrí Big; established direct and secret telegraphic links with Istanbul; took up residence in the house of 'Abdu'l-Ghaní Bayḍún, a collaborator of the Covenant-breakers; and began the task of collecting evidence. It was reported that they had located a few Palestinians

THE ARRIVAL OF SULTÁN 'ABDU'L-ḤAMÍD'S OFFICIALS 355

of that same clan whom, nineteen hundred years before, Jesus had addressed as the "generation of vipers", and that these had drafted testimonials in accordance with the Covenant-breakers' wishes and filed them with the Commission. The irony was that these were the same people who had frequently solicited 'Abdu'l-Bahá's assistance and had invariably received a favourable response.

In this turmoil the violators of the Covenant, who considered themselves to be the direct instigators of this investigation, arrogantly gave ultimatums to whoever they came in contact with, saying, "Your days of glory are numbered; tomorrow this and that will happen." Even the Centre of Sedition, who for a long time had secluded himself in his ignominious lair, leapt out of his hole and began to accompany his comrades, visiting friends and celebrating their seemingly fast-approaching victory.

The residents of 'Akká, some gloomy and upset, others dazed and dumbfounded, were making preparations either to attend the imminent auctions of Bahá'í possessions to get what they could at knock-down prices, or simply to pillage such belongings once their Bahá'í owners were arrested and exiled. Such was the condition of the Covenant-breakers and mischief-makers at that period.

The believers, relying on the Master's words that "a good end is the reward of the pious", tolerated the rebukes and taunts of the opposition in a spirit of peace and forbearance, and reacted with dignity and composure, smiling off the insults while at the same time eagerly awaiting with all their hearts the appearance of the heavenly angels of mercy and confirmation.

The area around the House of 'Abdu'l-Bahá was deserted, for the non-Bahá'ís dared not approach, and the trouble-makers, who were lying in wait for the opportunity to do mischief, did not risk coming near the house. Even the Friday beggars stopped coming round to receive their customary handouts, for fear of being wrongly accused. Spies were on the move all around the house, while the general inspectors openly harassed those who came to visit.

The Centre of the Covenant, however, was in a state of utmost joy and serenity. Free of all concern, He spent His time planting trees and expanding the flowerbed. Any friend who came to call was in His presence suddenly uplifted into a world of cheerfulness and joy. This was a cause of astonishment and envy to the non-Bahá'ís. As reported by Mírzá Núru'd-Dín-i-Zayn in his note to this servant, in the midst of all the turmoil the Commission of Enquiry secretly sent Shaykh Muḥammad-i-Nabihání to the presence of 'Abdu'l-Bahá so that on the pretext of a social visit he could rebuke the Master for not having paid a courtesy call on the Commission inspectors when they arrived, and for having failed to show them the proper marks of respect and hospitality. They hoped that such words would strike fear and trepidation into the heart of the Master. However, he found 'Abdu'l-Bahá adamant and unyielding. This he passed on to those who had planned his visit, which in turn increased their resentment and enmity.

This Commission had been empowered by Royal Decree. Its authority was unchallengeable and its decisions were final, with no possibility of appeal. One Friday morning, the Commission set out for Haifa to inspect the Shrine of the Báb, which had been described to them as a storehouse of arms and ammunition. The plan was that having confirmed the charges, they were to descend upon 'Akká in the darkness of night and arrest and imprison all those who had already been marked out for such an action.

This was quite clear and obvious to the friends as they awaited the onslaught, and the pain and agony which it would entail. But suddenly Almighty God gave the signal to discharge the cannon blast of divine confirmation and mercy, and 'Abdu'l-Ḥamíd's commands were in turn cast into the pit of oblivion. The situation was reversed; a secret telegram summoned the inspectors back with all due haste. The details are as follows.

On that same Friday, when Sulṭán 'Abdu'l-Ḥamíd was returning to his palace from public prayers in all the pomp and grandeur of secular and religious sovereignty, his enemies hurled a bomb at his coach. While the attempt did not harm the Sultan, it caused many deaths. Having thus escaped death, he immediately summoned the inspectors – whom he considered astute and trustworthy – back to Court, so that they might through their considerable influence resolve the mystery and discover the source of the conspiracy. In the meantime, any further action regarding the matter of Haifa and 'Akká ceased.

The Master generally referred to this incident as the "cannon blast of divine confirmation".

This is the letter from Núru'd-Dín-i-Zayn

To Dr. Youness Khán Afroukhteh, may my life be a sacrifice for you. The following is a summary description of the events associated with the arrival of the inspectors in 'Akká, so far as my memory permits.

Briefly, the dispatch of a number of testimonials to Istanbul, prepared at the instigation of the violators of the Covenant and signed and sealed by the malicious enemies of the Cause in 'Akká, bore witness to charges and allegations against 'Abdu'l-Bahá, including His supposedly strong fortress and mighty stronghold on the slopes of Carmel, and His presumed secret communications with foreigners. Furthermore, it charged that groups of these foreigners, both men and women, were arriving in 'Akká regularly, taking up residence in the Master's House (this is a reference to the pilgrims from Europe and America who arrived in groups to visit 'Abdu'l-Bahá) and were being encouraged to join a new religion, which is entirely in conflict with the principles of Islám. And that, in addition, they had already deceived a number of residents of 'Akká. It is quite obvious that to create apprehension and concern in the mind of a suspicious and cowardly king such as 'Abdu'l-Hamíd, any one of these accusations would have sufficed to rob him of his self-control, how much more when he encountered such a variety of allegations and charges.

'Abdu'l-Bahá was aware of the nature of such documents sent to the headquarters of the Ottoman government, and thus warned the friends repeatedly that although the King was quite unconcerned about any mischief in these parts, yet the frequent transmission of such affidavits to the government would eventually trouble the King enough to bring about a state of turmoil and unrest.

One night, three or four days before the expected arrival of the inspectors, in a general meeting with all the friends 'Abdu'l-Bahá related, "Last night in a dream I witnessed the arrival of a ship at 'Akká. As it dropped anchor, I saw a number of birds in the shape of grenades fly up from the ship and over the city. They soared from one part of town to another, yet the grenades did not detonate, and the birds returned to the ship." He made no further comments. One of 'Abdu'l-Bahá's divine qualities was, as He Himself used to explain: "Whenever a difficult matter or an arduous circumstance presents itself, I say nothing until it passes, and then I make mention of it." It is clear that in His supreme compassion and divine wisdom, He concealed such situations, personally enduring all the associated hardship and torment and arising single-handed to diffuse the crisis and repel the assault.

In short, it was but a few days after the Master's dream that an Ottoman ship arrived in 'Akká and the four-member Commission of Enquiry entered the town and proceeded directly to the house of 'Abdu'l-Ghaní Bayḍun, near the Mansion of Bahá'u'lláh. Bayḍun was a prominent and wealthy resident of 'Akká and one of the few enemies of the Faith.

This created a major commotion in the town, for their arrival was quite unexpected, sudden and unannounced; neither the local government officials and senior military officers nor the political opposition had been informed about this sudden entry into 'Akká, and were ignorant of its true intent and purpose. And so a variety of rumours, speculations and conjectures began to spread like wildfire among the people.

'Abdu'l-Bahá now told us that his dream had come true and assured us that, God willing, the grenades would not explode. Yet to be on the safe side, He advised the majority of the friends in the Holy Land to leave 'Akká and travel in whatever direction they deemed suitable. Most of them went to Egypt, leaving their wives and children behind, and only a few remained in 'Akká.

Here, in order to clarify the authority of the inspectors in the performance of their duties, a point must be mentioned. Under Ottoman rule the administration of the affairs of the country proceeded from two centres of power: one was the Sublime Porte and the other was the Ottoman Court. Any command issued from the Sublime Porte, which was initiated by the Council of Ministers of the government of the day, was subject to revision, moderation, appeal and mitigation. But any instruction issued from the Ottoman Court, which was generally known as the Royal Decree – meaning the absolute command and injunction of the person of the Sultan – was definitive, unequivocal and unconditional and could not be modified, revised or mitigated.

For example, if an official or a commission was assigned the duty of investigating a certain area of the country by the Sublime Porte, it generally carried out an enquiry and then issued a report. Those accused or considered guilty had the right to defend themselves and prove their innocence; a further enquiry would then usually be carried out, which could ultimately lead to the vindication of the accused either through the payment of a large bribe, which was quite prevalent at the time, or through the recommendation of an influential party. In rare cases and by sheer luck, the accused would be exonerated through the fairness and justice of the officials responsible. Otherwise the government usually won the case and punished the guilty party, thus bringing the matter to a conclusion.

However, if an official or a commission was sent from the Ottoman Court to carry out an investigation, it was given the authority to simply prove the accusations or the substance of the charges under investigation without any effort to take into account any opposing evidence that might nullify the charges. In other words, regardless of what it took, the commission had to prove the accusations. On this basis the proper punishment would be issued directly by the Sultan himself. The severity of the punishment specified by Royal Decree was decided by the sovereign himself without any input from anyone else. The order was absolute and the command final.

This Commission of Enquiry had been sent by the Ottoman Court and was armed with the signed and sealed affidavits of the enemies of the Faith, as instigated by the intrigues of the Covenant-breakers. What was tragically comic was that they began their investigation by interrogating those who had signed the affidavits. In other words, the plaintiff and the witness were one and the same. The plaintiff was the witness, and the witness the plaintiff. And it goes without saying that a plaintiff witness does not reject his own plaint but rather confirms it, since it is clear that if he even for a single instant manifested the slightest hesitation regarding the truth of his charge, he himself could become the subject of chastisement.

Such was the due process of law during the tyrannical rule of 'Abdu'l-Ḥamíd, and examples were numerous. Since the government was notorious at that time for deception, craftiness, corruption and distortion, the Commission of Enquiry announced on arrival that it had come to investigate certain issues of national, military and political importance, that the enquiry into the charges against 'Abdu'l-Bahá was to be carried out as an adjunct to their main task; and that in order to achieve a quick resolution of these problems they had seen fit to dismiss and exile certain officials of the government and the army, including the Governor of the city.

The truth, however, was that the tone and contents of those depositions had aroused such fear and agitation in the heart of the King that the principal purpose of the Commission was to carry out the Royal Decree in confirming and proving the charges contained in those documents.

In the midst of all this, the Master paid no attention to the officials and conducted Himself with supreme dignity, serenity, majesty and power, all the while withholding the slightest demonstration of welcome or hospitality to these men, all of whom were officers of the highest rank and the direct representatives of the Royal Court. This lack of regard on the part of 'Abdu'l-Bahá increased their indignation, astonishment and consternation to such an extent that losing all patience they found one of 'Akká's Islamic scholars, known as Sha<u>yk</u>h Muḥammad-i-Nabihání – who outwardly appeared as a proponent of the Faith but was in fact a mischief-maker – instructed him appropriately and sent him to the sanctified presence of 'Abdu'l-Bahá. He arrived feigning humility, trepidation and concern, yet beheld the Master in a state of tranquillity, composure and grandeur, as if nothing had happened. And since he was only too aware of the deceptions and trickery of the Commission of Enquiry, he was astonished. He thought the Master's dignity, power and magnanimity to be due to His ignorance of the cruel plans they had in store for Him and the vicious practices of the people of tyranny. Otherwise surely this Lion of the Covenant would, like a fox at bay, adopt the ways of flattery, praise and appeasement of the Commission, if only for the sake of appearances, and would cease to evince such a disinterested and unconcerned attitude.

In any case, this insincere scholar pleadingly put forth his case: "O my Master, this Commission is exceedingly ruthless and is currently plotting many schemes. Its members have stated, 'We had heard that, regardless of rank and standing, whenever an official arrives in 'Akká the exalted 'Abbás Effendi treats him with deference and shows him hospitality and kindness. We, however, who have come directly from the

Sultan, each possessing high rank and position, and have now been in 'Akká for a number of days, have been totally disregarded, while all the city leaders as well as people of prominence and wealth have already paid their courtesy visits.' This has so outraged them that they are intent on harming 'Abdu'l-Bahá and there is a fear of great danger to His wellbeing. Therefore, it may be better for the Master to pay them a visit and show them kindness and consideration, so as to dispel hurt feelings and quench the fire of enmity which rages in their hearts."

'Abdu'l-Bahá smiled and replied, "Yes, that is true. I have always been the first to offer hospitality to a newly-arrived official, regardless of rank, and you yourself know well my gentle and loving nature. But this Commission has come to prove the false accusations made in those testimonials against me, and therefore if I express any greetings and or welcome them, or offer hospitality and friendliness, they may mistakenly consider my motive to be fear, flattery and appeasement, whereas we are innocent of these accusations. It is not befitting for me to express such sentiments, for they should be allowed to conduct their investigation free from all influences. 'We rely on none but God.'"

Astonished by such forthright words uttered with such supreme power, the enquirer received permission to take his leave.

In the meantime, one day the Commission collectively visited Haifa and Mount Carmel and looked over the Shrine of the Báb. One of them placed his hand on a corner of the building and commented in Turkish, "This is a solid fortress" – one of the accusations in the signed depositions.

In any event, from the date of their arrival they assigned a guard to the House of 'Abdu'l-Bahá so as to prevent people from visiting the Master. No one dared to approach the house anyway. They stayed for some twenty days, sometimes in 'Akká and at other times in Haifa. Anxiety and uneasiness dominated the hearts and minds of the residents all this time, until suddenly and without advance notice, news reached 'Akká one day at sunset that the Commission of Enquiry had boarded the Ottoman ship in Haifa. Rumour had already been spread that it was the Commission's intention to take 'Abdu'l-Bahá away with them. As the ship approached 'Akká, the Greatest Holy Leaf and the Master's household became deeply anxious and the few believers present began to weep, especially when 'Abdu'l-Bahá paced up and down in the central hall of the house all alone, awaiting the descent of divine will. This servant, forgetful of self and in a state of near insanity, left the house and ran to a point from where the ship could be observed. I tarried a moment watching the ship approach the shores of 'Akká, but suddenly its lights seemed to turn away; it changed direction and began to sail away from 'Akká. I ran back with all the speed I could muster and entering the house saw 'Abdu'l-Bahá still pacing the floor in the darksome night. I approached.

"Well, what news?" He enquired.

"The ship is leaving 'Akká," I reported.

Then I shared the news with the members of the household. It brought about some peace of mind. Other friends, who had also gone to various parts of the city to observe the ship's movements, brought back the same news, and the grief and sorrow of the denizens of the tabernacle of purity and the friends of God was turned into relief and inexpressible joy. In those days of hardship and danger to the person of 'Abdu'l-Bahá, there was an Italian citizen called Escobino, who has since passed away, but at the time was the Vice-Consul for both the Persian and the Italian consulates.[219] Moreover, along with his nephews he was the official agent for the Italian commercial shipping line which served the port of Haifa. One night this man and his wife, who bore a sincere love for 'Abdu'l-Bahá and His family and exhibited deep humility and devotion in His presence, arrived in 'Akká secretly. As soon as the government guard left for the night they presented themselves at the door of the Master's House and in a state of great agitation and apprehension asked to be permitted to enter the presence of 'Abdu'l-Bahá. On attaining the presence of the Master he pleaded and implored 'Abdu'l-Bahá in these words, "On the pretext of loading commercial freight I have kept an Italian ship in the port of 'Akká, and to ward off any suspicion I have told it to dock alternately at Haifa and 'Akká. At present the ship is at a preselected point between the two cities, and a small boat from the ship is currently at the shore in readiness. Time is short, the carriage is ready, there are no obstacles and the opportunity is at hand; therefore, it is best for the Master to accept to board the ship so that He may flee this tyranny and sail to whatever destination He chooses."

After a moment's pause, 'Abdu'l-Bahá responded to his request with words of encouragement: "My Lords the exalted Báb and Bahá'u'lláh, in situations far more dangerous than this, chose not to defend themselves and kept their peace and composure; so I, too, follow the path of those sanctified beings and choose to remain rather than flee. Therefore, I will not leave."

The more he persisted, the less 'Abdu'l-Bahá yielded. At last, he returned to Haifa that very night and released the ship to depart for its destination. Later I heard that the ship had been provided through the efforts of the American Bahá'ís in order to rescue the Master.

Now, what the reason was for the sudden departure of the Commission of Enquiry at the peak of their investigation, and why the unseen hand of divine power and might had chosen to put on such a show, was a mystery. All that was known was that a telegraph had been received from the Sultan commanding the Commission to return to Istanbul in haste.

Two or three days later came the news that on Friday, Sultán 'Abdu'l-Ḥamíd had officially attended the Jám'ih Mosque to participate with all due ceremony in the observance of the public obligatory prayer. As he was mounting his horse to depart, a bomb had exploded, damaging a few of the carriages and wounding some of the horses. The King, however, sustained no injury. This incident produced much commotion and agitation in the city of Istanbul and was the main reason for the return of the Commission. After a few days, the Commission prepared its report and submitted it to the King. But because of that incident the matter was hardly noticed, for every faculty of the government, and the King's entire attention, were focused on uncovering the conspiracy and arresting the plotters. Some six months passed before the Sultan decided to study the reports in detail. But yet again the unseen hand of divine power intervened. Struggling to establish a democratic system of government, the Young Turks Party, which 'Abdu'l-Ḥamíd had always feared and whose members he had over the course of his reign murdered by casting them in the sea in their hundreds – nay thousands – selected Salonika, which at the time was the headquarters of the ablest units of the Ottoman army, as the centre of their secret movement. They soon won the sympathy and cooperation of the military, and together marched on Istanbul to demand freedom and a constitutional government. Subsequently, by decree of the Sultan a constitutional government was established and all political prisoners were released; the people, overcome with joy, celebrated their deliverance in all four corners of the land.

But the hatred of the malicious, the personal prejudice of the local officials in 'Akká, and the viperous inclination of the people induced them to address a query to the central government asking whether or not the decree of the release of political prisoners also applied to 'Abbás Effendi. The immediate and affirmative response gave 'Abdu'l-Bahá complete and unconditional freedom. Some time later the King decided to go back on his word and dissolve the constitutional government. He was overthrown and exiled; the grand edifice of the supreme Sultanate began to tremble and finally collapsed, and that band of tyrants received their due chastisements.

He is the Exalted, the Powerful, the Mighty, the Everlasting.

1 November 1935/ 17 'Ilm 92 B.E.
Núru'd-Dín Zayn

The fulfilment of the prophecies of 'Abdu'l-Bahá, now and in the future

While the preparation of this book, *Memories of Nine Years*, has encountered many years of indolence and inactivity and its completion has been delayed for too long, yet fortunately the account of 'Abdu'l-Bahá's many promises and prophecies in the various chapters of the book regarding future triumphs of the Cause of God has coincided with the present realization of those promises. For example, the fall of the green, white and blue domes, the abasement of the clergy and the exaltation of the friends, the expansion of the Faith, the establishment of the great Bahá'í institutions, etc, etc, have all come true. And just as the truth of these has been established, so before long the rest of His promises will also be fulfilled.

In the course of His prophetic utterances regarding the friends, 'Abdu'l-Bahá would sometimes make reference to the enemies of the Faith, and at other times to the entire world and all that is therein. The significance of many of these was beyond my comprehension. For example, whenever the Persian friends complained of the cruelties and enmity of the people of sedition, the Master would give soul-stirring glad tidings that soon this or that would come to pass, the tabernacle of the Cause of God would be raised and the banner of the Faith would fly on the highest peaks. And yet, He would at times advise the youth and schoolchildren to the contrary: "I am not training you for a life of ease and comfort." His purpose was to assert that "during the descent of difficulties and afflictions, you must endure and persevere".

Sometimes, in response to the Western friends who desired to achieve the honour of martyrdom, 'Abdu'l-Bahá explained that in Europe and America too, the resistance and opposition of the enemies of the Faith would lead to the martyrdom of sanctified souls.

Today, too, the same truths may be perceived in the words of the beloved Guardian of the Faith of God. On the one hand, His recent telegrams bear the glad tidings of the establishment of new Spiritual Assemblies in Central and South America and the completion of the interior decoration of the American Mashriqu'l-Adhkár. These, of course, are the same dazzling triumphs which we have been anticipating for forty or fifty years. And then on the other hand, He cautions and warns the friends to be prepared for the emergence of events of major proportions.[220]

In short, the Master used to make references to the destructive World War, however implicitly.[221] I missed the point. He even mentioned it quite explicitly on one occasion, while interpreting a dream I had had, but again I could not understand His meaning and so in my ignorance I thought his utterances to be tactful words of wisdom, and proceeded to make my own interpretation. The details of this particular event follow.

In the days of the rebellion of Mírzá Áqá Ján known as Khadim'u'lláh, when the incessant hostile activities of the Covenant-breakers had forced the Ark of the Cause of God into the stormy waters of tests and difficulties, one day in the pilgrim house I had a strange and horrible dream. I saw myself, accompanied by a number of friends, sailing in a small fragile ship. I heard someone say, pointing to a gigantic ship approaching us from some distance away, that the ship was plague-ridden and that the government had ordered it to be destroyed.

As the ship approached, the officers of our small ship gave the command to attack. Cannons began to roar, mortar shells exploded and hand grenades were hurled. The large ship was on fire. Flames and a cloud of smoke, as well as the screams, weeping and wailing of those on board, rose heavenward. The shrieking sound of their weeping and sobbing was so heart-rending and harrowing that, as the ship began to sink, I awoke shaken and frightened. In that state of fear and shock, I interpreted the dream as signifying the destruction of the Covenant-breakers, and I was confident of the accuracy of my interpretation. Yet I waited for an opportunity to bring the matter to the attention of 'Abdu'l-Bahá, feeling quite certain that He would confirm my interpretation. The opportunity did not present itself until one day in the presence of a group of resident Bahá'ís and pilgrims, as I gazed in humility and adoration at the sublime countenance of 'Abdu'l-Bahá, He suddenly said, "Khán, why don't you say something?"

"I have had a dream," I responded. Receiving His permission, I recounted the details, anticipating His affirmation of my interpretation.

However, after a moment's pause, He spoke these words with power and authority: "The ship in which you found such comfort is the ship of the Cause of God and the large ship is the ship of the world. This ship is outwardly very small, but the ship of the world will sink, while the ship of the Cause of God will reach the safety of the shore."

He continued to speak for some time, but I can remember none of the details. He gave intimations of today's conflicts and wars, but at the time I was mentally incapable of understanding His allusions. At the time, I imagined that since a number of Covenant-breakers were also in attendance, 'Abdu'l-Bahá was being cautious in His comments so that they would not make of this a pretext to publish further false accusations and rumours. And for the past three or four years, the words and letters of the beloved Guardian are openly informing the friends of these same matters.

CHAPTER EIGHT

He is the Most Glorious!

Arrival at Beirut

'Abdu'l-Bahá's counsels on how to attract divine confirmations (presented in the last part of Chapter 6) left such an indelible impression on my otherwise confused and muddled memory that even now, after thirty or forty years, their highlights still endure in my thoughts. At the time they were imparted to me, they illumined the horizon of my future. Yet remoteness from that Threshold was very difficult to bear, especially when the inspectors were interrogating a number of people, some of whom had provided testimonies to please the Covenant-breakers, while others, forced to comply, signed whatever the Commission had already concluded.

A troubled heart, an anxious nature, and a confused mind did not leave me many resources to resist the onslaught of such agonizing hardships, and so I found solace in undamming the river of my tears. As it is said:

> *Tears are the cure for the incurable pain,*
> *A weeping eye is the fountain of God's grace.*

From friend and foe horrifying news continued to pour in, for the doors of direct correspondence and communication were closed, and people repeated whatever they had heard. It was rumoured that these tyrants of the earth [the Commission] had been summoning individuals from every class of people

– Muslims, Jews, Christians, Easterners, Westerners and even a number of 'Akká's political prisoners – and were preparing depositions against the Beloved of the world. Many people had signed these testimonials without a second look, while those who had refused to sign had been thrown into prison. A number of the friends who had not complied with 'Abdu'l-Bahá's many warnings to leave 'Akká, or who had failed to act quickly enough and had been left behind, had been arrested. Áqá Mírzá Jalál, the son of the King of Martyrs, who had delayed too long, was arrested on the road on his way out of 'Akká.

The exalted Mírzá Abu'l-Faḍl, that renowned veteran teacher of the Faith, the products of whose mighty pen have adorned the pages of Bahá'í literature and whose words and deeds had prompted the conversion of many Western believers, had returned to Egypt, having completed his teaching work in the United States of America. 'Abdu'l-Bahá had then invited him to move his residence to 'Akká, so that he might live out the remaining years of his life at that sanctified threshold near the Holy Shrines, forsaking the arduous task of speaking in order to engage himself in the rewarding work of disseminating the Holy Writings.

He had been living in 'Akká for some time, but now the prevailing unstable and chaotic conditions rendered any further stay dangerous. The Master therefore sent him to Beirut, which was relatively a safer place, and subsequently charged me with the honourable task of attending to him in that city. This bounty became a blessing for the entire community of friends at Beirut as well, since for a few days wonderful, spiritual gatherings were arranged. But before long, an urgent command was received from 'Abdu'l-Bahá, advising caution, "so that you may be safeguarded in the face of the hatred of the Ottoman tyrants". In a short Tablet in his honour sent in my care, He wrote about the harshness of the conditions: "To depict the severity of the situation, suffice it to say that the Arab grocer nearby, who refused to give testimony against Me, has been put in prison."

ARRIVAL AT BEIRUT

In brief, Abu'l-Faḍl departed from Beirut, which increased my solitude. In those lonely times my days were spent in the study of medicine, but my thoughts were so utterly occupied by the events in the Holy Land that even attending classes brought me sorrow and pain. At night the uneasiness of worry and anxiety allowed me no sleep; past events, and the infinite bounties and blessings of 'Abdu'l-Bahá, unfolded before my mind's eye. My thoughts were so confused that at every minute – nay, every second – I was entertaining the idea of considering other alternatives and taking some action. When I envisioned the loving-kindness of the Master I told myself: I will go back to 'Akká no matter what. But when I remembered His parting words, including His promises of reunion, I heartened myself by reciting the verse:

> *It is true that nothing is more difficult than remoteness from the Beloved,*
> *But if there is hope of reunion then it can be endured.*

When I became utterly hopeless, I beheld that heavenly Being before my mind's eye and recited to myself:

> *My day passes in pain and my night in wonder,*
> *How unbearable is the passing of time without You.*

In brief, all the verses of poetry I had ever memorized in my life – both Bahá'í and non-Bahá'í – passed through my thoughts. The poet Aḍar Túsí has written about separation:

> *Afflicted with the pain of separation, it is better to die,*
> *None knows the cure for this illness better than I.*

But I did not agree with this poem; I liked the one by Sa'dí better. His words speak from the depths of the heart:

> *To die in the path of search for the Beloved is easy,*
> *It is living that is difficult.*

I was not the only one burning in the fire of separation from Him; many of the friends in other parts of the world were faring much worse. When communication between even 'Akká and Haifa, a distance of no more than an hour, was cut off, it should be clear how terrible must have been its impact on the friends in far-off cities of the world.

At the beginning of the upheaval, the late Ḥájí Siyyid Taqí Manshádí was responsible for receiving and sending the mail. In accordance with the Master's instructions, he informed the Bahá'í world that any pilgrim who was on his way to 'Akká should suspend his travel and postpone his journey, and either stay wherever he was or return home. In the days of the Blessed Beauty incidents of this nature had also taken place, and in accordance with His instructions the pilgrim's journey changed into residence at whatever place he had reached. However, in those times the pilgrims did not come in large numbers, but now there were two or three in every city whose travel came to a halt. In Badkubih, Tbilisi, Istanbul, Egypt and Beirut a number of individuals bided their time in fear and anticipation. In Beirut this painful dart of separation had afflicted two people. One was that renowned teacher of the Faith, Mírzá Ṭarázu'lláh Samandarí. Much distressed, he was waiting out his time in pain and misery in a room at a local inn. Sometimes I visited him to cheer him up. I would tell him:

> *Come, all you heartbroken ones, let's console each other,*
> *For only the heartbroken knows the pain of a broken heart.*

To comfort him I recounted the glad tidings and promises that I had heard from the lips of 'Abdu'l-Bahá, using all my eloquence, and yet:

> *I heard a sweet word from the old man of Canaan,*
> *Separation from the Beloved cannot be expressed in words.*

How does a man look who has received a thousand horrifying

pieces of news during the day and has not slept a moment all night? That was exactly what I saw in the face of Samandarí. For a time things continued in this vein, but then we received a hopeful bit of news from Mr. Man<u>sh</u>ádí communicating a message from 'Abdu'l-Bahá: "A good end is the reward of the pious." This news brought relief; little by little tranquillity and peace were restored to 'Akká; Mr. Samandarí was summoned; and after a time the cannon blast of divine confirmation was heard and communications between this city and 'Akká were reopened. But I must add:

It is true that the fruit of the tree of separation is reunion,
Yet I wish the eternal Farmer had not such a seed sown.

What sort of place was Beirut?

The city of Beirut was at that time not only the centre of learning in the Ottoman Empire, but also the centre for the most important collection of educational institutions in the Middle East. There were numerous schools and (in today's terminology) two universities, one French and one American; these were attended by a large number of students. While the population of the city did not exceed 125,000 souls (25,000 Muslims, 100,000 Christians and a few Jews), yet its political importance was such that its Governor was more powerful than the governors of other provinces.

During 'Abdu'l-Bahá's journey to Beirut in the days of the Blessed Beauty, the Muslim religious scholars of that city had developed such devotion and affection for the Master that they continued to express these sincere and heartfelt sentiments in their later correspondence. The people in general, and all the Muslims in particular, considered 'Abdu'l-Bahá to be Master and Lord, the possessor of spiritual powers. The various Christian denominations, whose religious beliefs could not countenance the idea of ascribing to the Master the position of Messiah – as had been done by some – nevertheless admitted without hesitation the greatness of Bahá'u'lláh and the magnanimity and generosity of 'Abdu'l-Bahá, whose name they praised. All this was due to 'Abdu'l-Bahá's journey to Beirut.[222]

The Persians and other Shi'ites in the city, despite their hatred for the Faith while in Iran, here in Beirut as well as in other cities of Syria referred to 'Abdu'l-Bahá with great respect. The officials of the Ottoman government, whether high or low, regarded the Master as one of God's apostles in the field of spiritual knowledge and personal detachment, and thus considered assistance to His followers to be a religious duty. For example, in the majority of the Customs' offices there, whenever they discovered someone to be a follower of 'Abbás Effendi they treated him with perfect courtesy.

The Covenant-breakers, however, from the onset of their rebellion and the dissemination of their despicable literature, their provocation and inciting of the local populations of various cities against the Faith, their correspondence with the Islamic religious scholars of those regions ascribing to the Master a variety of charges, even presenting a long list of grievances and pleading for justice (as previously described under the title "*Kashkúl* or pumpkin bowl?"), made every effort to confuse the minds and hearts of the population with such deceptive practices in order to attract their sympathy and assistance. In the face of all these trials and tribulations, 'Abdu'l-Bahá's expressions of kindness and love towards those scholars did not diminish, nor did His customary practice of bestowing gifts and granting favours, which was one of His natural qualities. In fact, if anything, such bestowals of kindliness increased.

From the time the Commission of Enquiry arrived in 'Akká (when I had already reached Beirut), and especially in the course of those few days when a number of meetings were arranged in the presence of the exalted Mírzá Abu'l-Faḍl, the agents of the Covenant-breakers like birds of the night came to Beirut in the guise of businessmen. They said they were hoping to trade with the Iranian merchants, some of whom were the guardians or sponsors of Iranian students. In making such contacts they created an atmosphere of apprehension and mistrust with regard to the Faith of God. They also hoped to mislead and deceive the young students by sowing the seeds of discord and dissension. It is interesting to note that up to that time no followers of Yaḥyá had attended any of the schools. Now, however, a couple of them appeared during the course of my studies. Now let us see what the advice and admonitions of 'Abdu'l-Bahá would do for me.

The conditions of this servant in Beirut

In a collection of memoirs such as this, compiled with the purpose of contributing to the teaching work by acquainting the friends with the events of yesteryear, no space should be allotted for any description of the conditions of this unworthy servant. However, since everything that happened next in fact fulfilled 'Abdu'l-Bahá's promises and manifested the power of the admonitions of that loving Master, it deserves to be mentioned, as it will surely be of interest to any believer who wishes to gain a deeper understanding of the words of that sanctified personage regarding present and future events. For example, had I not paid close attention to His words when He mentioned, either in passing or in a quick reference, that a certain event would happen and gave advice as to how it should be encountered, when the event came to pass my disregard of His admonitions would have surely spelled the loss of a lifetime of work. One must therefore consider that in each divine utterance there exists a world of significance, as it is said: "One single utterance contains an ocean of meanings."

In brief, as described in the last section of Chapter 6, I arrived in Beirut filled with gloom and in a state of despair and hopelessness. With all the confidence that I had in the promises of the Master when His counsels and advice were uppermost in my mind, the past with all its divine blessings seemed like a bright and radiant day, while the future looked dark and sombre. So whenever I pondered this sombre future, I would recollect one of 'Abdu'l-Bahá's promises, and through that narrow opening I was able to behold a bright and brilliant world.

So, after finding a place to live and getting properly settled, I embarked on my study of the sciences. While the means of continuing my education was quickly provided, yet whenever I reviewed the curriculum and compared its requirements with my abilities and talents, I said to myself, "Alas, between love and attainment there are thousands of miles." I wondered about the seemingly endless distance between me and the mastery of all these sciences. But then, whenever the demon of despair spread its shadow over my head, I searched for deliverance in the utterances of 'Abdu'l-Bahá, until the light of hope shone with such power that my eyes were blinded by its intensity, and my being was thrilled by such joy and delight that I would spontaneously jump up from my seat.

Since I was constantly preoccupied with my past life in 'Akká, many of 'Abdu'l-Bahá's words uttered over the course of several years stood out clearly in my mind. Therefore, whenever I encountered problems or found a door closed to me, I was able to find the key in those utterances. At the same time, I was aware that to remain idle, awaiting the descent of divine confirmations, was sheer heresy, for the Master had on many occasions explained the meaning of this concept in emphatic terms: "Confirmation revolves around action, confirmation revolves around action." So I never shirked action and was never deprived of heavenly grace.

For example, although I had been away from the academic world for many years, and at the age of thirty-five had lost the patience required to deal with mathematics and its applications to chemistry and medical physics, yet my progress was so rapid that before long I found a number of pupils, and in the preliminary examinations in the medical sciences I almost achieved first place. In examinations in philosophy and literature, which are the natural talents of every Bahá'í, I excelled to the point of becoming well known among my peers. Entrance to the Medical School required certain other obstacles to be overcome. For example, the submission of a high school diploma and a copy of a birth certificate, which were not customary documents in Iran, were major prerequisites. For the high school diploma I presented as supporting documentation the licences I had acquired from the International Bank, and postponed the issue of the birth certificate with a promise to provide it as soon as I received a copy from Iran.

The other problem was that while the number of applicants was many, the Medical School would only admit the few who were capable of passing the entrance exams – just as it says in the Bible: "Many are called but few are chosen." I, however, was accepted with great deference. In fact, although I was a Persian and a Bahá'í, which in the opinion of certain opponents of the Faith was unacceptable, yet praised be God, during the entire course of my studies the grace and bounty of Bahá'u'lláh were so overwhelming that I was accorded perfect courtesy and cooperation in all matters and affairs. Why do you think that was? First, because I had set out to study medicine by the will of the Beloved of the world of existence: "When it is God's will, He saith 'Be', and it is." Secondly, during the entire period of my studies I constantly strove to live in accordance with each and every guideline imparted to me, and this truly was another heavenly blessing for which I can never find adequate words of thanksgiving.

Another problem, which by comparison was more difficult and critical, and which no powers of initiative or action could resolve, was the expense associated with the cost of the Medical School, as well as my living expenses in Beirut. When I left 'Akká, 'Abdu'l-Bahá had given me the equivalent of ten French liras; this was spent in a few days, and then I found myself faced with a problem which I did not seem to be able to resolve. The situation was clearly critical. Conditions in Iran were even worse. After the passing of my father some two years before, troublemakers and thugs had crowded around the house in order to take possession of the body and set it on fire. He had, therefore, been buried within the confines of the house. Furthermore, the aftermath of the uprising associated with the Constitutional Revolution had added to the problems. The only remaining alternative was what 'Abdu'l-Bahá had frequently advised: "Ask whatsoever thou wishest of Him alone; seek whatsoever thou seekest from Him alone,"[223] and so I recited this prayer: "Open unto me the doors of ease and comfort, free me from the world, and supply me with Thine unheralded gifts from heaven."[224]

One day the late Áqá Muḥammad Muṣṭafá Baghdádí, that intrepid believer whose outstanding services have illumined the annals of the Cause, and who was housebound because of his semi-blindness, summoned me to his presence and with great persistence asked me to do a favour for him. After I had accepted, he proposed to open a checking account for me at his business, at an interest rate of nine per cent for a number of years. It was agreed that the same rate would apply to whatever funds I might receive from Iran and deposit in that account. In the end, the account was opened and the issue of my living expenses was resolved.

A few months later I received a letter from my brother Mírzá Faḍlu'lláh, informing me that in the two years since the passing of our father the neighbours had made a lot of trouble, protesting that if the house eventually turned into a holy shrine for the Bahá'ís, the Muslims would flee the area and property values would fall. This had led to an uprising with the intent to attack the house and dig up and destroy my father's remains. The remains were, therefore, exhumed at night and removed to the Muslim Cemetery. The house was then sold and the funds transferred to me in Beirut. I was able to put this money into the checking account, and it supported me for several years. Some years later, after my return to Iran, Tehran's *golestán-i-jávíd*[225] was constructed and with the help of the same gentlemen who had removed my father's remains to the Muslim Cemetery, we transferred them to the *golestán-i-jávíd*.

That grenade that missed the breast of Sultán 'Abdu'l-Ḥamíd struck the liver of the Covenant-breakers

The above narrative has distracted our attention from the main theme, so let us return to the story. The news of the attack on the person of the Sultan by a group of political partisans, which 'Abdu'l-Bahá had humorously referred to as the "cannon blast of divine confirmation", at last reached Beirut. But as some of the pilgrims who had been biding their time in various cities in an agonizing state of wait-and-see were gradually granted permission to travel, it became clear that while those horrible events which had been rumoured among the friends had not come to pass, yet the banishment of 'Abdu'l-Bahá to the Fezzan Desert in Libya, though not destined to come about, had nevertheless been ordered. The Master frequently made mention of this point. However, now that the Covenant-breakers' last dart had missed its target, they realized that they were both inwardly and outwardly defeated. As their last hopes of a possible recovery were dashed, they crept back into the deep recesses of oblivion, and thus those birds of the night lost any hope of further flight – nay, of any movement at all.

Ordinarily, whenever the Covenant-breakers' attempts against the Faith ended in total failure, they would bide their time for a while in quiet contemplation, and then putting their heads together they would emerge with a fresh approach and a new trick. Now we have to see if this story of Gog and Magog[226] would be repeated.

In this connection, let us recall one of 'Abdu'l-Bahá's utterances. Some four years earlier, while at the dinner table He had spoken on the topic of misfortune and adversity, as well as the tyranny and rebellion of the Covenant-breakers. I was quite moved and saddened by His words, and so I asked, "Will these Covenant-breakers continue to thrive in this world?"

"What are you saying?" retorted 'Abdu'l-Bahá, seemingly

astonished at my question. "They will be finished in four years. Mírzá Badí'u'lláh himself told me: 'Master, we are done for.'" Then He added, "But a trace of the followers of Yaḥyá will remain."

The words "four years" which 'Abdu'l-Bahá had used as an example could have been understood to mean any length of time, even up to ten times that figure. I nevertheless took it to heart. At the end of the four years this prediction was entirely fulfilled. Moreover, a few months after the episode of the "blast of divine confirmation", when I was in 'Akká at the threshold of 'Abdu'l-Bahá, He spoke one day in the pilgrim house about the unseen Hand and heavenly power. In conclusion He said, "The attack made on the Ottoman Sultan, and consequently his being forced to ignore the report made by the inspectors of the Commission of Enquiry, were both part of the blast of divine confirmation."

As soon as I heard this, I told myself, "That dart of fate, which missed the breast of the Sultan, struck at the very liver of the Covenant-breakers."

Another look at Beirut

It had been some years since the honoured Muḥammad Muṣṭafá Baghdádí, together with his sons (Ḥusayn Iqbál, 'Alí Iḥsán, and Zia Mabsout) had established a substantial business venture in Beirut with a branch in Alexandria. This respected family had been an example of service to the Cause and was always recognized in that capacity. Their services to the Faith were so numerous, especially during the Ministry of the Centre of the Covenant, that they had aroused the hatred and jealousy of the Covenant-breakers who called them "the fathers of apostasy". There were many other friends residing in Beirut at that time, whose names I can no longer recall. From the time when the Iranian students arrived in the city, the Faith began to thrive. In the meantime, the Covenant-breakers sent their own teachers to the city in order to confuse the minds of the Muslim population.

After their defeat and the frustration of all their hopes, communications between 'Akká and Beirut were restored and news began to arrive every day. I used to spend the summer months of each year in 'Akká engaged in writing. The summers of the last two years, however, were spent in Haifa, in the proximity of the Shrine of the Báb. Some of the Bahá'í students whom I can remember from that time are Dr. Zia Mabsout Baghdádí, Valíyu'lláh Khán-i-Varqá, Dr. Mu'ayyad, Mírzá Badí' Bushru'í, Mírzá 'Abbás Ṭahirí, Dr. Muḥammad Ṣáliḥ from Egypt, Riaz Salím from Egypt, and Jináb-i-Bashárí, along with a few Bahá'ís from Tabriz. Every week on Sunday afternoons we came together in a large meeting in a corner of the gardens of the American School, which we referred to as Mashriqu'l-Adhkár. The school authorities were sympathetic towards the Bahá'í youth and encouraged such meetings.

The everlasting disgrace of the Covenant-breakers was simultaneous with the removal of Sulṭán 'Abdu'l-Ḥamíd

In the days when the violators of the Covenant had lost all hope of success for their seditious plans, had crept into their dark hovels and sunk into the abyss of misery, Sulṭán 'Abdu'l-Ḥamíd, their last hope and refuge, was beset by an endless array of misfortunes and disasters. The "blast of divine confirmation" was followed by other setbacks. Defection and rebellion were rampant everywhere. The effect of the incident in Yemen grew stronger, weakening the already ineffective government.[227] From every clime was raised a new cry of opposition to the Ottoman Caliphate. The flame of civil war became a blazing fire as neighbouring governments began hostile action, taking advantage of the internal chaos. The bitterest of these enemies was the Emperor of Austria who, although a member of the alliance of the four great powers – the Ottoman Empire, Germany, Italy and Austria – suddenly took the offensive and conquered vast tracts of Ottoman soil, namely Herzegovina and Bosnia.[228]

A great upheaval ensued. The Ottomans, enraged by the sudden attack, boycotted the wearing of the *fez*, the Ottoman headdress and a symbol of their national heritage, because it was manufactured in Austrian textile mills. Removing them from their heads, they hurled them to the ground and replaced them with Iranian and other unusual headgear. This was followed by angry demonstrations of protest in every Ottoman city. But all this was of no avail; that part of the Empire was lost forever.

Even more ominous, the German Emperor, who had up to that point been a close and friendly ally of the Ottoman Sultan, sent a telegram of congratulation to the Austrian Emperor complimenting him on his conquest. All these perilous events took place one after the other and were shortly followed by the uprising demanding a constitutional government. The Young Turk Party struck a bargain with the army, seized the Sultan and imprisoned him. Tripoli was snatched by Italy, as the World War began which resulted in the loss of all the countries of the Empire and the abolition of the Islamic Caliphate. Thus the Covenant-breakers lost the support of the Caliph whom they had served, and contrite and despairing met their ruin. Bahá'u'lláh's words are illuminating: "I fear lest, bereft of the melody of the dove of heaven, ye will sink back to the shades of utter loss, and, never having gazed upon the beauty of the rose, return to water and clay."[229]

When did Satan ever give me a chance?

My life in Beirut was filled with joy and excitement, as all the means for a happy and joyful life were readily available. First, communications between 'Akká and Beirut were well established, the bountiful tidings of the Beloved of the world were continuous and ever-flowing, and unseen confirmations streamed forth unabated. Spiritual affairs proceeded to my utter satisfaction and matters related to the material aspects of everyday life were in perfect order.

However dark and sombre the future had seemed in the initial months of my arrival, my enthusiasm and the excitement generated by success in my studies filled me with such hope and confidence in the ultimate attainment of the desired goal that suddenly that bleak future began to appear a hundred-fold brighter. The four-month-long summer vacations, which were spent at the sanctified threshold of 'Abdu'l-Bahá, were in themselves a source of joy and gladness. Moreover, I was blessed with the companionship of a group of loving friends, all of whom were devoted to the teaching work, and with whom spiritual gatherings were held twice a week. There were also a number of interested and sympathetic seekers who regularly attended our firesides. These associations created an atmosphere of understanding, sincere devotion, and happiness. But what could I do? When did Satan ever give me a chance to serve?

As has been previously mentioned, there were a few Azalí students[230] who had broken into the circle of the young Persians, some of whom had become quite enamoured of the teachings of the Faith. Since the Iranian Constitutional Revolution was now at its height, these Azalís had taken up the cause of patriotism and had under its guise dismissed religion as superstition; and so they endeavoured to deceive our sympathetic seekers. Among the Bahá'í youth there was a student who was related to a Covenant-breaker. His presence added to the already existing tension and led at last to disunity and conflict. Their animosity and jealousy towards me ultimately brought about the disruption of our community.

The more advice I gave them, the fewer were the results. Despite my sharing with them 'Abdu'l-Bahá's counsels and advice imparted to me at the time of my departure from 'Akká, I failed to discover a cure for the malady. With the coming of the summer holidays I travelled to 'Akká, and on my arrival I had in mind to bring the matter up to the attention of 'Abdu'l-Bahá at an opportune moment. One day as He walked in the streets of 'Akká, talking to me with great gentleness about the manners one should observe in dealing with people, His voice suddenly rose to a higher pitch as He revealed the following: "You must conduct yourself in such a way that your silence will serve as your highest reproach of any opponent." This utterance of 'Abdu'l-Bahá cured all my ills. I discovered that the giving of advice to my friends had been due to my inexperience, and that those words had reached the ears of the enemies and increased their enmity and rancour. The following year on my return to Beirut, I put the Master's advice into practice, and during the rest of my stay in that city the world was my paradise. I have thus brought back this story with me to share it as a gift with my esteemed readers.

Manufacturing a dream with the intention of slandering the Faith of God

The effects of 'Abdu'l-Bahá's words were often so overwhelming that His listeners actually experienced the realization of His promises and prophecies at that instant, even though the physical fulfilment of those events might take several years to emerge. For example, He had counselled the virtues of patience and fortitude as response to the hostile actions of the Covenant-breakers, as described in Chapter 6 of these memoirs. When He admonished me, "If you hear with your own ears that they are insulting me, do not allow into your heart any hatred for them," at that very moment I was certain that such an unpleasant event would take place and so I implored God to confirm me in my obedience to 'Abdu'l-Bahá's instructions. The details of the subsequent events are as follows.

After I returned from 'Akká and began my studies again in conformity with the guidelines of the Master, it was not long before my old friendships were renewed, the friends came together and the gatherings of fellowship began again. The breezes of love and faithfulness began to waft and the non-Bahá'ís found in us ready companions, as dissension and conceit disappeared.

As teaching work began to make substantial headway, the envy of the hateful came to the surface again. When their actions – intended to create disunity among the friends – met with defeat, they conspired to invent a dream and then ask this servant to interpret it, so that they might find a pretext to level the harshest of insults at the Centre of the Covenant. The dream was described to me in the presence of several people, all of whom anticipated a reaction of outrage from me and a possible scandal in the making. But instead, I suddenly and spontaneously began to laugh. This was not mocking laughter, but rather the result of extreme joy and gladness, for I was mentally seeing the blessed figure of 'Abdu'l-Bahá and hearing His admonitions ring in my ears. Those present became contrite and tried to make it appear as though something else had been intended, playing with words and changing the subject.

The person who initiated that episode is today an eminent statesman who is both inwardly and outwardly sympathetic towards the Cause.

I consider such words to be meaningless

During my stay in Beirut I sent to the holy presence of 'Abdu'l-Bahá a few individuals who had shown themselves to be sincerely interested and sympathetic, or who had unreservedly accepted the Faith of God. They all received His boundless blessings, and on their return spread the breezes of His love among the people. Once I took with me to 'Akká a man of prominence, and he too became utterly enthralled by 'Abdu'l-Bahá's loving-kindness.

One of those young men, Mr. Ghulam-Ḥusayn Karagozlu, was a libertine – a freeloading, bold individual who was also the ringleader of the group of the young students. When he travelled to 'Akká I was confident that he would return utterly intoxicated with the wine of the love of God. Yet I wondered how he would be able to handle his close friends and cronies, and tolerate their boisterous abuse and conduct. The week that Ghulam-Ḥusayn returned he was so spiritually on fire that he was hardly conscious of his surroundings. When his friends visited him, he spoke fearlessly and with great love in a manner that astonished everyone. One day they decided to embarrass him, so one of them asked, "Ghulam, if we say something insolent against 'Abdu'l-Bahá, what will you do? Will you be upset with us?"

"Of course not. God forbid!" he replied.

"Why is that?" they asked.

"Not a day goes by without all of you using the foulest language to describe the Holy Ones of your own Faith," he replied. "You don't even spare each other from words of abuse, so if you speak any such words against 'Abdu'l-Bahá, I shall consider them to be just as meaningless as all the others."

This wise yet frank and unassuming reply crushed those gentlemen and cut short their experiments in abuse. From then on they spoke with extreme respect and reverence. Ghulam later returned to Tehran and taught his own mother, and I once heard that he was sent by 'Abdu'l-Bahá to Egypt on an assignment which he completed successfully.

Conclusion of Chapter 8

The major theme of this chapter has been the actions of the last of the Covenant-breakers, and how they as well as the other faithless ones became the target of their own last strike which they had initiated against the Centre of God's Covenant. Not long after this defeat, Sulṭán 'Abdu'l-Ḥamíd too received his own chastisement for his actions. All these events were the manifestation and fulfilment of 'Abdu'l-Bahá's promises and assurances foretold over the years.

During my five-year stay in Beirut I attained the Master's presence three or four times each year, and during that time the communication links remained intact, except for the first year when the door of correspondence was closed to all. All the information presented in this chapter is reflected in the various written and telegraphic communications received in

Beirut, or in the stories that I heard first hand from the lips of 'Abdu'l-Bahá. Readers need not, therefore, entertain any doubts as to their veracity.

One significant event which took place after the downfall of the Covenant-breakers was the transportation of the casket containing the remains of the Blessed Báb to His Shrine. This most exalted and sanctified Shrine was already a holy place for pilgrims even before the sarcophagus, which had been brought from India, was placed in it. The Covenant-breakers' efforts to prevent the purchase of that property which had been selected for the site of the Shrine have already been described in Chapters 2 and 3 of this book. These actions caused much torment and agony to 'Abdu'l-Bahá. It finally reached a point where Mírzá Áqá Ján, that notorious enemy, had told the other Covenant-breakers, "Don't oppose the Master on this issue, for the establishment of this Shrine was prophesied thousands of years ago and is recorded in the Bible: 'Now He who is known as the Branch shall entomb the body of the Lord on Mount Carmel.'"[231]

So as the structure neared completion the Covenant-breakers proclaimed it to be a fortress and an ammunition dump, in the hope that the Ottoman government would demolish the building and raze it to the ground. When the inspectors came to investigate the allegations, they asked the workers on the site how many basements had been built underground, for the Covenant-breakers had spread the rumour that arms stores were kept in the lower basements.

The sacred remains of the exalted Báb, may my life be a sacrifice unto Him, which for so many years had been carried from one city to another, from one house to another and from one country to another, were finally laid to rest in that Shrine by the hands of the Centre of the Covenant Himself.

Well, we have strayed from the main theme. My other purpose in writing this chapter of the book was to describe that period of time when I was sent to study medicine, and the counsels vouchsafed to me on how to attract divine confirmations. These included advice on what to do in various situations whose emergence was foretold by the Master. All of these came to pass. Since there is insufficient space to present them all here, I have refrained from including them. Among the thousands of such experiences, I have presented those I remember best, in the hope that they will suffice for the study of young Bahá'ís, so that they may learn how to perform the most difficult of tasks with ease. For instance, if they wish to continue higher education at a mature age, the study of the instructions recorded in Chapter 6 of this narrative should suffice, as my five-year term of study was completed successfully by relying on the Master's promises and counsels.

Every year there were two major examinations. One was taken before the School examiners and the other before the Ottoman and French government examiners. Since the university belonged to the Pope, the atheistic French government did not pass the students easily; they had to prove that their competencies exceeded those of the students at the Paris Medical School. To the foreign students graduating from this School was granted the right to practise anywhere in France, whereas the Paris school did not bestow such diplomas.

The medical diploma from the [Beirut] School of Medicine entitled a foreign graduate to practise medicine everywhere, whereas a foreigner graduating from the Paris Medical School could not practise in France; this is sufficient evidence of the degree of difficulty of the medical curriculum of this school. Praise be to God, with divine assistance and strict obedience to the counsels of 'Abdu'l-Bahá, I achieved complete success. Young people should read and reflect on these counsels, and never forget His utterance: "Divine confirmation is dependent on action."

And now, to complete this chapter I present one of 'Abdu'l-Baha's Tablets[232] revealed in honour of one of the believers, at a time when the opposition of the Covenant-breakers was at its peak:

He is God!
O thou who art attracted by the rays of the light emanating

from the dawning place of mysteries! Hasten to attain true salvation; hasten towards the shining light; hasten towards eternal joy; hasten towards the wondrous grace; hasten towards the mighty Covenant. Verily the hearts of the heedless have been shaken by the convulsions of frequent calamities, by great tests and difficulties, and the horizons of their lives have been darkened by thick clouds of wickedness and rebellion. Thus the water of certitude dried up and in its place the boiling waters of idle fancies and vain imaginings welled forth. Doubts and illusions spread, as they abandoned the authorized Centre of the Covenant and the solid edifice of the Faith of God, and followed instead every rash and heedless one, the speakers who hear not, and the guides who see not.

Do they think that they shall be left alone to their own devices? Nay! When the nightingale sings in the eternal paradise, and the dove of holiness warbles its melody in the groves of the realm of grandeur, and the rays of confirmation beam forth from the midmost heart of heaven, and the lamps of oneness shine brightly within the hearts of His chosen ones, and the way is prepared, and the path made straight, and the trumpet of ecstasy is sounded, and the bugle of eternal life is blown, and the hosts of the Abhá Kingdom rush forth, and the angels of the Supreme Concourse spur on their chargers, and the standards of the Covenant are hoisted, and the sails of fidelity and harmony are unfurled – on that Day shalt thou see the steadfast ones abiding in the highest heaven, dwelling beneath His all-embracing shadow, occupying a glorious station, and partaking of His conspicuous favors, while the heedless shall be seen enshrouded in a black smoke, reduced to the seat of abasement, and fallen prey to distress, loss and sorrow, until the Day whereon they shall be raised again to life.

'Abdu'l-Bahá

CHAPTER NINE

He is the Most Glorious!

We believers were not without our faults

Praise be to God, that in the previous eight chapters of this book I have been able to describe those events at the Most Holy Threshold that impressed themselves indelibly on my confused and feeble mind, despite the passage of thirty to forty years. While the accounts of the treachery of the Covenant-breakers have no doubt distressed my esteemed readers, they also contain the glad-tidings of the process by which the enemies of the Faith met at last with utter defeat and ruin. They explain how the ringleaders and their accomplices were annihilated and how the banner of the Covenant was unfurled on the highest peaks. In short, as revealed in the above Tablet, everything that heavenly Reality had promised the loved ones of God came to pass.

I now wish to bring to the esteemed readers' attention this thought: let us beware lest we, the lovers of God, who are well acquainted with this painful history, should allow it to repeat itself today, when the heavenly essence of the Covenant has re-emerged attired in the sublime raiment of Guardianship.

Although in the past, during the ministry of 'Abdu'l-Bahá, we had all carefully studied the Kitáb-i-'Ahd and were intimately acquainted with its explicit divine verses, and although we longed to serve the Cause and sacrifice ourselves in the path of the Covenant, yet out of negligence and indifference to the nature of our deeds and conduct, many of us brought sadness to the heart of 'Abdu'l-Bahá.

The boundless blessings and bounty of that manifestation of grace and compassion had so enraptured us that we unwittingly became preoccupied with ourselves to such an extent that we imagined the Faith to be our own possession, and so we felt entitled to bring our often unreasonable and untimely requests to 'Abdu'l-Bahá's attention, taking up so much of His precious time as He responded to each and every one.

For the smallest personal matters we imposed on Him extraordinary requests. Several times I heard from 'Abdu'l-Bahá's lips, when He was somewhat indisposed, words such as these: "I have written to him only recently. He should open his chest and count the number of letters he has from me. The irony is that they do not obey my words; if they did, a single word I said would suffice the world."

The burden we imposed on the person of 'Abdu'l-Bahá was beyond endurance. I mention one or two as examples:

When He asked the resident friends to contribute, no matter how little, towards the construction of the Mashriqu'l-Adhkár in 'Ishqábád, the late Áqá Riḍáy-i-Qannád was assigned to collect all such contributions and send them. Since there were troublemakers in our midst and Áqá Riḍá wished to make sure that they would not find an opportunity to stir up conflict and disunity, he humbly asked that all receipts for such contributions be signed by 'Abdu'l-Bahá. This was to ensure that the Covenant-breakers would not be able to use this as a pretext for their mischievous purposes. The receipts were signed and sealed by the Master.

When the news reached Iran, the Persian friends in envy implored that their receipts too might be so adorned. Several thousand receipts in the amounts of 9 *shahi*, 19 *shahi* and 9 *qeran*[233] arrived in 'Akká, and all of them, one by one, received His signature and seal. There was so much of it that the insignia of the Master's seal wore out completely, and the Master's fingers could no longer function at times. One day I was going up the stairs as 'Abdu'l-Bahá was coming out of

His office. Suddenly He stopped, and leaning against the door remarked, "Jináb-i-<u>Kh</u>án, I am exhausted. Let us go for a walk. Today I have signed and sealed a thousand receipts for contributions to the Ma<u>sh</u>riqu'l-A<u>dh</u>kár." The extreme fatigue so evident in His face was heartrending. I was so saddened that I completely forgot the reason that had brought me to Him, and so instead began to relate a story from the Bible.[234]

As we walked the narrow, dark streets of 'Akká He continually expressed His satisfaction and happiness with all the friends. The irony was that at times He even went so far as to express feelings of embarrassment and – God forbid! – shame at the sacrifices made by a few of the friends.

Consider the benevolence of the Lord,
The servant is the sinner and yet He is contrite.

For example, certain letters from Iran sometimes recounted a disagreement between two of the friends. The matter was usually so insignificant and pointless as not to be worthy of mention. Yet they placed their hopes and expectations upon 'Abdu'l-Bahá's judgement. The Master, however, like a kind and compassionate father whose two children are fighting over the possession of a peach or a walnut, would tenderly soothe and reconcile them, never using a harsh tone lest a heart – the treasure-house of the love of Bahá'u'lláh – be broken.

These were among the burdens imposed on 'Abdu'l-Bahá by individuals. Strangely enough, the Bahá'í communities were no less blameworthy: "Thus this should serve as a warning for those who have eyes to see." I present one example:

During the Constitutional Revolution in Iran, opponents of the Faith on both sides of the struggle – namely the constitutionalists and the autocrats – maligned and vilified the friends. The leaders of both sides were members of the clergy. One *mullá* took the Aqdas into the pulpit and read aloud the verse: "...the reins of power [will] fall into the hands of the people,"[235] which seemed to express a view sympathetic towards the Constitution, while at the same time another *mullá* declared the Bahá'ís' lack of participation in revolutionary politics as a sure sign of their support for an autocratic system. This difficult problem was truly a divine test for the friends, who had just survived the terrible test of the Covenant-breakers' rebellion.

Since both sides accused the Bahá'ís of belonging to the wrong camp, any time one side seemed to be losing ground it would appeal to the Bahá'ís for help, promising victory if only it could be assured of their cooperation. And just as soon as the situation was reversed, the other side would beseech the friends for their assistance. It was at these times that various conflicting petitions and entreaties would reach the Holy Threshold.

Unfortunately, these events were taking place at an inopportune time. Barely a year or a year and a half had passed since the events of Yazd and Isfahan[236] and the Iranian nation was susceptible of rebellion, and capable of a bloodbath on the smallest excuse. Moreover, they were happening at a time when the Covenant-breakers' activities were at their peak, as they prepared their last assault on the Faith. Now you can see what 'Abdu'l-Bahá was going through. "Refrain from involvement in politics, even to the extent of uttering a single word," was continuously on His lips; similar words formed the opening passages of His Tablets.

These are a few examples of 'Abdu'l-Bahá's burdens and hardships. When He was distressed over this or other matters, He would also implicitly complain about those believers who were firm in the Cause. For example, He would say, "I wrote to Iran instructing the friends to do *this*. They replied, 'Since things are as they are, it would be better if we did *that*.' Do you know what that means? It means, 'You do not know, and we do.' Despite all this, I pray for them and implore God to aid and assist them."

Another time He said, "They have written to me from Iran that, 'We are being asked:

"Where is your pride? Where are your aspirations? What has happened to your courage and your audacity?'" How can we respond?'" Then He continued, "I wrote that they should say, 'If a mature, wise human being observes a few immature, ignorant children fighting over some imaginary object, is it worthy of that person to involve himself and participate in their feud, or should he counsel both sides and reconcile them?'"

In short, during the entire period of the Constitutional Revolution these matters imposed a burden which 'Abdu'l-Bahá had to endure in addition to the rebellion of the Covenant-breakers in 'Akká. This was due to the faults and shortcomings of us firm believers.

My point is that we, lovers of God, firm and steadfast in His Covenant, having weathered the tests and difficulties caused by the uprising of the Covenant-breakers as described in previous chapters – we who could recite the Tablet of the Covenant by heart, manifesting intense devotion and depth of faith, nevertheless constantly presented "our" opinions and expressed our "selves" at that sanctified threshold. And this is one category of hardship we imposed on 'Abdu'l-Bahá. Many a time He would say, "I don't claim sinlessness. I am the first of sinners (God forbid!) but the Ancient Beauty has bestowed upon me a station, and therefore whatever I say is what will be."

What is a homeland and who is a patriot?

At the height of the Constitutional Revolution, which coincided with the first year of the Ottoman Empire's constitutional government, all the Iranians in Beirut (including those who had fled Iran or had been exiled, and particularly two or three young men whose fathers had been killed in the uprising) assembled day and night demonstrating their patriotic fervour and expressing their devotion to their homeland and their love of freedom. They believed such sentiments to be the zenith of human perfections. This was their highest ideal, and they considered anyone who failed to share their convictions an outcast and devoid of all human virtue.

The words homeland, freedom and independence were to them the same as faith, devotion, God, prophet and love. In fact, this illusory freedom and independence had been won by utilizing foreign embassies as political sanctuaries, for fear of government reprisals. The [Bahá'í] friends, however, had no affiliation with foreign entities and so the young Bahá'ís in Beirut were, in their view, devoid of human merit. Fortunately, a few of these revolutionaries who were possessed of sound judgement and a pious spirit were my intimate friends. Once these friends became acquainted with the principles of the Faith I sent them, in accordance with the Master's previous instructions, to the sanctified threshold of 'Abdu'l-Bahá where they became inebriated with the wine of His bounty and love.

One of those whom I took with me to 'Akká was a proud young man from a noble family who is at present a man of prominence and has made his home in Europe. He became the recipient of 'Abdu'l-Bahá's infinite bounty and loving-kindness. In those days (which coincided with the opening stages of the Young Turks Revolution and the time when the Covenant-breakers had crept back into seclusion) the Western and Eastern pilgrims were beginning to receive permission again to travel to 'Akká and attain the presence of 'Abdu'l-Bahá. A respectable American believer and his wife arrived in 'Akká at this time, tasted the sweetness of reunion and became the recipients of divine blessings at the dinner table; they met this young man and developed a warm friendship with him. After a few days, when they received permission to depart, I was assigned to escort all three of them to Haifa to board the ship. The Americans were going to Egypt and the young Iranian was bound for Beirut. As they paid their farewells to 'Abdu'l-Bahá, kissing the hem of His '*abá*, the Master told the Americans, "Wherever you encounter Iranian Bahá'ís embrace them on my behalf, like this, and kiss them."

"What should I do?" asked the American lady.

"You can do the same with the ladies!" was 'Abdu'l-Bahá's response.

And so they said their goodbyes and we travelled to Haifa. As we arrived at the dock, several Bahá'ís from the remote villages of Azerbaijan were disembarking. These pilgrims, men, women and children, looked exhausted, dishevelled and unkempt. The men looked haggard with their shaved heads, untidy ruffled beards, unwashed faces and worn-out clothes. In order to attain the desired Ka'bih these pilgrims had probably walked some two-thirds of the way from Iran and borne all manner of hardships before reaching the passenger ship. They must have said to each other all the way,

> *The air of Ka'bih has me running with such joyful rush*
> *That the thornbushes in my path are like silk to the touch.*

Their extreme fatigue could therefore be clearly appreciated. My patriot friend, who was from an aristocratic family, was loath to meet people who were so obviously of the agricultural and working class, and so he turned his head and walked away. But as soon as the two American Bahá'ís discovered that these were Bahá'ís, in obedience to what the Master had told them they welcomed them joyfully. Like parents who have just found their lost children or, to use 'Abdu'l-Bahá's expression, "like two lovers" they embraced them, tears of joy streaming from their eyes. I called my friend who had walked away, and said, "Come and see what 'homeland' really means, and what is meant by 'patriotism'." He approached, only to witness that heart-warming emotional scene as tears of envy flowed from his eyes. Thus he recognized the true homeland and learned patriotism from us, and for some time this story went from mouth to mouth in Beirut.

What was happening on the moon?

As described in previous chapters, during my stay in Beirut I used to visit 'Akká and attain 'Abdu'l-Bahá's presence four months a year. In the first years the Master gave me some translation work, but in the following years, although He

Shoghi Effendi in childhood

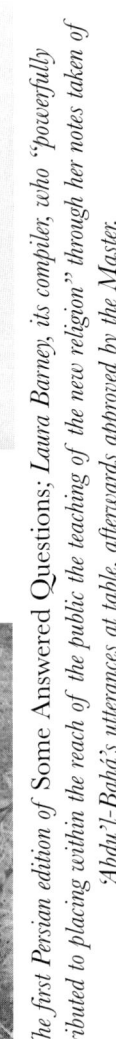

The first Persian edition of Some Answered Questions; Laura Barney, its compiler, who "powerfully contributed to placing within the reach of the public the teaching of the new religion" through her notes taken of 'Abdu'l-Bahá's utterances at table, afterwards approved by the Master.

Ethel Rosenberg, early English Bahá'í who assisted Laura Barney in transcribing Some Answered Questions; *Kanichi Yamamoto, the first Japanese Bahá'í*

Believers in Paris in the early 1900s. The photograph shows several of the early Paris group including Hippolyte Dreyfus, Edith Sanderson, and Edwin Scott in whose studio the photograph was taken; Mrs. Jackson is seated in the front row, second from left.

'Abdu'l-Bahá's tent in the courtyard of the House of 'Abdu'lláh Páshá. Here He used to rest, in the garden He planted during the investigations of the Commission of Enquiry (see p. 401).

Dr. Youness Khán Afroukhteh,
'Abdu'l-Bahá's trusted secretary and interpreter;
photograph taken about the time of writing these memoirs.

Left: Dr. Younes Afroukhteh with his wife Zarintaj and daughters Nirvana and Farzaneh in about 1926; right: doctors at the Sehat Hospital, Tehran, shortly after his return to Iran from the Holy Land: Dr. Younes Khán is in the second row, behind Dr. Susan Moody.

"The Holy One walks"

WHAT WAS HAPPENING ON THE MOON?

would invite me to "rest a few days and then be ready for work", there was nothing much for me to do, for the translation work was being performed by others. Later He instructed me to stay in Haifa near the Shrine of the Báb. Once, I asked to be permitted to move to another location, since I felt it was not befitting to use that sanctified Shrine as a place of rest or residence. 'Abdu'l-Bahá replied, "I forbade others, but you are the servant of that Shrine and therefore you must stay there." (This was one of the greatest honours of my life.)

Many of 'Abdu'l-Bahá's utterances, as before, contained glad tidings which brought joy and happiness to the hearts of the oppressed and persecuted Iranian friends. They had heard from the lips of Bahá'u'lláh: "This Faith is like an unstoppable flood, despite the Persians who wish to prevent it from flowing. Before long, it will rise in America." It was therefore necessary for the friends to know that "the All-Knowing is faithful to His promises".

At that time, all documents worth publishing were sent on the Master's instructions to the honoured Muḥibu'ṣ-Sulṭán Rawḥání to be printed and distributed. One day I was summoned to the presence of 'Abdu'l-Bahá. He handed me a small but thick envelope and told me: "Gather together all the English-language experts and translate this letter carefully."

The English-language experts at the time consisted of Mírzá Valíyu'lláh Khán Varqá, who had been attending the American school for just one year, Mírzá Badí' Bushru'í, and Mírzá Nurú'd-Dín Zayn and Mírzá Munír, who were studying English under my tutelage. We assembled in the pilgrim house and anxiously opened the letter. Unfortunately, in addition to the illegible handwriting, the contents were comprised of scientific and mathematical expressions with which none of us was familiar. Nobody had any knowledge of astronomy or astrophysics. All we understood was this: "On such and such a night when there was a full moon, using such and such a telescope located at the summit of such and such a mountain peak, I saw ... and recognized you, and therefore I profess my belief." This was followed by a number of emotional expressions, after which more scientific formulae followed.

When I submitted to 'Abdu'l-Bahá the translation along with the original petition, I apologized for our incompetence. Showering me with expressions of loving-kindness, He instructed me to send it to Tehran forthwith so that it might be published. This was done. Recently in Tehran I asked Muḥibu'ṣ-Sulṭán if he had the English version of that letter for me to review after all these years. He replied that he was no longer in possession of any of those papers. I even asked the honoured Varqá. He had forgotten the whole incident altogether.

The point here is that the old Persian friends had read in Bahá'u'lláh's Tablets that all the atoms of the universe testify to the greatness of this Cause (the moon being one such atom). In another place He reveals: "The tree bears witness and the sea professes: the Hidden Treasure has been manifested."[237] In His Tablet revealed in my honour when I was a youth, He writes, "All things rejoice and clap their hands ..." The Pen of the Covenant wrote, "Soon the banner of the Covenant will be raised aloft on the world's highest peaks." ('Abdu'l-Bahá)[238] There are many similar Writings of which the friends are aware and with which I, too, am somewhat familiar. However, I must admit, I have no clue as to what was going on inside that full moon!

Another work referring to the moon was prepared by the honoured Subḥání, who has sent me a copy for inclusion in this book. In Surih 180 of the exalted book Qayyúmu'l-Asmá',[239] the Surih known as "Alif, Lam, Mim", and also in Surih 111 of that same Book, known as the "Surih of 'Alí", a certain blessed verse has been revealed twice without the slightest change. From the billowing ocean of this verse, and through the power of inspiration granted to Mr. Subḥání, a single priceless pearl has emerged.[240] Here is the twice-revealed verse: "O people of God, hear My call from this shining moon." In abjad numerology the value of the term

WHAT WAS HAPPENING ON THE MOON? 399

qamaru'l-munír (shining moon) is equivalent to the value of "Shoghi Rabbani".

Shoghi Rabbani		Shining moon	
SH	300	Q	100
O	6	M	40
GH	100	R	200
I	10	L	30
R	200	M	40
B	2	N	50
A	1	I	10
N	50	R	200
I	10		670
(Value of the expression "shining moon")			9
679			679

This was the content of the honoured Subḥání's letter.

By God, you're right!

Having completed the last year of my studies and successfully passed the tests required by the Medical School, I now had to go through the State examinations required by the Ottoman and French governments. Since the examinations were to be held by a committee that was to arrive at the end of summer, I welcomed the opportunity to return to 'Akká for the summer.

Although the Persian Constitutional Revolution was in full swing, the non-partisanship of the believers had been clearly demonstrated by their actions and had served to keep them safe, so that news reaching 'Akká from Iran was not only devoid of horrifying reports, but actually gave tidings of the wellbeing, safety and tranquillity of the friends. This in turn brought joy to the hearts of the resident believers.

The Ottoman Constitutional Revolution had only just begun, and so no one was paying much attention to the machinations of the Covenant-breakers; defeated and broken, all their attempts having failed miserably, they burrowed into their holes like earthworms.

No longer were the Covenant-breakers even mentioned among the friends. Peace prevailed everywhere. The Eastern friends were beginning to arrive, and the pilgrim house was lively again. Most of 'Abdu'l-Bahá's utterances pertained to the days of the Blessed Beauty; these He recounted in the context of admonition and advice, so that in times of hardship and calamity the friends might be reminded to rely on the will of God. He gave examples of the virtues of courage and audacity; these excited every atom of one's being and prompted the desire to challenge any enemy to an encounter.

Speaking of Mírzá Asadu'lláh, who had the responsibility of sweeping the floors of His house, 'Abdu'l-Bahá said, "Áqá Asadu'lláh is a very small man, but he possesses a brave heart. He used to carry a broadsword and act as a guard at Bahá'u'lláh's house. In Baghdad, when whispers were heard that a plot was afoot by the enemies of Bahá'u'lláh to attack His house, the Blessed Beauty responded, 'I will send Áqá Asadu'lláh who will take care of the lot of them.'"

One of the stories the Master told frequently was about one of the Ottoman officials in 'Akká, who once planned to extract a large bribe from Bahá'u'lláh. To do so he began to create a great deal of trouble. Failing in his purpose, he summoned the Blessed Beauty to the Government House. When Bahá'u'lláh arrived, the officer intensified the pressure by threatening Him with a variety of ultimatums and penalties. Losing patience with the man, Bahá'u'lláh suddenly stood up and there and then began to perform the Obligatory Prayer, as the officer looked on incredulously. Once the prayer was completed He beckoned the officer. As he approached, suddenly the Blessed Beauty raised His hand, slapped him hard across the face and said, "I have telegraphed you the money," and walked out. The poor man, petrified, stood there like a statue. It so happened that that very evening he received a telegram from the Sublime Porte relieving him of his duties and summoning him to the capital. That night he presented himself at Bahá'u'lláh's door, threw himself at His feet and asked for forgiveness and blessing.

The point is this: that in those days, some time in mid-1908, no trace of concern and worry for the resident believers and pilgrims was left. 'Abdu'l-Bahá in utter joy and happiness Himself, was counting the victories of the Cause and explaining to us in pleasant stories and examples how those victories had been won.

It goes without saying what an ocean of joy flooded my heart, having completed the arduous courses of the medical curriculum, passed all the examinations, and then attained the presence of the Beloved. One afternoon, I walked from the pilgrim house to the Master's House. The Master was not at home and the *bírúní* area was deserted. As I waited, I began to pace back and forth in the front yard, the same spot where during the investigations of the Commission of Enquiry the Master had planted flowers and put up a tent as a place of rest. As I walked up and down this long pathway, sweet and wonderful thoughts so dominated my mind that utterly oblivious of my surroundings I was soaring in the heavenly atmosphere of a different realm. My thoughts centred around this: that ten or fifteen years ago, in my ignorance I had thought that the highest position that I could ever attain in this world was to merit a raise from the Bank, build a larger house for myself, gradually earn the right of signature in one of the departments of the Bank, and become this or that. O God, how unworthy were those desires for a human being who is filled with the love of God! Praised be God, that He had planned a different fate for me. The Master summoned me, and worthy or not I absorbed heavenly virtues and found myself in the company of the very personification of Truth. From the darkness of the material world I was guided towards the celestial light. Ultimately, I was encouraged to study medicine and the hosts of divine confirmations came to my aid every step of the way, not only in this achievement but for others which lay in the future. O, my God, what loss would I have experienced had I achieved my unworthy goals and become deprived of these blessings! How far from my desires was the divine will.

For about an hour I was deeply engrossed in these thoughts, as I continued to pace up and down waiting for 'Abdu'l-Bahá to arrive. In that state of thanksgiving, I raised my head and observed the crescent moon. I told myself how wonderful it would be if seeing this moon could coincide with beholding that matchless Beauty, as has been written:

It was the moon I sought,
But lo! It was the sun that rose.

As this thought crossed my mind, suddenly the voice of 'Abdu'l-Bahá rang out: "Jináb-i-K̲h̲án, come!"

O my God, how could I have been so mindless as to have missed the Master's presence in the tent? I ran towards it. With a feeling of utter joy mixed with a bit of embarrassment, and breathing hard, I bowed. With one of those loving smiles, He said, "So, what were you thinking? I want to know. Tell me truthfully now, I won't make you pay! But be honest."

I was so confused that I had not heard the Master repeatedly telling me to sit down. "I have come to understand something, and that is what I was thinking about just now," I replied. "Whatever a human being desires for himself brings him nothing but loss, and whatever God desires for him is gain upon gain." Immediately, He joyfully exclaimed three times, "By God, you're right!"

What is fortune?

If each hair of your head is endowed with manifold talents,
Not one will be of use if bad luck is its companion.

There is no doubt that it is the lack of true understanding of this issue on the part of the ignorant that has caused the deterioration of human society, and yet the existence in our everyday lives of the factor we call "luck" can neither be ignored nor discounted. Many a poet and philosopher has considered it an important element in the achievement of success and happiness. This belief, however, has diminished the value of initiative, action and effort by promoting an attitude of passivity and sloth, and has lured people into a deep slumber of indolence as they await the rising of the star of good fortune. As the poet says,

Banish from heaven the star of my fate, O Seer,
For my fate is doomed, and my sighs may burn away the sky, I fear.

This illusive fortune comes in a variety of colours. Black fortune, white fortune, sleeping fortune, sober fortune, beginner's luck, worn-out luck, feeble luck, hard luck, bright fortune, dark fortune, rebellious fortune, etc. In short, this many-coloured and multi-faceted fortune sometimes accompanies an individual from the moment of his birth and stays with him to the end; while at other times its star rises but then quickly fades. Luck can come and go. At times it comes only to disappear without trace.

So who should ask this significant philosophical question on the subject of luck? Who else but a young, illiterate, simple Pársí Bahá'í,[241] who apart from his qualities of total sincerity and complete honesty had no claim to learning or wisdom. In a gathering of friends and in the presence of 'Abdu'l-Bahá, he asked, in his peculiar native dialect. "May my life be a sacrifice for You, what is this luck? Is it real or just an invention?" This question from that simple and modest young man caused the ocean of utterance to surge, and thus for over a quarter of an hour those present were enraptured by the Master's words.

On our return to the pilgrim house everyone praised and applauded that young man who had been the instrument through whom many a truth had been discovered. 'Abdu'l-Bahá's utterances, as far as I can recall after these many years, were as follows:[242]

"In Bahá'í philosophy, luck is the same as divine confirmation, which is ceaseless and continuous, never subject to interruption or suspension. It is not limited to some to the exclusion of others. The capacity for its manifestation must be created. Showers of divine bounty and confirmation are always falling; if any spot experiences a suspension or delay, other areas shall receive these effusions. The clouds of divine bounty bestow blessings on all. It is sanctified of exclusivity. The significant point is that he who sows a seed or plants a sapling becomes the recipient of bounty, he becomes the possessor of good fortune, otherwise he remains deprived. The sun of mercy is eternal and ever-abiding; it is not specific to some. The loved ones of God must strive to become worthy of divine confirmations. Misfortune has no true existence. It is simply deprivation of divine bounty. Darkness is the absence of light, otherwise darkness has no outer reality. Darkness should be eliminated through the light of the recognition of God. For example, a storm is a universal blessing. It is a prelude to cool and temperate weather. It is one of nature's features, an essential part of natural phenomena. However, if it strikes a ship which is incapable of resisting its force, this is not due to the ship's misfortune. The storm did not come to sink the ship but to follow its own natural course. Now, the more substantial and sturdy the ship, the better it can endure the force of the storm. Tests of the world of nature are of the same kind.

"So good fortune, or luck, is the ceaseless bounty of God, and misfortune is a chance event that represents its absence. Praise be to God that all of you are fortunate. What fortune is greater than divine knowledge? What fortune is greater than the love of God, which is the source of all divine effusions?"

In short, He spoke in this vein for some time as we all sat utterly spellbound.

Return to Beirut

The summer was over. The happy, enchanted days of reunion had come to an end. Never before had 'Akká seemed happier or more accommodating. It was cleansed of evil individuals and free from the unfaithful. This was an historic moment, culminating in the lifting of the condition of incarceration and its associated restrictions.

Once I arrived back in Beirut, I was confronted with manifold problems. The late Áqá Muḥammad Muṣṭafá's commercial firm had fallen into disorder through the duplicity of his partners; my account there had been closed and any prospect of establishing credit at another financial institution was non-existent. The day of the arrival of the State Examiners was near, and not only was there no hope of any financial help from the school authorities, who were Jesuit priests, but rather, I could count on their antagonism and opposition.

Before the arrival of the examiners I was in dire need of 30 *liras*, without which all the work of the previous five years would have gone for naught, and further, my financial reputation would have been ruined. While I was away, the general chaos caused by the Iranian Revolution and the continuing violence and slaughter between the Constitutionalists and the autocrats had become so fierce that all communications to Iran had been suspended. Moreover, within the Ottoman realm, the triumph of the Young Turks and the rebellion of the Armenians had brought business to a standstill. My application to the Ottoman Bank was turned down. As the State Examiners arrived the problem remained unsolved. When no hope remained, I resorted to prayer and supplication. If within the next six hours of that day the required fees were duly paid, I would be able to sit for the State examinations next morning; otherwise the process would be delayed for one year, and who knew what might happen between now and then?

In short, the hardships of those first few days were substantially more acute than the difficulties in the first year of my studies. But praised be God, those promises of divine confirmations were realized; rebellious fortune was tamed and the pathway to deliverance was made manifest when Áqá Mírzá Enayat'u'lláh Cha'ichi, having run all the way and arriving quite out of breath, brought the news that such and such a Jewish currency exchange firm had agreed to lend the required amount and had accepted my promissory note, which no one else had been willing to recognize and no bank would have accepted as collateral. In short, within the space of six hours the deal was done and the fee was paid just before closing time.

Next morning I was summoned before the examiners. Three State tests were given, in addition to the annual examinations held by the School. Were these tests easy or difficult? Difficult for the one who did not know the real meaning of good fortune and had not heard the true definition of the word from the lips of 'Abdu'l-Bahá. Within a few days all the examinations were completed with great success and the promises of divine confirmations were fulfilled once again. Afterwards, I set out for 'Akká straight away and presented to 'Abdu'l-Bahá the document issued by the Medical School authorizing me to practise medicine pending the receipt of the actual medical diplomas from Paris and Istanbul.

Three medical cases

In the section entitled "Six years of hard work did not go to waste!", reference was made to the fact that 'Abdu'l-Bahá was not very satisfied with the doctors in 'Akká. Typically, whenever one of the pilgrims or resident Bahá'ís was taken ill, he visited a doctor selected by 'Abdu'l-Bahá and it was the Master who paid the doctor's fees and the cost of all the required medications. The doctors, who had no formal training and yet practised medicine, were also entitled to a fee. It was during the time of turmoil brought about by the investigations of the Commission of Enquiry that the Master had sent me to Beirut, after preparing me for the challenge of attending medical school through the bounty of His counsel and advice. Once, before I left, He had addressed me in these words, "Go and get an education, maybe you can save us from these doctors." Then He had added, "Who knows where we may be at that time?"

The point is, He was not happy with the doctors. The only doctors who had been trained abroad were the American Protestant physician who ran a missionary hospital, a Greek Cypriot who had come from Istanbul, and two other Arab doctors who were licensed to practice. The members of 'Abdu'l-Bahá's family were usually sent to Beirut for medical care.

My first opportunity to practise medicine came during my first two months in medical school, when I had just begun the study of the science of anatomy and dissection. The Greatest Holy Leaf and one of 'Abdu'l-Bahá's daughters, accompanied by Mírzá Hadí Afnán, arrived in Beirut for medical treatment. As soon as I heard the news, I rushed to the home of the late Muḥammad Muṣṭafá Baghdádí to pay my respects.

The honoured Afnán emerged from the inner apartments in an agitated state. "She [the Greatest Holy Leaf] has been visiting Dr. Debron for the last two days, but she is feeling quite poorly," he informed me. "She is experiencing severe dizziness and nausea and asks that you should write a prescription and give proper advice for the condition."

"I have just begun the alphabet of medicine," I replied. "How can I give any instructions when I know nothing?"

He went back inside to relay the message, but returned forthwith. "Whatever it takes, you must give some advice," he pleaded. "It is her wish that you should prescribe medication."

No matter how hard I thought, nothing came to mind except expressions of helplessness and ignorance. When they brought her message for the third time, insisting on the same thing and emphasizing the same instructions, the honoured Afnán made a personal plea, "We have no power of our own.

Healing comes from God. You prescribe something, maybe it is your good faith and strong devotion which she feels will properly guide you."

Without a second thought I said, brew a pinch of mint like tea and have her drink it with candy sugar. Having said this, I sat down to wait it out.

An hour later they brought the happy news that the nausea had abated and that she had prayed for me in gratitude for my contribution. The next morning, I received the honour of being admitted into her presence to offer my wishes for her speedy recovery. It is a pity that the loving friends could not have been present at such an occasion. I was rewarded with a package of high-quality silk handkerchiefs, some candy sugar from the Holy Land, a bottle of attar of rose, and many kind words. So this was my first fee from my first opportunity to practise medicine before completing the requirements of the Medical School.

My second opportunity to practise medicine took place when I had passed the last examination of the Medical School and was duly recognized by the school authorities as a Doctor of Medicine. While I was waiting for the State Examiners to arrive and preparing myself for those tests, a young aristocratic Iranian was taken ill. Because of the turmoil in Iran he had received no communications from his parents. I undertook to treat this young man for five Turkish *liras*, and made a personal guarantee at a reputable pharmacy for the payment of all the medication before starting my treatment.

In my first years at Medical School I had made a vow that when I completed my studies, I would present my very first earnings to 'Abdu'l-Bahá as an act of love and devotion. I was emulating the renowned Mr. Remey, who while studying engineering in Paris had sent an amount of $9, his very first fee, to 'Abdu'l-Bahá. This was the same amount that He had granted to me on my departure for Beirut. At that time I had no hope that my patient would receive funds any time soon, thus enabling me to collect my first fee. However, since the arrival of the funds was still within the realm of possibility, and because my intentions were good and I had learned the true meaning of good fortune, my patient was cured within two weeks, the money was received from Iran, he paid his debt at the pharmacy and fulfilled his responsibility to me. I, too, stayed true to my vow, and before long received the receipt for the amount from the sanctified threshold of 'Abdu'l-Bahá. This was the result of my second attempt to practise medicine before I was officially granted the licence to do so. But oh, how I needed God's help on my third attempt!

The third attempt: When I returned to 'Akká after completing the examination and receiving my licence, I overheard a conversation in the pilgrim house to the effect that the Centre of the Covenant was experiencing chronic fever. About an hour after attaining His presence and presenting Him with my licence, 'Abdu'l-Bahá, showering me with endless expressions of His loving-kindness, told me, "I run a fever every night. It is a nervous condition. Give it some thought." The idea of treating 'Abdu'l-Bahá as a patient had never occurred to me, and so I took His utterance as a kindly but humorous comment and I bowed my head in response.

Two or three days later while a few of us were in His presence, the Master said in passing, "At night I run a temperature and develop severe headaches." Then, addressing this servant, He said, "Prescribe something."

Again, I did not think that 'Abdu'l-Bahá had actual medical treatment in mind, and in my heart I said,

May Thy pain come to the hearts of all Thy lovers,
May their lives be sacrificed for Thine.

That night, like the night before, He did not come downstairs. Next morning Mírzá Ḥaydar-'Alí and I attained His presence. The Master was in a happy mood and so in turn all of us were filled with joy and gladness. Suddenly He said, "Khán, whatever has happened? Come closer and check my pulse."

Since whenever 'Abdu'l-Bahá's hand fell into my grasp by chance, I would kiss it as He smiled at me, so this time, too, I jumped at the chance with abandon, took His hand and kissed it three times. Smiling broadly, He said, "My dear man, I said check my pulse!"

I checked His pulse. It was quite regular and smooth, somewhat slow, but otherwise like the pulse of a young person. He said, "It is all right now, but at nights I have a temperature." He then rose and began to pace up and down the front area of the *bírúní*. After a few minutes, He summoned me alone to His presence and said, "Really now, prescribe something. I have been ill for more than a month."

Only then did I realize that aside from bestowing kind words, He really was referring to actual medical treatment. Furthermore, He Himself had already diagnosed the problem. And since I was never a shy or silent type, I boldly jumped at the opportunity and replied, "I have received from America a number of half-milligram sample pills of arsenate of strychnine."

"Yes, yes, that is good," said the Master approvingly.

"I will immediately go to the pharmacy and prepare several doses of quinine for four or five days," I added.

"Very well," he agreed, "proceed."

Overwhelmed, I ran all the way to the pilgrim house and then to the pharmacy and in a world of excitement I prepared the medicine, wrote the instructions for its use, placed it neatly in a box and returned. It was before noon and 'Abdu'l-Bahá was still in the guest room. I presented the box.

"Well?" mused 'Abdu'l-Bahá. "So you want to put me under your medical care. And without a fee? You think I am going to take your medicine without paying the expenses?"

He walked over to where Mírzá Haydar-'Alí was standing and addressed him: "Listen to what Khán has to say. He is offering to treat me and provide all the medication for no fee. Many a physician has come to me, but I did not accept them, and now Khán, who became a doctor only yesterday, prescribes medicine for me today and all for free."

The honoured Mírzá continually confirmed 'Abdu'l-

Bahá's utterances by repeated bows. I was beside myself with joy. As He began to climb the stairs, He turned and said, "Very well, I will start now."

In the afternoon, we attained the Master's presence again, but He made no further reference to the matter. Since in those days 'Abdu'l-Bahá did not normally receive the friends in the evenings, we too had reduced our expectations of being granted that pleasure, but unfortunately that night someone brought the news that He was very ill. It should be obvious how a newly qualified doctor would feel when faced with such tidings in handling his very first case. A few minutes later someone else brought further news that 'Abdu'l-Bahá's condition had not improved.

The joy and happiness of the late morning had suddenly been replaced by the horror of this hour. I was summoned to His presence. He was resting on the couch in the upstairs guest room when I entered. I cannot express the depth of my dismay and anxiety.

"Nothing has happened," He said quickly. Then He asked about the exact components, one by one, of the mixture. Since I myself had prepared the medicine I was quite certain that no wrong ingredient had mistakenly found its way into the mixture. I enumerated each component and its quantity. "Yes, the quantity of the quinine must have been somewhat excessive," He said. "Do not worry," He went on to assure me, "everything will turn out all right." After showering me with boundless expressions of loving-kindness, He dismissed me with "May God go with you."

Feeling terrible, I returned to the pilgrim house. Only God knows what I went through that night. All night long I either sat up in bed or lay down wide awake, and sometimes in my delirium I repeated,

O Thou Who art the Recipient and Answerer of every prayer,
O Thou Who art the healing balm and the true healer,
At this night's end the sun shall not its promise keep.
Endless thoughts play through my mind but the one bestowing sleep.

Dost Thou know why the morning breeze I love so well?
It resembles my Beloved's face when He removes his veil!

At sunrise, noiselessly and without alarming anyone, I hastened to the House of 'Abdu'l-Bahá. And what did I see in the front yard of the *bírúní?* Áqá Asadu'lláh, that old sword-carrying guard of the Blessed Beauty, was sweeping and cleaning the area. He shouted from some distance away, "Jináb-i-<u>Kh</u>án, glad tidings, glad tidings, you should be very happy! 'Abdu'l-Bahá has offered prayers in your name! He said, 'For some time I have not been able to go to the public bathhouse. I feel so well today that I am able to go this morning, thanks to Jináb-i-<u>Kh</u>án.'"

This happy news was so dramatic that suddenly I found myself sitting in a corner weeping uncontrollably, as a flood of tears of joy quenched the burning fire in my heart. After a while, I regained my senses and began to pace back and forth while the sun began to rise on the eastern horizon.

Suddenly 'Abdu'l-Bahá appeared at the doorway of the front entrance. And what did He say? "Jináb-i-<u>Kh</u>án, I felt so well that I went to the bathhouse and prayed for your well-being. I will continue to take the rest of the medicine."

He praised me further with kind words and I, half dancing, half running, returned to the pilgrim house; and since I had concealed the events of the previous night from the pilgrims, I now shared the whole story with them.

> *Thy name was whispered, yet the lovers heard it plain;*
> *They jumped up dancing, he who heard and he who named.*
> *On the forehead of this crazed one they placed kiss after kiss,*
> *And then they snapped their fingers in happy joyful bliss.*
> *From pure joy the friends into frenzied dance broke*
> *And eagerly grasped the hem of the Beloved's robe.*

News from Iran and the Ottoman States

These opening days of the Fall of 1909 were the best times in

'Akká, for the hearts of the pilgrims and the resident believers were filled with joy and gladness. The loathsome noises of the troublemakers and antagonists were no longer to be heard; instead, the soul-stirring melodies of the steadfast believers sounded sweet to our ears in this divine flower garden.

While both Iran and the Ottoman realms had been subjected to extreme hardship and both lands were afflicted by the ever-growing fires of rebellion and revolution, the friends, in obedience to the emphatic instructions of 'Abdu'l-Bahá, had remained uninvolved in any of the political issues and struggles. Thus the reality of the verse "God keeps tyrants busy with tyrants" was manifested, as the corrupt and hostile thoughts and actions of both the Constitutionalists and the autocrats received their chastisement, while the peace-loving, gentle Bahá'ís were kept safe in the midst of these dangerous times.

Every report that reached the Holy Land contained glad tidings of the friends' wellbeing and safety, as well as their feelings of unbounded zeal and devotion. Even more remarkable was that the enemies of the Faith in both camps, and in both the Persian and Ottoman realms, invariably received due chastisement for their actions. In Iran, whenever the Constitutionalists had the upper hand, those antagonists who had tried to deceive the public by accusing the Bahá'ís of initiating the rebellion, themselves became the targets of suspicion and experienced the horrors of the gallows; and conversely, when there was a reversal of fortune and the autocrats regained power, again it was the enemies of the Faith and the trouble-makers who were caught in the web of their own conspiracies and who paid dearly for their actions. All this was entirely due to 'Abdu'l-Bahá's unequivocal instructions.

Because of this general state of tranquillity and order, the teaching work improved tremendously both in the East and in the West, and 1909 turned out to be a blessed year. For example, in Iran when several of the enemies of the Faith were executed by the autocrats, at the same time the

"Utuzbir" incident took place in Istanbul where some thirty-one ministers and high-ranking pashas, all inveterate enemies of the Faith, were arrested and immediately hanged the same day. This unforgettable incident was one of the most significant events of the Young Turks Revolution.[243] And so this year witnessed the doom of the Covenant-breakers, the demise of the mischief-makers, and finally, the end of the Most Great Prison.

The end of the Most Great Prison of 'Akká

The Young Turks Revolution and the imprisonment of 'Abdu'l-Ḥamíd had created such an atmosphere of suspicion and fear that none of the Ottoman Muslims residing in Palestine and Syria dared even to mention it. Some of the die-hard autocrats either gave no credence to the reports or spread a thousand absurd stories about the Sultan having ascended to the heavens and the liberals having managed to imprison only his statue. Meanwhile, in their deeply rooted hatred the Armenians let no opportunity go by in publishing caricatures and taunting and insulting pictures of the King.

The friends, however, considered all this noise as nothing but the buzzing of flies, and thus continued their spiritual feast, receiving heavenly blessings. In these words they expressed their sentiments of gratitude and thanksgiving:

> *If there is enmity and war among the Arabs;*
> *There is nothing but love and joy between Laylí and Majnún.*[244]

News at last reached 'Akká that the Sublime Porte had issued a decree freeing all political prisoners. This news was of course unworthy of mention in the presence of 'Abdu'l-Bahá, yet among the friends it created great commotion and excitement. The believers began to anticipate the departure of the Master from 'Akká to the city of Haifa, while in that city, friends and non-Bahá'ís alike awaited His arrival with great eagerness.

THE END OF THE MOST GREAT PRISON OF 'AKKÁ

In those days, I had just arrived in Haifa from 'Akká and witnessed the excitement of the friends who, having tasted the bitter poison of separation during the reincarceration of 'Abdu'l-Bahá, were now impatiently and anxiously awaiting His arrival.

How long shall I wait anxiously for a glance of Thee,
As I stand in the street looking longingly at the gate?
In my sore longing after Thee
It is my eye that you will see,
O misery, roll down my face,
So that my tears it may replace.

Everyone asked me, "Why is He not coming?" Some said they had heard that the Governor of 'Akká had proclaimed the Master to be free of all restrictions. But others said that 'Abdu'l-Bahá had indicated that any order freeing Him must come from Istanbul and be specifically in His name. Some said that the Governor had already asked for such specific instructions, but with all the chaos in Istanbul only God knew when a reply might be forthcoming.

Of course, I had heard all these stories in 'Akká too, but because there we were all submerged in the ocean of His presence, 'Abdu'l-Bahá's dignified and serene bearing prevented us from asking any questions about it. Here, however, there was a great deal of clamour and excitement among the friends; the cup of their patience had so overflowed that in accordance with the expression, "A drowning man clutches at any straw", they found me to be their last resort. They told me, "You are the one who brought us the news of the reincarceration of 'Abdu'l-Bahá a few years ago, and so now you are the one who must present our petition and entreaty at His threshold." And I, who had been undeservedly spoiled by the Master, abandoned my manners and humbly brought the matter to His attention.

Praised be God, after a day or two their petition received the honour of His acceptance and that peerless Beauty repaired to the city of Haifa. On His arrival in the city He said to me, "We have accepted your request and rejected Sulṭán 'Abdu'l-Ḥamíd's command. What more do you want?" and then He entered His residence. Observing the unfinished building, He remarked, "We are not of this world and have no need of such a house. But man has the duty to develop and cultivate God's earth."

The foundations of the house had been laid by the late Mrs. Jackson, who did not live long enough to complete its construction;[245] the building work was finished at 'Abdu'l-Bahá's expense and the House is now the residence of His family.

In brief, those were days of joy, celebration and thanksgiving for the friends. Nor did the non-Bahá'ís fall short in expressing their own delight, and so feasts and festivities abounded. One point that I shall never forget was the marked change in 'Abdu'l-Bahá's attitude and conduct towards people of prominence and government dignitaries. All forms of discretion and caution, which had been practised from the time of the Blessed Beauty, gave way to open declaration of the Faith. From that point I understood that the line of the Caliphate had been broken once and for all. For instance, to the die-hard pro-Caliphate officers the Master spoke about the Tradition: "Wonder of wonders between Jamadí and Rajáb."[246] He even declared, "The days which fall within this duration are the time for me to arise for the triumph of the Cause of God and the promotion of the divine teachings." At these words, those in attendance evinced such humility and lowliness that we were astounded.

Describing the indescribable

In this collection of memoirs now nearing completion, I have recorded many of my experiences and observations which I felt were worthy of mention. For example, in each chapter I have presented a brief description of the manners, bearing and many burdens of 'Abdu'l-Bahá. In the sections on love, generosity, helping the poor and others I have recounted whatever my feeble and confused memory can recall after all these years. But alas, there are a number of subjects commonly regarded as indescribable, that I, like a dumb-mute who has dreamed a vision but is incapable of enunciating a word, have kept in the treasure-house of my heart, withholding them from the eyes and thoughts of the readers.

These subjects I have referred to as "describing the indescribable". Why indescribable? Because, first, where is the power of expression, where is the wisdom and knowledge that would enable me to adequately express and convey true understanding? Secondly, where are those who can truly hear and understand?

In any case, with trembling and feeble hand I now present some samples of such secrets, sharing with the friends a few drops of that ocean. One is the effect of 'Abdu'l-Bahá's glance. Not a description of the Master's eyes; such descriptions have already been recorded by many of the believers, and are all entirely true. Nobody, in fact, could look directly into 'Abdu'l-Bahá's eyes. On His arrival in America (as recounted by the members of His retinue), when the optometrist arrived to examine the Master's eyes he was unable to look directly into them. This matter is well known to those who have attained His presence.

> *Many a king is ensnared by the mystery of thine eyes,*
> *Many a wise one inebriated by the sweet wine of thy love.*

The effect of His glance, however, is my real purpose. First, the look of anger, for which "I seek refuge in God from His wrath". But this look, praised be God, was very rare. Secondly, the glance of love and compassion. This was His permanent and all-encompassing glance, bringing joy and delight. Third, that magnetic, captivating and all-conquering gaze. On many an occasion in the narrow, dark alleys of 'Akká, I have observed non-Bahá'ís who followed us utterly attracted and captivated by 'Abdu'l-Bahá, until dismissed by

Him. This glance had certain characteristics which I cannot even begin to describe.

With a glance, the kings conquer a realm,
With a glance, to the kingdom of hearts you lay claim.

Fourth, the look of satisfaction, which meant "I am well-pleased with you". This look was the same for both the obedient and the rebellious. Fifth, the gaze which perceives through divine power the desire of the one beheld. In this state, I felt that if I asked for sovereignty over the earth and heavens, He would grant it to me – but in that instant one could have no other wish but that which was the will of God. I saw this look many a time. Under its influence, one desires suffering in the path of God. Varqá the martyr, and certain others, hastened to the field of martyrdom under the influence of such a gaze. Sixth, the searching glance, so that the one beheld realized that everything in his heart and mind, from past to future, was laid bare before Him.

Those secrets and deceit that in man may lie hidden,
Before God are clear as daylight, so it is written.

Seventh, and above all, the look that bestows knowledge and understanding. For example, we were witnesses to two individuals who became enraptured with such a glance and received true understanding. One was the late Fáḍil-i-Shírází and the other Shaykh 'Alí-Akbar-i-Qúchání. At the time of their pilgrimage both these believers were men of literary talent and illumined hearts, yet by their own admission they were bereft of true understanding. The Master frequently used to say about both of them with some humour, "You teach the Faith and I teach the Faith. I summoned Shaykh 'Alí-Akbar and said a few words to him. Wait and see how I taught him."

He said the same thing about Fáḍil. We put many questions to these two believers about their experiences while they were in 'Akká, but their answers were not convincing. Yet they both spoke out on the subject of teaching.

Although I was never worthy of that glance, yet I have seen it many times, and will give one example here. One day a number of us were accompanying the Master to one of the houses where Bahá'u'lláh had formerly resided, and He was talking to us on a variety of subjects. Suddenly and quite unexpectedly, He asked, "Khán, how long have you been with us?"

"Five years," I replied

"Five years," He repeated. "The time has come for me to cease speaking and for you to begin understanding. Protect the friends. Go in the care of God," He remarked, and so dismissed me from His presence.

At that moment, not only did I understand 'Abdu'l-Bahá's allusion, but I also knew what had to be done. Siyyid Mihdí-i-Dahají, known as 'Alí-Akbar, outwardly seemed to enjoy 'Abdu'l-Bahá's trust, yet I knew that he was secretly a troublemaker and that unless he himself divulged his true intentions, the Master would never expose him. At present he had deceitfully gathered about him a group of innocent and naïve young men from both the pilgrim and resident groups, and by recounting the details of his time spent in prison in Tehran and Bahá'u'lláh's sentiments of loving-kindness and bounty towards him, had charmed and captivated every one. But, praised be God, by the grace of God I was able to safeguard the friends. His expulsion from the Faith, however, did not become known until three years later, when he himself revealed his true nature.

This, then, was how 'Abdu'l-Bahá looked at us. As for how we looked at that all-powerful Master, the words of Ḥáfiẓ should suffice:

How can any glance perceive you as you really are?
Each one sees only what he can understand.

Return to Iran

During the entire time of my stay at 'Abdu'l-Bahá's threshold, whether during my residency in 'Akká or during my frequent trips to and from that city, I had never given any thought to my ultimate departure and permanent separation from the Beloved of the world. However, as soon as the Most Great Prison was ended and the hands of the Covenant-breakers could no longer weave any more conspiracies or rebellions, I was reminded of 'Abdu'l-Bahá's words before the renewal of the prison conditions. He often said, "Were it not for safeguarding the Most Holy Shrine – for these gentlemen (meaning the Covenant-breakers) will not protect these holy sites – I would travel and teach the Faith." And again, after the overthrow of the Sultanate and Caliphate of 'Abdu'l-Ḥamíd, He used to openly explain to the die-hard Ottomans: "I have to spread the teachings of God around the world."

From these words, it became clear that He considered the security of 'Akká as well as that of the Shrine of the Báb an established fact, the destruction of the Covenant-breakers conclusive, and the probability of His travelling to various destinations very likely.

His words to this servant were similar to those which He had imparted to me during my first visit (twelve years before) as I was departing for Iran. All His instructions were about serving the Faith of God. While the thought of separation and remoteness from that Threshold was unpleasant, yet praised be God, the prevalent atmosphere of joy and happiness that accompanied the defeat of the enemies of the Faith both within and without, and the pleasure and joy of nearness to the Beloved of the world during His time of freedom as He planned His travels to various regions of the world, so delighted our hearts that each living cell of our bodies was in a state of utter bliss.

This time conditions were quite different from the time of my departure for Beirut, for at that time the Beloved of the world had been suffering in the clutches of the people of malice. But this separation did not entail such distressful feelings. As the poet says:

It would take hemlock more bitter than the poison of remoteness
To make me forget the ecstasy of your nearness.

One day we were in the presence of 'Abdu'l-Bahá in Haifa. I was deep in thought and feeling exceptionally happy. I do not know what could have been detected from my face, but suddenly 'Abdu'l-Bahá asked, "Tell me, what are you thinking? Where are you? Tell me the truth now!"

This increased my joy. "I was thinking about the power of God," I explained, "and how divine confirmation has descended upon the whole world, and how within a month's time a group of the enemies of the Faith in Iran received their due punishment at the hand of the dictatorial regime, while simultaneously the Utuzbir incident took place in Turkey whereby thirty-one high-ranking ministers and senior government officials, all inveterate enemies of the Faith, were dispatched to the realm of perdition by the power of the constitutionalists."

The Beloved replied, "It is exactly as you say."

It should not go unstated that one of those enemies of the Faith who was able to escape with his life in the Utuzbir incident was Jamál Páshá. During his administration as Governor he had caused much mischief, but escaped its consequences at the time. Later, he led the Ottoman armies in the First World War, and in the Battle of Egypt vowed to hang the Master once victory was achieved. However, after his defeat he himself was subsequently hanged, and joined the other thirty-one of his colleagues at last.[247]

In brief, it became quite clear from 'Abdu'l-Bahá's utterances that I had to return to Iran. When the Master spoke about my journey, Mírzá Ḥaydar-'Alí commented, "It would be good for him to go to 'Ishqábád and stay there for a while. This would be of much benefit all round."

But 'Abdu'l-Bahá advised, "No, his mother misses him too

much. First he must go to Tehran. Then he may go wherever is suitable."

At that time, Tehran was quite a safe place to live. The Spiritual Assembly, however, was not elected by the body of the friends. The Hands of the Cause elected a number of individuals based on majority vote. There were nineteen of them, and therefore, because of differences in taste and talent, the administration of affairs always lagged behind schedule.

For a few days 'Abdu'l-Bahá continued to speak about Iran until my departure became definite. The kindly and bountiful utterances heaped upon this unworthy sinner by 'Abdu'l-Bahá were now so profuse as to be beyond estimation. The night before my departure, He asked me, "How long have you been with us?"

"Nine years," I replied.

"A sacred number. You will go to Iran and you will do well because your intentions are pure. We are also doing well, because our intentions too are pure." He then pointed towards a large German warship, which had dropped anchor in the port of Haifa, and said, "We have no such fighting ships. But then, all these ships will eventually sink, while our frail skiff will reach its destination."

He spoke at great length in praise of my unworthy services. His words prompted me to look inside myself carefully. I saw nothing but sinfulness, shortcomings, weakness and shame. And yet He had closed His eyes to all that and had accounted them as my service and sacrifice. Then I realized how well the poet Khayyám had written:

> *Where there is blessing, things thou hast not performed*
> *Are considered as done.*

Or in the words of Sá'dí:

> *Let me weep, O heart, as the falling spring rain,*
> *For even the rock laments the lovers' parting pain.*
> *He who has once of parting's bitter wine tasted*

Knows the pain of hope abandoned in those so tested.
Tell the state of my tearful eyes to the caravan driver's men
So they as on a rainy day may pack the beasts of burden.

His words added to my shame and embarrassment. That night I spent sleepless; my tears would not cease.

The next day from morning until dinnertime, I was permitted to attain the presence of 'Abdu'l-Bahá several times. During the entire time I was filled with joy and delight. After dinner, as I took my leave, the Master spoke to me in confidence on some matters that filled my soul with joy and faith. The heavenly breezes that He wafted over me kept me in a state of exaltation as I departed from His presence. A few of the friends, in accordance with the Master's instructions, accompanied me to the dock. As the ship lifted anchor and began to move into open sea, I kept my eyes unwaveringly and as long as I could see, on Mount Carmel.

To heart, the breast is but its home,
And you to heart are a guest well known.

Those with insightful hearts do well
To have you in their hearts forever dwell.

As heart within, so to us are you part,
As life within, so are you our very heart.

To conquer my heart how easy for Thee,
To free it from your love, how hard for me.

The stars, O Thou shining bright as the sun,
Are but the point to which all reverence is done.

True beloved art Thou in Thy lovers' sight,
Thou shining in every assemblage like candle light.

Once the heart's mirror finds a place
Before the light of Thine incomparable face

*Like unto Sinai will it brightly shine
And become the recipient of mysteries divine.*

*If seeing you is but hopeless desire,
Seeking you is hope fulfilled, spirits rising higher.*

*Happy the one whose love for Thee
Resolves every difficulty.*

*In this tempest of love, what my heart hopes for
Is that my ship of wisdom never reaches the shore.*

*My tears fail to extinguish my love's fiery glow,
How can mere mud cover the sun-fountain's flow?*

*O fire burning bright in longing hearts,
Burn away the veils of superstitions and doubts,*

*Burn away this temple, this mortal cage,
So that naught between my beloved and I may emerge.*

*Thy nearness for Afroukhteh, a joy eternally true,
Woe is his lot whose heart is bereft of You.*

Apology

Dear friends, this account which has been presented to you under the title *Memories of Nine Years in 'Akká* is an unworthy attempt on my part to depict that Heavenly Reality, that Celestial Beauty. But no words, whether written or spoken, can describe Him, so that any such attempt is doomed to failure. Furthermore, the literary style of this epistle is quite undeserving of any notice by those friends who have drunk deep of the fountainhead of erudition, literary knowledge and divine wisdom. Considering my lack of the necessary literary skills, and especially the long period which separates me from that pilgrimage, it might have been better for me to have spent the remaining years of my life in silence, wonder and astonishment, for what I witnessed and experienced, compared to this earthly and material life, was heavenly intoxication; it now seems like a dream that ended all too soon. And while pondering on that dream, amazing and unforgettable as it was, I feel that I should begin to interpret it and understand its implications, or at least arise to perform a service to fulfil its ideals. For at that time and in that place, "I was an angel, and the heavenly paradise was my home."[248] And now, if someone were to ask me what I have brought back with me from that other world, I would have to respond hopelessly, "Nothing, nothing".

> *I have neither blooms, not leaves, nor fruits,*
> *I wonder why the wise Gardener planted a seed like me?*

As you read, you will note that this collection is filled with flaws and deficiencies. First, the rules of philosophy, literature and composition have not been observed, and so every line of this story is the product of the natural expression of my feelings, and in no way complies with the requirements of reason and logic. Secondly, I have reflected here the thoughts and emotions of my youth, through the sluggish and all too feeble faculties of my old age, recording these events after the passing of some forty years. Obviously, such a jump across so extensive a time is bound to have invited a good many errors into the text, to say nothing of what may have been lost to mere forgetfulness. Of course, if after so many years no change in the intensity of my feelings and views is detected here, it is strictly due to the bounty of faith and devotion and has nothing to do with any literary or philosophical achievement.

I ask, therefore, that if during the reading of these chapters you have come across stories pleasing or heartwarming to you, you may rest assured that they did not originate in me but rather are the reflections of divine bounty and heavenly confirmations. And if you have found flaws and errors, you may also be assured that they are the reflections of the deficiencies and faults of this unworthy servant, for which I offer my deepest apology.

SELECTED BIOGRAPHICAL NOTES

'Abdu'lláh Khán-i-Núrí, Hájí Mírzá The father-in-law of Várqá the martyr (see below). A resident of Tabriz, he served as attendant to the Crown Prince. See Balyuzi, *Eminent Bahá'ís*, pp. 76–7.

'Abdu'lláh, Mírzá (c. 1843–1918) "kitáb-i-músíqí-i-Írán" ("the book of Persian music"), he was a master of the sitár and the tár. He was the son of 'Alí Akbar Farahání, the foremost court musician under Nasiru'd-Dín Sháh, and followed in his father's footsteps; his system and teaching of Persian classical music is still followed today in Iran's conservatories. 'Abdu'l-Bahá's Tablets to him urge him to "elevate and transform classical music". See Caton, "Bahá'í Influences on Mírzá 'Abdu'lláh", which discusses these Tablets.

'Abdu'l-Ghaní Baydún "A wealthy and influential man who was living in close proximity to the Mansion of Bahjí and had friendly association with the violators of the Covenant" (Taherzadeh, *Covenant*, p. 234). The Commission of Enquiry stayed at his house in 1907; the family had lived on this property since at least the eighteenth century.

'Abdu'l-Hamíd II (ruled 1876–1909) Sultan of the Ottoman Turkish Empire. As a result of the plotting of Mírzá Muhammad-'Alí in 1901 he restricted 'Abdu'l-Bahá's freedom, confining Him and His family within the city walls of 'Akká. He later sent two Commissions of Enquiry to investigate false charges made against 'Abdu'l-Bahá by the Covenant-breakers. He was deposed in 1909 following the Young Turks Revolution of 1908. See Shoghi Effendi, *God Passes By*, pp. 269–72.

Abu'l-Faḍl Gulpáygání, Mírzá (1844–1914) The most celebrated Bahá'í scholar of his generation, noted for his learned treatises on the Bahá'í Faith. *Fará'id* (Priceless Jewels), his response to a critical work by an influential cleric of the time, is considered his masterpiece. It is as yet unpublished in English, although a translation is in preparation. In 1901 'Abdu'l-Bahá sent him to the United States to deepen the American Bahá'ís and to counter the attempts of Kheiralla to create a division within the American Bahá'í community. His grave in Egypt is next to the grave of Lua Getsinger. He was named an Apostle of Bahá'u'lláh by Shoghi Effendi. See Balyuzi, *Eminent Bahá'ís*, pp. 263–5.

Afnán, Áqá Siyyid Aḥmad The rank of martyr was bestowed on him posthumously. See Fayḍí, *Khanidán-i-Afnán*.

Afnán, Áqá Mírzá Hadí The father of Shoghi Effendi, he was the son of Áqá Siyyid Ḥusayn-i-Afnán of Shíráz. See Balyuzi, *Eminent Bahá'ís*, p. 219 (photograph); Taherzadeh, *Covenant*, p. 358.

Afnán, Ḥájí Mírzá Muḥammad-Taqí (Vakílu'd-Dawlih) On reading the Kitáb-i-Íqán he sought out Bahá'u'lláh in Baghdad before returning to Persia to teach the Faith. After the passing of Bahá'u'lláh he carried out the building of the Mashriqu'l-Adhkár in 'Ishqábád. "Never did he fail in servitude, in devotion, and he would set about a major undertaking with alacrity and joy" ('Abdu'l-Bahá, *Memorials*, p. 127). His last days were spent in Haifa; he was named an Apostle of Bahá'u'lláh by Shoghi Effendi. See 'Abdu'l-Bahá, *Memorials*, pp. 126–9; Balyuzi, *Eminent Bahá'ís*, pp. 266–8.

Ahmadov brothers Believers living in Tbilisi, Georgia, whose father Ḥájí Aḥmad met the Báb in Tabriz and hid the remains of the Báb after His martyrdom.

Ákhund, Ḥájí 'Alí-Akbar (Hand of the Cause), see **'Alí-Akbar-i-Shahmírzádí**

'Alí-Akbar-i-Qúchání, Shaykh (d. 1915) A learned and respected Bahá'í teacher, he served the Faith in the Caucasus and India. He was shot while making purchases in the bazaar of his native town and was named a martyr. See Balyuzi, *'Abdu'l-Bahá*, p. 416.

'Alí-Akbar-i-Shahmírzádí, Hájí Mullá (c. 1842–1910) Known as Hájí Ákhund, he was one of the four Hands of the Cause of God appointed by Bahá'u'lláh. On his conversion in about 1861 his religious students in Mashhad forced him to leave the town and thereafter he was frequently arrested and imprisoned. He was responsible for much of the teaching and administration of the Persian Bahá'í community and was named an Apostle of Bahá'u'lláh by Shoghi Effendi. See 'Abdu'l-Bahá, *Memorials*, pp. 9–12; Balyuzi, *Eminent Bahá'ís*, pp. 265–6; Taherzadeh, *Revelation*, vol. 4, pp. 294–301.

'Alí-Muhammad Khán Bahá'í Of Yazd. Once a close associate of Jalálu'd-Dawlih, the Governor of Yazd who instigated the persecutions of 1903, he later became a teacher and principal of the Tarbiyát School for boys in Tehran. See Sulaymání, *Masábíh-i-Hidáyat*.

'Alí-Qulí Khán (Ali Kuli Khan, Nabílu'd-Dawlih, 1879–1966) Distinguished Bahá'í and diplomat who served 'Abdu'l-Bahá in 'Akká as translator before going to the United States in 1901 to translate for Mírzá Abu'l-Fadl. His marriage to Florence Breed in 1904 was the first marriage between a Persian and an American Bahá'í. He was an early translator of some of the most important works of Bahá'u'lláh into English. See Gail, *Summon Up Remembrance* and *Arches of the Years*.

Áqá Ján, Mírzá (d. 1901) The amanuensis of Bahá'u'lláh. As a youth he met Bahá'u'lláh in Karbilá and there became the first to whom Bahá'u'lláh gave a glimpse of His station. He served Bahá'u'lláh for forty years as amanuensis and personal attendant, and was given the title Khádimu'lláh (Servant in attendance). After the passing of Bahá'u'lláh he broke the Covenant and turned against 'Abdu'l-Bahá. See Taherzadeh, *Covenant*, ch. 15.

Áqáy-i-Kalím Mírzá Músá, Muhammad-Qulí. Faithful brother of Bahá'u'lláh, named first among the Apostles of Bahá'u'lláh by Shoghi Effendi. He accompanied Bahá'u'lláh in all His exiles. See 'Abdu'l-Bahá, *Memorials*, pp. 86–90; Balyuzi, *Bahá'u'lláh, The King of Glory*, passim.

Arastú Khán Hakím, Dr. (1877–1934) The grandson of Hakím Masih, the first Bahá'í of Jewish descent. After studying at the American School in Tehran he went to 'Akká in 1900 and stayed for a year. He later practised medicine in Tehran. See *Bahá'í World*, vol. 5, pp. 414–16.

Arjmand, Ḥáj Mihdí (1861–1941) Of Jewish background, he became a well-known teacher of the Bahá'í Faith in Hamadan. His book *Gulshán-i-Ḥaqáyiq* (Rose Garden of Truths) is admired for its apologetic treatment of the relationship of the Bahá'í Faith to Judaism and Christianity. His family established the Haj Mehdi Memorial Trust in his name. See Ayman, "Ḥáj Mihdí Arjmand".

Aṣadu'lláh, Áqá From the city of Qúm, he was a well-known travelling teacher, and remained faithful to the Cause to the end of his life. One of those responsible for making purchases on behalf of 'Abdu'l-Bahá.

Asadu'lláh-i-Iṣfáhání, Mírzá A trusted believer, he was charged with bringing the sacred remains of the Báb from Iran to the Holy Land. After the defection of his son Amín'u'lláh Faríd, he, too, broke the Covenant.

Áshchí, Áqá Ḥusayn Originally from Káshán, he served as cook in the household of Bahá'u'lláh in Adrianople and later in 'Akká. ("Áshchí" means "one who cooks soup".) He also kept the household pharmacy. His memoirs are notable for their eyewitness accounts of the life and times of Bahá'u'lláh. He was one of those involved in the murder of three Azalís in 'Akká, owing to his devotion to Bahá'u'lláh. See Taherzadeh, *Revelation*, vol. 2, pp. 169, 404–8; vol. 3, pp. 13,18, 235–6, 410.

Badí'u'lláh, Mírzá Son of Bahá'u'lláh by his second wife Fáṭimih Khánum (Mahd-i-'Ulyá), he was the younger brother of the Arch-breaker of the Covenant Muḥammad-'Alí and a half-

BIOGRAPHICAL NOTES   431

brother of 'Abdu'l-Bahá. Although he did not initially question
the Will and Testament of Bahá'u'lláh, his activities against
'Abdu'l-Bahá led to his becoming a Covenant-breaker. His short-
lived repentance is recounted in this book. See Taherzadeh,
Covenant, pp. 117, 150–53.

Baghdádí, Áqá Muḥammad Muṣṭafá Devoted believer in
Baghdad from the time of Bahá'u'lláh's sojourn in Iraq. "He was
the leader, among all the friends in 'Iráq, and after the great separation, when the convoy of the Beloved left for Constantinople,
he remained loyal and staunch, and openly, publicly, observed by
all, taught the Faith" ('Abdu'l-Bahá, *Memorials*, p. 132). He later
asked for permission to live nearer 'Akká, and was granted leave
to establish his residence in Beirut. Here he assisted travelling
pilgrims. His son **Zia Mabsout Baghdádí** (d. 1937) was a student in Beirut during the author's time there. After qualifying as
a medical doctor he settled in the United States in 1909 and was
a prominent member of the Chicago Bahá'í community. See
Bahá'í World, vol. 7, pp. 535–9.

Báqiroff (Khamsi), Siyyid Naṣru'lláh (1857–1925) One of
five brothers who were honoured by Bahá'u'lláh with the title
"Sádat-i-Khams". He used his considerable wealth in the service
of the Cause, particularly in offering the major share of the
expenses of 'Abdu'l-Bahá's travels in Europe and America. A
member for many years of the Spiritual Assembly of Tehran,
when news of the passing of 'Abdu'l-Bahá reached that body but
before His Will and Testament was read, in the midst of shock
and grief Báqiroff is reported to have said, "Praised be God, the
Faith has become young." See Balyuzi, *Eminent Bahá'ís*, p. 64
(and photograph); Mehrabkhani, *Sádat-i-Khams*, a history of the
Khamsi family.

Breakwell, Thomas (1872–1902) Early English Bahá'í. He
became a Bahá'í in Paris in 1901, and died there of consumption
after his pilgrimage to 'Akká. Shoghi Effendi called him a "lumi-
nary in the firmament of the Faith of Bahá'u'lláh". See *Bahá'í
World*, vol. 7, pp. 801–2; Balyuzi, *'Abdu'l-Bahá*, pp. 74–80. 'Abdu'l-
Bahá's Tablet in his memory is printed in *Selections*, pp. 187–9.

Brittingham, Isabella (1852–1924) Eminent American Bahá'í teacher and travelling teacher. Author of *The Revelation of Bahä-ulläh in a sequence of four lessons*; first published in 1902 by the Bahai Publishing Society in Chicago, it went into at least nine editions. She went on pilgrimage in 1901 shortly after the renewal of restrictions on 'Abdu'l-Bahá, and again in 1909. She travelled the United States, teaching constantly and sending letters from new believers to 'Abdu'l-Bahá. Named a Disciple of 'Abdu'l-Bahá by Shoghi Effendi. See Whitehead, *Some Early Bahá'ís*, pp. 131–8.

Búrújirdí, Áqá Jamál During the lifetime of Bahá'u'lláh he received much praise and various honorary titles such as Ismu'lláh'u'l-Jamál (The Name of God, Jamál) due to his many services, but broke the Covenant after the ascension of Bahá'u'lláh and rose in opposition to the Centre of the Covenant, 'Abdu'l-Bahá. He was known in the Bahá'í community as "Hyena" or "Old Hyena" (*pír-i-kaftár*). See Taherzadeh, *Revelation*, vol. 2, pp. 118–19, 264–7.

Bushru'í, Mírzá Badí'. A student contemporary with the author at the Syrian Protestant College in Beirut. During World War I he ran a school at the village of Abú-Sinán for the children of the Bahá'ís. A companion of 'Abdu'l-Bahá for many years in the Holy Land.

Canavarro, Countess Marie de Souza Known as Sister Sanghamitta, she was the first woman to convert to Buddhism on American soil, in 1897. She lectured on Buddhism in Asia and the West, wrote books and articles about the religion, and ran a Buddhist school for girls in Sri Lanka. See Tweed, *The American Encounter with Buddhism*; Bartholomeusz, *Women under the Bo Tree*.

Díyá'u'lláh, Mírzá Son of Bahá'u'lláh by His second wife Fátimih Khánúm (Mahd-i-'Ulyá), he was the younger brother of the Arch-breaker of the Covenant Muhammad-'Alí, full brother of Mírzá Badí'u'llah, and a half-brother of 'Abdu'l-Bahá. A weak, vacillating man, he eventually broke the Covenant. See Taherzadeh, *Covenant*, pp. 117, 150–53.

BIOGRAPHICAL NOTES 433

Dodge, Arthur Pillsbury (1849–1915) Lawyer, publisher, and inventor, he became a Bahá'í in 1897. He was named a Disciple of 'Abdu'l-Bahá by Shoghi Effendi. See Stockman, *Bahá'í Faith in America*, vol. 1, pp. 116–17 and *Star of the West*, vol. 6, no. 13, pp. 100–101. His sons **Wendell Phillips Dodge** and **William Copeland Dodge** studied the Faith as young men with Ibrahim Kheiralla. Following their pilgrimage in 1901 they published *Utterances of Abdul Beha Abbas to two young men, American pilgrims to Acre, 1901*.

Dreyfus, Hippolyte (1873–1928) The first French Bahá'í, in 1901. A prominent French lawyer, he wrote a number of works on the Bahá'í Faith and translated several of Bahá'u'lláh's writings into French. He was instrumental in writing and presenting petitions to the Shah in September 1902 in Paris and again during the Yazd and Isfahan persecutions of 1903 (see *Star of the West*, vol. 15, p. 230, and Metelmann, *Lua Getsinger*, pp. 59–61). In 1911 he married Laura Clifford Barney with whom he had worked on a French translation of *Some Answered Questions*. Dreyfus was a devoted Bahá'í and was named a Disciple of 'Abdu'l-Bahá by Shoghi Effendi. See Shoghi Effendi's appreciation of him in *Bahá'í World*, vol. 3, pp. 210–14.

Dreyfus-Barney, Laura (1879–1974) From a prominent American family, she accepted the Faith in Paris around 1900. She made a number of extended visits to 'Akká, asking questions of 'Abdu'l-Bahá, the answers to which she later compiled as *Some Answered Questions* (see the description in this book, pp. 314–19, 342–4.) She was active in the promotion of the human rights of women and was twice decorated by the French government for services to humanity. See *Bahá'í World*, vol. 16, pp. 535–8.

Fádil-i-Shírází (Shaykh Muḥammad Ibráhim, 1863–1935) An eminent Muslim scholar of literature and philosophy, he accepted the Bahá'í Faith through reading the Writings of Bahá'u'lláh, who gave him the title "Fáḍil" (learned, man of culture and refinement). His own writings are mainly in logic and apologetics. He undertook the pilgrimage to 'Akká during the ministry of 'Abdu'l-Bahá and received several Tablets from Him. See Sulaymání, *Maṣábíḥ-i-Hidáyat*, vol. 1.

Faezeh Khánum (Gulsurkh Begum, c. 1856–c.1930) A courageous believer during the ministry of 'Abdu'l-Bahá, she was the daughter of a Muslim cleric who secretly believed in the Báb and advised her to seek Him out. She became a Bahá'í in Tehran, upsetting her husband who however came to accept the Faith. She was given the name "Faezeh" (the one who attains, victorious) by 'Abdu'l-Bahá. Her services to the Faith were many and varied: teaching, writing a plea to the Shah for justice together with other Bahá'í women, and selling her house as a contribution to the construction of the House of Worship in 'Ishqábád. Often persecuted, she was on one occasion so badly beaten by a mob that she lost the sight of one eye. She received numerous Tablets from 'Abdu'l-Bahá and wrote poems addressed to Him. Her pilgrimage took place in 1898. See Arbáb, *Akhtaran-i-Tábán*, vol. 1.

Faríd (Fareed), Amín'u'lláh Son of Mírzá Asadu'lláh-i-Iṣfáhání. Faríd was educated by the Master and accompanied him to the United States as one of His translators, but caused 'Abdu'l-Bahá much anxiety and grief because of his "erratic and damaging behaviour" (Balyuzi, *'Abdu'l-Bahá*, p. 230). He became a Covenant-breaker in 1914.

Faríq Páshá Turkish government official in 'Akká. As General he led the Turks against the Greeks in 1897 in Syria.

Farmer, Sarah Jane (1847–1916) American philanthropist who became a Bahá'í upon meeting 'Abdu'l-Bahá in 'Akká in 1900. She gave Green Acre, her property in Eliot, Maine, to the Faith for use as a permanent Bahá'í summer school. She was named a Disciple of 'Abdu'l-Bahá by Shoghi Effendi. See Martin, *Life and Work*.

Getsinger, Lua (Louisa Moore, 1871–1916) Outstanding American Bahá'í who accepted the Faith in Chicago in April 1897. She and her husband, Edward, played a central role in opposing Kheiralla and other Covenant-breakers. Lua devoted nearly all her time to teaching the Faith and spent much time away from home; she also made several extended visits to 'Akká. She died in Egypt of an illness she had contracted in India, and

BIOGRAPHICAL NOTES

is buried in Cairo next to Mírzá Abu'l-Faḍl. She was given the title "Herald of the Covenant" by 'Abdu'l-Bahá and was named a Disciple of 'Abdu'l-Bahá and "Mother Teacher of the West" by Shoghi Effendi. See *Bahá'í World*, vol.8, pp. 642–3 and Metelmann, *Lua Getsinger*.

Goodall, Helen (1847–1922). She accepted the Faith in 1898 and with her daughter Ella Cooper helped establish the first Bahá'í community on the West Coast of the United States, in Oakland. After her first pilgrimage in 1908 she and her daughter published *Daily Lessons Received at Acca*. She was named a Disciple of 'Abdu'l-Bahá by Shoghi Effendi. See Whitehead, *Some Early Bahá'ís of the West*, pp. 21–34.

Greatest Holy Leaf, Bahíyyih Khánum (1846–1932) Daughter of Bahá'u'lláh and Navváb, and sister of 'Abdu'l-Bahá, she was designated by Shoghi Effendi as "the outstanding heroine of the Bahá'í Dispensation". She accompanied Bahá'u'lláh in every stage of His exiles and imprisonment, and after His passing stood by her brother 'Abdu'l-Bahá and assisted Him greatly when the activities of the Covenant-breakers were at their height. After the passing of 'Abdu'l-Bahá, the youthful Guardian, overwhelmed by the responsibilities thrust upon him, left the affairs of the Cause in the hands of Bahíyyih Khánum while he retired to recuperate and contemplate the tasks ahead. See Shoghi Effendi, *God Passes By*, p. 216; *Bahíyyih Khánum, The Greatest Holy Leaf*.

Ḥaydar-'Alí, Ḥájí Mírzá, of Iṣfáhán (c. 1834–1920) He became first a Bábí and later met Bahá'u'lláh in Adrianople. For fifty years he served the Cause of God and endured much hardship including imprisonment in Egypt and Sudan. In his later years he served the Master in Haifa. His best-known publications are the partially translated *Bihjatu's-Ṣudúr* (Delight of Hearts) and *Dalail'u'l-Irfán* (Proofs of the Knowledge of God). See Balyuzi, "The Angel of Mount Carmel", in *Eminent Bahá'ís*, pp. 237–50.

Hoar, William H. (1856–1922) Hoar heard of the Faith at the World Parliament of Religions in Chicago in 1893 and became a Bahá'í in 1896. In 1900 he was instrumental in forming the first Bahá'í consultative body in New York, the New York Board of Counsel. He served on the Executive Board of the Bahá'í Temple Unity from 1909–1912. He was named a Disciple of 'Abdu'l-Bahá by Shoghi Effendi. See Harris, "William H. Hoar".

Ḥusayn Effendi Tabrízí Resident in Haifa, "he faithfully waited upon the believers, and his home was a way station for Bahá'í travellers". His life is described by 'Abdu'l-Bahá, *Memorials*, pp. 118–19.

Ḥusayn Effendi, buried in 'Akká. Son of 'Abdu'l-Bahá who died in childhood.

Ismá'íl Áqá (d. 1939). Servant in the household of 'Abdu'l-Bahá, also gardener. He served 'Abdu'l-Bahá devotedly for thirty years and was present at His passing. See *Bahá'í World*, vol. 8, p. 681.

Ismu'lláh'u'l-Jamál, see **Búrújirdí**.

Jackson, Mrs. Tewksbury American Bahá'í resident in Paris in the late 19th and early 20th centuries. She made the pilgrimage to 'Akká several times and used her considerable wealth in the service of the Faith. Her apartment in Paris gave hospitality to Bahá'ís such as Lua Getsinger and May Bolles. Thomas Breakwell's first encounter with the Faith took place there. 'Abdu'l-Bahá visited her there in 1911 on hearing she was in ill health.

Jahrumí, Mullá Ḥusayn Notorious Covenant-breaker in Bombay (see note 64).

Jalál, Mírzá A son of the King of Martyrs and a son-in law of 'Abdu'l-Bahá, he later broke the Covenant.

Jamál Páshá, Ahmad (1872–1922) Turkish politician and general. One of the chiefs of the Committee of Union and Progress during World War I. He was Minister of Public Works (1913) and

BIOGRAPHICAL NOTES 437

Minister for the Navy (1914), and Commander of the 4th Army in Syria from 1915–1917, His meetings with 'Abdu'l-Bahá are described by Balyuzi, *'Abdu'l-Bahá*, pp. 412–14. However, swayed by the accusations of the Covenant-breakers, he vowed to crucify the Master. After the War he became a refugee in Berlin, and then in Switzerland. In Afghanistan as inspector general of the Afghan Army, he made contact with the Bolsheviks in Moscow and in Tashkent in 1920. He was assassinated at Tiflis in 1922. See Larousse, *Grand dictionnaire encyclopédique*.

Kern, Margaret Early American believer in New York City by about 1897. Her poem "The Rustle of His Robe" was published in 1901. See Stockman, vol. 1, pp. 121, 226.

Kheiralla (Khayru'lláh), Ibráhím George (1849–1929) Syrian Christian who became a Bahá'í around 1888. He migrated to the United States in 1892 and was instrumental in establishing the Faith there. He began to question the authority of 'Abdu'l-Bahá in 1900 and eventually broke with the Bahá'í Faith, creating a crisis in the Bahá'í community. See Stockman, *Bahá'í Faith in America*, vol. 1, pp. 158–84.

Khusraw Servant in the household of 'Abdu'l-Bahá. Of Burmese origin, he was the Master's personal servant, accompanying Him to Eygypt, but was prevented from continuing to the United States. His marriage took place in the week before 'Abdu'l-Bahá's passing. See Balyuzi, *'Abdu'l-Bahá*, p. 400.

Majdu'd-Dín, Mírzá The son of Áqáy-i-Kalím, the faithful brother of Bahá'u'lláh. Majdu'd-Dín became a Covenant-breaker and one of the bitterest enemies of 'Abdu'l-Bahá. See Taherzadeh, *Covenant*, p. 148.

Manshádí, Hájí Siyyid Muhammad Taqí A faithful and devoted servant of Bahá'u'lláh who with his brother Ja'far followed Him from Adrianople to 'Akká. The Covenant-breakers attempted to win him to their cause but he remained loyal to 'Abdu'l-Bahá. Tablets and letters were sent and received through him, at first through his residence in Haifa and later in Port Said at 'Abdu'l-Bahá's request. See 'Abdu'l-Bahá, *Memorials*, pp. 54–57.

Mihdí-i-Dahají, Siyyid known as 'Alí-Akbar. Entitled by Bahá'u'lláh "Ismu'lláh'u'l- Mihdí" (The Name of God, He who is guided) he became a Covenant-breaker during the Ministry of 'Abdu'l-Bahá. The name 'Alí-Akbar was also bestowed on him by Bahá'u'lláh in remembrance of Siyyid Mihdí's nephew, a faithful believer greatly loved by Bahá'u'lláh and for whom the Fire Tablet was revealed. See Taherzadeh, *Revelation*, vol. 2, pp. 272–275.

Mishkín-Qalam Title of Mírzá Ḥusayn Iṣfáhání, the famous Bahá'í calligrapher, who attained the presence of Bahá'u'lláh in Adrianople. He was banished to Cyprus by the Ottoman government in 1868. After gaining his freedom he returned to 'Akká and continued to work at his art producing a range of magnificent calligraphies over the years. He was named an Apostle of Bahá'u'lláh by Shoghi Effendi. See Balyuzi, *Eminent Bahá'ís*, pp. 270–72.

Mu'ayyad, Dr Ḥabíbu'lláh Khudábakhsh (1888–1971) Born to a Bahá'í family of Jewish heritage, he was a student contemporary of the author at the Syrian Protestant College in Beirut in 1909, Dr. Mu'ayyad served the Master in several capacities. In 1914 he was sent to Germany to counter the activities of Dr. Faríd. During World War I he ran a dispensary at Abú-Sinán where he carried out operations with the assistance of Lua Getsinger (Balyuzi, *'Abdu'l-Bahá*, p. 411). His memoirs *Khátirát-i-Ḥabíb* are notable for their pen-pictures of 'Abdu'l-Bahá. His poem "Dastam-Beguir" is well known in the West. He was a member of the National Spiritual Assembly of Iran for many years.

Moody, Dr. Susan I. (1851–1934) American physician who became a Bahá'í in 1903 in Chicago. At 'Abdu'l-Bahá's invitation she went to Persia in 1909 to provide medical care for the Bahá'í women. She founded the Tarbiyát Girls' School in Tehran in 1910, and lived in Persia for 15 years. See *Bahá'í World*, vol. 11, pp. 483–6.

Muḥammad-'Alí, Mírzá (1853–1937) Younger half-brother of 'Abdu'l-Bahá. The Arch-breaker of Bahá'u'lláh's Covenant after

His ascension, he was given the title "Centre of Sedition" by the Master. See Shoghi Effendi, *God Passes By*, pp. 246, 249, and Taherzadeh, *Covenant*, pp. 125–34.

Muḥammad Ḥasan, Áqá Caretaker of the pilgrim house in 'Akká. "Single-handedly, thrice a day he prepared the pilgrims' meals, cleared the rooms, shopped for provisions, cooked, washed the dishes ... [he] greatly loved to engage in discussion ... he was truly learned, particularly in the areas of mysticism, philosophy and proofs." (Mu'ayyad, *Khátirát-i-Habíb*).

Muḥammad Javád-i-Qazvíní "One of the most inveterate adversaries of 'Abdu'l-Bahá" (Balyuzi, *'Abdu'l-Bahá*, p. 86). A devoted believer during the time of Bahá'u'lláh, Who gave him the title Ismulláh'u'l-Jud (the name of God, the Generous). He became a Covenant-breaker during the ministry of 'Abdu'l-Bahá. His son **Ghulámu'lláh** was one of those sent to America by the Covenant-breakers to help Kheiralla in his bid for power.

Muḥammad-i-Qá'iní, Áqá (Nabíl-i-Akbar) A "man without likeness or peer ... a universal man" ('Abdu'l-Bahá, *Memorials*, p. 1). A scholar and mujtahid, he met Bahá'u'lláh in Baghdad and became a believer. The title "Nabíl-i-Akbar" was given him by Bahá'u'lláh; he was also known as Fáḍil-i-Qá'iní (the learned one of Qá'in). Bahá'u'lláh's Lawḥ-i-Hikmat (Tablet of Wisdom) was addressed to him. A fearless teacher of the Cause, he was persecuted and died in poverty. Named by 'Abdu'l-Bahá posthumously as a Hand of the Cause. See 'Abdu'l-Bahá, *Memorials*, pp. 1–5.

Munír, Áqá Mírzá Son of Mírzá Muḥammad-Qulí, Áqáy-i-Kalím. Served as amanuensis for the Persian text of *Some Answered Questions*.

Munír-i-Zayn A son of Zaynu'l-Muqarrabin, he served as one of the Master's secretaries, accompanying Him to Egypt in 1910, but was prevented from going to America with Him. See Balyuzi, *'Abdu'l-Bahá*, pp. 135, 176, 399.

Músá-i-Javahirí, Ḥájí Mírzá Surnamed Ḥarf-i-Baqá (Letter of Eternity, Immortal Letter), a title bestowed on him by Bahá'u'lláh). He was the original owner of the House of Bahá'u'lláh in Baghdad, and a devoted servant of Bahá'u'lláh. See 'Abdu'l-Bahá, *Memorials*, pp. 108–16 under Mírzá Muḥammad-i-Vakíl; Taherzadeh, *Revelation*, vol. 1, pp. 211–12.

Nabíl-i-Akbar see **Muḥammad-i-Qá'iní**

Nabíl-i-Zarandi, Nabíl-i-A'ẓam (d. 1892) Title of Muḥammad-i-Zarandí, a devoted and fearless follower of Bahà'u'llàh who served the Cause in various capacities. He was a tireless teacher of the Faith and an accomplished poet and scholar. Among others, he taught the Faith to Áqá Buzurg Khurásání known as Badí', Bahá'u'lláh's emissary to Náṣiri'd-Dín Sháh who sacrificed his life to complete his mission, as well as to the wife of the Báb who became a devoted believer in the Cause of God. Nabíl was given the title Nabíl-i-A'ẓam (the most great Nabíl) by Bahá'u'lláh and is referred to by the beloved Guardian as "His Poet-Laureate, His chronicler and His indefatigable disciple" (Shoghi Effendi, *God Passes By*, p. 130). Grief-stricken, he drowned himself after the passing of the Blessed Beauty. He is the author of the well-known history, *The Dawn-Breakers*. He was named an Apostle of Bahá'u'lláh by Shoghi Effendi. See Balyuzi, *Eminent Bahá'ís*, pp. 268–70.

Na'ím, Mírzá Muḥammad Eminent Bahá'í poet and teacher. See Sulaymani, *Masáabiḥ-i-Hidáyat*; Taherzadeh, *Revelation*, vol.3, pp. 389–93.

Núru'd-Dín-i-Zayn, Mírzá Son of Zaynu'l-Muqarrabín. He later attended 'Abdu'l-Bahá to Egypt in 1910. See Balyuzi, *'Abdu'l-Bahá*, p. 135.

Phelps, Myron H. A prominent member of the New York Bar, he heard of the Bahá'í Faith in London. Although he never became a Bahá'í, his book *Abbas Effendi, His Life and Teachings* was for many years one of the best-known accounts of 'Abdu'l-Bahá in English, despite its various inaccuracies. These are well described by Stockman, vol. 2, pp. 236–8, and in Marzieh Gail's

BIOGRAPHICAL NOTES 441

Preface to the 1985 edition of Phelps' book (*The Master in 'Akká*, Los Angeles: Kalimát Press).

Remey, Charles Mason (1874–1974) Remey became a Bahá'í in Paris in 1899 and served the Faith devotedly for many years in various capacities. Appointed a Hand of the Cause of God in 1951, he was appointed president of the International Bahá'í Council the same year, but after the passing of Shoghi Effendi in 1957 he broke the Covenant and was declared a Covenantbreaker in 1960. See Harper, *Lights of Fortitude*, pp. 287–306.

Riḍáy-i-Qannád, Áqá Muḥammad Also known as Áqá Riḍá of Shiraz. Believer exiled with Bahá'u'lláh to 'Akká. Between Baghdad and Constantinople he and Áqá Mírzá Maḥmúd travelled ahead of the party to prepare the food and make arrangements for the comfort of the believers. In 'Akká he continued to serve the Holy Family, purchasing goods and keeping accounts. See 'Abdu'l-Bahá, *Memorials*, pp. 39–41.

Rawḥání, Mírzá 'Alí-Akbar Khán, Muḥibu'ṣ-Sulṭán. Secretary of the Spiritual Assembly of Tehran for many years and responsible for publishing in Tehran. Known also as a calligrapher.

Ruḥú'lláh see **Varqá**.

Ṣadru'l-'ulamá, Ḥájí Áqá Honoured by the pen of 'Abdu'l-Bahá with the title of **Ṣadru's-Ṣudur**. Islamic scholar originally from Hamadan, "reportedly eulogized and praised by 'Abdu'l-Bahá" (Ayman, "Ḥáj Mihdí Arjmand", pp. 9–10). He was the first to receive instructions from 'Abdu'l-Bahá to initiate teacher-training classes in Tehran. See also Rastigár's biography of him.

Salmán, Shaykh Early believer who made the journey from Persia to 'Akká every year on foot to carry Tablets from Bahá'u'lláh for distribution among the friends in Persia. He also conducted Munírih Khánum to 'Akká before her marriage to 'Abdu'l-Bahá. See 'Abdu'l-Bahá, *Memorials*, pp. 13–16; Taherzadeh, *Revelation*, vol. 1, p. 113; Balyuzi, *King of Glory*, pp. 344–7, 441–4.

Samandar, title of **Shaykh** Kazim **Qazvíní**, the recipient of the Tablet of Fu'ád. He was the son of Muḥammad Nabíl. This title was bestowed upon him by Bahá'u'lláh during whose ministry, as well as the ministry of 'Abdu'l-Bahá, he performed exemplary service in the teaching work as well as the promotion of solidarity and love within the Bahá'í community.

Samandarí, Ṭarázu'lláh (d. 1968) Son of Samandar (see above). In his youth he attained the presence of Bahá'u'lláh. He served with distinction during the ministries of 'Abdu'l-Bahá and the Guardian, and was among the first contingent to be named a Hand of the Cause by the beloved Guardian in December 1951. His services continued until his death at the age of 94.

Sanderson, Edith Early American Bahá'í in Paris, from 1901. She went on pilgrimage several times and had the honour of receiving 'Abdu'l-Bahá in her mother's home in Paris in 1912. Shoghi Effendi refers to her "long record [of] historic services" (*Bahá'í World*, vol. 13, pp. 889–90).

Shu'á'u'lláh, Mírzá Son of the Arch-breaker of the Covenant Mírzá Muḥammad-'Alí, who sent him to the United States in 1905 to help Kheiralla in creating a breach in the ranks of the Bahá'í Community. In 1912 during 'Abdu'l-Bahá's visit he made every effort to neutralize the influence of the Master but was unsuccessful in winning converts to his father's cause.

Spencer, Louise, see **Waite**.

Sulaymán Khán One of the leaders of the Bábí Faith, martyred by having his body pierced in several places and inserting lighted candles in the wounds. He danced the whole time singing songs of love for his beloved Báb.

Ṭáhirih Khánum Notable Bahá'í in Tehran, described as "an enlightened soul, holding advanced ideas, not gleaned from foreign sources, but evolved through personal work and service" (Remey, *Observations*, 2nd ed., p. 106, quoted in Stockman, vol. 2, p. 292).

BIOGRAPHICAL NOTES 443

Vakílu'd-Dawlih see **Afnán, Ḥájí Mírzá Muḥammad-Taqí**

Varqá, Mírzá 'Alí-Muḥammad With his 13-year-old son **Rúḥú'lláh** he was martyred in Tehran by the brutal Ḥájibu'd-Dawlih under the most cruel circumstances in May 1896. Rúḥu'lláh was forced to watch the murder of his father but nevertheless refused to renounce his faith and was strangled by the executioner. Varqá is considered to be one of the most distinguished teachers and poets of the Bahá'í Faith. He was named by 'Abdu'l-Bahá posthumously as a Hand of the Cause of God. See 'Abdu'l-Bahá, *Memorials*, p. 5; Shoghi Effendi, *God Passes By*, p. 296; Balyuzi, *Eminent Bahá'ís*, Ch. 7.

Varqá, Mírzá 'Azízu'lláh Khán Son of the martyred Mírzá 'Alí-Muḥammad Várqá, brother of the Hand of the Cause Mírzá Valíyu'lláh Khán Várqá, and uncle of the Hand of the Cause Dr. 'Ali Muḥammad Várqá. See photograph in Balyuzi, *Eminent Bahá'ís*, p. 81.

Vujdání, Yúsuf Khán (d. 1934) A well-known teacher whose life spanned the ministries of Bahá'u'lláh, 'Abdu'l-Bahá and Shoghi Effendi. A descendant of Fatḥ-'Alí Sháh, his early life was spent at Court, but this could not satisfy his quest for truth. After becoming a Bahá'í he received a Tablet from Bahá'u'lláh and later served 'Abdu'l-Bahá in India and Iran, where he was injured by fanatical mobs and subsequently exiled. In the early years of the twentieth century he resided in Haifa where he taught the young Bahá'í children. See Sulaymání, *Maṣábiḥ-i-Hidáyat*, vol. 2, p. 3; *Bahá'í World*, vol. 5, p. 413 (photograph only).

Waite, Louise Spencer Given the Persian name "Sháhnaz" by 'Abdu'l-Bahá. American Bahá'í, musician and poet. See *Bahá'í World*, vol. 8, pp. 661–64.

Winterburn, G.T. and Rosa Winterburn Early American Bahá'ís in Paris, they were among the signatories of the 1903 petition to the Sháh presented by Hippolyte Dreyfus and Lua Getsinger, appealing to him to stop the persecutions of Bahá'ís in Yazd and Isfahan. Their account of their six-day pilgrimage in February 1904, *Table Talks with 'Abdu'l-Bahá*, was translated by Youness Khán and published in 1915. On their return to the United States they settled in Tropico, California.

Yaḥyá, Mírzá, Subḥ-i-Azal (c.1832–1912) Younger half-brother of Bahá'u'lláh, he rebelled against Him and claimed to be the successor of the Báb. When Bahá'u'lláh was banished to 'Akka in 1868, Azal was exiled to Cyprus where he spent the rest of his life. See Shoghi Effendi, *God Passes By*, pp. 112–27; Taherzadeh, *Covenant*, pp. 60–96.

Yamamoto, Kanichi (1879–1961) First Japanese Bahá'í. He learned of the Faith in Hawaii and became a Bahá'í in 1902 at the age of 23. In 1903 he left Hawaii to become a butler to Helen Goodall's family in Oakland, California. He arranged the meeting at the Japanese YMCA at which 'Abdu'l-Bahá spoke on 7 October 1912. See *Bahá'í World*, vol. 13, pp. 931–3; Whitehead, *Some Bahá'ís to Remember*, pp. 176–86.

Zaynu'l-Muqarrabín (1818–1903) Title of Mullá Zaynu'l-'Ábidín of Najafábád, Iṣfáhán, who according to 'Abdu'l-Bahá is accounted among the Disciples of the Báb and Apostles of Bahá'u'lláh. From a clerical family, he was persecuted for his Bahá'í belief and exiled to Mosul with other believers from Baghdad; there his leadership and guidance were instrumental in building a model Bahá'í community. "Noted among the companions of Bahá'u'lláh for his wit and humour, his learning and calligraphy, but above all for Bahá'u'lláh's high regard for him." (Balyuzi, *Eminent Bahá'ís*, p. 274.) Because of his skills, Bahá'u'lláh instructed him to transcribe His Tablets. All Tablets in the hand of Zaynu'l-'Ábidín, according to 'Abdu'l-Bahá, are considered authentic. See 'Abdu'l-Bahá, *Memorials*, pp. 150–53.

BIBLIOGRAPHY

'Abdu'l-Bahá. *Memorials of the Faithful.* Trans. Marzieh Gail. Wilmette, Ill.: Bahá'í Publishing Trust, 1971.
—*The Promulgation of Universal Peace.* Compiled by Howard MacNutt. Wilmette, Ill.: Bahá'í Publishing Trust, 2nd edn. 1982.
—*Selections from the Writings of 'Abdu'l-Bahá.* Comp. Research Dept. Trans. Marzieh Gail et al. Haifa: Bahá'í World Centre, 1978.
—*Some Answered Questions.* Comp. and Trans. Laura Clifford Barney. Wilmette, Ill.: Bahá'í Publishing Trust, 4th edn. 1981. First published as *Some Answered Questions*, and *An-Núru'l-Abhá Fí Mufáwaḍat 'Abdi'l-Bahá*, collected by Laura Clifford Barney (Kegan Paul, Trench, Trubner & Co.Ltd., London, 1908); *Les Leçons de St-Jean-d'Acre* (Leroux, Paris, 1908).
Afroukhteh, Youness. *Irtibat-i-Sharq va Gharb* (Union of the East and West). Unpublished.
Alexander, Agnes Baldwin. *Forty Years of the Bahá'í Cause in Hawaii, 1904–1942. Personal Recollections of a Bahá'í Life in the Hawaiian Islands.* Rev. edn. Honolulu: National Spiritual Assembly of the Bahá'ís of the Hawaiian Islands, 1974.
Arbáb, Forúq. *'Akhtarán-i-Tábán.* Vol.1. Tehran, 126 B.E. (1969).
Ayman, Iraj. "Ḥáj Mihdí Arjmand", in Moojan Momen (ed.), *Scripture and Revelation.* Bahá'í Studies Series, vol. 3. Oxford: George Ronald, 1997.
Bahá'í Prayers.A Selection of Prayers Revealed by Bahá'u'lláh, the Báb and 'Abdu'l-Bahá. Wilmette, Ill.: Bahá'í Publishing Trust, 1982.
Bahá'í World, The. Vol. 3, 1928–1930; vol. 5, 1932–1934; vol. 7, 1936–1938; vol. 8, 1938–1940; vol. 11, 1946–1950. Wilmette, Ill.: Bahá'í Publishing Trust, various years. Vol. 13, 1954–1963. Haifa: The Universal House of Justice, 1970. Vol. 16, 1976–1979. Haifa: Bahá'í World Centre, 1981.

Bahá'u'lláh. *Epistle to the Son of the Wolf*. Trans. Shoghi Effendi. Wilmette, Ill.: Bahá'í Publishing Trust, 1962.
—*The Hidden Words*. Trans. Shoghi Effendi. Wilmette, Ill.: Bahá'í Publishing Trust, 1985.
—*The Kitáb-i-Aqdas: The Most Holy Book*. Haifa: Bahá'í World Centre, 1992.
—*Tablets of Bahá'u'lláh Revealed after the Kitáb-i-Aqdas*. Comp. Research Department. Trans. Habib Taherzadeh et al. Wilmette, Ill: Bahá'í Publishing Trust, 2nd edn. 1978.
Bahíyyih Khánum: The Greatest Holy Leaf. Research Department of the Universal House of Justice. Haifa: Bahá'í World Centre, 1982.
Balyuzi, H. M. *'Abdu'l-Baha: The Centre of the Covenant of Bahá'u'lláh*. George Ronald: Oxford, 1971.
—*Bahá'u'lláh, the King of Glory*. Oxford: George Ronald, 2nd edn. 1991.
—*Eminent Bahá'ís in the Time of Bahá'u'lláh*. Oxford: George Ronald, 1985.
—*Muhammad and the Course of Islám*. George Ronald: Oxford, 1976.
Bartholomeusz, Tessa. *Women Under the Bo Tree*. New York: Cambridge University Press, 1994.
Baudelaire, Charles. *L'étranger*, in *Le spleen de Paris*. Paris: Le Livre de Poche, Librairie Générale Française, 1964.
Bezai, N. Z., *Tasqirih-i-Shua'ráyyih Qam-i-Avval-Bahá'í* (Biographies of the Poets of the First Bahá'í Century) vol. 2. Tehran: Bahá'í Publishing Trust, 1970.
Bible. *Holy Bible*. Revised Standard Version. London: Collins, 1952.
Book of Common Prayer.
Canavarro, Marie de Souza. "Insight into the Far East", (1925), in T.A. Tweed and Stephen Prothero (eds.), *Asian Religions in America: A Documentary History*. New York and Oxford: Oxford University Press, 1999.
Carus, Paul. *The Gospel of Buddha according to old records*. New York: Open Court Publishing Co, 1894.
Caton, Margaret L. "Bahá'í Influences on Mírzá 'Abdu'lláh, Qájár Court Musician and Master of the *Radíf*", in Cole and Momen, 1984.
Compilation of Compilations, The. Research Department of the Universal House of Justice, 1963–1990. 2 vols. Sydney: Bahá'í Publications Australia, 1991.
Cole, Juan R., and Momen, Moojan. *From Iran East and West*.

Studies in Bábí and Bahá'í History, vol.2. Los Angeles: Kalimát Press, 1984.
Dodge, Wendell Phillips, and Dodge, William Copeland. *Utterances of Abdul Beha Abbas to two young men, American pilgrims to Acre, 1901*. Board of Counsel in New York (n.d.).
Dreyfus, Hippolyte. *The Universal Religion: Bahaism*. London: Cope & Fenwick, 1909.
Esslemont, J.E. *Bahá'u'lláh and the New Era*. First published 1921. London: Bahá'í Publishing Trust, 1974.
Faydí, Muhammad-'Alí. *Khánidán-i-Afnán* (History of the Afnán Family). Tehran: BE 128 (1971).
Gail, Marzieh. *Arches of the Years*. Oxford: George Ronald, 1991.
—*Summon Up Remembrance*. Oxford: George Ronald, 1987.
Harper, Barron Deems. *Lights of Fortitude*. Oxford: George Ronald, 1997.
Harris, W. Hooper. "William H. Hoar", in *Star of the West*, vol. 12, no. 19 (2 March 1922).
Haydar-'Alí, Hájí Mírzá. *Bahai Martyrdoms in Persia in the Year 1903, A.D.* Translated by Dr. Youness Khan Afroukhteh. Chicago: Bahai Publishing Society, 1904.
—*Stories from the Delight of Hearts: The Memoirs of Hájí Mírzá Haydar-'Alí*. (Originally published as *Bihjatu's-Sudúr*, Bombay, 1913.) Trans. and abridged A.Q. Faizi. Los Angeles: Kalimát Press, 1980.
Health and Healing. Compiled by the Research Department of the Universal House of Justice. New Delhi: Bahá'í Publishing Trust, 1986.
Hollinger, Richard. "Ibrahim George Kheiralla and the Bahá'í Faith in America", in Cole and Momen, 1984.
Huqúqu'lláh: The Right of God. Comp. Research Department of the Universal House of Justice. London: Bahá'í Publishing Trust, rev. edn. 1989.
Kern, Margaret. *The Rustle of His Robe* (1901).
Lights of Guidance: A Bahá'í Reference File. Comp. Helen Bassett Hornby. New Delhi: Bahá'í Publishing Trust, 3rd rev. edn. 1994.
Martin, Douglas James. *The Life and Work of Sarah Jane Farmer, 1947–1916*. Diss. University of Waterloo, 1967.
Matthews, Gary L. *He Cometh With Clouds: A Bahá'í View of Christ's Return*. Oxford: George Ronald, 1996.
Mehrabkhani, R. *Sádat-i-Khams* (History of the Khamsi Family).

Metelmann, Zelda Piff. *Lua Getsinger: Herald of the Covenant*. Oxford: George Ronald, 1997.

Momen, Moojan. *The Bábi and Bahá'í Religions, 1844–1944: Some Contemporary Western Accounts* (ed.). Oxford: George Ronald, 1981.

—*An Introduction to Shi'i Islam: The History and Doctrines of Twelver Shi'ism*. Oxford: George Ronald, 1985.

—*Scripture and Revelation* (ed.). Bahá'í Studies Series, vol. 3. Oxford: George Ronald, 1997.

Momen, Wendi (ed.) *A Basic Bahá'í Dictionary*. Oxford: George Ronald, 1989.

Mu'ayyad, Ḥabíb. *Khátirát-i-Ḥabíb* (Memoirs of Ḥabíb). Tehran: 1961.

Phelps, M. H. *Abbas Effendi: His Life and Teachings*. Introduction by Edward Granville Browne. First published 1903. 2nd rev. ed: *Life and Teachings of Abbas Effendi*. New York: G. P. Putnam's Sons, 1912.

Qur'án. Rodwell, J.M. (trans.). *The Koran*. London: J.M.Dent, 1909.

Rabbani, Rúḥíyyih. *The Priceless Pearl*. London: Bahá'í Publishing Trust, 1969.

Rastigár, Nasr'u'llah. *Tarikh-i-Haḍrat-i Ṣadru'ṣ-Sudúr*. Biography of Ṣadru'ṣ-Sudúr. Tehran: Bahá'í Publishing Trust, 1947.

Remey, Charles Mason. *Observations of a Bahai Traveller*. 2nd ed. Washington: 1914.

Rochefoucauld, François, Duc de La. *Réflexions ou sentences et maximes morales* (1665).

Ruhe, David S. *Door of Hope: The Bahá'í Faith in the Holy Land*. George Ronald: Oxford, 2nd rev. edn. 2001.

Sears, William. *Thief in the Night: The Case of the Missing Millenium*. Oxford: George Ronald, 1961.

Shoghi Effendi. *God Passes By*. Wilmette, Ill.: Bahá'í Publishing Trust, rev. edn. 1974.

—*Messages to America 1932–1946*. Wilmette, Ill.: Bahá'í Publishing Committee, 1947.

Sims, Barbara. *Japan Will Turn Ablaze! Tablets of 'Abdu'l-Bahá, Letters of Shoghi Effendi and the Universal House of Justice, and Historical Notes about Japan*. Rev.edn. Osaka: Bahá'í Publishing Trust, 1992.

Star of the West (8 vols.). Chicago: Bahá'í News Service, 1910–1935. Oxford: George Ronald. Reprinted 1978 and 1984.

Stockman, Robert H. *The Bahá'í Faith in America*. Vol.1: *Origins, 1892–1900*. Wilmette, Ill.: Bahá'í Publishing Trust, 1985. Vol.2: *Early Expansion, 1900–1912*. Oxford: George Ronald, 1995.

Sulaymání, 'Azízu'lláh. *Maṣábiḥ-i-Hidáyat* (Biographies of early Bahá'ís). 8 vols. Tehran: Bahá'í Publishing Trust, 1947–1972.
Taherzadeh, Adib. *The Child of the Covenant: A Study Guide to the Will and Testament of 'Abdu'l-Bahá*. George Ronald, Oxford, 2000.
— *The Covenant of Bahá'u'lláh*. Oxford: George Ronald, 1992.
—*The Revelation of Bahá'u'lláh*. Four volumes. Oxford: George Ronald, 1974–1988.
Tweed, T. A. *The American Encounter with Buddhism 1844–1912: Victorian Culture and the Limits of Dissent*. Rev. edn. Chapel Hill: University of North Carolina Press, 2000.
Waite, Louise. *Bahai Hymns and Poems written by Mrs. Louise Spencer-Waite*. Chicago, Bahai Publishing Society, 1904.
—*Bahai Hymns of Peace and Praise*. L.R. Waite. (n.p.). 1908.
Whitehead, O. Z. *Some Bahá'ís to Remember*. Oxford: George Ronald, 1983.
—*Some Bahá'ís of the West*. Oxford: George Ronald, 1976.
Whitmore, Bruce W. *The Dawning Place: The Building of a Temple, the Forging of the North American Bahá'í Community*. Wilmette, Ill.: Bahá'í Publishing Trust, 1984.
Winterburn, Mr. and Mrs. Geo. T. *Table Talks with Abdul-Baha in February, 1904*. Notes taken by Mr. and Mrs. Geo. T. Winterburn. Translated by Mirza Youness Khan. Chicago: Bahai Publishing Society, 1915.

NOTES AND REFERENCES

1. *abjad*: from the four letters of the Arabic alphabet "A", "B", "J" and "D". The letters of the alphabet were given corresponding numerical values and thus each word had both a literal meaning and a numerical significance. Shoghi Effendi wrote in 1932: "This practice is no more in use but during the time of Bahá'u'lláh and the Báb it was quite in vogue among the educated classes, and we find it very much used in the Bayán." (Letter written on behalf of Shoghi Effendi, 10 February 1932, in *Lights of Guidance*, no.828.) The abjad was used to codify messages or observe significant dates in verse or prose. For example, Bahá'u'lláh refers to Adrianople as the "Land of Mystery", both of which have the same numerical value. At the time of the passing of Bahá'u'lláh, Nabíl "found that the numerical value of the word 'shídád' – year of stress – was 309, and it thus became evident that Bahá'u'lláh foretold what had now come to pass" ('Abdu'l-Bahá, *Memorials*, p. 35). 1892, the year of Bahá'u'lláh's ascension, was 1309 A.H. For more on the abjad system see Momen, *Basic Bahá'í Dictionary*, p. 6.

2. Shokuhi: pen-name of Áqá Mírzá 'Abdu'l-Ḥusayn Shírází, who lived in Tehran (d.1918). See Bezai, *Poets of the First Bahá'í Century*.

3. lit. "The Book of My Covenant": the Will and Testament of Bahá'u'lláh, written entirely in His own hand and unsealed on the ninth day after His passing. "Referred to by Him as the 'Most Great Tablet' and 'the Crimson Book', it designates 'Abdu'l-Bahá as Bahá'u'lláh's successor and the one to whom all should turn for guidance after Bahá'u'lláh's death. As a

written covenant clearly stating the succession of authority by a Manifestation of God, this document is unique in religious scripture. The Will and Testament of Bahá'u'lláh, Shoghi Effendi has written, together with the Kitáb-i-Aqdas and those Tablets describing the station of 'Abdu'l-Bahá, 'constitute the chief buttresses designed by the Lord of the Covenant Himself to shield and support, after His ascension, the appointed Centre of His Faith and the Delineator of its future institutions' (*God Passes By*, p. 239)." (Momen, *Basic Bahá'í Dictionary*, p. 132.) The Kitáb-i-'Ahdí is published in English in *Tablets of Bahá'u'lláh*, pp. 219–223.

4. *Ghusn-i-Akbar*, the title given by Bahá'u'lláh to Muḥammad-'Alí, younger half-brother of 'Abdu'l-Bahá who broke Bahá'u'lláh's Covenant after His ascension. He was given the title "Centre of Sedition" by the Master.

5. Aghṣán, the kindred of Bahá'u'lláh. Plural of *ghuṣn*, branch. In His Writings, Bahá'u'lláh refers to His sons as Branches. 'Abdu'l-Bahá is *Ghuṣn-i-A'ẓam*, the Most Great Branch.

6. Karbilá and Najaf: cities in Iraq and sites of significant Islamic shrines. It was at Karbilá that the horrendous martyrdom of the Imám Ḥusayn, grandson of the Prophet Muḥammad, took place; while Najaf is the site of the Shrine of 'Alí, the first Imám. These two cities together with Kazimayn are the main centres of pilgrimage and scholarship in Shí'í Islam.

7. This refers to Bahá'u'lláh's statement in His Will and Testament, the Kitáb-i-'Ahd: "Verily God hath ordained the station of the Greater Branch [Muḥammad 'Alí] to be beneath that of the Most Great Branch ['Abdu'l-Bahá]. He is in truth the Ordainer, the All-Wise. We have chosen 'the Greater' after 'the Most Great', as decreed by Him Who is the All-Knowing, the All Informed." *Tablets of Bahá'u'lláh*, p. 222.

8. Mírzá Yaḥyá, the Arch-breaker of the Covenant of the Báb. Muḥammad-'Alí was named the Arch-breaker of Bahá'u'lláh's Covenant. See Shoghi Effendi, *God Passes By*, pp. 246, 249, and Taherzadeh, *Covenant*, pp. 125–34.

NOTES AND REFERENCES

9. Shoghi Effendi describes this period in the "newly-born Covenant of Bahá'u'lláh": "A crisis, almost as severe as that which had assailed the Faith in its earliest infancy in Baghdád, was to shake that Covenant to its foundations at the very moment of its inception, and subject afresh the Cause of which it was the noblest fruit to one of the most grievous ordeals experienced in the course of an entire century." *God Passes By*, p. 246.

10. Title given by Bahá'u'lláh to the members of the family of the Báb and their descendants.

11. "When the ocean of My presence hath ebbed and the Book of My Revelation is ended, turn your faces toward Him Whom God hath purposed, Who hath branched from this Ancient Root." Kitáb-i-Aqdas, v. 121. See also *Kitáb-i-Aqdas*, notes 145 and 184.

12. A city west of Tehran and the first stop on the way to Russia. Qazvín is the birthplace of the immortal Ṭáhirih.

13. A coastal town on the Caspian Sea.

14. A port on the Caspian Sea and a departure point for various Russian ports.

15. Present city of Baku, capital of Azerbaijan.

16. Capital of Georgia.

17. A Georgian port on the Black Sea.

18. "Shrouded in mystery is the ancient use of the cave near the base of the mountain [Carmel] at its western tip ... Elijah traditionally is said to have lived there ... During Arab times some new legends were evolved concerning al-Khiḍr (the Green or Immortal One) and both Druze and Arabs venerate the site ... Bahá'u'lláh visited the lower cave some time after His visit to the Carmelite monastery, thereby also hallowing it for the generations to come ... Following Bahá'u'lláh's passing in May 1892, 'Abdu'l-Bahá came that summer to Haifa, living

in the upper apartment of the western building near the cave mouth. There, in sorrow at the machinations of the Covenant-breakers and in relative isolation at this cool spot by the sea, the Master spent one month ... and He stayed there in subsequent years" (Ruhe, *Door of Hope*, pp. 187–90, with photographs).

19. The author's self-confessed emotional state at this first meeting with 'Abdu'l-Bahá may have caused confusion here. According to Christian doctrine, Jesus spent the three days between the Crucifixion and the Resurrection in hell, not heaven: "He suffered under Pontius Pilate, was crucified, dead and buried. He descended into hell; the third day He rose again from the dead; He ascended into heaven ..." (Creed, *Book of Common Prayer*).

20. A loose outer garment like a cape or a long coat, without pockets or buttons.

21. Bahjí: lit. place of delight. The site on the plain of 'Akká which gives its name to the Mansion that was the residence of Bahá'u'lláh during the last years of His earthly life. When Bahá'u'lláh passed away He was interred in the small house adjacent to the Mansion. This became His Shrine, the holiest spot of earth and the Qiblih of the Bahá'í Faith. However, the Mansion was occupied by the Covenant-breakers; not until 1929 did Shoghi Effendi regain custody of the building. See Ruhe, *Door of Hope*, pp. 101–18; Momen, *Basic Bahá'í Dictionary*, pp. 42–3.

22. A beautiful garden near 'Akká, named Riḍván (Paradise) by Bahá'u'lláh, which served as a place of rest and leisure. The river Na'mayn runs through it. The Riḍván Garden should not be confused with the garden of the same name in Baghdad, the site of Bahá'u'lláh's Declaration. See Ruhe, *Door of Hope*, pp. 91–96.

23. This refers to the Muslim Cemetery of 'Akká where Navváb, Ásíyih Khánum, wife of Bahá'u'lláh and mother of 'Abdu'l-Bahá, was laid to rest in 1886. Her remains were later transferred to the Monument Gardens in Haifa. See Ruhe, *Door of Hope*, pp. 79–80.

NOTES AND REFERENCES

24. "The Nabí Ṣáliḥ, patron saint of 'Akká, after whom the cemetery is named, is unlikely to be the Ṣáliḥ mentioned by Muḥammad in Qur'án vii.71-7 ... Ṣáliḥ was an Arabian prophet who followed Noah and Húd in the Qur'ánic ordering. In the Kitáb-i-Íqán, p. 9, Bahá'u'lláh refers to Ṣáliḥ and his hundred years of mission, but nowhere later connects the prophet with the holy man of 'Akká, whoever he may have been." (Ruhe, *Door of Hope*, p. 224.)

25. Probably referring to the son of 'Abdu'l-Bahá who died at the age of 4. See Ruhe, *Door of Hope*, p. 51.

26. The caravanserai Khán-i-'Avámíd served for decades as a residence and pilgrim house for Bahá'ís. See Ruhe, *Door of Hope*, pp. 72-3.

27. White tea: *aq-par* in Turkish, meaning untreated leaves of tea.

28. The main building of the former Governorate of 'Abdu'lláh Pashá, it was rented to 'Abdu'l-Bahá in October 1896 and served as the residence of 'Abdu'l-Bahá and His family for nearly two decades. Today it is one of the sites visited by pilgrims in the course of their pilgrimage. The Guardian of the Faith, Shoghi Effendi, was born in this house. The casket containing the remains of the Báb were hidden here in the room of the Greatest Holy Leaf from 1899 to 1909. It was here that the first Western pilgrims visited 'Abdu'l-Bahá; *Some Answered Questions* was revealed by 'Abdu'l-Bahá in the dining room of the upper floor of this house. See Ruhe, *Door of Hope*, pp. 56-68.

29. Old Persian homes were constructed so as to divide the outer quarters, the *bírúní*, which served as a general reception area where male guests were received and entertained, from the inner apartment, the *andárúní*, consisting of the family area which housed the ladies of the household and a private reception area where intimate friends were received.

30. *darb-khánih*: lit. the door of the house. The residential palaces of the Qajar kings in Tehran were referred to as the *darb-khánih*. It refers to the *bírúní* of the residence of 'Abdu'l-Bahá.

31. *abgusht*: a common Persian dish made of lamb, yellow split peas, beans, potatoes and tomatoes, with dried lemon. When cooked the liquid is separated from the other ingredients which are then mashed to a paste in a pestle and mortar and eaten with the liquid poured over.

32. About 1892 'Abdu'l-Bahá rented the house known as the Pilgrim House, adjoining the Shrine of Bahá'u'lláh, from its Christian owner; He also had the use of the house known as the Tea House. See Ruhe, *Door of Hope*, pp. 110, 226.

33. In Islamic countries prominent people had in their service a reciter of the Qur'án who had the daily task of chanting verses from the Qur'án in the evening, while the whole household listened to the words of God.

34. Revealed in Constantinople, "a masterpiece of Persian poetry, noted for the beauty and power of its composition, and acclaimed as one of the most soul-stirring among His poems" (Taherzadeh, *Revelation*, vol.2, p. 29).

35. Revealed in Kurdistán, this poem is known as Sáqí-Az-Ghayb-i-Baqá. See Taherzadeh, *Revelation*, vol. 1, p. 64.

36. Provisional translation.

37. "Hallelujah, Hallelujah, O Glad Tidings."

38. Provisional translation.

39. Chopped onion is placed at the bottom of the pot in a small amount of oil; short skewers of lamb meat are then placed over the onion. Another layer of chopped onion and a smidgen of minced garlic are added. The pot is then placed on the stove to cook at low heat.

40. "placed on the table in European style" i.e. rather than set out on a tablecloth at floor level in the Persian manner.

41. These included the believers named as "companions" of

Bahá'u'lláh. Those who entered the Most Great Prison with Him in 1868 are listed by Balyuzi, *King of Glory*, p. 277.

42 Ḥájí Mírzá Ḥaydar-'Alí writes of this time: "The ministry of 'Abdu'l-Bahá began so vigorously that Bahá'í communities everywhere were overwhelmed. Letters from the Master poured into every village, town and country like the drops of the rains of spring. The friends were cheered and enamoured by His life-giving words." *Stories from the Delight of Hearts*, p. 121.

43. "The centre of violation purloined, in its entirety, the Divine trust which specifically appertained to this servant. He took everything and returned nothing. To this day the usurper unjustly remains in possession. Although each single item is more precious for 'Abdu'l-Bahá than the dominion of earth and heaven, till now I have kept silent and have not breathed a word lest it bring us into disrepute amongst strangers. This was a severe blow to me. I suffered, I sorrowed, I wept, but I spoke not" ('Abdu'l-Bahá, Tablet to Mírzá Muḥammad-Báqir K͟hán of S͟hírá́z, quoted in Balyuzi, *'Abdu'l-Bahá*, p. 53). See also the Will and Testament of 'Abdu'l-Bahá, verses 6, 32, 38, described in Taherzadeh, *Child of the Covenant*, ch.16; Shoghi Effendi, *God Passes By*, pp. 248–9; Taherzadeh, *Covenant of Bahá'u'lláh*, pp. 126–134.

44. According to S͟hí'í belief, 'Alí Ibn Abí-Ṭálib, the cousin of the Prophet Muḥammad, was His intended successor. However, it was Abú-Bakr Ibn Abí-Quḥáfah, a wealthy and influential leader of the Muslims and the father-in-law of Muḥammad, who became the first Caliph of the world of Islam. "For 'Alí the supreme necessity of preserving the unity of Islam, of stemming the tide of secession, took precedence over the assertion of his own rights" (Balyuzi, *Muḥammad*, p. 168). Abú-Bakr was succeeded by 'Umar Ibn al-Khaṭṭáb, a courageous and fiery man, "stern but just" (Balyuzi, p. 70), and then by 'Ut͟hmán Ibn 'Affán. 'Alí was passed over until 23 years after the death of the Prophet, and became the fourth Caliph in 656 A.D. Here and elsewhere in this book the position of 'Abdu'l-Bahá is likened to that of 'Alí, alluding to the Covenant-breakers' attempts to usurp His divinely ordained position.

458   MEMORIES OF NINE YEARS IN 'AKKÁ

45. "Him Whom God hath purposed": Kitáb-i-Aqdas, v. 121. See note 11 above. "Him round Whom all names revolve": Lawḥ-i-Arḍ-i-Bá (Tablet of the Land of Bá, Beirut), in Bahá'u'lláh, *Tablets*, p. 227, revealed on the occasion of 'Abdu'l-Bahá's visit to Beirut at the invitation of the Governor of the Province of Syria. See Balyuzi, *King of Glory*, p. 378–9; Taherzadeh, *Revelation*, vol. 4, pp. 240–41. On the use of the title "Master" (Áqá), see Taherzadeh, *Covenant*, pp. 138–9, where Bahá'u'lláh is recorded as having admonished someone who "referred to certain individuals as the Áqá. On hearing this Bahá'u'lláh was heard to say with a commanding voice: 'Who is the Áqá? There is only one Áqá, and He is the Most Great Branch.'"

46. Kitáb-i-Aqdas, v. 121, quoted by Bahá'u'lláh in his Will and Testament.

47. Provisional translation from Arabic; "the company that returned from the banks of the Euphrates ..." refers to the army of the Umayyad usurpers under the brutal generalship of 'Ubaydu'lláh ibn Ziyád, who slew the Imám Ḥusayn at Karbilá and brought his only surviving son 'Alí as a prisoner to Damascus. "Men and women, misguided, misinformed, misled, thronged the route to the palace of Yazíd and heaped abuse upon them. 'You are seceders,' they shouted; 'you have put yourselves outside the pale.' 'Alí ... replied: 'Nay, by God, we are his servants who believed in Him and His proofs. Through us the gladsome visage of Faith was revealed and the signs of the merciful God shone forth.' But the people retorted: 'Did you not forbid what God made lawful; did you not make lawful what God forbade?' And 'Alí answered: 'Nay, we were the first to follow the commandments of God. We are the root of this Cause and its origin. We are the sign of God, His word amidst mankind.'" (Balyuzi, *Muḥammad and the Course of Islám*, p. 196.) See also Momen, *Shí'í Islam*, pp. 30–32. These events eventually led to the sack of the holy city of Medina, where 80 of the remaining companions of the Prophet were put to the sword (Balyuzi, p. 197).

48. *Khádimú'lláh*: servant of God; *Abd-i-Haḍír*: servant in waiting; titles given to Mírzá Áqá Ján by Bahá'u'lláh when

NOTES AND REFERENCES 459

he served as Bahá'u'lláh's amanuensis. See Taherzadeh, *Covenant*, ch.15.

49. Ḥuqúqu'lláh: literally, the Right of God. It is a sum equivalent to 19 per cent of the assets of a Bahá'í after all expenses; according to Bahá'í law it should be paid to the Head of the Faith. This is not to be confused with optional donations contributed by Bahá'ís. See *Ḥuqúqu'lláh: The Right of God*.

50. Kitáb-i-Aqdas, v. 121. The event referred to is the passing of Bahá'u'lláh.

51. *Báb-ed-Dín: The Door of True Religion* (1897). See Hollinger, "Ibrahim George Kheiralla ...", in Cole and Momen, *From Iran East and West*, p. 113 and note 117.

52. The Battle of Khandaq (moat or fosse) took place in 627 A.D. It was one of the most significant victories of the Prophet over the idolators. Also known as the Battle of the Confederates, it was occasioned by the last attempt of the Meccans to destroy Muḥammad and His followers. A huge army laid siege to Medina, which the Muslims defended by digging a moat or trench around the city, at the suggestion of Salmán the Persian. See Balyuzi, *Muḥammad*, pp. 93–101.

53. Point of Adoration: Qiblih. The Shrine of Bahá'u'lláh is the Qiblih or the Point of Adoration for the Bahá'ís of the world. Obligatory prayers are recited while facing in that direction.

54. An example of 'Abdu'l-Bahá's prophecies concerning Haifa is given by Dr. Ḥabíb Mu'ayyad: "The future of Mount Carmel is very bright. I can see it now covered all over with a blanket of light. I can see many ships anchored at the Port of Haifa. I can see the kings of the earth with vases of flowers in their hands walking solemnly toward the Shrine of Bahá'u'lláh and the Báb with absolute devotion and in a state of prayer and supplication" (*Kháṭirát-i-Ḥabíb*, vol.1, p. 81, cited in Taherzadeh, *Covenant*, p. 226).

55. The superstructure was completed on 1 May 1931, but not

until 8 January 1943 was the exterior ornamentation complete. Work on the interior and the gardens still remained; the public dedication of the House of Worship took place in May 1953. See Whitmore, *Dawning Place*.

56. Ḥaẓíratu'l-Quds (lit. Paradise). The term was first used by the beloved Guardian in his message of the summer of 1925 and refers to a site which is to be used for assemblage, consultation and fellowship of the believers as well as the holding of various meetings and assemblies.

57. Well-known Islamic tradition referring to God and His creation. References and allusions to it are found throughout the Bahá'í writings. See *Kitáb-i-Aqdas*, note 43.

58. *Rawdih-khání*: a recital of the tragedy of Karbilá where Ḥusayn, grandson of the prophet Muḥammad and third Imám of Shí'í Islám, was martyred with his family in the 7th century A.D. See Momen, *Introduction to Shi'i Islám*, p. 240 and fig. 41.

59. Provisional translation. Here 'Abdu'l-Bahá alludes to the story of Joseph who was betrayed by His brothers, thrown into a water well and left for dead. He was rescued and taken to Egypt where He gained high office and was able to save His tribe. The analogy is found in several places in the Bahá'í Writings, referring to both Bahá'u'lláh and 'Abdu'l-Bahá. 'Abdu'l-Bahá too was betrayed by His brothers, and rescued the Faith of God from their clutches. 'Abdu'l-Bahá here compares the Joseph story to the Covenant-breakers' treatment of Him after the ascension of Bahá'u'lláh.

60. On the significance of the Hidden Words Bahá'u'lláh Himself reveals: "This is that which hath descended from the realm of glory, uttered by the tongue of power and might, and revealed unto the Prophets of old. We have taken the inner essence thereof and clothed it in the garment of brevity, as a token of grace unto the righteous, that they may stand faithful unto the Covenant of God, may fulfil in their lives His trust, and in the realm of spirit obtain the gem of

NOTES AND REFERENCES   461

Divine virtue." On the Tablets such as Ṭarázát [Ornaments], Iṣhráqát [Splendours], Tajallíyát [Effulgences] and others published in English in *Tablets of Bahá'u'lláh*, Shoghi Effendi has written: "These Tablets ... must rank among the choicest fruits which His mind has yielded, and mark the consummation of His forty-year-long ministry" (*God Passes By*, p. 216).

61. Kitáb-i-Aqdas, v. 121.

62. Mírzá Hadí Afnán, the father of Shoghi Effendi.

63. 29 May, the anniversary of the Ascension of Bahá'u'lláh.

64. "... the Aghṣán and a few others ... decided to address a letter to Mírzá Áqá Ján purporting to be on behalf of all the Bahá'ís of Persia. The gist of the letter was as follows: 'O Khádem! How long will you remain silent? For how long should we tarry in the wilderness of error? All of us look for your guidance ...' ...The Aghṣán sent the above draft to Mullá Ḥusayn-i-Jahrumí who was residing in Bombay, India, and instructed him to copy it in his own handwriting and post it to Mírza Áqá Ján, care of the Arch-breaker of the Covenant ... They arranged to hand the letter to him in the Shrine of Bahá'u'lláh. Usually when Mírzá Áqá Ján went to the Shrine, he would sit down for about an hour, close his eyes and raise his hands upwards saying prayers. One day when he was seated in this manner ... the letter [was placed] in his hands. Later, he opened his eyes and saw the letter, but did not know who had placed it there ... We can guess what kind of thoughts must have come to him when he read it. He imagined that as soon as he made a statement, all the believers in Persia would respond positively to him. The fire of pride and rebellion began to burn within his heart ..." (Account by Ḥájí 'Alíy-i-Yazdí, quoted in Taherzadeh, *Covenant*, p. 185).

65. *Man*: a unit of measurement equivalent to approximately three kilograms.

66. The Black Stone (*Hajaru'l-Aswad*) which adjoins the Ka'bih is the Point of Adoration (*Qiblih*) to which Muslims turn in

prayer and where the annual rites of pilgrimage (*Ḥajj*) are carried out. According to some traditions, this is "the stone which, it is said, the Angel Gabriel brought to Abraham from Paradise" (Balyuzi, *Muḥammad*, p. 18); for some it is the same rock upon which Abraham was commanded by God to sacrifice His son.

67. Kitáb-i-'Ahd, in Bahá'u'lláh, *Tablets*, p. 222.

68. Provisional translation.

69. They meant that 'Abdu'l-Bahá had replaced the customary Bahá'í greeting of "Alláh'u'Abhá" with the term "Alláh'u'A'ẓam" in order to emphasize His own rank and thus assume a new station superseding that of Bahá'u'lláh.

70. Alláh'u'Abhá, God, the Most Glorious; Alláh'u'A'ẓam, God the Most Great; Alláh'u'Ajmal, God, the Most Beauteous; Alláh'u'Akbar, God the Great One.

71. Provisional translation.

72. "obviously a man of various indulgences and pleasures": this reflects centuries-old Islamic attitudes to music and musicians. The author would have drawn this conclusion simply from the fact that Mírzá 'Abdu'lláh was a musician, and worse, had been at court. The statement reflects the reputation of musicians within Iranian Islamic society and demonstrates that these traditional attitudes had not yet been shed by the Bahá'ís at this time. In fact, "a number of musicians have spoken of the good character of Mírzá 'Abdu'lláh, that he had a spiritual temperament, was *darvísh* (humble) and exemplified the ideal of the spiritual master of music" (Caton, "Bahá'í Influences on Mírzá 'Abdu'lláh", p. 54). See also Biographical Notes in this book. The Islamic prohibition against music has been lifted in the Bahá'í Faith and music is regarded as "divine and effective" ('Abdu'l-Bahá), "an exalted and worthy art" (Caton, p. 54).

73. This refers to the legal concept in Islám of the necessity for two witnesses to prove a case: a main witness and a supporting

witness. There are legal qualifications for a person to be allowed as a witness. Women and children are not considered to possess the qualifications of a witness and are therefore not recognised in law as witnesses.

74. Salmán was the first Persian to believe in Islám. He is therefore considered a supporting witness. Abu'l-Ḥikam (literally, the father of wisdom, father of philosophy) is a title given by Bahá'u'lláh to Socrates in a number of His Tablets (see, for example, the Lawḥ-i-Ḥikmat, in *Tablets*, p. 147). In other words, many wise men bore negative testimony to the truth of Muḥammad and yet Salmán, an ordinary man, accepted the Cause.

75. *mubáhilih*: a confrontation designed to prove the veracity or falsity of a claim. "The two parties come together face to face and it is believed that in such a confrontation the power of truth will destroy the ungodly" (Taherzadeh, *Child of the Covenant*, p. 125).

76. Kitáb-i-Aqdas, v. 121.

77. ibid. verses 122 and 123.

78. Provisional translation.

79. A northern province of Iran crossed by travellers on their way to Russia and other northern destinations; it was the native province of Bahá'u'lláh.

80. 'Abdu'l-Bahá is alluding to his spiritual demise because of his violation of the Covenant.

81. Reference to the future Dr. Amín'u'lláh Faríd, who in 1914 broke the Covenant. His mother was a sister of Munírih Khánum, wife of 'Abdu'l-Bahá.

82. The pilgrim house for Westerners, at the end of Haparsim Street nearest the sea, is among the Bahá'í properties and has been restored. Other houses in Haifa from this period have

been demolished or their whereabouts are not known at this time.

83. *Hidden Words*, Persian no.13.

84. The author is probably referring here to the years following the Young Turks Revolution in 1908, when the House of the Master was completed and pilgrims were once more welcomed in larger numbers, since elsewhere in this chapter he refers to pilgrimages being curtailed in 1900.

85. which He considered to be poorly translated.

86. The construction of the Shrine began in 1899–1900. See Shoghi Effendi, *God Passes By*, pp. 274–5.

87. The author is referring here to the Shrine constructed by 'Abdu'l-Bahá, not to the superstructure completed in 1953 by Shoghi Effendi after the present book was published.

88. Possibly in one of the Templar houses in the German colony; see Ruhe, *Door of Hope*, illustration p. 194. The author refers to three houses having been rented in Haifa in 1900.

89. *Bahá'í Prayers*, p. 60.

90. See note 59.

91. Since 1866 when the Cretans rose in revolt against Turkish rule there had been a dispute over Greek claims to Crete and Macedonia which had never been satisfactorily resolved. Violence broke out in May 1896 and continued sporadically over the following months. In February 1897 Greece sent an armed force to annex the island of Crete, whereupon Austria, Britain, France, Germany, Italy and Russia proclaimed an international protectorate and landed troops. This intervention only exasperated the situation, however, and the Greeks prepared for war, which was declared by Turkey in April 1897. After a brief campaign Greece was defeated, a peace treaty being signed on 4 December 1897. The political question of

NOTES AND REFERENCES 465

Crete remained, however, giving rise to sporadic violence for the next fifteen years until the outbreak of the First Balkan War in 1912–13.

92. This Tablet is published in English in 'Abdu'l-Bahá, *Selections*, no. 158 (pp. 187–9).

93. See the account by May Maxwell in *Bahá'í World*, vol. 7, pp. 707–11.

94. The House of 'Abbúd; see Ruhe, *Door of Hope*, p. 47.

95. Wendell Phillips Dodge and William Copeland Dodge, sons of Arthur Pillsbury Dodge. Their account of their pilgrimage: *Utterances of Abdul Beha Abbas to two young men, American pilgrims to Acre, 1901*, was published by the Board of Counsel in New York (n.d.). See Stockman, *Bahá'í Faith in America*, vol. 2, p. 79.

96. i.e. the House of 'Abbúd.

97. This well-known book on Buddhism for Western readers was by Paul Carus (1852–1919): *The Gospel of Buddha according to old records*. Told by P. Carus. New York: Open Court Publishing Co, 1894, and many other editions. Madame de Canavarro was a prominent American Buddhist at this time; see Biographical Notes.

98. Phelps, M. H. *Abbas Effendi: His Life and Teachings*. Introduction by Edward Granville Browne. First published 1903. 2nd rev.ed: *Life and Teachings of Abbas Effendi*. New York: G. P. Putnam's Sons, 1912. Passages from this book are quoted in Balyuzi, 'Abdu'l-Bahá, pp. 98–102.

99. "In 1894 Captain Alfred Dreyfus (1859–1935), an Alsatian Jewish officer of the French army, was falsely accused of giving information to the German military attaché in Paris. Subsequent efforts to exonerate Dreyfus led to a prolonged political crisis, perhaps the most important in the history of the Third Republic. Although the evidence against him was insufficient, he was convicted and sent to Devil's Island in

October of 1894. Twelve years later he was vindicated and readmitted to the army" (*Grolier Encyclopedia*).

100. No information about this person has been found so far.

101. The Getsingers were members of the first group of Western pilgrims to 'Akká, December 1898–March 1899. They made a second pilgrimage in the autumn of 1900, staying in Haifa until 1 January 1901 before going to Port Said to study the Bahá'í teachings with Mírzá Abu'l-Faḍl ... Lua Getsinger "visited the Holy Land at least eight times, and spent two long periods of time in the Master's household, once about 1902–3 and again in 1915" (Metelmann, *Lua Getsinger*, p. 50). Correspondence between Youness Khán and Lua Getsinger is quoted in Metelmann's book (pp. 53–5).

102. See note 109.

103. *qadír*: omnipotent, equal to 144 in *abjad* reckoning. The author thus agreed to recite the Báb's prayer 144 times in accordance with Lua's request.

104. The original of this poem has not been found. The attempt to retranslate into English from the fine Persian translation by Youness Khán has been undertaken by the present translator.

105. He had been implicated in the rebellion of Mírzá Áqá Ján. See note 64 above.

106. Emigrants: *muhájirún*. Here the analogy is drawn between those families who were the companions of Bahá'u'lláh in His exiles, and the early believers in Islám who accompanied the Prophet Muḥammad to Medina in 622 A.D., the year of the Hijra (Hegira) or Emigration. The Muslim calendar dates from that year.

107. On the 1903 persecutions in Yazd and Isfahan, see Balyuzi, *'Abdu'l-Bahá*, pp. 102–107; Momen, *Bábí and Bahá'í Religions*, ch. 27, pp. 373–404.

108. Ḥaydar-'Alí, Ḥájí Mírzá. *Bahai Martyrdoms in Persia in the Year 1903, A.D.* Translated by Dr. Yúnis Khán Afrúkhtih. Chicago: Bahai Publishing Society, 1904.

109. Written in 1935/36.

110. Compare 'Abdu'l-Bahá's statement in *Some Answered Questions*, ch. 45: "Know that infallibility is of two kinds: essential infallibility and acquired infallibility ... Essential infallibility is peculiar to the supreme Manifestation, for it is His essential requirement, and an essential requirement cannot be separated from the thing itself ... But acquired infallibility is not a natural necessity; on the contrary, it is a ray of the bounty of infallibility which shines from the Sun of Reality upon hearts, and grants a share and portion of itself to souls. Although these souls have not essential infallibility, still they are under the protection of God – that is to say, God preserves them from error ... For instance, the Universal House of Justice, if it be established under the necessary conditions – with members elected from all the people – that House of Justice will be under the protection and the unerring guidance of God. If that House of Justice shall decide unanimously, or by a majority, upon any question not mentioned in the Book, that decision and command will be guarded from mistake. Now the members of the House of Justice have not, individually, essential infallibility; but the body of the House of Justice is under the protection and unerring guidance of God: this is called conferred infallibility."

111. Bahá'u'lláh, *Tablets*, p. 222.

112. Bahá'u'lláh, *Epistle to the Son of the Wolf*, p. 55.

113. 'Abdu'l-Bahá, quoted in Esslemont, *Bahá'u'lláh and the New Era*, p. 108.

114. Provisional translation.

115. Provisional translation.

116. Mírzá Muḥammad-'Alí.

117. Khalíl: Ḥájí Muḥammad-Ibráhím of Qazvín, the recipient of the Lawḥ-i-Khalíl revealed by Bahá'u'lláh. See Taherzadeh, *Revelation*, vol. 2, pp. 259–61.

118. See note 44.

119. This Tablet, revealed in Arabic and as yet untranslated into English, begins with the words, "In My Name, the Humourist". In a Memorandum to the Universal House of Justice dated 12 January 1997, the Research Department states: "…it is a serious mystical poem, revealed in the form of a prayer. The text does not illuminate the reference to the 'Humourist'. It is, however, interesting to note that, while dealing with an exalted theme, the language of expression is, unexpectedly, that of the common people – light, simple, and even colloquial."

120. Lit. "They mix wine (*sharáb*) with liquor (*araq*) and call it *sharaq*." The combination of the words "wine" and "whisky" into "wineky" is the translator's attempt to replace a term used by the author which if used here would fail to communicate the meaning and humour of the original.

121. Provisional translation.

122. 'Abdu'l-Bahá, *Haḍrat-i-'Abdu'l-Bahá Majmuiyyij-Munajatha*. Langenhain: Bahá'í-Verlag, 1992, p. 176, prayer no. 157. The author here uses the description "revealed verse" in a general rather than specific sense, as the term is usually used only for the Writings of Bahá'u'lláh or the Báb.

123. Qur'an 2.151.

124. Phelps, *Abbas Effendi*, pp. 2–10. His description is reprinted in Balyuzi, *'Abdu'l-Bahá*, pp. 98–102.

125. Authorized translation.

126. *ghazal* in Persian.

127. *ghassideh* in Persian.

128. No information about this believer has been found. The opening lines of the poem are retranslated here.

129. Margaret Kern, *The Rustle of His Robe*, 1901. The opening lines of her poem are retranslated here.

130. Louise Waite. This poem appears in *Bahai Hymns and Poems written by Mrs. Louise Spencer-Waite* (Chicago, Bahai Publishing Society, 1904), p. 7, under the title "A Bahai Hymn". It is set to music in Waite, *Bahai Hymns of Peace and Praise* (1908).

131. "Ottoman-style *fez*": a tall narrow circular hat, typically red, in common use at that time and place. Pilgrims wearing Western headgear would have been too easily identifiable.

132. Pársís are Zoroastrians of Iranian heritage who fled the persecution of the Islamic clergy and settled in India and Pakistan from about the 8th century A.D. The largest community of Pársís is in Bombay. The first Iranian Zoroastrians to accept the Faith of Bahá'u'lláh already belonged to a persecuted minority. See Taherzadeh, *Revelation*, vol.3, pp. 267–73, on these early conversions and also about the survival of "pure Persian" in the Zoroastrian community, in contrast to the present Persian language which incorporates many words originally from Arabic.

133. The Winterburns described this incident in their account of their pilgrimage, which took place between 5–11 February 1904: "While we were in Acca, there was also visiting Abdul-Baha a man from Bombay, one who had been a Zoroastrian. He was accompanied by his little son, a child of perhaps eleven or twelve. He heard that two Americans were there, and he begged to be allowed to see us, because in the sacred book of the Zoroastrians, written thousands of years ago, it was prophesied that a new world should be discovered, and that in the "last days" people from this new world should meet with the people of Zoroaster, that they should meet in the worship of the same God, in the same place. To him it was the

literal fulfilment of the prophecy, and he wanted to see us. He was a tall man with a great simplicity of manner, that simplicity that comes of great earnestness. He said: 'I can not tell you how happy I am to see you, or what my heart feels to meet you here. My words can not express it, but I would give my life for you.' He added that he should always remember having seen us. Neither shall we ever forget that meeting." *(Table Talks with Abdul-Baha*, p. 27.) Of their meetings with 'Abdu'l-Bahá, the Winterburns wrote: "We saw Abdul-Baha every day at luncheon and at dinner, and some days He would come to us for a little while in the morning or for a few minutes in the afternoon, and once He spent a long time with us at night after dinner. At the table, between courses, or when He was not eating, He would talk to us, giving us the teachings, the proofs of this great Manifestation. Always His words came with graciousness, with kindness and encouragement, and over and over again did He impress upon us the necessity of service in the Cause. For myself, I had not those great experiences of emotion that some visitors to his Presence have been seized with; but a great peace fell upon my soul, a tranquility and a surety took possession of me, such as comes nowhere else. That is the pervading atmosphere of the Holy House, a calm security that no cataclysm can shake; a love that encircles one, that is expressed by every person there, the great love of service, of doing something for another, of losing one's self completely in the absolute love that comes only from God. The love shown us there I can never forget. May God grant that I may be able to carry the message of it to others!" (ibid. p. 26).

134. This probably refers to Ḥájí Muḥammad Riḍáy-i-Iṣfahání who was martyred in 'Ishqábád in 1889. His martyrdom, foretold by Bahá'u'lláh in a Tablet to him, led to a prolonged legal case which his murderers were sentenced to death. The Bahá'í community made representations to the government on their behalf and obtained from the Czar the commutation of their sentences to life imprisonment. "This act of intercession on behalf of their enemies was acclaimed by Bahá'u'lláh as a princely deed" (see Taherzadeh, *Revelation*, vol. 4, pp. 342–6 and photograph).

NOTES AND REFERENCES 471

135. Vakílu'd-Dawlih, title of Ḥájí Mírzá Muḥammad-Taqí Afnán, the builder of the Ma<u>sh</u>riqu'l-A<u>dh</u>kár in 'I<u>sh</u>qábád. See Biographical Notes.

136. emigrants: see note 106.

137. See note 52.

138. Amatu'lláh: Handmaid of God.

139. Tel al-Fa<u>khkh</u>ár, the Hill of the Shards, also known as Napoleon's Hill.

140. "Whoso layeth claim to a Revelation direct from God, ere the expiration of a full thousand years, such a man is assuredly a lying imposter" (Kitáb-i-Aqdas, v. 37); "We have chosen 'the Greater' after 'the Most Great' (Kitáb-i-'Ahd, in Bahá'u'lláh, *Tablets*, p. 222). i.e. the Covenant-breakers claimed that 'Abdu'l-Bahá had claimed to be a Manifestation of God, whereas such a claim was strictly condemned by Bahá'u'lláh, and that because of this the succession should now fall to his half-brother, Mírzá Muḥammad-'Alí, the "Greater Branch".

141. Fundamental principles: *muhkamat*; allegorical verses: *muteshabehat*. Verses of the Qur'án are considered to be of these two types. *Muhkamat* are verses whose meanings are clear and require no interpretation or clarification, while *muteshabehat* refers to verses which have an allegorical or symbolic meaning, and require interpretation.

142. Persian proverb.

143. the two mischief-makers of Tabriz: supporters of Muḥammad-'Alí. One of these was Jalíl-i-<u>Kh</u>ú'í, for whom Bahá'u'lláh had revealed the Tablet of I<u>sh</u>ráqát. See Taherzadeh, *Revelation*, vol. 4, pp. 145–6.

144. This was the Russo-Japanese War of 1904–5, which ended with a peace treaty in September 1905.

145. Seat of the Ottoman government in Istanbul.

146. Two international conferences (1899 and 1907) held at The Hague became known as World Peace Conferences. The first (1899) which is referred to here, was convened by Count Muravyov, Minister for Foreign Affairs of Tsar Nicholas II of Russia. Twenty-six nations were represented. Although the Conference failed to realise its primary objective of arms limitation, it did succeed in passing three Conventions or Declarations prohibiting the use of asphyxiating gases, expanding bullets, and projectiles or explosives fired from balloons; also, by adopting a Convention for the Pacific Settlement of International Disputes it laid the groundwork for the Permanent Court of Arbitration. The second Peace Conference (1907) was proposed by U.S. President Theodore Roosevelt but was officially convened by Tsar Nicholas II, with 44 participating nations. 'Abdu'l-Bahá's well-known Tablet addressed to the Central Organization for a Durable Peace at the Hague was sent to neither of these Peace Conferences, but after World War I in 1919 and 1920.

147. "Praise be to Him Who hath honoured the Land of Bá through the presence of Him round Whom all names revolve": the first sentence of the Lawḥ-i-Arḍ-i-Bá, revealed by Bahá'u'lláh in honour of 'Abdu'l-Bahá on the occasion of 'Abdu'l-Bahá's visit to Beirut. See Bahá'u'lláh, *Tablets*, p. 227.

148. Kitáb-i-'Ahd, in Bahá'u'lláh, *Tablets*, p. 222.

149. This paragraph refers in several places to the passages in the Kitáb-i-Aqdas and the Kitáb-i-'Ahd already quoted. The whole passage in the Kitáb-i-'Ahd is as follows: "The Will of the divine Testator is this: It is incumbent upon the Agḥsán, the Afnán and My kindred to turn, one and all, their faces toward the Most Mighty Branch. Consider that which We have revealed in Our Most Holy Book: 'When the ocean of My presence hath ebbed and the Book of My Revelation is ended, turn your faces toward Him Whom God hath purposed, Who hath branched from this Ancient Root.' The object of this sacred Verse is none other except the Most

Mighty Branch ['Abdu'l-Bahá]. Thus have We graciously revealed unto you our potent Will, and I am verily the Gracious, the All-Powerful. Verily God hath ordained the station of the Greater Branch [Muḥammad 'Alí] to be beneath that of the Most Great Branch ['Abdu'l-Bahá]. He is in truth the Ordainer, the All-Wise. We have chosen 'the Greater' after 'the Most Great' as decreed by Him Who is the All-Knowing, the All Informed" (Bahá'u'lláh, *Tablets*, pp. 22 1–22).

150. Nuṣayrí: followers of 'Alí rather than the Prophet Muḥammad. See Balyuzi, *Muḥammad*, pp. 223–4.

151. 'Alíyu'lláhí: "those who equate 'Alí with God". Also known as Ahl-i-Ḥaqq, the people of truth. See Balyuzi, *Muḥammad*, p. 224.

152. The House of 'Abdu'l-Bahá. See note 30.

153. Qiblih or the Point of Adoration, the holy site towards which faithful believers direct their attention while reciting the obligatory prayer. The Shrine of Bahá'u'lláh at Bahjí is the Qiblih of the Bahá'í community, according to the text of the Kitáb-i-Aqdas (verses 6 and 137). The verse quoted by Mírzá Yúsuf Khán-i-Vujdání is from the Qur'án, ii: 109, the Súrih of the Cow (*al-baqarah*), which alludes to the question of the Qiblih in Islám.

154. See Chapter 1, pp. 95–6.

155. In most Bahá'í prayer books.

156. 'Abdu'l-Bahá, *Promulgation*, p. 453.

157. Áqáy-i-Kalím, Mírzá Músá, the faithful brother of Bahá'u'lláh. See Biographical Notes.

158. Kitáb-i-Aqdas, v. 113.

159. The drawing of blood, or blood-letting, was used to cure a variety of illnesses.

160. See Ruhe, *Door of Hope*, pp. 211–12 for a description the Druze community and beliefs. There were several Druze villages on Carmel and in the Galilee at the time, often visited by 'Abdu'l-Bahá. In World War I some of these villages provided shelter to local Bahá'ís. The present-day Druze community in the region numbers some 100,000.

161. "Signs of the Day of Revelation" (*yom-i-zuhur*: day of advent, appearance, manifestation, revelation): contradictions such as these are prophesied, for example, by Isaiah: "The wolf also shall dwell with the lamb, and the leopard shall lie down with the kid; and the calf and the young lion and the fatling together.... they shall not hurt nor destroy in all my holy mountain: for the earth shall be full of the knowledge of the Lord, as the waters cover the sea" (11:6–9).

162. This passage, from "when 'Abdu'l-Bahá was walking.... triumph of the Cause of God is in his hands!'" is reprinted with permission from Rabbani, *Priceless Pearl*, pp. 2–3.

163. See note 147.

164. i.e. Shoghi Effendi. The author here uses indirect allusion as a mark of respect.

165. This translation of 'Abdu'l-Bahá's Tablet is reprinted from Rabbani, *Priceless Pearl*, p. 2.

166. See Momen, *Shi'i Islam*, p. 249–50 for a short account of these struggles. The Constitution was signed in early 1907, was briefly overturned in a *coup d'état* in 1908 but triumphed in 1909. The "two black and white domes" refer to clerical turbans.

167. Aḥmad Sháh.

168. This passage refers to the policy of the Pahlavi dynasty under Riḍá Sháh, who proclaimed himself Shah in 1925. He curtailed the power of the ulama, and in 1928 made Western dress compulsory. See Momen, *Shi'i Islam*, pp. 250–51.

169. Kirmán, in Iran, was a centre of Azalí activity.

170. Millerites: followers of William Miller, one of the many nineteenth-century Christian scholars who calculated from Bible prophecies that Christ would return in 1843 or 1844. The Millerite movement was the precursor of today's Seventh Day Adventist church. For the basis of these calculations and a description of this and other millenial movements, see Sears, *Thief in the Night*, pp. 1–11; Matthews, *He Cometh with Clouds*, pp. 89–111.

171. 23 May 1844.

172. Kanichi Yamamoto was already a Bahá'í when he went to work for Mrs. Goodall in 1903. For accounts of his accepting the Faith in Honolulu in 1902 see Whitehead, *Some Bahá'ís to Remember*, pp. 176–186; *Bahá'í World*, vol. 13, p. 932; Alexander, *Forty Years of the Bahá'í Cause in Hawaii*, pp. 8–12. Mrs. Goodall had in fact taught Elizabeth Muther, who taught Kanichi Yamamoto while he was working in the household of Mr. and Mrs. William Owen Smith, the parents of Clarence Smith. Yamamoto had already written twice to the Master in Japanese and received two Tablets in reply, before the event described here by Youness Khán. It refers to the third Tablet revealed by 'Abdu'l-Bahá on 4 August 1904; by this time Yamamoto had moved to California where he was working as butler to Mrs. Goodall. On this occasion Mrs. Goodall sent his letter and her own in the same envelope to the Master.

173. 4 August 1904. In Sims, *Japan Will Turn Ablaze!*, pp. 22–23.

174. An illustration of this bathhouse appears in Taherzadeh, *Revelation*, vol. 3, between pages 60–61. See also p. 74, note, in that book.

175. Compare other statements by the Master, e.g. "... the food of man is cereals and fruit ... he is not in need of meat, nor is he obliged to eat it. Even without eating meat he would live with the utmost vigour and energy." "Meat is nourishing and containeth the elements of herbs, seed and fruits; therefore

sometimes it is essential for the sick and for the rehabilitation of health. There is no objection in the Law of God to the eating of meat if it is required" (From Tablets to individual believers, in *Health and Healing*, compiled by the Research Department of the Universal House of Justice).

176. *qábá*: a long shirt worn under the *'abá*, the overdress.

177. "duláb" disease = diabetes.

178. Hidden Words, Persian no. 49.

179. Qur'án 104:1–2.

180. This refers to 'Alí ibn Abú Ṭálib, cousin of the Prophet and the first Imám.

181. Ḥátem-i-Ṭá'í: legendary figure in Persian folklore; "Ṭá'í" = generous.

182. François, Duc de La Rochefoucauld (1612–1680), author, famous for his epigrams on manners and behaviour. In 1665 he published *Réflexions ou sentences et maximes morales*, which went into five editions in his lifetime under the title *Maximes*. Self-interest, a quality he found in all human actions, is a recurrent theme of the *Maximes*: "Les vertus se perdent dans l'intérêt commes les fleuves se perdent dans la mer" – virtues are lost in self-interest as rivers are lost in the sea (quoted in *Encyclopedia Britannica*).

183. Bahá'u'lláh, *Prayers and Meditations*, section CLIII.

184. Tyre and Sidon, two of the oldest Phoenician towns, which today are located in Lebanon.

185. Stigmatized by Bahá'u'lláh as "The Tyrant of Yazd" (*God Passes By*, p. 232), Prince Jalálu'd-Dawlih was a son of Ẓillu's-Sulṭán.

186. 'Aynu'l-Baqar: Spring of the Cow; see Ruhe, *Door of Hope*, pp. 122, 227.

187. By "Traditions" here the author means Islamic ḥadíth, and in this case a Tradition "attributed to the Apostle of God Himself" (Ruhe, *Door of Hope*, p. 122). The translation is by Shoghi Effendi in *Epistle to the Son of the Wolf*, p. 180.

188. On the aqueduct, see Ruhe, *Door of Hope*, pp. 123–5; on the Gardens of Riḍván and Firdaws see Ruhe, pp. 91–100.

189. Tongue of Glory: Bahá'u'lláh.

190. As translated in 'Abdu'l-Bahá, *Selections*, no.206, p. 256.

191. The first paragraph is a provisional translation. The authorized translation of the remainder of the Tablet has been taken from 'Abdu'l-Bahá, *Selections*, no. 12, pp. 27–28.

192. Provisional translation.

193. See Taherzadeh, *Covenant*, p. 235. The Fezzan Desert is in the North Sahara, in present-day Libya south of Tripoli.

194. The three parts of the Will and Testament were written at different periods of 'Abdu'l-Bahá's life. The first part, in which Shoghi Effendi is appointed Guardian of the Cause, was probably written around 1906; it was then buried underground for safety. See Taherzadeh, *Child of the Covenant*, p. 7.

195. The chanter of the Muslim call to prayer, the *adhán*.

196. Amatu'l-Bahá: "Handmaiden of Bahá". Laura Barney's visits took place before her marriage mentioned in the previous paragraph.

197. Lit. "Table talks of 'Abdu'l-Bahá". It was published simultaneously in English, French and Persian: *Some Answered Questions*, and *An-Núru'l-Abhá Fí Mufáwaḍat 'Abdi'l-Bahá*, collected by Laura Clifford Barney (Kegan Paul, Trench, Trubner & Co.Ltd., London, 1908); *Les Leçons de St-Jean-d'Acre* (Leroux, Paris, 1908). The contribution of this book to the knowledge of the Bahá'í teachings in the West was well

described by Hippolyte Dreyfus (who translated it into French) in the Preface to his own book published in the same year: "By this work, Laura Clifford Barney has powerfully contributed to placing within the reach of the public the teaching of the new religion, for she has given, in the very simple form in which they were held, the conversations she had with the "Master of 'Akká". Till now, in fact, considering the small number of works translated into any one of the European languages, the knowledge of the philosophy and theology of Bahaism was limited only to the Orientalists who could read in the text the works of Bahá'u'lláh or of 'Abdu'l-Bahá, and to the adepts among whom the Master's Tablets are in circulation. *Some Answered Questions*, therefore, covers a deficiency particularly perceptible in the West." (*The Universal Religion: Bahaism*, pp. 9–10). See also Shoghi Effendi, *God Passes By*, pp. 107, 260, 268 and 305.

198. See *Some Answered Questions*, Ch. 74: "The Nonexistence of Evil", pp. 263–4.

199. It has not been possible to ascertain who is referred to here.

200. Provisional translation.

201. The assassination of Náṣiri'd-Dín S͟háh took place on 1 May 1896.

202. *Irtibat-i-S͟harq va G͟harb:* Union of the East and West; the author's diary of his teaching trip to Europe.

203. These reports were the result of mischief-making by partisans of Mírzá Muḥammad-'Alí. See Balyuzi, *'Abdu'l-Bahá*, p. 111.

204. "And he brought him forth abroad, and said, Look now toward heaven, and tell the stars, if thou be able to number them; and he said unto him, So shall thy seed be. And he believed in the Lord; and he counted it to him for righteousness" (Gen 15:5–6).

205. i.e. a follower of Mírzá Yaḥyá had joined the followers of Mírzá Muḥammad-'Alí.

206. In most Bahá'í prayer books.

207. The father of Shoghi Effendi.

208. Retranslated into English from the published Persian translation.

209. This can be read in the 1981 edition: "Preface to the First Edition", *Some Answered Questions*, pp. xvii–xviii. See also note 197 above.

210. One of these was the section "Strikes", published as an "Appendix to London 1908 edition" in 1918 by the Bahai Publishing Society, Chicago.

211. The French translation was in fact made in collaboration with Hippolyte Dreyfus (see note 197 above), "and, as she later related, it was during this undertaking that they discovered how well they could work together". *Bahá'í World*, vol. 16, p. 536.

212. i.e. the Covenant-breakers.

213. See note 194 above for the date of 'Abdu'l-Bahá's Will and Testament.

214. Although an Italian national, he was Acting Consul for Spain at the time; for accounts of this incident see Balyuzi, *'Abdu'l-Bahá*, p. 121; Taherzadeh, *Child of the Covenant*, p. 218.

215. The author refers here to Iranian history with which his readers would be familiar. Ḥájí Mírzá Áqásí was Prime Minister of Iran during the reign of Muḥammad S͟háh (1834–1848), and was bitterly opposed to the mission of the Báb. Mullá Baqír Májlisí (1628–1700) enjoyed similar power and influence at the 17th-century Safavid court.

216. Mawlaví and Yektai: two of the many sects of Sunní Islám practised in the Ottoman Empire, both inclined towards mysticism.

217. See 'Abdu'l-Bahá's own account of these charges in *Selections*, pp. 216–21.

218. Hájí Mírzá Haydar-'Alí describes this visit in *Stories from the Delight of Hearts*, p. 152; it seems to have taken place in 1903, i.e. before the Commission of Enquiry.

219. See note 214 above.

220. These events took place in 1951 during the Second Seven Year Plan in the United States, but were announced by Shoghi Effendi in 1946, e.g. in his cable of 25 April 1946 to the American Convention inaugurating the Plan (*Messages to America*, p. 88). This date coincides with the writing of the last three chapters of the present book, although the book was not published until 1953 (109 B.E.)

221. World War I.

222. On the Master's journey to Beirut in 1879, see Shoghi Effendi, *God Passes By*, p. 193; Balyuzi, *'Abdu'l-Bahá*, pp. 37–9; Taherzadeh, *Revelation*, vol.4, pp. 240–41, which quotes Bahá'u'lláh's Tablet revealed on that occasion, the Lawh-i-Ard-i-Bá (Tablet of the Land of Bá). This Tablet is also found in Bahá'u'lláh, *Tablets*, pp. 227-8.

223. 'Abdu'l-Bahá, *Selections*, no. 22, p. 51.

224. Provisional translation.

225. Lit: 'eternal rose-garden', the term applied to Bahá'í cemeteries.

226. Gog and Magog: according to biblical prophecy (Rev. 20:8–9), these nations went to war against the Kingdom of God under the leadership of Satan: "and they went up on the breadth of the earth, and compassed the camp of the saints about, and the beloved city: and fire came down from God out of heaven, and devoured them."

NOTES AND REFERENCES

227. "the incident in Yemen": possibly the continuing confrontation between the British and the Ottomans, or an incident concerning the continued Zaydí opposition to Ottoman rule; the Zaydí leader was Yaḥyá ibn Muḥammad.

228. This took place on 5 October 1908, taking advantage of the opportunity arising from the Young Turks Revolution that summer.

229. Bahá'u'lláh, Hidden Words, Persian no. 13.

230. Followers of Mírzá Yaḥyá, the Arch-breaker of the Covenant of the Báb.

231. "Of this event Zechariah had written: 'Thus speaketh the Lord of hosts, saying, Behold the man whose name is The Branch; and he shall grow up out of his place, and he shall build the temple of the Lord' (Zech. 6:12). How mysteriously and indubitably had his prophecy come true. 'The Branch' had built 'the temple of the Lord', had raised His 'tabernacle' on His Mountain – on Carmel – the Mountain of God." (Balyuzi, *'Abdu'l-Bahá*, p. 129.)

232. Provisional translation. The original is in Arabic.

233. Persian coins of negligible value.

234. See Chapter 4, pp. 226–7.

235. Kitáb-i-Aqdas, v. 93.

236. In 1903, see above, p. 160.

237. Provisional translation.

238. Provisional translation.

239. This book is the Báb's interpretation of the Surih of Joseph, one of the Surihs of the Qur'án renowned as the Aḥsánu'l-Qisas (the Best of Stories). The first chapter of the Báb's

interpretation, known as the Suratu'l-Mulk, was revealed by Him on the night of His Declaration in His house in S̲h̲íráz in the presence of Mullá Ḥusayn Bushruí, on 23 May 1844.

240. Here the author alludes to the passage in the Will and Testament of 'Abdu'l-Bahá referring to Shoghi Effendi as "the most wondrous, unique and priceless pearl that doth gleam from out the Twin surging seas" (*Will and Testament*, para. 2).

241. Pársí Bahá'í: typically, a Bahá'í of Persian Zoroastrian descent who lives in India.

242. Provisional translation.

243. *Utuzbir*: thirty-one. Among those executed that day was 'Árif Bey, head of the Commission of Enquiry. See Balyuzi, *'Abdu'l-Bahá*, p. 124.

244. Laylí and Majnún: legendary lovers enjoying the same fame in the East as Romeo and Juliet do in the West.

245. "At the request of Mrs. Tewksbury Jackson who on one occasion accompanied her to the Holy Land, Laura Barney helped in the project... In relating this episode to the writer later, Mme. Dreyfus-Barney said: 'For some time, therefore, and meeting with many obstacles, I was occupied with purchasing the land, having a design for the house made – of course with the approval of the Master – and seeing that its construction was carried out efficiently and promptly. All this kept me occupied for some time.'"(Account by Ugo Giachery in *Bahá'í World*, vol. 16, p. 537.) Mrs. Jackson, an American, lived mainly in Paris, where she was visited by 'Abdu'l-Bahá in 1911.

246. Jamádí and Rajab: two months of the lunar calendar observed by the Islamic world.

247. On Jamál Pás̲h̲á and his threat against the Master, see Balyuzi, *'Abdu'l-Bahá*, pp. 412–14.

248. Ḥáfiẓ.

INDEX

'Abdu'l-Bahá
  burdens on, 83, 134, 177–80, 298, 391–4
  chants Tablet of Visitation, 24, 25–6, 28, 61, 137
  his character, 31, 180, 339
    dignity, 186, 321, 346, 362, 415
    forbearance, 228, 286–7, 288
    forgiveness, 112–13
    gentleness, 241
    generosity, 112, 117, 133, 169, 179, 203–4, 284–7
    hospitality, 29–30, 197–9, 220, 301
    humility, 286, 302
    humour, 73, 182, 184, 205–6, 269, 272–3, 291, 309, 318
    justice, 219
    kindness, 13, 15, 48, 72, 74, 81, 84–5, 145, 168, 179, 285, 328, 339, 422
    love, 303–7, 334, 339
    mercy, 112, 285
    perseverance, 298
    serenity, 228, 328, 346, 356
    tenderness, 142, 145, 180, 334
    understanding, 146
    will, 253, 330
    wisdom, 75, 253, 320–21, 338
  concern for wellbeing of Bahá'ís, 230, 248, 320–21, 333–4, 392
  concealment of actions of Covenant-breakers, 7, 77, 112, 114
  daily life of, 11–12, 22, 124, 178–80, 274–6
    Fridays, 202–6
    Sundays, 206
  described by author, 416–17
    His glance, 417
    His walk, 125, 270–71
  and difficulties, 180–83
  and education of children, 159–60, 202, 204–6, 218, 366
  eloquence of, 40, 57–8, 201
    in different languages, 58, 195
  family of, 147, 150, 315, 363
  and healing, 117, 249–52, 290
  health of, 178, 275–6, 295–7, 299–301, 409–12
  House of,
    in 'Akká, 21–2, 25, 27, 29, 105, 161, 163, 167–8, 214, 241–2, 254, 346, 355–6, 357, 362, 455, 456, illus.
    in Haifa, 110–11, 130, 416, 464
  intercedes for Covenant-breakers, 135, 208–9
  journey to Beirut, 373–4, 458, 472, 480
  ministry of, 457
  and the poor, 117, 179, 202–4
  and Shrine of the Báb, 111, 116–21, 129, 134, 387

at Shrine of Bahá'u'lláh,
    24–6, 28, 61–5, 69, 109, 137,
    456
reincarceration in 'Akká,
    128–31, 132–3, 136–7, 208–9
sorrow of, 8, 14, 72, 85–6, 156,
    161–3, 177–8, 180–83, 187,
    298, 457
station of, 5–7, 36, 39, 77, 82,
    232, 242–8, 453, 471
stories told by, 272
    the Arab and his starving
        dog, 281–2
    the Arab without a hat, 273
    attempt to extract bribe
        from Bahá'u'lláh, 400
    Battle of <u>Kh</u>andaq, 49
    physiognomy, 276–9
Tablets *see* Writings
utterances of, 58, 79–80,
    194–5, 376, 397; *about*
action, 333–4, 376
adversity, 184, 310, 311, 329
advice to believers to leave
    'Akká, 311–12, 319–20, 322,
    331, 354, 359, 370
audacity, 400
Bahá'ís, 15, 84–6, 248,
    279–80, 299–301, 391, 392,
    395–6
Bahá'u'lláh, 57, 235, 400
charity, 279–80
Christianity, 49
concentration, power of,
    331, 333
conduct, 384
courage, 400
Covenant, 389, 398
Covenant-breakers, 16,
    38–41, 54–6, 78, 84, 107,
    121–2, 128–9, 154, 164,
    169, 180, 192–3, 261,
    263–4, 287, 304–5, 379–80,
    389, 420, 457
deepening new believers,
    56–7
diet, 274, 475
disunity, 299

divine confirmation, 333–4,
    369, 376, 404
divisiveness, 282–3
dreams, 367–8
education, 330, 331, 333
evil, non-existence of, 317
feasts, 302
fear of God, 335
forbearance, 335–6, 384
generosity, 280–82
God, 239
Greatest Name, 95–6
Guardian of the Cause,
    258–60
health, 54–5, 252, 273
Houses of Worship, 50–51,
    223–4, 226
hypocrisy, 279–80
Ibráhím <u>Kh</u>ayru'lláh, 106
His imprisonment, 210, 353,
    416
infiltrating the Faith, 282–3
Islám, 49, 73
Iranians, 335–6, 338
Joseph (in Bible and
    Qur'án), 57, 126, 460
Laura Barney, 316
love, 302, 303–7, 335–6
Lua Getsinger, 154
luck, 404
martyrdom, 51–4, 153, 366
miserliness, 280–81
moral education, 57
patience, 335–6, 339, 354, 384
persecution, 181–2
perseverance, 186–7, 334–5,
    354, 366
politics, involvement in, 393
His promotion of the
    Cause, 416, 420
prophecies, 32, 49–51, 126,
    133, 163–6, 260–62, 366,
    375–6, 380, 459
pure intentions, 422
service, 329, 420, 470
Shrine of the Báb, 119–20,
    129
silence, 384, 457

INDEX

Some Answered Questions,
  342–3
Spiritual Assemblies, 170
spiritual concepts, 86, 147
His station, 245, 247
strengthening one's faith,
  335
success in undertakings, 331,
  333–4
tests, 221–2, 226,
translation, 115–16, 234–5
Thomas Breakwell, 139–41
ultimate triumph of Cause,
  49–50, 227, 258, 353, 366,
  368, 397, 22
unity, 282, 302
Universal House of Justice,
  169–72, 282, 467
universal participation,
  223–4
upheavals, impending, 353,
  358
Will and Testament of
  Bahá'u'lláh, 77
wine-drinking 184
Word of God, 302
World War I, 237–8, 367
His Writings, 3, 176
visitors to, 22, 199–202,
  233–42
workload of, 309, 315
Writings of, 3, 32, 40, 48, 87,
  96, 101–2, 141–2, 158–9, 176,
  180–81, 185, 195, 201–2,
  206–7, 209, 230, 256, 260,
  266, 269–70, 289, 309,
  310–11, 340, 348, 370, 388–9
circumstances, 195–9
Will and Testament, 60,
  259, 310, 346, 477
'Abdu'lláh Khán-i-Núrí, 84, 427
'Abdu'lláh, Mírzá (musician), 97–8,
  427, 462
'Abdu'lláh Pashá, House of, 455,
  illus. *see also* 'Abdu'l-Bahá, House
  of, in 'Akká
'Abdu'l-Ghaní Baydún, 354, 358,
  427

'Abdu'l-Hamíd II, Sultan, 86, 122,
  129, 134, 350–51, 356–7, 359–61,
  364–5, 379, 381–2, 414, 415, 427
Abu'l-Fadl Gulpáygání, Mírzá, 38,
  70, 176, 177, 229, 231, 370, 374,
  428, 466
Abu'l-Hikam, 99, 463
Abu'l-Húdá, Shaykhu'l-Islám,
  351–2
abjad system, 3, 398–9, 451
Abraham, 333, 462
Adrianople, 30
Afnán (family of the Báb), 6, 31,
  33, 77, 453
Afnán, Siyyid Ahmad, 297, 428
Afnán, Mírzá Hadí, 59, 73–4, 341,
  407, 428
Afnán, Muhammad, 103
Afnán, Muhammad-Taqí
  (Vakílu'd-Dawlih), 223, 428, illus.
Afroukhteh, Youness,
  instructions received from
  'Abdu'l-Bahá, 46–7, 74–5,
    83–5, 86–90, 103, 107, 108,
    110, 115–16, 129–30, 139–40,
    141, 156, 158–9, 200, 218,
    235, 244, 264–5, 323–4, 330,
    331, 333–7, 397, 402, 409–10,
    420–22
  and language teaching, 45,
    158–9
  and medicine, 327, 330, 332–3,
    376–7, 387–8, 399, 405–12
  and poetry, 48, 61–3, 72–3,
    159, 423
  Tablets revealed for, 28–9, 87,
    96, 398
  and translation, 46–7, 105, 110,
    115–16, 136, 141, 145–8,
    153–4, 158–9, 210–13, 235,
    240, 264–5, 269, 302, 312,
    316, 318, 327, 396–9
Aghsán, 4, 5, 6, 31, 33, 44, 77, 171,
  452, 461
Ahmadov brothers, 10, 92, 104, 428
Ákhund, 'Alí-Akbar (Hand of the
  Cause), *see* 'Alí-Akbar-i-
  Shahmírzádí

'Akká, 17, 18, 76, 105, 109, 113, 123, 156, 164–5, 179, 182, 230, 255, 275, 291–4, 312–13, 353, 365, 405, 412, illus.
  'Aynu'l-Baqar well (Spring of the Cow), 292
  bathhouse in, 272, 475
  Christians in, 21, 206, 305–6, 320
  dignitaries of, 22, 24–5, 31, 199, 321, 365, 400
  doctors in, 406–7
  Governor of, 132, 208, 349–50, 354, 415
  Mufti of, 41, 189–92, 350
  Muslims in, 295, 320
  pilgrim house, 18–22, 105, 136, 150, 161, 455, illus.
  Persian Consul in, 251, 313–4
  reincarceration in, see 'Abdu'l-Bahá
'Alí, Imám, 73, 167, 180, 283, 457, 458, 476
'Alí-Akbar, Siyyid, 82
'Alí-Akbar, Mírzá, 64–6, 69
'Alí-Akbar-i-Qúchání, Shaykh, 418, 428
'Alí-Akbar-i-Shahmírzádí, Mullá, 5, 429
'Alí-Muḥammad Khán (Khán-i-Bahá'í), 289–91, 429
'Alí-Qulí Khán (Ali Kuli Khan), 158, 429
Alíyu'lláhís, 244, 473
Alláh'u'Abhá, 95–6, 171, 218, 283, 299, 462
America, Americans, 46–7, 106, 111, 126, 136, 158, 169, 176, 213, 231, 2346, 237, 239–42, 258–60, 266–7, 326–7, 364
Amín see Faríd
Anzali, 9, 92
Áqá Ján (Khádimu'lláh), 41–2, 60, 64–70, 74–5, 78, 93–4, 111, 134–5, 177, 181, 183, 244, 298, 350, 367, 387, 429, 458, 461
Áqásí, Mírzá, 351, 479
Áqáy-i-Kalím see Muḥammad-Qulí

Arabs, 198, 273, 281–2
Arastú Khán Hakím, 97, 141,144, 150, 152, 250, 430, illus.
Arbáb, Mírzá, of Rasht, 9
Arch-breaker of the Covenant, see Muḥammad-'Alí, Mírzá
Armenians, 405, 414
Arjmand, Ḥáj Mihdí, 101, 430
Aṣadu'lláh, Áqá, 43, 400, 412, 430
Asadu'lláh-i-Iṣfáhání, 108, 114, 347–8, 430
Ascension of Bahá'u'lláh, commemoration, 60–62
Áshchí, Ḥusayn, 252, 430, illus.
astronomy, 397–8
atheists, 239–40
Austria, 381–2, 464
Azalís see Yaḥyá

Báb, the, 95, 98, 364, 387, 455
  prayers revealed by, 120, 152–3
  Remover of Difficulties, 71, 153, 466
  Qayyúmu'l-Asmá', 398–9, 481
  Shrine of, 111, 116–21, 129, 134, 209, 215, 356, 362, 387, 397, 464, illus.
backbiting, 114
Badkubih, 9, 92, 104, 372
Badí'u'lláh, 34, 44–5, 55–6, 115, 164, 165–9, 172–5, 231, 260–61, 380, 430
Badrí Bíg, 350, 354
Baghdad, 2, 4, 20, 30, 73, 256, 400
Baghdádí, Dr. Zia Mabsout, 380, 381, 431
Baghdádí, Muḥammad Muṣṭafá, 378, 380, 405, 407, 431
Bahá'ís, 158, 213, 243–6, 298–301, 364, 372, 377, 390–94, 395–6, 413
  in America, 106, 144, 213, 218, 221, 230–31, 266–8
  in Beirut, 273, 331–2, 335, 338, 395
  in India, 227
  in Iran, 8, 15, 19, 46, 98, 161–3, 177, 221–2, 225, 227, 392–4

INDEX

in Iraq, 15
martyrs, 152-3, 161-2
in Paris, 326-9
Persian, 221-2, 391-4, 395-6
resident in Holy Land, 30-32,
35, 46, 47-8, 59-60, 70-72,
74, 113, 132, 160, 161-3, 166,
168, 183, 187-8, 208, 243-4,
300, 320-21, 322, 346, 355,
363, 391, 412-16
in Russia, 227, illus.
see also pilgrims; West
Bahá'í terminology, 239-40,
316-17, 327
Bahá'u'lláh, 18, 30, 68, 73, 76-7,
95-6,118, 144, 147, 170, 182, 249,
263, 271, 292-4, 352, 364, 400
photograph of, 220-21
Shrine of, 16, 18, 22, 24-9,
61-5, 69, 109,111, 127, 137,
163, 230, 255, 349-50, 420,
454, 461, illus.
Will and Testament of, 3, 33,
77, 171, 242, 390, 451, 452,
472
Writings of, 28, 33, 124, 171,
182-3, 398, 468, 472
Hálih-Hálih-Yá-Bi<u>sh</u>árát,
28, 456
Hidden Words, 57, 111, 382,
460
I<u>sh</u>ráqát, 57, 461
Kitáb-i-'Ahd *see* Bahá'u'lláh,
Will and Testament
Kitáb-i-Aqdas, 101, 392-3,
453
Ma<u>th</u>naví, 28, 456
Sáqí Namih, 28, 456
Tajallíyát, 57, 461
Ṭarázát, 57, 461
Bahjí, 16-18, 108, 109, 454
Mansion of, 17, 42-4, 69, 111,
209, 271, 454, illus.
Balá, Áqá, 272-3
Baladieh park, 293
Báqiroff (Khamsi), Siyyid
Nasrullah, 259, 431
Barney, Laura *see* Dreyfus-Barney

Ba<u>sh</u>árí, Jináb-i-, 381
Bayán, 98
Bible, 115, 138, 167, 226, 377
Beirut, 31, 69, 84, 90-91, 104, 273,
330, 331-2, 345, 370-75, 394-5
Black Stone (Ka'bih), 73, 461
Bolurih, 'Abdu'lláh, 110, 116
Bombay, 33, 156, 216, 227, 232,
461, 469
Bosnia, 381
Boston, 240
Breakwell, Thomas, 138-42, 266,
431, illus.
Brittingham, Isabella, 228, 432,
illus.
Buddhism, Buddhists, 144-5, 302,
465
Búrújirdí, Áqá Jamál (Old Hyena),
5, 6-8, 33, 55, 92, 96, 100-101,
114, 177, 232, 264, 432
Bu<u>sh</u>ru'í, Badí', 381, 397, 432

Caliphate, 167, 176, 352, 381-2,
416, 457
Canavarro, Countess Marie de
Souza (Sister Sanghamitta),
144-8, 317, 344, 432, 465
Carmel, 10, 111, 118, illus.
Centre of Sedition *see*
Muḥammad-'Alí
Cha'ichi, Enayat'u'lláh, 406
Chicago, 230
China, 149
Christians, 21, 122, 206, 218-20,
302, 352, 373
see also 'Akká
Commission of Enquiry, 233, 254,
335, 343, 352-3, 354-7, 358-65,
369, 380, 482
Constitutional Revolution
Iranian, 261-3, 378, 383,
392-4, 399, 405, 474
Ottoman, 399
Covenant, 57, 59, 85, 176, 390,
398-9, 452, 453
Covenant-breakers, 4-5, 10, 17-18,
42-5, 47, 64, 78-9, 103, 111-13,
123, 137, 154, 157, 162, 167, 169,

174–7, 243–4, 253–4, 298–9,
    349–55, 367, 379–80, 382, 400
  allegations against 'Abdu'l-
    Bahá, 31, 40, 68, 76, 118, 134,
    143, 191, 209, 215, 229, 311,
    345–6, 351–3, 357–8
  bribery by, 34, 134
  and Shrine of the Báb, 119–20
  strategies of, 20, 33–41, 43–4,
    66–9, 75–7, 92–3, 113, 177,
    188–92, 231–3, 350–52, 374–5
  writings of, 19, 32, 37–41,
    66–70, 74–5, 85, 174, 175
Crete, 464–5

Dahají, Siyyid 'Alí-Akbar, 114, 419
Damascus, 31
Di Santo Amini, 149
disunity, 298–9
Díyá'u'lláh, 44–5, 111, 164, 189, 432
Dodge, Arthur Pillsbury, 142, 143,
  433, 465
Dodge, Wendell Phillips, 143–4,
  433, 465
Dodge, William Copeland, 143–4,
  433, 465
Dreyfus, Alfred, 148, 465
Dreyfus, Hippolyte, 142, 148–50,
  228, 326, 433, 479, illus.
Dreyfus-Barney, Laura, 149–50,
  215, 314–19, 328, 332, 341–5, 433,
  482, illus.
Druze community, 251, 474

education, 143–4, 154, 330–33
  of children, 159–60
Egypt, 20, 80–83, 85, 86, 107, 126,
  177, 332, 343, 359, 372
    Battle of, 421
Elijah, Shrine of, 10–16, 453–4,
  illus.
Emigrants, 160, 456–7, 466
Engleman, Mr., 327
English language, 110, 158–60, 173,
  214–15, 269, 302, 397
Escobino (Consul), 346, 363–4, 479
Europe, Europeans, 126, 145, 159,
  169, 176, 231

Faḍíl-i-Shírází, 418, 433
Faḍlu'lláh, Ibn-i-Ashraf, 8, 15, 21,
  24, 53–4, 61, 62, 70, 84
Faezeh Khánum (Gulsurkh
  Begum), 95, 434
Farid (Fareed), Amín'u'lláh, 108–9,
  110, 434, 463
Faríq Páshá, 133, 320, 350, 354,
  434
Farmer, Sarah Jane, 213, 434
fasting, 294–7
feasts, 301
Fezzan Desert, 310, 346, 379, 477
finance, 112, 115, 120
Firdaws Garden, 22, 255, 293
fortune, 402–4
Frank Frank, 217–21, 234
French government, 388, 399
French language, 45, 110, 148, 149

George, Walter, 211
German colony, 118, 464
Germany, 381–2, 464
Getsinger, Lua, 141, 150–58, 173,
  215, 434, 466, illus.
Ghulámu'lláh, 177, 231, 439
Gog and Magog, 379, 480
Goodall, Helen, 268–9, 435, 475
Greatest Holy Leaf, Bahíyyih
  Khánum, 147, 363, 407–8, 435,
  455
Greatest Name *see* Alláh'u'Abhá
Greece, Greeks, 86, 133, 464
Green Acre Bahá'í School, 213
Guardian *see* Shoghi Effendi

Ḥabíb, Mírzá, ('Aynu'l-Mulk), 327
Ḥabíb Mesgar, 224
Haddad, Anton, 177
Hádí Khán, Dr., 55
Hádí, Shaykh, 159, 200–02
Ḥáfiẓ, 419, 482
Hague, The, 238, 472
Haifa, 10–11, 31, 50, 104–5, 110–27,
  130, 138, 143, 151, 163, 209, 314,
  346, 414–16, 459, 464
Hands of the Cause of God, 5,
  171, 264, 421

INDEX

Harf-i-Baqá, see Músá-i-Javáhirí
Ḥasan, Mírzá (of Egypt), 80–83, 99, 236
Ḥátem-i-Ṭá'í, 284, 476
hats, 143, 213–4, 234, 261–3, 302, 366, 382, 469
Ḥaydar-'Alí, Ḥájí Mírzá, 60, 104, 136, 150, 153, 156–7, 161, 182, 200, 210, 215, 258, 272, 300, 309, 354, 409–10, 421, 435, 457, 480, illus.
Herzegovina, 381
Hidden Words see Bahá'u'lláh, Writings of
Hindus, 302
Hoar, William H., 104–9, 265–6, 435, illus.
Holy Days, 108, 109, 127, 137
Holy Family, 30, 111, 132
Ḥubb'u'lláh, 96, 264
Ḥuqúqu'lláh, 43, 188, 459
Huron desert, 165–6, 312
Ḥusayn Effendi Tabrízí, 14, 436
Ḥusayn Effendi (son of 'Abdu'l-Bahá), 17, 436, 455

India, 20, 85, 86, 137, 144, 176, 222
infallibility, 467
intellect, 236
Iran, Iranians, 85, 86, 89, 149, 161, 169, 177, 222, 335–6, 377–8, 413, 479
  in Beirut, 394
  religious leaders, 261–3
  see also Constitutional Revolution
Iraq, 4
Isfahan, 152, 162, 175, 177, 181, 267, 288, 466
Isfandíyár, 25, illus.
'Is̲h̲qábád, 176, 215, 223, 225, 231–2, 300, 421, 470, illus.
  see also Mas̲h̲riqu'l-Ad̲h̲kár
Islám, 73
  divines, 97, 175, 199–202
  history of, 457, 458, 459–60
  Holy Shrines of, 4, 452
  Imáms, 243
  legal concepts in, 463
  Sunní, 352
    Mawlaví, 352, 479
    Yektai, 352, 479
  Traditions, 98–9, 292, 477
  see also 'Alí, Imám
Ismá'íl Áqá, 199, 274, 436
Ismu'lláh'u'l-Jamál, see Búrújirdí
Istanbul, 10, 30, 69, 84, 89, 91–2, 104, 261, 345, 347, 372, 413, 415
Italy, 381–2, 464

Japan, 233, 238, 269–70
Jackson, Mrs. Tewksbury, 215, 228, 301, 416, 436, 482, illus.
Jahrumí, Ḥusayn-'Alí (Fiṭrat), 156–8, 232, 436, 461
Jalál, Mírzá, 116, 117, 130, 370, 436
Jalálu'd-Dawlih, 289, 476
Jamál Pás̲h̲á, 421, 436, 483
jealousy, 173
Jesus Christ, 13, 49, 60, 139, 158, 202, 213, 226, 310, 355, 454
Jews, 237, 302, 373
Jonah, 13
Joseph, 57, 126, 460, 481

Kaiser Wilhelm, 34–5
Karagozlu, G̲h̲ulam-Ḥusayn, 385–6
Káẓim Pás̲h̲á, 229
Karbilá, 4, 452, 460
Kern, Margaret, 212, 437
K̲h̲alíl, Muḥammad-Ibráhím, 177, 468
K̲h̲andaq, Battle of, 49, 227, 459
K̲h̲án-i-'Avámíd, 455, illus, see also 'Akká, pilgrim house
K̲h̲án-i-Bahá'í see 'Alí-Muḥammad K̲h̲án
K̲h̲ayyám, Omar, 422
Kheiralla (K̲h̲ayru'lláh), Ibrahim George, 47, 106, 177, 231, 428, 433, 434, 437, 439, 442
K̲h̲usraw, 72, 437
Kirmán, 263, 475
Kitáb-i-'Ahd see Bahá'u'lláh, Will and Testament

Lává Páshá, 199, 320, 350, 354
London, 139
luck, 402–4

Mahmúd Káshání, 64
Mahmúd, Shaykh, 251–2
Majdu'd-Dín, 68, 164, 180, 437
Májlisí, Mullá Baqír, 351, 479
Manshádí, Siyyid Muhammad Taqí, 11, 90, 110, 116, 209, 372–3, 437
Marseilles, 165–6, 312, 322–6
martyrdom, martyrs, 152–4, 161–2
material world, 103
Mashriqu'l-Adhkár, 50–51, 176, 223–7, 231–2, 367, 381, 391–2, 459–60, illus.
Mawlaví, see Islám; Rúmí
Mázindarán, 104
Mecca, 36, 73
medicine, 406–12 see also 'Abdu'l-Bahá, utterances about health; Afroukhteh, Youness, and medicine
Messiah, 267–8
Mihdí-i-Dahají, Siyyid 'Ali-Akbar (Ismu'lláhu'l-Mihdí), 438
Millenium, 213
Millerites, 267, 475
Mishkín Qalam (Mírzá Husayn Isfáhání), 19, 88,136, 150, 160, 438, illus.
Moody, Dr. Susan I., 228, 438, illus.
Moscow, 323, 325
Most Great Prison, see 'Akká
Mu'ayyad, Dr Habíbu'lláh Khudábakhsh, 381, 438, 459
Muhammad, the Prophet, 49, 73, 100, 466
Muhammad-'Alí (Centre of Sedition), 4, 5–6, 33, 37–39, 44, 59, 77, 121, 156, 157–8, 164,168, 180, 189–90, 232, 242, 304–5, 355, 438, 452
Muhammad-'Alí Nabílí, Shaykh, 328
Muhammad-'Alí, Ustád, 124, 125–6

Muhammad Hasan, Áqá, 20–21, 23, 84, 250–51, 439
Muhammad-Ja'far Mírzá, 94–5
Muhammad Javád-i-Qazvíní, 177, 299, 304, 439
Muhammad Mihdí Khán, 309
Muhammad-i-Qá'íní (Nabíl-i-Akbar), 57, 439
Muhammad-Qulí, Áqáy-i-Kalím, 178, 249, 429–30
Muhammad Sháh, 351, 479
Munír (son of Áqáy-i-Kalím), 178, 318–19, 343, 439
Munír-i-Zayn, 158, 164–5, 178, 397, 439
Músá-i-Javáhirí (Harf-i-Baqá), 4, 255–6, 440
Muslims, 302, 373 see also Islám
Muzaffaru'd-Dín Sháh, 265
mysticism, 144, 212–13, 480

Nabihání, Shaykh Muhammad, 356, 361
Nabíl-i-Akbar see Muhammad-i-Qá'íní
Nabíl-i-Zarandi, Nabíl-i-A'zam, 2, 440
Na'ím, Muhammad, 6, 126, 440
Najaf, 4, 452
Násiri'd-Dín Sháh, 292, 325, 478
Napoleonic wars, 292
Navváb (Ásíyih Khánum, wife of Bahá'u'lláh), 17, 454
Níyáz, Hájí, 107
Núru'd-Dín Zayn, 158–60, 164–5, 178–9, 196, 201, 218–9, 311, 341, 345, 347–8, 357–65, 397, 440
Nusayrís, 244, 473

Old Hyena, see Burujirdí
Ottoman Empire, 76, 77, 86, 133, 381–2, 413–14
Ottoman government, Ottoman officials, 34, 86, 118, 122, 127–8, 143, 215, 227, 234, 237, 311, 321, 345, 348, 350–52, 359–60, 374, 399, 400
  see also Commission of Enquiry

Pacific Ocean, 207
Palestine, 133, 237, 263, 352
Paris, 138, 142, 215, 323, 326–9, 388
Pársís *see* Zoroastrians
persecutions, 152, 161–3, 175, 177–8, 466
Persian language, 158–9, 302, 318, 469
Phelps, Myron H., 144–5, 147–8, 179, 202, 317, 344, 440
patriotism, 394–6
pilgrimage, pilgrims, 16–30, 35–7, 80–83, 109, 111,112, 113, 137, 143–144, 150, 173, 193–8, 216–7, 204, 208, 210, 254–5, 288–9, 357, 372, 395–6
pistols, 123, 125
Port Said, 84, 209, 214, 215, 323–4
Prison City, *see* 'Akká

Qájár dynasty, 262
Qazvín, 8, 92, 453
Qiblih, 245, 454, 458, 461–2, 472
Qur'án, 471
chanting of, 27, 322, 328, 337, 456

Ramaḍán, 294–5
Ramsey, Mrs., 305–6
Rasht, 9, 92
reincarnation, 145
Remey, Charles Mason, 408, 441
Riḍá-Iṣfahání, Muḥammad, 223, 470
Riḍáy-i-Qannád, Muḥammad, 43–4, 171–2, 174, 183, 221, 224–5, 287, 297, 391, 441, illus.
Riḍván, 109,
Riḍván Garden, 17, 22, 127, 230, 236, 249–50, 255, 293, 454
Rawhání, Alí-Akbar Khán (Muhibu'ṣ-Sulṭán), 47, 211, 213, 397, 398, 441
Rochefoucauld, 284–5, 476
Rosenberg, Ethel, 314, 316, 342–4, illus.
Ruḥú'lláh, martyred son of Varqá, 51, 52, 443

Rúmí, 135, 167
Russia, 176, 222, 233, 237–8, 464

Sa'dí, 13, 51, 268, 371, 422
Ṣadru'l-'ulamá, Hájí Áqá (Ṣadru's-Ṣudur), 97–102, 441
Safavids, 351, 479
Ṣáliḥ, Shaykh ,251–2
Ṣáliḥ, Dr. Muḥammad, 381
Ṣáliḥ, 17, 455
Salím, Riaz, 381
Salmán (first Persian believer in Islám), 99, 463
Salmán, Shaykh, 228, 441
Samandar (Shaykh Kazim Qazvíní), 8–9, 442
Samandarí, Ṭarazu'lláh, 372–3, 442
Sanderson, Edith, 148, 442
Sanghamitta, Sister, *see* Canavarro
service to the Cause, 54, 56 *see also* 'Abdu'l-Bahá, utterances about
Shoghi Effendi, Guardian of the Bahá'í Faith, 27, 59–60, 196, 258–60, 310, 341, 343, 366, 368, 399, 455, 482, illus.
Shu'á'u'lláh, 177, 231, 442
Sinai, 101
Socrates *see* Abu'l-Ḥikam
Some Answered Questions, 179, 314–19, 342–5, 455, 467, 477, illus.
Spencer, Louise, see Waite.
Spiritual Assemblies, 95, 170, 222, 367
of Latin America, 367
of Chicago, 230–31
of Tehran, 171, 258, 421
Subhání, Mr. 398–9
Sublime Porte *see* Ottoman government
Suez Canal, 293
Sulaymán Khán, 51, 53, 442
Switzerland, 315
Syria, 133, 263, 352

Tablets of Visitation, 16, 137, 246
Tabriz, 232, 381, 471

Tabrízí, Angiz, 343
Ṭabúr Áqásí, 11, 66, 68–9, 75, 112
Ṭáhirih, 152
Ṭáhiri, 'Abbás
Ṭáhirih Khánum, 246, 442
Tbilisi, 10, 92, 104, 372
teaching, 8, 158, 175–6, 227–8, 385, 413 *see also* West
Tehran, 5, 8, 53, 92–3, 97, 103, 258, 398, 421
Trebizond, 92
Tripoli, 382
Turks, 86, 198, 464
Túsí, Aḍar, 371

'Umar, 180
Universal House of Justice, 169–72, 467
Utuzbir incident, 413–14, 421, 482

Vakílu'd-Dawlih, *see* Afnán, Muḥammad-Taqí
Varqá, 'Alí-Muḥammad, 48, 51, 52, 443
Varqá, 'Azízu'lláh Khán, 19, 84, 443
Varqá, Valíyu'lláh Khán, 381, 397–8
vegetarianism, 274, 475–6
Vujdání, Yusif Khán, 245, 443

Waite, Louise Spencer, 212, 443
West, Westerners, 31, 46, 175–6, 210–15, 228–9, 254–5, 349
wheat sifting, 23–4, 45
Winterburn, G.T and Rosa, 215–7, 254, 443–4, 469–70
women, 158
World War I, 237–8, 344, 367, 382, 421

Yaḥyá, Mírzá, Subḥ-i-Azal, 5, 36, 59, 73, 85, 200, 221–2, 261, 263. 335, 375, 380, 383, 444, 452
Yamamoto, Kanichi, 268–70, 444, 475, illus.
Yazd, 152, 161–3, 175, 181–2, 222, 288–9, 466
  Governor of, 289
Yazdí, Áqá Aḥmad, 209, 236, 324
Yazdí, Muḥammad, 259
Yektai, 352, 479
Yemen, 381, 481
Young Turks, 365, 405, 414, 464, 481

Zaynu'l-Muqarrabín, 19, 88, 136, 150, 160, 444, illus.
Zoroastrians, 216–7, 302, 403, 469, 482